REALIZING REPARATIVE JUSTICE FOR INTERNATIONAL CRIMES: FROM THEORY TO PRACTICE

This book provides a timely and systematic study of reparations in international criminal justice, which goes beyond a theoretical analysis of the system established at the International Criminal Court (ICC). It originally engages with recent decisions and filings at the ICC relating to reparation and how the criminal and reparative dimensions of international criminal justice can be reconciled. This book is equally innovative in its extensive treatment of the significant challenges of adjudicating on reparations, and proposing recommendations based on concrete experiences. With recent and imminent decisions from the ICC, as well as developments in national courts and beyond, Miriam Cohen provides a critical analysis of the theory and emerging jurisprudence of reparations for international crimes, their impact on victims and stakeholders.

Miriam Cohen is an Assistant Professor of International Law and Human Rights at Université de Montréal. She is the recipient of various prestigious awards, fellowships and research grants, including from the Government of Canada research agency for her research on international justice and victims' rights, and from the Canadian Bar Association. She has published over 20 papers in international law and human rights in renowned publications. Prior to her academic career, she practised international law at the International Court of Justice (United Nations) and at the International Criminal Court. She holds a Ph.D. in international law from Leiden University, a Master of Law (LLM) in human rights from Harvard Law School, a Master of law (LLM) in international law from the University of Cambridge, and a Master of law (LLM) from Université de Montréal. She is an international lawyer (Quebec Bar) and has appeared as Counsel before the International Tribunal for the Law of the Sea.

Realizing Reparative Justice for International Crimes

FROM THEORY TO PRACTICE

MIRIAM COHEN
Université de Montréal

CAMBRIDGE
UNIVERSITY PRESS

University Printing House, Cambridge CB2 8BS, United Kingdom

One Liberty Plaza, 20th Floor, New York, NY 10006, USA

477 Williamstown Road, Port Melbourne, VIC 3207, Australia

314–321, 3rd Floor, Plot 3, Splendor Forum, Jasola District Centre,
New Delhi – 110025, India

79 Anson Road, #06–04/06, Singapore 079906

Cambridge University Press is part of the University of Cambridge.

It furthers the University's mission by disseminating knowledge in the pursuit of
education, learning, and research at the highest international levels of excellence.

www.cambridge.org
Information on this title: www.cambridge.org/9781108472685
DOI: 10.1017/9781108574846

© Miriam Cohen 2020

This publication is in copyright. Subject to statutory exception
and to the provisions of relevant collective licensing agreements,
no reproduction of any part may take place without the written
permission of Cambridge University Press.

First published 2020

A catalogue record for this publication is available from the British Library.

Library of Congress Cataloging-in-Publication Data
NAMES: Cohen, Miriam, 1983– author.
TITLE: Realizing reparative justice for international crimes / Miriam Cohen.
DESCRIPTION: 1. | New York : Cambridge University Press, 2020. | Includes
bibliographical references and index.
IDENTIFIERS: LCCN 2019046505 (print) | LCCN 2019046506 (ebook) | ISBN
9781108472685 (hardback) | ISBN 9781108622851 (ebook)
SUBJECTS: LCSH: Restorative justice. | Transitional justice. | International crimes. |
Crimes against humanity. | Reparations for historical injustices. | Criminal justice,
Administration of.
CLASSIFICATION: LCC K5250 .C64 2020 (print) | LCC K5250 (ebook) | DDC 340/.115–dc23
LC record available at https://lccn.loc.gov/2019046505
LC ebook record available at https://lccn.loc.gov/2019046506

ISBN 978-1-108-47268-5 Hardback

Cambridge University Press has no responsibility for the persistence or accuracy of
URLs for external or third-party internet websites referred to in this publication
and does not guarantee that any content on such websites is, or will remain,
accurate or appropriate.

To my boys
Jayden, Joshua, and Steve

Contents

Foreword		*page* xiii
Acknowledgments		xvii
Table of Cases		xix
List of Abbreviations		xxiv
Prologue		xxvi
Introduction		1
I.1	General Parameters	4
I.2	Themes and the Scope of the Book	5
	I.2.1 Themes and Key Concepts	7
	I.2.2 Scope and Limitations	9
	I.2.3 Book Structure	10
1	**Punishment and Reparation: Construing the Legal Basis of a Duty to Repair in International Criminal Law**	**12**
1.1	Of Crimes and Punishment	13
1.2	Victims, Reparation, and Restorative Justice Theory	18
1.3	The Genesis of International Criminal Law and the Shift from State Responsibility to Individual Accountability	19
1.4	Paving the Way to Reparations for Mass Crimes: Overview of the Legal Duty of Reparations in Other Fields of International Law	23
	1.4.1 The Purposes of Reparations	24
	1.4.2 The Multifaceted Dimensions of Reparations	25
	1.4.3 The Duty of Reparation in International Law from a State Responsibility Dimension	27

viii   *Contents*

1.4.4   International Human Rights Law and the Principles
        Developed in the Jurisprudence of the Inter-American
        Court of Human Rights   29
1.4.5   International Humanitarian Law: Reparation and its
        Enforcement   41
1.4.6   The Legal Duty of Reparations   45
1.4.7   The Beneficiaries of Reparations Under
        International Law   47

**2   Reparative Justice at International and Hybrid Criminal
     Tribunals**   52

2.1   Historical Account: Reparations and the Nuremberg
      and Tokyo Trials   54
2.2   The Ad Hoc Tribunals for the Former Yugoslavia
      and Rwanda   55
2.3   Other International or Hybrid Criminal Tribunals   62
      2.3.1   The Special Tribunal for Lebanon   63
      2.3.2   The Special Court for Sierra Leone   65
      2.3.3   Parting with the Trend: The Cambodian Extraordinary
              Chambers' (ECCC) Approach to Victims' Redress   66
2.4   The Development of the Long Road to Reparations   73

**3   The Construction of a Reparative Dimension of International
     Justice Before the International Criminal Court (ICC)**   75

3.1   The Codification of Reparations Within the Rome Statute   76
3.2   The Search for Victims' Justice Before the ICC: Recent
      Case Law on Reparations   81
      3.2.1   The Trailblazing Case of *The Prosecutor* v. *Thomas
              Lubanga Dyilo*   81
      3.2.2   *The Prosecutor* v. *Germain Katanga* Case: Individual
              Awards for the First Time   91
      3.2.3   *The Prosecutor* v. *Ahmad Al Faqi Al Mahdi* Case:
              Individual, Collective and Symbolic Reparations   94
      3.2.4   *The Prosecutor* v. *Jean-Pierre Bemba* Case:
              The Unfortunate Reparations Outcome   98
      3.2.5   A Reparative Dimension in Terminated Cases?   100
3.3   Assessing the Case Law on Reparations to Date:
      Inconsistencies, Delays, and the Need for Change   102
      3.3.1   Key Features of the Reparations System at
              the ICC   102

	3.3.2	Tackling the Difficult Dilemmas: Reconciling Reparations Before the ICC with Conflicting Perspectives and Paradigms	111
3.4		Conclusions	124

4 Victims of International Crimes Within Administrative Mechanisms: The Example of the ICC Trust Fund for Victims (TFV) — 126

4.1		The Road to the TFV and its Legal Framework	128
	4.1.1	Relevant Legal Provisions	129
	4.1.2	The Mandates of the TFV	132
	4.1.3	Functioning of the TFV: Budget and Programs	133
	4.1.4	Rationales for Channeling Reparations Through the TFV	135
4.2		The Reparations Mandate: Lessons from First Cases	139
4.3		Bridging the Gap: The TFV's Assistance Mandate	142
4.4		The Road Ahead: The Challenges of the TFV and Administrative Mechanisms in the Aftermath of Mass Victimization	146

5 The Role of National Courts and Mechanisms in Realizing Reparative Justice for International Crimes — 150

5.1		Diverging Domestic Approaches to Reparations Within Criminal Law Proceedings	151
	5.1.1	Romano-Germanic Systems	152
	5.1.2	Common Law Systems	154
5.2		Domestic Case Study: Missed Opportunities in the Former Yugoslavia	155
	5.2.1	International Mechanisms	156
	5.2.2	Seeking Redress Domestically: Mechanisms in Bosnia and Herzegovina	159
	5.2.3	Proceedings Before Domestic Courts in Bosnia and Herzegovina	162
5.3		Reparations for Victims of Hissène Habré and Beyond: Breaking New Ground?	164
5.4		Fostering Civil Redress for International Crimes in Domestic Courts: Rationales and Challenges	165
5.5		Universal Civil Jurisdiction as an Alternative Avenue to Seek Redress for International Crimes?	167
	5.5.1	The Doctrine of Universal Criminal Jurisdiction	168

	5.5.2	Towards a Victim-Orientated Approach: A Civil Dimension of Universal Jurisdiction?	180
	5.5.3	Assessing Universal Civil Jurisdiction as a Way to Seek Redress for Victims of International Crimes	195
5.6	Conclusions		196

6 Conclusions

198

6.1	The Theory and Practice of Reparative Justice for International Crimes	198
6.2	Key Themes: The Emerging Reparative Dimension of International Justice and New Paradigms	201

	6.2.1	Reparation Is Only One Facet of the Broader Goal of Delivering "Justice for Victims" of International Crimes	201
	6.2.2	Individual Perpetrators Have a Legal Duty to Provide Reparations to Victims of International Crimes, in Certain Circumstances, and Victims Have a Corollary Right to Receive Reparations	202
	6.2.3	The Contents of the Legal Duty to Repair Imposed on Individual Perpetrators are Still Under Formation in International Criminal Justice and Lessons Can Be Learned from Other Reparations Initiatives	203
	6.2.4	An Individualized Approach to Reparations Remains Complementary to State Responsibility for Reparations for International Crimes	203
	6.2.5	Disconnect Between the Rhetoric that Included Reparations in International Criminal Justice, Supported by the Idea of Justice for Victims, and the Substantive Realization of Reparations	204
	6.2.6	A Reparative Dimension of International Criminal Justice, Including Reparations for Victims of International Crimes, Is Not Limited to the ICC	205
	6.2.7	In the ICC Context, Expectations with Regards to Reparations Have to Be Measured	206
	6.2.8	Victims' Provisions at the ICC Have a Significant Symbolic Value and Could Be a Catalyst for the Implementation of Reparations in Other Fora	206
	6.2.9	Adding a Civil Dimension to Universal Jurisdiction May Provide an Avenue for Victims' Claims for Reparation	207

6.3		Realizing Reparative Justice: The Road Ahead	207
	6.3.1	A New Phase of International Justice: The Need to Move Reparative Justice Forward	208
	6.3.2	Realizing Reparative Justice for International Crimes Requires Global Efforts	208
	6.3.3	To Be Effective, Reparative Justice Needs to Be Expeditious	209
	6.3.4	Seeing the Victims, Not the Perpetrators: Reparations Unconditioned to Convictions	210
	6.3.5	At the ICC, There Should Be a Collaborative Effort Towards Realizing the Reparations Mandate	212
	6.3.6	More Efforts Have to Be Put into Bridging Informational Gaps and Managing Victims' Understanding and Expectations of the Mandate and Limitations of the ICC	213
	6.3.7	States Parties Should Engage in Realizing Reparations	213
	6.3.8	The Context in Which Reparation Is Sought Is Important	214
6.4		Final Remarks	216

Bibliography	218
Index	249

v

Foreword

It is with particular satisfaction that I write this Foreword to the book by Dr. Miriam Cohen, *Realizing Reparative Justice for International Crimes: from Theory to Practice*, for three main reasons. First, the book is inspired on the Ph.D. thesis of the author, which she brilliantly presented at Leiden University, on 28 June 2017. On the occasion, I was in the examining board, and, in approving her thesis *cum laude*, we all recognized her engagement on the cause, her dedication to the research, and the excellence of her work.

Secondly, the current topicality of the subject is attracting growing attention in our days, such as the one devoted to it by the author in her present book. And thirdly, the fact that I have been accompanying Dr. Miriam Cohen's academic and professional trajectory, both here at the International Court of Justice at The Hague, where she worked in my Chamber for four years, as well as in her doctoral studies at Leiden University and in her professional work thereafter.

Dr. Miriam Cohen is nowadays Professor of International Law at the University of Montréal, being moreover active in participation in academic and judicial events in distinct countries; she is likewise author of successive studies published in international legal periodicals in distinct continents. I much value her academic vocation, and her dedication to facing the challenges examined in the present book, with a humanitarian outlook, so as to secure redress to the vulnerable victims of mass crimes.

In effect, ever since humanity came to exist, there have been armed conflicts and grave human rights violations. Countless persons have been victimized as a result of wars, oppressive and dictatorial regimes, and violent conflicts. Criminal punishment and inter-State reparations have, for a long

xiv *Foreword*

time, taken precedence over redress for human beings and groups who have suffered most, as a result of such grave violations. At the inception of international criminal justice, reparations for victims of international crimes were not included in the practice of international tribunals. More recently, reparative justice in the aftermath of conflicts has attracted more attention in juridical writings.

Yet, most studies focus on one aspect of reparative justice, with the system developed at the International Criminal Court (ICC) often occupying a central place. The present book by Dr. Miriam Cohen comes in good time, as an in-depth study, like hers, of the way reparations for international crimes has developed in systems beyond the ICC, and how it can further evolve, was largely lacking in international law scholarship. Such study of reparations for mass human rights violations, including international crimes, is a remarkable endeavour, given the fluidity and complexity of the theme.

The present book, on *Realizing Reparative Justice for International Crimes: from Theory to Practice*, fills this gap with a timely, thorough, and holistic analysis of the challenges and potentials of reparative justice for the most heinous conduct. In this book, Professor Miriam Cohen brilliantly develops a theory that realizing reparative justice is an interconnected endeavour, one which must be undertaken in multiple frameworks, at domestic, regional, and international levels.

The author devotes the first part of the book to the construction of the legal basis of a duty of reparation in international criminal law (chapter 1). She then focuses on the shift from State to individual responsibility, and takes into consideration the experience gathered in the International Law of Human Rights, in particular in the adjudication of cases of massacres by the Inter-American Court of Human Rights and its pioneering jurisprudence ensuing therefrom.

Dr. Miriam Cohen then turns to the second part of the book, on the case-law of the former *ad hoc* International Criminal Tribunals (for the Former Yugoslavia - ICTY, and for Rwanda - ICTR), as well as of other internationalized or hybrid tribunals (for Lebanon - STL, for Sierra Leone - SCSL, for Cambodia - ECCC) (chapter 2), and the gradual development towards reparations. Following that, the author examines the case-law of the International Criminal Court (ICC) in the construction of the domain of reparations (chapter 3); in this respect, she presents her assessment of that case-law, encompassing inconsistencies, delays, and the need for change.

In the following part of the book, the author considers the position of victims of international crimes within administrative mechanisms, with particular attention to the ICC Trust Fund for Victims (TFV) (chapter 4). She

Foreword

extracts lessons from the first cases pertaining to the reparations mandate, and identifies the challenges of the TFV and administrative mechanisms in the aftermath of mass crimes. This is completed by the remaining part of the book (chapter 5), on the role of national courts and mechanisms (in distinct legal systems) for securing redress to victims of mass crimes.

The study as a whole provides a fresh outlook on recent and significant jurisprudential developments at the ICC and other international tribunals, while also dwelling on administrative mechanisms and domestic cases as potentially the way forward in realizing reparative justice. Dr. Miriam Cohen engages in a thoughtful study of the contribution of human rights mechanisms and the pioneering jurisprudence of the Inter-American Court of Human Rights (particularly at the time I presided it), of the International Law of Human Rights as a whole, and other fields beyond International Criminal Law, and she argues for a synergy of endeavours to realize fully reparative justice for victims.

Dr. Miriam Cohen's book calls for a greater engagement with reparative justice mechanisms as a response to victimization in conflicts, and proposes some areas for further development, so that victims' right to reparations can be truly realized. In the present study, rather than focusing on the "criminal" of international criminal law, those affected by international crimes take correctly the centre-stage. The author's approach is particularly important at present, given the current development of the international adjudication of cases of grave violations of rights of the human persons.

Such approach grows in importance, considering that time regrettably has not yet come when reparations to victims become part of all post-conflict responses, be they judicial, administrative, or others; much stills needs to be done. The present study recognizes the endeavours undertaken for the realization of reparative justice for victims of heinous conduct; it makes a significant and timely contribution in this reparative domain, as it unprecedently engages with synergies of distinct systems in place, as well as possibilities for future development.

In addition to the five chapters of the book, Dr. Miriam Cohen presents the substantial conclusions of her in-depth study with thoughts on the evolution of reparations to victims of international crimes, encompassing theoretical endeavours as well as the practical application by distinct national and international institutions. As the author clearly posits, while some advances can here be perceived, more remains to be done in order to achieve truly the realization of reparative justice for victims of mass violations of human rights and international law.

The present book proposes recommendations anchored on theory and practice, so as to move from the ideal to the concrete realization of reparations. The author supports, as the way forward, a holistic cross-fertilization of distinct systems and mechanisms, working in synergy for the achievement of reparative justice for victims of humanity's worst atrocities. Professor Miriam Cohen's book constitutes a timely and most valuable contribution to the important matter so well examined herein, and to the emerging bibliography on the matter. Her book will attract wide readership, surely on the part of the new generation of scholars, and of all those engaged in the realization of justice in the realm of International Criminal Law as well as International Law of Human Rights and International Humanitarian Law.

The Hague, 22 November 2019.

Antônio Augusto CANÇADO TRINDADE
Judge of the International Court of Justice; Former President of the Inter-American Court of Human Rights; Emeritus Professor of International Law of the University of Brasília, Brazil

Acknowledgments

Many people have been fundamental in the making of this book, without whom this project would not have been possible. I wish to express here a few words of gratitude. This book is inspired by, and further develops, the topic of my Ph.D. thesis completed in 2017 at Leiden University, Grotius Centre for International Legal Studies. I would first like to extend a special "thank you" to my principal supervisor, Professor Larissa Van den Herik, for her guidance and feedback throughout the process. Her support, inspiration, and extensive knowledge have meant so much in this journey, and I am indebted to her for having believed in this project, and for trusting me, from the very beginning. I also wish to express my gratitude to Professor Carsten Stahn whose invaluable suggestions, and ongoing support, have greatly improved my ideas. I would also like to thank the members of the Doctoral Committee at Leiden University, who provided excellent comments and challenged me during my viva: Professor Cançado Trindade, Professor William Schabas, Professor Caroline Fournet, Professor Afshin Ellian, Dr. Alejandro Kiss, and Dr. Sergey Vasiliev.

My former supervisor at the International Court of Justice, and life mentor, H. E. Judge Antônio Augusto Cançado Trindade, has been a continuous source of inspiration and guidance. I cannot thank him enough for supporting this book and my doctoral studies during the four years I worked in his Chambers at the International Court of Justice, and thereafter, and for all the encouraging discussions and scholarly opportunities he has provided me throughout the years.

My gratitude also goes to Professor Martha Minow with whom I first discussed the foundational ideas that would give rise, years later, to the topic of this book.

I also wish to thank the production and editorial staff at Cambridge University Press who have tirelessly thoroughly worked with me and provided useful comments throughout the completion of the book. I am deeply indebted to anonymous peer reviewers for their insightful and helpful comments and suggestions, all of which greatly improved the manuscript.

A very special thank you is particularly owed to my family who have always stood by me. My spouse and life partner, Steven Geneau, for his unconditional love and trust, for his peaceful inspiration, and for always reminding me that dreams can come true. This book would not have been possible without his support and motivation. My parents, Erlinda and Moises, who have taught me diligence, hard work, perseverance, and kindness, and who have always believed in my wildest projects, ever since my childhood in Brazil. My sister, Alessandra, for her invaluable support especially in the final stages of this project. I could not have done this without all of you. Last but certainly not least, my young sons, Joshua and Jayden, who continuously inspire me to strive for a better world, and who have been, at such young ages, generous and patient to share my attention and my time with this project. Their large smiles and *joie de vivre* have kept me focused and pushed me forward: it is my hope that one day they will find some source of inspiration in this book.

Table of Cases

CASES

ADC Affiliate Limited and ADC & ADMC Management Limited v. *Republic of Hungary*, Case No. ARB/03/16, Award of 2 October 2006, ICSID

Amoco International Finance Corporation v. *The Islamic Republic of Iran et al.*, Partial Award No. 310–56-3 of 14 July 1987, 15 Iran-United States Claims Tribunal Reports 189

Bautista de Arellana v. *Columbia* (563/93), CCPR/C/55/D/563/1993 (1995)

Blancov v. *Nicaragua* (328/88), CCPR/C/51/D/328/1988 (1994)

Bridge of Varvarin case, Landgericht (LG) Bonn, 1 O 361/02, NJW 2004, 525, HuV-I 2/2004, 111–113, confirmed by *Oberlandesgericht* (OLG) Köln, 7 U 8/04

Cyprus: Supreme Court, *Ttofinis* v. *Theochandes* (1983) 2 Cyprus Law Reports 363

Divisional Court, *Jones* v. *Whalley* [2006] 2 Criminal Law Review 67 on appeal to the House of Lords, *Jones* v. *Whalley* [2006] 4 All ER 113

ECtHR, *Kalougeropoulou and Others* v. *Greece and Germany*, Admissibility, 12 December 2002, Application No. 59021/00

ECtHR, *Varnava et al.* v. *Turkey*, Merits, Grand Chamber, 18 September 2009, unreported, Application No. 16064/90

ECCC, "Appeal Judgment," Case File/Dossier No. 001/18–07-2007-ECCC /SC, 3 February 2012, 116

ECCC, "Case 002/01 Judgment," Case File/ Dossier No. 002/19–09-2007/ ECCC/TC, 7 August 2014

ECCC, "Judgment," Case File/Dossier No. 001/18–07-2007/ECCC/TC, 26 July 2010

ECCC, "Decision on Civil Party Co-Lawyers' Joint Request for a Ruling on the Standing of Civil Party lawyers to Make Submissions on Sentencing and Directions Concerning the Questioning of the Accused, Experts and xx *Table of Cases*

Witnesses Testifying on Character," Case 001: Kaing Guek Eav (001/18–07-2007/ECCC/TC), 9 October 2009

El-Hojouj v. Amer Derbas et al., 21 March 2012, Case No. 400882/HA ZA 11–2252

Factory at Chorzów, Jurisdiction, Judgment No. 8, 1927, PCIJ, Series A, no. 17

Ferida Selimović et al. v. the Republika Srpska, Decision on Admissibility and the Merits, 7 March 2003, CH/01/8365 et al.

Ferrini v. Federal Republic of Germany, Corte di Cassazione (Sezioni Unite), 11 March 2004, 87 *Rivista di diritto internazionale* 539

Fitfield v. Ins. Co. of Pa., 47 Pa. 166, 187 (1864)

IACtHR, *Baldeón-García v. Peru*, Merits, Reparations and Costs, 6 April 2006, Series C No. 147

IACtHR, *Velásquez-Rodríguez v. Honduras*, Merits Judgment, 29 July 1988

ICC, "Decision on Applications for Participation in Proceedings a/0004/06 to a/0009/06, a/001606, a/0063/06, a/0071/06 to a/0080/06 and a/01/05/06," in the case of *The Prosecutor v. Thomas Lubanga Dyilo*, 20 October 2006, ICC-01/04–01/06–601

ICC, Decision on the Applications for Participation in the Proceedings of VPRS1, VPRS2, VPRS3, VPRS4, VPRS5, and VPRS6, ICC-01/04-101-t-ENG-Crr, 17 January 2006

ICC, Decision on the Applications for Participation in the Proceedings of VPRS1, VPRS2, VPRS3, VPRS4, VPRS5, and VPRS6, 17 January 2006, ICC-01–04-101-t-ENG-Corr

ICC, Decision on Victims' Application for Participation a/0010/06, a/0064/06 to a/0/0070/06, a/0081/06, a/0082/06, a/0084/06 to a/0089/06, a/0091/06 to a/0097/06, a/0099/06, a/0100/06, a/0102/06 to a/0104/06, a/0111/06, a/0113/06 to a/0117/06, a/0120/06, a/0121/06 and a/0123/06 to a/0127/06, in the case of *The Prosecutor v. Joseph Kony, Vincent Otti, Okot Odhiambo, Dominic Ongwen*, 14 March 2008, ICC-02/04–01/05–282 (pre-trial phase)

ICC, *The Prosecutor v. Thomas Lubanga*, "Judgment on the Appeals of the Prosecutor and The Defence against Trial Chamber I's Decision on Victims' Participation," 18 January 2008, ICC-01/04–01/06–1432

ICC, *The Prosecutor v. Lubanga*, "Observations of the V02 Group of Victims on Sentencing and Reparations," (V02 Group), 18 April 2012, ICC-01/04–01/06

ICC, *The Prosecutor v. Lubanga*, "Observations on the Sentence and Reparations by Victims" (V01 Group), 18 April 2012, ICC-01/04–01/06

ICC, *The Prosecutor v. Thomas Lubanga Dyilo*, "Decision Establishing the Principles and Procedures to be applied to Reparations," 7 August 2012, ICC-01/04–01/06, Trial Chamber I, 134, 135, 175, 179, 214

ICC, *Situation in the Democratic Republic of Congo*, "Decision on the Application for Participation in the Proceedings of VPRS1, VPRS2, VPRS3, VPRS4, VPRS5 and VPRS6," 17 January 2006, ICC-01/04–101-tEN-Corr

ICC, *Situation in Uganda*, "Notification of the Board of Directors of the Trust Fund for Victims in accordance with Regulation 50 of the Regulations of the Trust Fund for Victims," 25 January 2008, ICC-02/04

ICC, *The Prosecutor v. Thomas Lubanga*, "Judgment on the Appeals of the Prosecutor and The Defence against Trial Chamber I's Decision on Victims' Participation," 18 January 2008, ICC-01/04–01/06–1432

ICC, *The Prosecutor v. William Samoei Ruto and Joshua Arap Sang*, "Decision on the Requests Regarding Reparations," ICC-01/09–01/11–2038, 1 July 2016, 159, 160

ICC, Trial Chamber II, *The Prosecutor v. Thomas Lubanga Dyilo*, "Order Approving the Proposed Plan of the Trust Fund for Victims in Relation to Symbolic Collective Reparations," ICC-01/04–01/06, 21 October 2016, 219, 308

ICJ, Application of the Convention on the Prevention and Punishment of the Crime of Genocide (*Bosnia and Herzegovina v. Serbia and Montenegro*), Judgment, 26 February 2007

ICJ, Case Concerning Ahmadou Sadio Diallo (*Republic of Guinea v. Democratic Republic of the Congo*), Judgment, ICJ Reports 2010

ICJ, Case Concerning Application of the Convention on the Prevention and Punishment of the Crime of Genocide (*Bosnia and Herzegovina v. Serbia and Montenegro*), Judgment, ICJ Reports 2007

ICJ, Case Concerning Armed Activities on the Territory of the Congo (*Democratic Republic of the Congo v. Uganda*), Judgment, ICJ Reports 2005

ICJ, Case Concerning Avena and Other Mexican Nationals (*Mexico v. United States of America*), Judgment, ICJ Reports 2004, 56

ICJ, Case Concerning Gabčíkovo-Nagymaros Project (*Hungary v. Slovakia*), Judgment, ICJ Reports 1997

ICJ, Case Concerning Pulp Mills on the River Uruguay (*Argentina v. Uruguay*), Judgment, ICJ Reports 2010, 56

ICJ, Case Concerning the Jurisdictional Immunities of the State (*Germany v. Italy*: Greece intervening), Judgment, 3 February 2012, 85

ICJ, Reparation for Injuries Suffered in the Service of the United Nations, Advisory Opinion, ICJ Reports 1949

ICTY, *Prosecutor v. Furundžija*, Trial Chamber, Judgment of 10 December 1998 (no. IT-95–17/1-T)

xxii   *Table of Cases*

Ivica Kevesevic v. *the Federation of Bosnia and Herzegovina*, 10 September 1998, Case No. CH/97/46

Josip, Bozana and Tomislav Matanovic v. *the Republika Srpska*, Decision on Admissibility, 13 September 1996, Decision on the Merits, 6 August 1997, Decisions on Admissibility and Merits, March 1996–December 1997, Case No. CH/96/01

Kadic v. *Karadžić*, 70 F.3d 232 (2d. Circ. 1995), cert. denied, 518 US 1005 (1996)

Kadic v. *Karadžić*, No. 93 Civ. 1163, judgment (S.D.N. August 16, 2000)

Khatsiyeva et al. v. *Russia*, Merits, 17 January 2008, unreported, Application No. 5108/02

Kiobel v. *Royal Dutch Petroleum Co.*, 132 S. Ct. 1738 (2012)

Kiobel v. *Royal Dutch Petroleum Co.*, 133 S. Ct. 1659 (2013) (No 10–1491), 295

LG&E Energy Corp., LG&E Capital Corp., LG&E International Inc. v. *Argentine Republic*, Case No. ARB/02/1, Award of 25 July 2007, ICSID

M/V "Saiga" (No. 2) (Saint Vincent and the Grenadines v. *Guinea)*, Judgment, ITLOS Reports 1999

Mehinovic, Kemal, et al. 2009. v. *Nikola Vuckovic*, Civil Section 1:98-cv-2470-MHS US District Court, Northern District of Georgia, 29 July 2009

Palic v. *Republika Srpska*, Decision on Admissibility and Merits, 11 January 2001, Case No. CH/99/3196

Prefecture Voiotia v. *Federal Republic of Germany*, Hellenic Supreme Court, 4 May 2000, Case No. 11/2000

Prosecutor v. *Charles Ghankay Taylor*, Appeals Judgment, Special Court for Sierra Leone, 26 September 2013, SCSL, 03–01-A

Prosecutor v. *Charles Ghankay Taylor*, Judgment, Special Court for Sierra Leone, 18 May 2012, SCSL, 03–01-T

Prosecutor v. *Thomas Lubanga Dyilo*, "Decision of the Appeals Chamber on the Joint Application of Victims a/0001/06 to a/0003/06 and a/0105/06 Concerning the Directions and Decision of the Appeals Chamber," 2 February 2007, ICC-01/04–01/06–925, Separate opinion of Judge Pikis

Queen's Bench Division R (on the application of Gladstone Pic) v. *Manchester City Magistrates* [2005] All ER 56 (All England Law Reports)

Rasim Jusufović v. *the Republika Srpska*, Decision on Admissibility and Merits, 9 June 2000, Case No. CH/98/698

Rodriquez v. *Uruguay* (322/88), CCPR/C/51/D/322/1988 (1994)

Sosa v. *Alvarez-Machain*, 124 U.S. 2739, 2775 (2004)

Sosa v. *Alvarez-Machain*, Supreme Court, 542 U.S. 692 (2004)

Stockholms Tingsrätt (Stockholm District Court), case no. B 382–10, 8 April 2011

Supreme Court of Norway Judgment, case no. 2010/934, 3 December 2010

The Public Prosecuting Authority v. *Mirsad Repak*, Oslo District Court case
no: 08-018985MEDOTIR/08, 2 December 2008

The S.S. Lotus Case PCIJ Ser. A, No. 10, p. 4 (1927)

Trial of Major War Criminals before the International Military Tribunal,
Nuremberg, 14 November 1945–1 October 1946 (Nuremberg: International
Military Tribunal, 1947), 43

Unkovic v. *Federation of Bosnia and Herzogovina*, Decision on Admissibility
and Merits, 9 November 2001, Case No. CH/99/2150

Abbreviations

ACHR	American Convention on Human Rights
AC	Appeals Chamber
ASP	Assembly of States Parties
CRPC	Commission for Real Property Claims of Refugees and Displaced Persons
EAC	Extraordinary African Chamber
ECCC	Extraordinary Chambers in the Courts of Cambodia
ECHR	European Convention on Human Rights
ECnHR	European Commission of Human Rights
ECtHR	European Court of Human Rights
IACnHR	Inter-American Commission on Human Rights
IACtHR	Inter-American Court of Human Rights
ICTs	International Criminal Courts and Tribunals
ICC	International Criminal Court
ICJ	International Court of Justice
ICCPR	International Covenant on Civil and Political Rights
ICTY	International Criminal Tribunal for the former Yugoslavia
ICTR	International Criminal Tribunal for Rwanda
IHL	International Humanitarian Law
ILC	International Law Commission
IMT	International Military Tribunal
OPCV	Office of Public Counsel for Victims
OTP	Office of the Prosecutor
PCIJ	Permanent Court of International Justice
RPE	Rules of Procedure and Evidence

SCSL	Special Court for Sierra Leone
STL	Special Tribunal for Lebanon
TC	Trial Chamber
TFV	Trust Fund for Victims
UN	United Nations

Prologue

Whatever the reparations will be, we are aware of the fact that we have lost what money can and will never buy: our dignity. We lost in a few days what we had built during our entire lives. In my case, I was raped by several men from the MLC, in front of my children. My dignity as a mother, as a woman, as a human being, I lost it that day. The bond of mother with my children has been distorted and tarnished by this act. My children and I will forever bear the weight of rape. This heavy silence, these avoidances in each other's eyes translate not only our pain but also the shame we are carrying. My boys became rebels in the society, ready to join any militia in the country in order to take revenge for my rape. It is difficult for me to admit that tomorrow they could do to another woman, another mother, what our persecutors did to us. We are eagerly waiting for justice to play its deterring role.[1]

This is a book permeated by stories of human suffering and pain, loss and tragedy. It is also a tale of hope for the victims, striving to find ways to mend what is forever broken, in search for a more humane world. It is a book about how the rule of law and diverse redress systems can be part of responses to mass atrocity. It is hoped that it can contribute to crucial dialogues that honor victims and survivors, and how we can move forward as humanity.

---

[1] ICC, *The Prosecutor* v. *Jean-Pierre Bemba*, "Legal Representatives of Victims' joint submissions on the consequences of the Appeals Chamber's Judgment dated 8 June 2018 on the reparations proceedings," ICC-01/05–01/08–3649, 12 July 2018, para. 23 (cited as "Meeting with victim a/0588/08 in Bangui in September 2017").

Introduction

The concept of justice, in all its dimensions,[1] is one of the most ancient, complex, and controversial notions known to humanity. Yet, horrific crimes and mass victimization have remained a defining feature of humankind. In the past, this criminal conduct has been met with a variety of responses, most of which claim to fit within a narrative of "justice."

In recent decades, the search for justice in the context of international crimes and mass human rights violations has garnered increased attention in international legal scholarship.[2] In large part, this scholarship has focused upon the conceptual dichotomy between punishment of offenders on the one hand, and reparations[3] for victims on the other. A dominant assumption is that

---

[1] See e.g., Amartya Sen, "Global Justice: Beyond International Equity," in *Global Public Goods: International Cooperation in the 21st Century*, ed. I. Kaul, UNDP, 1999 (for the concept of justice as a global public good). See also, D. D. Raphael, *Concepts of Justice*, Oxford University Press, 2003; Judith N. Shklar, *The Faces of Injustice*, Yale University Press, 1992; John Rawls, *A Theory of Justice*, Harvard University Press, 1971.

[2] See generally, Steven Ratner, Jason Abrams, and James Bischoff, *Accountability for Human Rights Atrocities in International Law: Beyond the Nuremberg Legacy*, Oxford University Press, 3rd ed., 2009; William Driscoll et al., *The International Criminal Court: Global Politics and the Quest for Justice*, International Debate Education Association, 2004. See also, Steven R. Ratner et al., *Accountability for Human Rights Atrocities in International Law*, Oxford University Press, 1997; Antonio Cassese, "On the Current Trends Towards Criminal Prosecution and Punishment of Breaches of International Humanitarian Law," *European Journal of International Law* 9 (1998), p. 2.

[3] Reparations include "restitution, compensation, rehabilitation, satisfaction and guarantees of non-repetition," see Basic Principles and Guidelines on the Right to Remedy and Reparation for Victims of Gross Violations of International Human Rights Law and Serious Violations of International Humanitarian Law, G.A. Res. 60/147 U.N. Doc. A/RES/60/147 (Mar. 21, 2006). See also, ICJ, Case Concerning Ahmadou Sadio Diallo (*Republic of Guinea* v. *Democratic Republic of the Congo*), Judgment, 30 November 2010, Separate Opinion of Judge Cançado Trindade, paras. 209–212. The terms "redress" and "reparation" will be used interchangeably throughout this book.

2 *Reparative Justice for International Crimes*

human rights law conceptually encompasses redress for victims of violations.[4] This same assumption is not typically found within international criminal law literature, which has traditionally focused on the criminal liability and the punishment of perpetrators, rather than on the rights of the victims.

Dealing with the aftermath of conflicts and mass victimization imposes difficult questions regarding the appropriate response to these crimes. At its inception, the concept of justice for mass crimes focused on accountability and punishment of the offender. More recently, international criminal law discourse embraces the notion of reparative justice for victims as an additional goal of international justice.[5] Some scholars have claimed that "justice for victims" is one of the core tenets of the international criminal justice enterprise.[6] Victims are viewed as "both the reason for and objective of international criminal justice."[7] This raises questions about what delivering justice to victims of international crimes entails, and whether the criminal prosecution and punishment of perpetrators is sufficient to achieve this goal.

In relation to international crimes and mass atrocities, the justice divide has been traditionally characterized by the total separation of criminal processes and remedies (pursued, in the international plane, mainly by international or hybrid criminal tribunals), and victim redress (for example, pursued through interstate agreements, mass claims processes, human rights mechanisms, or civil claims

---

[4] See Thomas M. Antkowiak, "Remedial Approaches to Human Rights Violations: The Inter-American Court of Human Rights and Beyond," *Columbia Journal of Transnational Law* 46 (2008), pp. 351–419 (examining the jurisprudence of the Inter-American Court of Human Rights and European Court of Human Rights and noting that human rights mechanisms concern obtaining reparation from states and not from criminal offenders). See also, Dinah Shelton, *Remedies in International Human Rights Law*, Oxford University Press, 2nd ed., 2005.

[5] See e.g., ICTY Annual Report to the General Assembly, A/50/365-S/1995/728, 1995, paras. 198–199; Statement of the ICC Deputy Prosecutor in the opening of the Prosecutor's case in Katanga and Chui, "ICC Cases and Opportunity for Communities in Ituri to Come Together and Move Forward," ICC-OTP-20080627-PR332, 27 June 2008.

[6] See *inter alia* Luke Moffett, *Justice for Victims Before the International Criminal Court*, Routledge, 2014; Luke Moffett, "Meaningful and Effective? Considering Victims Interests Through Participation at the International Criminal Court," *Criminal Law Forum* 26 (2015), pp. 255–289; Luke Moffett, "Elaborating Justice for Victims at the International Criminal Court: Beyond Rhetoric and The Hague," *Journal of International Criminal Justice* 13 (2015), pp. 281–311; Luke Moffett, "Realising Justice for Victims Before the International Criminal Court," *International Crimes Database*, 2014; Luke Moffett, "Reparative Complementarity: Ensuring an Effective Remedy for Victims in the Reparation Regime of the International Criminal Court," *International Journal of Human Rights* 17 (2013), pp. 368–390.

[7] Cited in Emily Haslam, "Victim Participation at the International Criminal Court: A Triumph of Hope over Experience," in D. McGoldrick (ed.), *The Permanent International Criminal Court*, ed. D. McGoldrick, Hart, 2004, pp. 315–334, p. 316 (statement of former French Minister of Justice Elizabeth Guigou).

Introduction

before domestic courts). New developments in international law, at both the international and domestic levels, have begun to blur the apparent normative, doctrinal, and practical criminal/reparative divide which has historically existed between the prosecution and punishment of individual perpetrators of international crimes on the one hand, and civil remedies including reparation for victims of those crimes, on the other. This dichotomy of criminal and reparations processes meant that international (or hybrid) criminal tribunals pursuing the prosecution and eventual punishment of perpetrators excluded the possibility of redress for victims from the proceedings.

The advent of the Rome Statute for the International Criminal Court[8] brought about a change in the traditional conception of international justice at the international level, and resituated the role of victims therein. The ICC Statute provided the possibility for both a criminal dimension – the investigation, prosecution, and the eventual punishment of perpetrators of international crimes[9] (encompassing retribution, accountability, and the fight against impunity) - and also a restorative dimension, including reparations[10] and assistance for victims within the proceedings of a given case.

At the domestic level, in addition to civil claims for reparations brought before national courts, cases relying on the doctrine of universal jurisdiction may have the potential to bridge the gap between the criminal and reparative dimensions of justice for international crimes. While victims' right to reparation for violations they have suffered is well-established under international law, and in most domestic systems a perpetrator of a crime will often not only be subject to criminal proceedings, but may also face civil action brought by the injured party (through a tort system or another form of civil liability system), the civil dimension of universal jurisdiction remains controversial under international law.[11]

---

[8] Rome Statute of the International Criminal Court, U.N. Doc. A/CONF.183/9 was adopted on 17 July 1998. It came into force on 1 July 2002 (hereinafter: "Rome Statute" or "ICC Statute") and it established the International Criminal Court (hereinafter: "ICC").

[9] The jurisdiction of the ICC over international crimes is limited to genocide, crimes against humanity, war crimes, and the crime of aggression, see Rome Statute, art. 8. The definition of international crimes for the purpose of this book is further explained below.

[10] See Rome Statute, art. 75. See also, Claude Jorda and Jerome de Hamptinne, "The Status and Role of the Victims," in *The Rome Statute of the International Criminal Court: A Commentary*, eds. Antonio Cassese, et al., Oxford University Press, 2002, pp. 1387–1388; Linda M. Keller, "Seeking Justice at the International Criminal Court: Victims' Reparations," *Thomas Jefferson Law Review* 29 (2006–2007), p. 189.

[11] See Donald Francis Donovan and Anthea Roberts, "The Emerging Recognition of Universal Civil Jurisdiction," *American Journal of International Law* 100 (2006), p. 142. See also a discussion in Chapter 5.

Against this backdrop, an analysis of the various systems operating at the national and international levels, and their approach to victim reparations for international crimes, is important and timely. The discussion aims to fit within a wider range of related themes and inquiries concerning victimhood and a critical analysis of international criminal justice.

This book both draws from relevant existing literature on these themes and aims to contribute to the dialogue by providing an analysis of reparations for international crimes, especially focusing on the systems developed at international and national levels. In pursuing this larger analysis, some tangential questions are examined: what other effects may adding a reparative dimension to international criminal justice have on current trends? We currently see certain archetypes of victims, such as children and sexual and gender-based violence victims. Is it proper to differentiate and prioritize, and how does adding a reparative dimension to criminal justice influence these dynamics? Further in this vein, some overarching themes present in the analysis concern the collective versus the individual and perceptions/constructions of victimhood. The discussion also engages with critical scholarship pertaining to the detrimental effects that criminal justice may produce for victims, and accordingly dwells upon whether the differentiated application of victims' rights in criminal contexts might ultimately be an argument against mixing criminal and reparation processes.

The present book focuses on the development of reparations for victims in international criminal law and looks into the emerging reparative dimension of international criminal justice. The conception of "reparative dimension" of international justice includes reparation or redress to victims of international crimes and it is juxtaposed to a criminal dimension in the sense of criminal investigations and prosecutions of international crimes. Ultimately, it inquires whether international justice should be moving towards a blend of the two dimensions within the international criminal process, or a *sui generis* model altogether. The research also explores how reparative justice for international crimes is best shaped and how it should further develop. These questions underlie the analytical framework, and are addressed directly or implicitly in the chapters of this book.

1.1 GENERAL PARAMETERS

The question of whether an individualized approach to reparations for international crimes is always preferable to the state-based approach that has historically existed to deal with reparations for international crimes is at the heart of this book. International criminal law rests on the premise that

Introduction

individuals should be held criminally accountable for international crimes they commit, but should this approach be transposed when it comes to reparations for victims? In this sense, this book questions whether such an individualized approach to reparations could be a mismatch with the collective nature of international crimes. In other words, should the individualized approach that international criminal law proposes for reparations for victims be favored, and what is the legal basis for imposing a duty of reparations directly on individuals? If international criminal justice is to place a duty of reparation directly on individuals, what is the content of this duty (which may be different from state duties to repair), and how can it be operationalized?

Throughout the analysis contained in this book, it is posited that the architecture of international criminal justice cannot be grounded solely on a criminal dimension concerning the trial and punishment of the *offender*, without attaching a role for *victims*. This vision of international criminal justice rests upon a synergy of efforts at international and national levels. The chapters of this book aim to reflect on and justify this claim.

There are two conceptual parameters within this book which guide its direction and inform its analysis. First, this book concerns international criminal justice, thus, conceptually, proceedings against *individuals*, and *not* states; second, it concerns a *reparative* dimension of international justice. As such, criminal accountability and criminal prosecutions for international crimes and mass atrocities are not the main focus of this book. In short, this book aims to examine the challenges and possibilities of a greater emphasis on victim reparation for international crimes at national and international levels, including through avenues such as national courts and administrative mechanisms which adjudicate civil claims pertaining to international crimes.

1.2 THEMES AND THE SCOPE OF THE BOOK

This book aims to provide a timely, comprehensive, and systematic legal analysis of reparations for international crimes which goes beyond a purely theoretical discussion of the system established at the ICC. It discusses the evolution of reparations for international crimes from theory to practice. This book originally engages with recent decisions and filings at the ICC relating to reparation to provide some suggestions on how concretely the criminal and reparative dimensions of international criminal justice can be reconciled. Previous studies on this topic were primarily theoretical, so a true assessment and recommendations on how to reconcile reparative and criminal dimensions of justice for international crimes could not be undertaken. This book looks at the development of reparations in practice through filings and decisions to critically assess the outcome against a careful theoretical framework. Furthermore, this book is innovative in its proposal to study reparations within international criminal justice at the broader international (including the ICC, but also other courts and tribunals in international criminal law) and national levels (by the study of how the application of international criminal law should develop at the national level), as well as administrative mechanisms (primarily through a careful discussion of the ICC Trust Fund for Victims' activities and its unique challenges).

A highlight of this book, compared to existing titles in the field, is that it sets itself apart from previous studies undertaken when reparative justice was still an ideological endeavor in international criminal law, and where the ICC had not yet delivered any concrete judgments against which to assess the system. With recent and imminent decisions from the ICC, and developments in national courts, this book aims to offer a timely critical analysis of the theory and practice of reparations, through a study of the jurisprudence and their real impact on victims and stakeholders, and to propose concrete suggestions for the future development of reparations in the field of international justice.

There exists a rich literature on reparations for international crimes. This book was greatly inspired by previous works in this field and it aims to contribute new insights to the debate. There are published monographs specifically on the subject of reparations for international crimes, such as: Luke Moffett, *Justice for Victims Before the International Criminal Court* (Routledge, 2014; analysing the ICC system of reparation through the creation of a theory of justice for victims and drawing on field research); Eva Dwertmann, *The Reparation System of the International Criminal Court* (Martinus Nijhoff, 2010) and Connor McCarthy, *Reparations and Victim Support in the International Criminal Court* (Cambridge University Press, 2012) (both analyzing the ICC system of reparation); Ilaria Bottigliero, *Redress for Victims of Crimes Under International Law* (Martinus Nijhoff, 2004). There are also other important works that address reparations for international human rights violations or international crimes from multidisciplinary dimensions (e.g., Jo-Anne Wemmers's edited collection on *Reparations for Crimes Against Humanity*, Routledge, 2014).

Existing books were published prior to the first decision on reparations at the ICC – which had a major impact on the law on reparations at the ICC and beyond – thus are limited in their discussion on the implications of reparative justice for international crimes and their recommendations. This book provides a critical assessment of the effectiveness and actual impact of the system devised at the ICC and beyond, by looking at decisions of national courts and other tribunals, such as the ECCC.

Introduction 7

In summary, there are distinguishing features in this book that contribute to the debate concerning reparations for international crimes. First, it aims to explore and provide a comprehensive analysis of reparation for victims of international crimes not only as it applies to the ICC but also to other national and international fora. Second, the book examines reparations in a holistic manner, showing their historical and conceptual backgrounds, contrasting different systems, and drawing some lessons from international human rights jurisprudence. Third, it examines the role of domestic courts in providing reparations for victims, including through an analysis of recent cases and the emerging doctrine of universal jurisdiction. Fourth, it contributes some ideas on the implementation of decisions on reparations at the ICC. Fifth, and importantly, this book goes beyond a theoretical analysis of reparations in the field of international criminal law, carefully analyses submissions of the parties and court decisions, and offers recommendations for development based on recent practice.

It is important to explain and define some key concepts and terms which surface throughout the book.

I.2.1 *Themes and Key Concepts*

1. **"International crimes"** in this book refers to the core crimes defined in the ICC Statute, that is: genocide, war crimes, crimes against humanity, and aggression, in light of their mass victimization nature. This book does not focus on torture[12] as it does not always have the collective dimension of the international crimes and is not an independent crime recognized by the ICC. Transnational crimes[13] are also excluded as different rules and regimes apply to them. It is a conscious decision to

---

[12] See Convention against Torture and Other Cruel, Inhuman or Degrading Treatment or Punishment, United Nations, Treaty Series, vol. 1465, p. 85.

[13] Transnational crime is understood as "offences whose inception, prevention and/or direct or indirect effects involved more than one country," UN Doc. A.CONF. 169/15/Add.1 (1995). The crimes listed in the UN document include *inter alia*: money laundering, terrorist activities, theft of art and cultural objects, theft of intellectual property, illicit arms trafficking, aircraft hijacking, sea piracy, insurance fraud, computer crime, environmental crime, trafficking in persons, trade in human body parts, illicit drug trafficking, fraudulent bankruptcy, infiltration of legal business, corruption, and bribery of public or party officials. See also, Neil Boister and Robert J. Currie, *Routledge Handbook of Transnational Criminal Law*, Routledge, 2014; Philip Reichel and Jay S. Albanese, *Handbook of Transnational Crime and Justice*, Sage Publications, 2nd ed., 2014.

focus solely on international crimes, acknowledging that such an analysis is limited and inherently selective, leaving out many other mass atrocities and human rights violations that do not fall within the above definition of international crimes.

3. **"International criminal law"** and **"international criminal justice"** are treated, respectively, as a doctrine and a system. Therefore, they are not limited to the examination of one particular institution (e.g., the ICC). Rather, they encompass the fabric of numerous procedures, institutions, and mechanisms which address international criminal conduct and reparation thereof. This book encompasses the reparative dimension of both international criminal law and international criminal justice.

4. **"Victims"** in the context of this book refers to those who have suffered as a result of international crimes. The project takes a broad approach to the meaning of victims and goes beyond the definition within one specific institution or framework (e.g., the concept of victim in the ICC).

5. **"Reparations"** in this book follows the guidelines of the *Basic Principles and Guidelines on the Right to Remedy and Reparation for Victims of Gross Violations of International Human Rights Law and Serious Violations of International Humanitarian Law.* They include: "restitution, compensation, rehabilitation, satisfaction and guarantees of non-repetition."[4] The focus of this book is on a right to reparation, and a corresponding legal duty to reparation. While this book will not discuss the right to remedy per se, such right includes: "(*a*) Equal and effective access to justice; (*b*) Adequate, effective and prompt reparation for harm suffered; (*c*) Access to relevant information concerning violations and reparation mechanisms."[5]

6. **"Justice for victims"** is widely referred to in this book. The purpose is not to provide a conclusive definition, or how to attain it. The notion of justice for victims in the aftermath of international crimes is complex and its scope is open to debate. It is acknowledged that justice for victims encompasses much more than reparations.[16]

---

[4] Basic Principles and Guidelines on the Right to Remedy and Reparation for Victims of Gross Violations of International Human Rights Law and Serious Violations of International Humanitarian Law, G.A. Res. 60/147 U.N. Doc. A/RES/60/147 (21 March 2006) ("Basic Principles"), Article 18.

[5] Ibid., Article 11.

[16] For an excellent study of the conceptualization of justice for victims of international crimes, see Luke Moffett, *Justice for Victims Before the International Criminal Court*, Routledge, 2014.

Introduction

I.2.2 Scope and Limitations

The analysis in this book aims to be as comprehensive as possible, but limitations of scope and selections of focus are inherently necessary in a vast and fast-changing field such as that of reparations for international crimes. In addition to defining key concepts and terms, it is important to delineate the scope of the research and analysis that underscore this book, as well as what is *excluded* from the scope of the book. Furthermore, the reader should note at the outset that the law in this field is complex and very fluid; this book considers key developments in law and jurisprudence, up to mid-2019. Conceptual exclusions from this book include the following.

I.2.2.1 State Responsibility

State responsibility is conceptually excluded since this book concerns the development of a reparative dimension of international criminal law and focuses on individuals.

Although the book does refer to state responsibility in the first part concerning theoretical dimensions, this is done purely in a complementary, informative, and comparative manner without it being the main focus. State responsibility is looked at in order to assess whether an individualized approach to reparations (i.e., seeking reparations from individuals rather than the state) is well-suited for dealing with redress for international crimes. This book also examines to what extent principles and case law on state responsibility for reparations can inform the content of an individual legal duty to repair.

I.2.2.2 International/Regional Human Rights Mechanisms

Similarly, because they deal with *state* responsibility for *human rights* violations (as opposed to a focus on international crimes), and have a different set of rules, the detailed study of human rights mechanisms is outside the scope of this book. This research overviews the jurisprudence of a selected pertinent regional human rights court purely to inform the analysis of the principles of reparations in international criminal law.

I.2.2.3 Domestic (Transnational) Human Rights Litigation

In a similar vein, the focus of this book is not to review all (transnational) human rights civil litigation in domestic courts. Although some civil litigation of this nature may be referenced to inform the analysis, the focus primarily centers on the possibilities of civil redress for international crimes (and not for all kinds of human rights violations) in domestic proceedings.

I.2.2.4 Truth and Reconciliation Commissions

Truth and reconciliation mechanisms are distinct responses in dealing with the aftermath of international crimes. Studying truth and reconciliation commissions would shift the focus away from the study of reparations in international criminal justice, which is the main theme of the book.

I.2.2.5 Mass Claims and Processes

This book does not discuss mass claims and processes relating to state responsibility for international crimes.

I.2.3 Book Structure

The book is divided in six chapters which provide a careful survey and analysis of the intricacies of international, national, and administrative mechanisms that are being developed to address reparative justice for international crimes, their unique challenges, and some suggestions on how reparative justice for international crimes should develop.

Chapter 1 provides an overview of different theories of justice and how they can inform the development of a reparative dimension of international criminal law. This chapter also traces the evolution of paradigms on the legal duty and the right to reparation: from perspectives of state versus state, to state versus individuals, to individuals versus individuals. It also outlines the development of a duty to repair for individual perpetrators alongside states' duty to repair. This introductory chapter thus provides the theoretical foundation that supports the analysis in the following chapters and it sets out the main themes that are discussed throughout the book. This chapter also discusses the jurisprudence of the Inter-American Court of Human Rights (IACtHR) on reparations, especially assessing victimhood, defining harm, awarding collective and individual reparations, and how the Court has played a role in developing reparative justice in the context of mass human rights violations in the context of state responsibility.

Chapter 2 dwells upon the operationalization of the reparative dimension of international criminal justice at the international level, with a focus on the historical evolution of reparations by international criminal courts and tribunals prior to the ICC, and the reparative justice model devised by the

Extraordinary Chambers in the Courts of Cambodia (ECCC). This chapter retraces the diverse models in place in international criminal tribunals in regards to reparations and analyses in-depth the reparation regime developed at the ECCC.

Chapter 3 focuses entirely on the reparation system at the ICC. The purpose of this chapter is to engage in an in-depth discussion of the development of reparative justice at the ICC, from theory to practice. This chapter is fully devoted to analysing the issues emerging from adding a reparative dimension in a primarily criminal process and how the criminal and reparative dimensions are intertwined, since reparations are conditional upon criminal conviction, how both dimensions are reconciled in practice by the Court, and how they should be reconciled in the future. It also provides a timely discussion of the first four cases dealing with reparations, which will pave the way and lay the foundation for the reparation system at the ICC for years to come. The discussion of cases is one of the factors that distinguishes this book from previous works in the field.

Chapter 4 examines the legal framework and experience of the ICC Trust Fund for Victims (TFV), as the main administrative mechanism dealing with reparations for international crimes. Considering the important questions that the TFV raises regarding reparations and the central role it has played thus far in the ICC context, the book devotes a separate chapter to the TFV to fully engage with the unique dimensions of its mandates, the challenges it faces and whether it can serve as a model for the development of other administrative mechanisms for reparations for international crimes.

Chapter 5 addresses the potential role of domestic courts and mechanisms in the adjudication and award of reparations for international crimes. It draws from existing studies in the field and examines the role that domestic courts may have in adjudicating claims of reparations for international crimes. It analyses these questions through, on one hand, a case study of domestic reparations for international crimes in Bosnia and Herzegovina, where the international criminal tribunal did not have a reparative dimension. On the other hand, it discusses the development of universal civil jurisdiction, including the challenges, some recent case law from different countries and the United States through the Alien Tort Claims Act (ATCA).

The book concludes with Chapter 6, a summary of the analysis of the key questions and related inquiries, bringing together the main themes discussed in the different chapters. It also offers some recommendations, in light of recent developments, of how the criminal and reparative dimensions of justice in the aftermath of international crimes can be reconciled in practice and how they should be reconciled in the future.

1

Punishment and Reparation

Construing the Legal Basis of a Duty to Repair in International Criminal Law

In order to understand how punishment of the offender and reparations for victims of international crimes fits into the fabric of modern international criminal justice, one needs to first engage with justice theories that inform international criminal law. The aftermath of international crimes can be dealt with in different forms of post-conflict justice: for example, with criminal trials, truth and reconciliation processes, amnesties, and peace accords (which often may have a provision for state-based reparations).[1]

In contrast to other possible responses to mass atrocities, punishment and retributive justice theory have provided an important model for international criminal justice. Responding to criminal conduct with criminal prosecution represents a commitment to the rule of law and the recognition that alleged perpetrators should be held accountable for their crimes.[2] International criminal trials represent an opportunity to seek the truth, they generate a historical account of events, they produce retribution for criminal conduct, and they may provide deterrence.[3] Furthermore,

---

[1] This important question goes beyond the scope of this chapter. See generally on this topic, Darryl Robinson, "Serving the Interests of Justice: Amnesties, Truth Commissions, and the International Criminal Court," *European Journal of International Law* 14 (2003), p. 3; Charles Villa-Vicencio, "Why Perpetrators Should Not Always Be Prosecuted: Where the International Criminal Court and Truth Commissions Meet," *Emory Law Journal* 49 (2000), p. 205; Martha Minow, *Between Vengeance and Forgiveness: Facing History after Genocide and Mass Violence*, Beacon Press, 1998.

[2] Martha Minow, ibid., p. 25.

[3] But see Brianne N. McGonigle, "Two for the Price of One: Attempts by the Extraordinary Chambers in the Courts of Cambodia to Combine Retributive and Restorative Justice Principles," *Leiden Journal of International Law* 22 (2009), p. 129, who claims that there is no empirical evidence that criminal trials have a deterrent effect. See also generally, Payam Akhavan, "Beyond Impunity: Can International Criminal Justice Prevent Future Atrocities?" *American Journal of International Law* 95 (2001), p. 12.

Punishment and Reparation

punishment and international criminal trials may also be seen in the light of their expressive roles.[4]

This chapter thus aims at an overview of different theories of justice and how they can inform the development of reparative justice in international criminal law. This chapter also traces the evolution of different dichotomies of the legal duty to provide reparations and the right to reparation: from the perspectives of state versus state, to state versus individual, to individual versus individual, as well as outlining the development of a duty to repair for individual perpetrators alongside states' duty to repair. It is not intended to be an exhaustive or in-depth discussion of all justice theories; rather, its goal is to provide the theoretical foundation that supports the analysis in the following chapters and to set out the main themes that are discussed throughout the book.

1.1 OF CRIMES AND PUNISHMENT

There are a few different rationales that underpin the idea of punishment as a response to criminal conduct. It is often claimed that punishment may deter future criminal conduct. Members of a given society, knowing that a certain conduct entails a given punishment, might abstain from pursuing that conduct. This idea finds support in the writings of authors throughout the centuries, among whom Plato, who stated that "he who desires to inflict rational punishment does not retaliate for a past wrong which cannot be undone; he has regard to the future, and is desirous that the man who is punished, may be deterred from doing wrong again. He punishes for the sake of prevention."[5] Inflicting punishment in relation to a given criminal conduct can be regarded as a way to prevent future crimes. In modern international criminal justice, this deterrent role is often debatable and some scholars question whether international criminal law as applied by international courts actually has a deterrent role.[6]

In the same vein, another theoretical justification for punishment as a response to criminal conduct is the rehabilitation of the criminal; the

---

[4] See generally in this regard, Anthony Duff, "Authority and Responsibility in International Criminal Law," in *The Philosophy of International Law*, eds. Samantha Besson and John Tasioulas, Oxford University Press, 2010, pp. 589–604; Bill Wringe, "Why Punish War Crimes? Victor's Justice and Expressive Justifications of Punishment," *Law and Philosophy* 25 (2006), p. 159.

[5] Plato, "Protagoras," in *Works of Plato*, ed. Irwin Edman, The Modern Library, 1956, pp. 193, 211.

[6] David Wippman, "Atrocities, Deterrence, and the Limits of International Justice," *Fordham International Law Journal* 23 (1999), p. 12; Payam Akhavan, "Beyond Impunity: Can International Criminal Justice Prevent Future Atrocities?" *American Journal of International Law* 95 (2001), pp. 7–31.

proponents of this justification focus on punishment for the *criminal*, as opposed to a focus on the *crime*.[7] The goal of punishment, so the theory goes, is to effect a change in the behavior of the criminal to decrease the likelihood of the commission of a crime in the future.[8] In this sense, it is based on the premise that punishment can change behavior. For Hart, "announcing certain standards of behavior and attaching penalties for deviating ... [leaves] individuals to choose. This is a method of social control which maximizes individual freedom within the framework of the law."[9]

A further theoretical rationalization of punishment is retribution.[10] Responding to international crimes with criminal trials and punishment can be seen through the lens of retributive justice theory. In classical retributive justice theory, a crime is responded to by punishing the perpetrator in a way that is proportional to the crime committed. The focus in this kind of response is not the individual victim(s); the crime is seen to have been committed against the state as a whole. A crime is first and foremost a violation of a law, a legal norm enacted by the state. The affected community and the victim are represented by the state.

Retributive theorists' view of punishment is that it produces a proper response to crime because it "cancels out" the crime, restoring the proper balance in society.[11] For Kant, punishment

> can never be inflicted merely as a means to promote some other good for the criminal himself or for civil society. It must always be inflicted upon him only because he has committed a crime. For a human being can never be treated merely as a means to the purposes of another or be put among the objects of rights to things: his innate personality protects him from this, even though he can be condemned to lose his civil personality.[12]

In this light, the focus of retributive justice theory is on finding guilt and imposing blame. The offender is seen as a danger to society as a whole. As such, the individual is believed to deserve punishment once guilt is found and is often taken out of society. This kind of justice is based on the premise that punishment is an effective response to a crime.

---

[7] Farooq Hassan, "The Theoretical Basis of Punishment in International Criminal Law," *Case Western Reserve Journal of International Law* 15 (1983), p. 49.

[8] George Whitecross Patton, *A Textbook of Jurisprudence*, eds. George Whitecross Patton and David P. Derham (4th ed.), Clarendon Press, 1972, p. 360.

[9] Herbert Lionel Adolphus Hart, *Punishment and Responsibility*, Clarendon Press, 1968, p. 23.

[10] Anthony Platt, "The Meaning of Punishment," *Issues in Criminology* 2 (1966), p. 79.

[11] David Dolinko, "Punishment" in *The Oxford Handbook of Philosophy of Criminal Law*, eds. John Deigh and David Dolinko, Oxford University Press, 2011, p. 406.

[12] Immanuel Kant, *The Metaphysics of Morals*, translation by Mary Gregor, Cambridge University Press, 1996, p. 105.

Retribution theory has a long history. Retributive justice is illustrated in the *lex talioni*, where reciprocity should equate to the crime committed. In ancient history, the Code of Hamurabi recognized retributive justice and it has been a form of justice for centuries ever since. As a consequence of the centralization of the state, sustained attention was given to the punishment of the offender and retribution, which brought about a proliferation of criminal codes and penalties.[13] This focus on retribution, and the marginalized role of victims in the administration of justice, lasted until the end of the eighteenth century at which time victims began playing a more active role in the administration of justice.[14]

Retribution, from the inception of international criminal law in the twentieth century, has been a leading justification for punishment of offenders in international law.[15] As one author has put it "[r]etribution ... though not historically a significant part of the evolutionary trends of international criminal law, was a definite component of at least the punishments awarded by the International Military Tribunal at Nuremberg."[16] The idea of fighting impunity, which is symbolic of international criminal justice and the establishment of international and ad hoc criminal tribunals, speaks to the justification of punishment as a form of retribution.

At the end of the Second World War, when the world became aware of the atrocities that were committed by Nazi forces, something needed to be done against those who perpetrated acts that shocked the conscience of humankind. It can be argued that at a moment of global recovery, following the horrors of the war, an international criminal tribunal poured the rule of law back into the international legal order. Setting up an international tribunal to try and punish the alleged offenders reestablished law and order in a world devastated by war. One of the most famous statements emanating from the Nuremberg trials refers specifically to the idea that those crimes could not go unpunished due to their nature and level of gravity: "[...] only by punishing individuals who commit such crimes can the provisions of international law be enforced."[17]

---

[13] Ilaria Bottigliero, *Redress for Victims of Crimes under International Law*, Nijhoff, 2004, p. 24.

[14] Lucia Zedner, "England," in *Reparation in Criminal Law: International Perspectives*, eds. Albin Eser and Susanne Walther (vol. 1), Iuscrim, Max-Planck Institute Für Ausländisches und International Strafrecht, 1996, pp. 109–227.

[15] For a thorough review of the goals and functions of punishment in international criminal law, see Mark A. Drumbl, *Atrocity, Punishment, and International Law*, Cambridge University Press, 2007.

[16] Farooq Hassan, "The Theoretical Basis of Punishment in International Criminal Law," *Case Western Reserve Journal of International Law* 15 (1983), p. 55.

[17] Trial of Major War Criminals before the International Military Tribunal, Nuremberg, 14 November 1945–1 October 1946 (Nuremberg: International Military Tribunal, 1947), p. 223.

Be that as it may, retribution is not the only justification for trying and punishing offenders. One of the claimed underlying rationales for punishment in international criminal law is deterrence.[18] If a criminal is punished, as the theory goes, everyone will know that act is wrongful under international law which entails consequences, thus deterring others from taking the same course of action. Deterrence and prevention of future crimes seem to have served as the justification for inflicting punishment on those found responsible for the crimes committed by Nazi Germany.[19] This is illustrated by the famous statement by Justice Jackson: "It is high time that we act on the juridical principles that aggressive war-making is illegal and criminal ... so as to make war less attractive to those who have governments and the destinies of people in their power."[20]

Punishment is also said to aid in the maintenance of the international legal order.[21] One author has posited in regard to this justification for punishment that "[j]ust as the general welfare of citizens and the supreme need for maintaining the social order in the domestic scene are considered paramount, the need for ensuring the sanctity of the most fundamental values of the international community also demands that potential violators be forewarned from committing breaches of the international legal order."[22]

Since there are no central enforcing institutions or agencies in the international legal order, punishment could be one way to enforce international rules. This said, it is difficult to grasp whether the punishment with which individual perpetrators are being sentenced fulfills the role of retribution or deterrence, there is a growing debate as to whether punishment of individuals contributes to the prevention of future crimes.[23] It is also premature at this point in the development of international criminal justice to determine whether, and how, punishment can influence and modify an individual's

---

[18] See generally, Farooq Hassan, "The Theoretical Basis of Punishment in International Criminal Law," *Case Western Reserve Journal of International Law* 15 (1983), pp. 48 et seq.

[19] Ibid., at p. 50.

[20] *Report to the President by Mr. Justice Jackson*, June 6, 1945, "International Conference on Military Trials," pp. 42, 52–53. See also, Robert Jackson, *The Case against the Nazi War Criminals*, Alfred A. Knopf, 1946.

[21] See generally, Cesare Beccaria cited in Elio Monachesi, "Pioneers in Criminology IX: Cesare Beccaria (1738–1794)," *Journal of Criminal Law, Criminology & Political Science* 46 (1955), p. 445.

[22] Farooq Hassan, "The Theoretical Basis of Punishment in International Criminal Law," *Case Western Reserve Journal of International Law* 15 (1983), p. 56.

[23] See generally, David Wippman, "Atrocities, Deterrence, and the Limits of International Justice," *Fordham International Law Journal* 23 (1999), pp. 473, 488; Payam Akhavan, "Beyond Impunity: Can International Criminal Justice Prevent Future Atrocities?," *American Journal of International Law* 95 (2001), pp. 7–31.

conduct. As international criminal law developed, retribution began to lose its importance as the main justification for inflicting punishment on offenders.[24] Many now claim that international criminal law (and punishment) is not producing the magnificent effect that its proponents were hoping for.[25]

Given the less important role of retribution as a justification for punishment in this context, it is understandable how victim redress could make its way into international criminal law. In a framework where reparation does not take the form of punitive damages, but rather comes from the concern with victims' justice, it is difficult to reconcile how reparation for victims would contribute to retributive justice theory.[26] Retribution provides no justification for including reparation within the realm of international criminal law remedies. Reparations in international criminal law are not equated to punishment; they are not punitive in nature. This is confirmed, at least within the ICC framework, by the negotiating history of the Rome Statute, and the reparation provisions within the Statute.[27]

Beyond the issue of the driving rationale for including reparation within international criminal justice, an interesting question is whether reparations could contribute to the main goals with which trial and punishment are concerned: prevention and deterrence.[28]

The relationship between reparation and deterrence is closely linked to the forms of reparation available within the realm of international criminal justice

---

[24] See generally, Farooq Hassan, "The Theoretical Basis of Punishment in International Criminal Law," *Case Western Reserve Journal of International Law* 15 (1983), p. 56.

[25] David Wippman, "Atrocities, Deterrence, and the Limits of International Justice," *Fordham International Law Journal* 23 (1999), pp. 473, 488.

[26] On the question of the dichotomy between reparation and retribution, see Charles F. Abel and Frank H. Marsh, *Punishment and Restitution: A Restitutionary Approach to Crime and the Criminal*, Greenwood Press, 1984; Ezzat A. Fattah, "From a Guilt Orientation to a Consequence Orientation: A Proposed New Paradigm for the Criminal Law in the 21st Century," in *Beitraege zur Rechtswissenschaft*, eds. Wilfried Küper and Jürgen Welp, C. F. Mueller Juristischer Verlag, 1993, pp. 771–792. See also, David Watson, Jacky Boucherat, and Gwynn Davis, "Reparation for Retributivists," in *Mediation and Criminal Justice: Victims, Offenders and Community*, eds. Martin Wright and Burt Galaway, Sage Publications, 1989, cited in Lucia Zedner, "Reparation and Retribution: Are they Reconcilable?" *Modern Law Review* 57 (1994), p. 228.

[27] See on this point, Conor McCarthy, "Victim Redress and International Criminal Justice: Competing Paradigms, or Compatible Forms of Justice?" *Journal of International Criminal Justice* 10 (2012), pp. 361–362.

[28] The following questions are outside the scope of this chapter: whether reparation for victims within international criminal proceedings, and at the ICC as its main example, is compatible with the traditional goals of international criminal justice; and whether it is appropriate and how it should develop. These will be addressed in the following chapters of this book. The inquiry at this juncture fits within the broader discussion of theories of justification for punishment in international criminal justice.

and the involvement of the offender in the reparation process. If reparation is given in the form of compensation, through a sum of money from the accused, this may provide a degree of deterrence similar to that of criminal liability. The possibility of facing criminal prosecution, as well as paying compensation to the victims, may deter individuals from committing a crime.

Perhaps, however, the most significant way in which reparations or victim redress may impact the prevention of future atrocities can be evaluated in a more holistic way. The integration of victims' concerns in the international criminal justice process may affect the way in which criminal conduct is dealt with. Including victims in the process, and implementing reparation-based awards (i.e., where the offenders will have to face the victim and respond to their actions), as opposed to treating crime simply as a public matter, might indeed contribute to the preventive effect that punishment is intended to have.

Thus, looking solely through the retributive justice lens, international criminal justice would have a purely criminal dimension, focusing mainly on the perpetrator, the crime, and the degree of punishment. A reparative dimension, that is, one which includes victims in the process, does not fit within this paradigm. Thus, including this dimension in international criminal justice requires further analysis of other theoretical underpinning(s).

1.2 VICTIMS, REPARATION, AND RESTORATIVE JUSTICE THEORY

Like retributive justice, restorative justice has been present in many civilizations through history. Since the Roman law period, there have been possibilities for remedies for wrongful conduct.[29] The shift to retribution as a way to respond to criminal conduct seems to have occurred between the twelfth and thirteenth centuries. When a wrongful act was committed against the state, retribution demanded that the interests of society as a whole be emphasized above and beyond those of individual victims.

Restorative justice,[30] as opposed to retributive justice, focuses on the needs of victims and seeks to provide some form of redress. Restorative justice is concerned with bringing victims and offenders together. The perpetrator is encouraged to make amends and repair the harm caused to the victim. Thus, restorative justice has a distinct forward-looking approach.

---

[29] Arlette Lebigre, *Quelques Aspects de la Responsabilité Pénale en Droit Romain Classique,* Presses Universitaires de France, 1967.

[30] See e.g., Conor McCarthy, "Reparations under the Rome Statute of the International Criminal Court and Reparative Justice Theory," *International Journal of Transitional Justice* 3 (2009), pp. 250–271.

John Braithwaite, a leading author in restorative justice theory, has defined restorative justice as:

> a process where all stakeholders affected by an injustice have an opportunity to discuss how they have been affected by the injustice and to decide what should be done to repair the harm. With crime, restorative justice is about the idea that because crime hurts, justice should heal. It follows that conversations with those who have been hurt and with those who have afflicted the harm must be central to the process.[31]

As far as reparations are concerned, it has been noted that "[restorative justice] places particular emphasis on the principles and aims of human dignity, strong relationships and morality [which] allows a more holistic approach to reparations," to the extent that "restorative justice provides a persuasive theoretical rationale for reparations."[32]

An important concern of restorative justice is whether the criminal justice process addresses the full complexity of the criminal conduct. Under this theory, criminal conduct is not a wrong committed against some abstract community, but instead should be dealt with as a dispute between the offender and the victim.[33] From this perspective, reparations to victims of international crimes are more in line with the premises of restorative justice. The question that remains is whether a blend of retributive and restorative justice theories makes sense in international criminal law. Similarly, this book dwells upon whether a mixture of criminal and reparative dimensions, and thus influences from diverse justice theories, is desirable or feasible in international criminal justice. These are the inquiries in the following chapters.

1.3 THE GENESIS OF INTERNATIONAL CRIMINAL LAW AND THE SHIFT FROM STATE RESPONSIBILITY TO INDIVIDUAL ACCOUNTABILITY

To understand the theoretical framework that guided the development of the doctrinal foundations of international criminal law, the latter must be

---

[31] John Braithwaite, "Restorative Justice and De-Professionalization," *The Good Society* 13 (2004), pp. 28–31.

[32] Antonio Buti, "The Notion of Reparations as a Restorative Justice Measure," in *One Country, Two Systems, Three Legal Orders – Perspectives of Evolution: Essays on Macau's Autonomy after the Resumption of Sovereignty by China*, eds. Jorge Costa Oliveira and Paulo Cardinal, Springer, 2009, p. 198.

[33] Conor McCarthy, "Reparations under the Rome Statute of the International Criminal Court and Reparative Justice Theory," *International Journal of Transitional Justice* 3 (2009), p. 253.

positioned within the broader context of international law at the time of its inception.

Modern international criminal law developed as a response to the atrocities committed during the Second World War. In the aftermath of the war, it became clear that the international crimes committed during the war needed to be accounted for and that the punishment of individual perpetrators was crucial for the reestablishment of the international legal order. Making the state, an abstract entity, solely responsible, without reaching those who individually perpetrated mass atrocities, was no longer desirable or acceptable, and remained disconnected from domestic criminal law systems. In the wake of the end of the Second World War, the framework for allocating responsibility in the international legal order focused on the state. Importantly, the development of international criminal law represented a shift from a state-centered approach.[34] For many centuries, international law was concerned solely with inter-state relations, and the idea of individuals being a (passive) subject of international law, standing trial and being punished, would have been inconceivable within the traditional framework of international law.[35]

In this sense, it can be said that the mere advent of international criminal law represents a turning point in the conceptual framework of international law. This paradigm shift is well illustrated by the famous statement of the International Military Tribunal at Nuremberg, noted above, that "crimes against international law are committed by men, not by abstract entities, and only by punishing individuals who commit such crimes can the provisions of international law be enforced."[36] This statement also demonstrates that, since its inception, international criminal law has focused on the trial and punishment of perpetrators as a means to enforce international law. Individual accountability, and punishment, has informed the formative stages of international criminal law. This can be explained by the need to hold individual perpetrators accountable for their crimes. Therefore, the shift from a state-based responsibility for international wrongs to individual accountability for international crimes marks the modern development of international criminal law. However, although individual perpetrators were held criminally

---

[34] See generally, Hersch Lauterpacht, "The Law of Nations and the Punishment of War Crimes," *British Yearbook of International Law* 21 (1944), p. 58.

[35] See e.g., the 1912 edition of the Lassa Oppenheim treatise on international law, stating that "the Law of Nations is a law between States, and ... individuals cannot be subjects of this law," Lassa Oppenheim, *International Law: A Treatise*, Longmans, Green, 2nd ed., 1912, p. 367, 368. The later edition was modified to take into account the growing position of individuals as subjects of international law.

[36] *Trial of Major War Criminals Before the International Military Tribunal*, Nuremberg, 14 November 1945–1 October 1946 (Nuremberg: International Military Tribunal, 1947), p. 223.

accountable, civil redress for victims of the crimes perpetrated during the war was left to be resolved by inter-state agreements.[37]

Holding individual perpetrators accountable for international crimes, rather than the states for which they acted, had put the focus on prosecution and punishment of the offender, while steering away from victims and civil redress. The idea of redress for victims of international crimes was thus not present in the early development of international criminal law[38] and, as we shall see in later chapters, only gained relevance with the advent of the ICC.

International criminal law, in its first phase, solidified the foundation of a system based on individual accountability and punishment, as opposed to collective responsibility. This dichotomy was explained by Hans Kelsen in the following terms: "the difference between the punishment provided by national law and the specific sanctions of international law ... consists of the fact that punishment in criminal law constitutes individual responsibility, whereas the specific sanctions of international law constitute collective responsibility."[39] The focus on the criminal accountability of individual perpetrators, as opposed to a framework that included criminal accountability and victim redress, in the shaping of the architecture of international criminal law at its formative stages can be understood in the context of the position of the individual as a subject of international law. The battle of that time was to pierce the veil of state responsibility, in order to be able to put the individuals responsible for the atrocities of the Second World War on trial.[40] Thus, at its inception, international criminal justice was focused on the criminal dimension.

---

[37] Indeed, according to Ariel Colonomos and Andrea Armstrong: "[t]raditionally, reparations were part of the framework of relations between nations following a conflict and obligated the losing State to compensate damages incurred by its opponents during the course of the war," Ariel Colonomos and Andrea Armstrong, "German Reparations to the Jews after World War II: A Turning Point in the History of Reparations," in *Handbook of Reparations*, ed. Pablo de Greiff, Oxford University Press, 2006, p. 390. See also Pierre d'Argent, *Les Réparations de Guerre en Droit International Public*, LGDJ, 2002; Richard Lillich et al., *International Claims: Their Settlement by Lump-Sum Agreement*, University Press of Virginia, vol. 1, 1975.

[38] See Conor McCarthy, "Victim Redress and International Criminal Justice: Competing Paradigms, or Compatible Forms of Justice?" *Journal of International Criminal Justice* 10 (2012), p. 359, where the author concludes that "international criminal law was conceptualized as a system of law little concerned with victims but rather one which was concerned with perpetrators and the enforcement of the rules of international law itself."

[39] Hans Kelsen, "Collective and Individual Responsibility in International Law with Particular Regard to the Punishment of War Criminals," *California Law Review* 31 (1943), p. 530.

[40] Even prior to the Second World War, John Westlake had stated that "the same tone of thought will again be evil if it allows us to forget that ... the action of our State is that of ourselves," John Westlake, *The Collected Papers of John Westlake on Public International Law*, ed. Lassa Oppenheim, Cambridge University Press, 1914, p. 411.

22   *Reparative Justice for International Crimes*

Hersch Lauterpacht had warned of the risks of continuing to maintain a purely state-centered approach: "[t]here is little hope for international law if an individual, acting as an organ of the state, can in violation of international law, effectively shelter behind the abstract and artificial notion of the state."[41] The necessary rationale to shift to a system that includes individuals' accountability for international crimes was the idea that individuals should not be shielded by the state when assigning responsibility for certain acts, which were ultimately performed by individuals. This had the effect of sometimes creating systems of concurrent state responsibility and individual criminal liability for certain international acts.[42] Thus, the focus on retribution and punishment of the perpetrator, in contrast with reparations, at this early stage of international criminal law can be explained by the idea that "[individual] punishment, in contrast to [interstate] reparation, satisfies ... the need for guarantees against future infractions of the law."[43]

The dogma of state sovereignty remained, at least as far as reparations for victims were concerned. If there was any claim for reparation from an individual victim it was for the sovereign state to "represent" their interests, and reparations for international crimes were to be sought from states. In other words, victim redress for international crimes was centered on a state-based approach.[44]

In sum, with the advent of international criminal law, individuals could be criminally prosecuted in a personal capacity. This remained, however, a

---

[41] Hersch Lauterpacht, "Règles générales du droit de la paix," *Recueil des Cours* 62 (1937), p. 351 (translation).

[42] See André Nollkaemper, "Concurrence Between Individual Responsibility and State Responsibility in International Law," *International and Comparative Law Quarterly* 52 (2003), pp. 615–640, citing emerging work in this field: Pierre-Marie Dupuy, "International Criminal Responsibility of the Individual and International Responsibility of the State," in *The Rome Statute of the International Criminal Court: A Commentary*, eds. Antonio Cassese, et al., Oxford University Press, 2002, pp. 1085–1100; Hazel Fox, "The International Court of Justice's Treatment of Acts of the State and in Particular the Attribution of Acts of Individuals to States," in *Liber Amicorum Judge Shigeru Oda*, eds. Nisuke Ando, Kluwer Law International, 2002, p. 147; Marina Spinedi, "State Responsibility *v* Individual Responsibility for International Crimes: Tertium Non Datu," *European Journal of International Law* 13 (2002), p. 895; Malcolm Evans, "International Wrongs and National Jurisdiction," in *Remedies in International Law: The Institutional Dilemma*, Malcolm Evans, Hart Publishing, 1998, p. 173; Otto Triffterer, "Prosecution of States for Crimes of State," *Revue Internationale de Droit Penal* 67 (1996), p. 341.

[43] Hersch Lauterpacht, "Règles générales du droit de la paix," *Recueil des Cours* 62 (1937), p. 352 (translation).

[44] Ariel Colonomos and Andrea Armstrong, "German Reparations to the Jews after World War II: A Turning Point in the History of Reparations," in *Handbook of Reparations*, ed. Pablo de Greiff, Oxford University Press, 2006, p. 390.

passive role for individuals in international law as they were the object of prosecutions. At this point in history (in the wake of the Second World War and the development of international criminal law in the twentieth century) individuals could not yet play an active role, separate from their state of origin. Individuals could not yet personally claim reparations for themselves in international law. As Connor McCarthy sums it up, "international criminal law was concerned primarily with perpetrators and the enforcement of the rules of international law itself."[45]

Thus, international criminal law, as it originally developed, was concerned with a criminal dimension. The reparative dimension for victims was not included. Reparations for victims followed a state-based approach.

1.4 PAVING THE WAY TO REPARATIONS FOR MASS CRIMES: OVERVIEW OF THE LEGAL DUTY OF REPARATIONS IN OTHER FIELDS OF INTERNATIONAL LAW

Reparations for victims of international crimes rest on two premises: the right to obtain reparations and the legal duty to provide reparations. Two questions underpin this analysis. Who bears the legal duty of reparation (i.e., the state, the individual, both)? And to whom is the reparation owed (i.e., to individuals and/or to the state)? In relation to the latter, another matter which must be addressed is whether the individual (i.e., the victim) has a legal *right* to reparation under international law. And importantly, does this by implication create an international obligation on *individuals* rather than (or in addition to) *states* concerning reparation? Would this not be a mismatch with the collective nature of international crimes? Not necessarily. Just like in a criminal dimension, state responsibility and individual criminal accountability are not mutually exclusive, in a reparation dimension, state responsibility and individual liability concerning reparations need not necessarily be either.

Alongside the development and solidification of international criminal law procedures, victim redress mechanisms have developed in other fields of international law. This has slowly given rise to an individual *right* to reparation for international wrongs, including human rights violations and international crimes. In order to better understand the shift from a purely retribution-oriented international criminal justice to a system which has a more active

---

[45] Conor McCarthy, *Reparations and Victim Support in the International Criminal Court*, Cambridge University Press, 2012, p. 43.

24   *Reparative Justice for International Crimes*

role for victims,[46] including the right to seek reparations within the international criminal proceedings, it is crucial to review the wider legal framework, and the development of a right to reparation under international law. There are two fields in particular that are closely linked to international criminal law (pertaining to the duty of reparation imposed on the state rather than the individual): international human rights law and international humanitarian law. Evaluating the state-based approach to reparations will inform the construction of a legal basis of a duty to repair imposed on the individual, and the contents of this duty.

1.4.1 *The Purposes of Reparations*

It goes without saying that reparations may serve varied purposes and be based on different theoretical underpinnings.[47] A brief overview of different goals of reparations is useful to set the context of the discussion in the following chapters. A common purpose of reparations is that of remedial justice. Remedial justice serves to correct the wrong done and rectify injustice by restoring the *status quo ante*. As Professor Dinah Shelton puts it, this rationale "appears to be the basis for most international decisions on reparations, including the *Chorzów Factory* case."[48]

Reparations may also serve as a form of retribution, to punish the offender and deter the wrongful conduct in the future.[49] Under this theoretical explanation, the form and extent of reparations could bring about a deterrent factor in future wrongdoing. In this sense, reparations can include a form of punitive damages. Another purpose of reparation speaks to restoration of victims and affected communities. The goal in this perspective would be to reconcile and restore, as well as induce positive future behavior.[50]

---

[46]   The question of the inclusion of reparation within international criminal proceedings will be reviewed in Chapters 2 and 3.

[47]   This chapter is not aimed at examining or discussing the purpose of reparations specifically in international criminal law. This topic will be addressed in following chapters.

[48]   See generally, Dinah Shelton, "Righting Wrongs: Reparations in the Articles on State Responsibility," *American Journal of International Law* 96 (2002), pp. 833–856.

[49]   See Antônio Augusto Cançado Trindade, *International Law for Humankind: Towards a New Jus Gentium*, Nijhoff, 2010, p. 371.

[50]   See generally on theories of restorative justice: Daniel W. Van Ness and Karen Heetderks Strong, *Restoring Justice*, Routledge, 2nd ed., 2002; Nigel Bigger, *Burying the Past: Making Peace and Doing Justice After Civil Conflict*, Georgetown University Press, 2003; Heather Strang and John Braithwaite, *Restorative Justice and Civil Society*, Cambridge University Press, 2001; Gerry Johnstone, *Restorative Justice: Ideas, Values, Debates*, Willan, 2002.

Some aspects of this overview are worth emphasizing. First, it may be noted that the system of reparations could be different depending on its context (i.e., the society where it is applied or the purpose it is devised to achieve). This aspect of reparations sheds light on the interconnectedness of victims and offenders, and the community in which they may belong. When a wrongful act is committed (e.g., a crime), various relationships are broken, values shattered, and the situation that existed before the wrongful conduct is no longer in place. Thus, the theoretical framework of the purpose of reparations evidences the tight relationship between crimes (a wrongful conduct) and redress (reparation), offenders and victims, the past and the future. It also exposes the weaknesses of a compartmentalized study of different fields of international law, in parallel, and with different aims, even though in essence they often pertain to the same conduct.

In the same line of reasoning, a broader discussion pertains to the considerations of international law and international justice: if different disciplines of international law do not interact and feed off each other, in a synergetic communication, the ultimate goal of justice may not be fully achieved. As Judge Cançado Trindade puts it,

> While an international tribunal of human rights (such as the European and Inter-American Courts, and more recently, the African Court) cannot determine the international criminal responsibility of the individual, and an international criminal tribunal (such as the ad hoc International Criminal Tribunals for the Former Yugoslavia [ICTFY] and for Rwanda [ICTR], and the ICC) cannot determine the responsibility of the State, impunity is most likely bound to persist, being only partially sanctioned by one and not the other.[51]

1.4.2 *The Multifaceted Dimensions of Reparations*

The former United Nations Special Rapporteur on the promotion of truth, justice, reparations, and guarantees of nonrecurrence, Dr. Pablo de Greiff, prepared a report focusing on reparations for mass violations of human rights and international humanitarian law. His report focused on the challenges of reparation, including implementation, exclusion of certain "categories of victims on the basis of political considerations ... and the gender insensitivity of a majority of reparation programmes,

---

[51] See Antônio Augusto Cançado Trindade, *International Law for Humankind: Towards a New Jus Gentium*, Nijhoff, 2010, p. 371.

which results in too few victims of gender-related violations receiving any reparation."[52]

Significantly, the report discussed the important dimensions of reparations. In particular, it warned against looking at reparations from a singular dimension and posited that: "to count as reparation and to be understood as a justice measure, it has to be accompanied by an acknowledgment of responsibility and needs to be linked with other justice initiatives such as efforts aimed at achieving truth, criminal prosecutions and guarantees of non-recurrence".[53] In a similar vein, he added that "[o]ffering reparations to victims should not be part of an effort, for example, to make impunity more acceptable."[54]

Specifically relating to the participation of victims in the reparation process, the Special Rapporteur:

> call[ed] on Governments to establish mechanisms for the meaningful participation of victims and their representatives. This requires guaranteeing their safety. ... Victim participation can help improve the reach and completeness of programmes, enhance comprehensiveness, better determine the types of violations that need to be redressed, improve the fit between benefits and expectations and, in general, secure the meaningfulness of symbolic and material benefits alike. Moreover, active and engaged participation may offer some relief in the light of the dismal record in the implementation of reparations.[55]

This discussion is crucial since it is argued in this book, precisely as the Special Rapporteur does, that reparation must be seen as complementary to the criminal liability of perpetrators of international crimes. In other words, the criminal and reparative dimensions of international justice are not mutually exclusive and should supplement one another, as two facets of justice in the aftermath of international crimes. The conclusion of the Special Rapporteur's report is thus a guiding chart.

Finally, the report makes another important point concerning the different dimensions of reparation. It calls on those responsible to design "reparation programmes to consider the great advantages of distributing benefits of

---

[52] United Nations, General Assembly, "Report of the Special Rapporteur on the Promotion of Truth, Justice, Reparation and Guarantees of Non-Recurrence," A/69/518, 14 October 2014 (hereinafter "the report").

[53] Ibid., para. 83.

[54] Ibid.

[55] Ibid., paras. 91 and 92.

Punishment and Reparation

different kinds and to not reduce reparation to a single dimension, be it material or symbolic. The great harms that reparation is supposed to redress require a broad array of coherently organized measures."[56] The report, and the guidelines provided therein, are useful for the development of reparative justice for victims of international crimes and provide some insight for the analysis throughout this book.

1.4.3 The Duty of Reparation in International Law from a State Responsibility Dimension

The duty to make reparation for an internationally wrongful act is a well-established principle of international law.[57] While much has been written on the right of states to obtain reparation,[58] the focus of this book rests on victims of international crimes, and thus on reparations for the benefit of individuals.

The principle underlying the legal duty to make reparation is that every breach of an international obligation carries with it a duty to repair the harm caused by the breach.[59] This has been confirmed in a number of international instruments and within the jurisprudence of international and regional courts. It has been crystallized in an often-cited passage by the Permanent Court of International Justice, in the *Chorzów Factory* judgment, wherein it is stated that:

---

[56] Ibid., para. 84.

[57] See e.g., on the duty to reparation for wrongful conduct under international law, Paul Fauchille, *Traité de Droit international public*, vol. I, Part I, Paris, Librairie A. Rousseau, 1922, p. 515; Ladislas Reitzer, *La réparation comme conséquence de l'acte illicite en Droit international*, Paris, Recueil Sirey, 1938, p. 30; Jean Personnaz, *La réparation du préjudice en Droit international public*, Paris, Libr. Rec. Sirey (1939), pp. 53–60; Hildebrando Accioly, "Principes généraux de la responsabilité internationale d'après la doctrine et la jurisprudence," *Recueil des Cours de l'Académie de Droit International de La Haye* 96 (1953), p. 415.

[58] See e.g., Christian Dominicé, *Observations sur les droits de l'Etat victime d'un fait internationalement illicite*, in *Droit international 2*, ed. C. Dominicé, Paris: Pedone, 1982, pp. 1–70; Francisco V. García-Amador, *The Changing Law of International Claims*, New York: Oceana, 1984; Francisco V. García Amador, *Principios de derecho internacional que rigen la responsabilidad: análisis crítico de la concepción tradicional*, Madrid: Escuela de funcionarios internacionales, 1963. See also, Dionisio Anzilotti, "La responsabilité internationale des États a raison des dommages soufferts par des étrangers," *Revue générale de droit international public*, p. 13; Paul Fauchille, *Traité de Droit International Public*, Vol. I, Librairie A. Rousseau.

[59] See Dinah Shelton, "Righting Wrongs: Reparations in the Articles on State Responsibility," *American Journal of International Law* 96 (2002), p. 835.

The essential principle contained in the actual notion of an illegal act ... is that reparation must, so far as possible, wipe-out all the consequences of the illegal act and reestablish the situation which would, in all probability, have existed if that act had not been committed. Restitution in kind, or, if this is not possible, payment of a sum corresponding to the value which a restitution in kind would bear; the award, if need be, of damages for loss sustained which would not be covered by restitution in kind or payment in place of it—such are the principles which should serve to determine the amount of compensation due for an act contrary to international law.[60]

It is further stated in the same case that: "It is a principle of international law, and even a general conception of the law, that any breach of an engagement involves an obligation to make reparation ... Reparation is the indispensable complement of a failure to apply a convention, and there is no necessity for this to be stated in the convention itself."[61]

This traditional conception of reparations has been applied in the jurisprudence of international bodies[62] such as the International Court of Justice,[63]

---

[60] *Factory at Chorzów*, Jurisdiction, Judgment No. 8, 1927, PCIJ, Series A, no. 17, p. 29.

[61] Ibid. See also PCIJ Statute, Article 36, which states that

> the States Parties to the present Statute may at any time declare that they recognize as compulsory *ipso facto* and without special agreement, in relation to any other state accepting the same obligation, the jurisdiction of the Court in all legal disputes concerning: ... (d) the nature or extent of the reparation to be made for the breach of an international obligation. Article 36 of the ICJ Statute is written similarly.

[62] See, for example, *M/V "Saiga" (No. 2) (Saint Vincent and the Grenadines v. Guinea)*, Judgment, ITLOS Reports 1999, para. 170.

[63] ICJ, *Reparation for Injuries Suffered in the Service of the United Nations*, Advisory Opinion, ICJ Reports 1949, p. 184; ICJ, *Case Concerning Gabčíkovo-Nagymaros Project (Hungary v. Slovakia)*, Judgment, ICJ. Reports 1997, p. 81, para. 152; ICJ, *Case Concerning Avena and Other Mexican Nationals (Mexico v. United States of America)*, Judgment, ICJ Reports 2004, p. 59, para. 119; ICJ, *Legal Consequences of the Construction of a Wall in the Occupied Palestinian Territory*, Advisory Opinion, ICJ Reports 2004, p. 198, para. 152; ICJ, *Case Concerning Armed Activities on the Territory of the Congo (Democratic Republic of the Congo v. Uganda)*, Judgment, ICJ Reports 2005, p. 257, para. 259; ICJ, *Case Concerning the Application of the Convention on the Prevention and Punishment of the Crime of Genocide (Bosnia and Herzegovina v. Serbia and Montenegro)*, Judgment, ICJ Reports 2007, pp. 232–233, para. 460; ICJ, *Case Concerning Pulp Mills on the River Uruguay (Argentina v. Uruguay)*, Judgment, ICJ Reports 2010, p. 77, paras. 273–274; ICJ, *Case Concerning Ahmadou Sadio Diallo (Republic of Guinea v. Democratic Republic of the Congo)*, Judgment, ICJ Reports 2010, p. 48, para. 161.

regional human rights courts, and other human rights bodies,[64] arbitral tribunals,[65] claims tribunals, and commissions.[66]

The principle of a state's duty to make reparations for international wrongful acts (including international crimes) has also been explicitly recognized in Article 31 of the 2001 International Law Commission Articles, which reads as follows: "[t]he responsible State is under an obligation to make full reparation for the injury caused by the internationally wrongful act."[67]

The International Court of Justice clarified in the *Avena and Other Mexican Nationals* case that "[w]hat constitutes 'reparation in an adequate form' clearly varies depending upon the concrete circumstances surrounding each case and the precise nature and scope of the injury, since the question has to be examined from the viewpoint of what is the 'reparation in an adequate form' that corresponds to the injury."[68]

1.4.4 International Human Rights Law and the Principles Developed in the Jurisprudence of the Inter-American Court of Human Rights

As seen above, the early stages of international criminal law in the twentieth century were focused primarily on prosecution and punishment. Other areas of international law developed alongside international criminal law which had some impact on the development of reparations for victims of conflicts.

---

[64] See, for example, IACtHR, *Velásquez-Rodríguez* v. *Honduras*, Merits Judgment, 29 July 1988, para. 174; see also *Papamichalopoulos and Others* v. *Greece*, Application No. 14556/89, Judgment, 31 October 1995, ECtHR, Series A, No. 330-B, para. 36.

[65] See, for example, *LG&E Energy Corp., LG&E Capital Corp., LG&E International Inc.* v. *Argentine Republic*, Case No. ARB/02/1, Award of 25 July 2007, ICSID, para. 31; ADC Affiliate Limited and ADC & ADMC Management Limited v. Republic of Hungary, Case No. ARB/03/16, Award of 2 October 2006, ICSID, para. 484.

[66] See, for example, Final Award, *Eritrea's Damages Claims Between the State of Eritrea and the Federal Democratic Republic of Ethiopia*, 17 August 2009, Eritrea-Ethiopia Claims Commission, available at www.pca-cpa.org/upload/files/ER%20Final%20Damages%20Awar d%20complete.pdf (accessed 12 January 2012), pp. 7–8, para. 24; Final Award, *Ethiopia's Damages Claims Between the State of Eritrea and the Federal Democratic Republic of Ethiopia*, 17 August 2009, Eritrea-Ethiopia Claims Commission, available at www.pca-cpa .org/upload/files/ET%20Final%20Damages%20Award%20complete.pdf (accessed 12 January 2012), p. 8, para. 24; *Amoco International Finance Corporation* v. *The Islamic Republic of Iran et al.*, Partial Award No. 310-56-3 of 14 July 1987, 15 Iran-United States Claims Tribunal Reports 189, paras. 189–206.

[67] Paragraph 2 of Article 31 defines "injury" as: "any damage, whether material or moral, caused by the internationally wrongful act of a State."

[68] ICJ, *Case Concerning Avena and Other Mexican Nationals (Mexico* v. *United States of America)*, Judgment, ICJ Reports 2004 (I), p. 59, para. 119; see also ICJ, *Case Concerning Pulp Mills on the River Uruguay (Argentina* v. *Uruguay)*, Judgment, 20 April 2010, p. 77, para. 273.

The most significant development in this area was the advent of international human rights law, which, through its mechanisms, empowered victims to seek and obtain reparations from the state for violations of their rights. International human rights law does not concern a criminal dimension (i.e., it is not directly focused on criminal prosecutions or punishment of individual perpetrators), but rather focuses on victims of human rights violations.

The advent of international human rights law has provided avenues for individuals to seek reparations from states for human rights violations.[69] It has significantly expanded the possibility for individuals to seek and obtain redress. The trailblazing instrument was the *Universal Declaration of Human Rights*,[70] which then prompted the adoption of many other similar instruments.[71] A victim's right to seek and obtain a remedy has been codified into human rights treaties and instruments. It has also been firmly reiterated and expanded upon by international jurisprudence.[72] The *European Convention on Human Rights*,[73] the *American Convention on Human Rights*,[74] and the *Optional Protocol to the African Charter* establishing an African Court of Human Rights,[75] all provide their respective courts with the authority to order reparations in order to compensate victims for violations of a conventional right.

---

[69] Riccardo Pisillo Mazzeschi, "International Obligations to Provide for Reparation Claims," in *State Responsibility and the Individual – Reparations in Instances of Grave Violations of Human Rights*, eds. Albrecht Randelzhofer and Christian Tomuschat, Kluwer Law International, 1999, p. 149.

[70] Proclaimed by General Assembly Resolution 217A (III), 10 December 1948.

[71] See generally, e.g., Universal Declaration of Human Rights (art. 8); the International Covenant on Civil and Political Rights (art. 2[3], 9[5] and 14[6]); the International Convention on the Elimination of All Forms of Racial Discrimination (art. 6); the Convention of the Rights of the Child (art. 39); the Convention against Torture and other forms of Cruel, Inhuman and Degrading Treatment (art. 14); the European Convention on Human Rights (arts. 5[5], 13, and 41); the Inter-American Convention on Human Rights (arts. 25, 68, and 63[1]); the African Charter of Human and Peoples' Rights (art. 21[2]).

[72] See e.g., *Velásquez Rodríguez* Case, Inter-American Court of Human Rights, Serial C, No. 4 (1989), par. 174. See also *Papamichalopoulos* v. *Greece*, ECHR Serial A, No 330-B (1995), p. 36. See e.g., *Rodriquez* v. *Uruguay* (322/88), CCPR/C/51/D/322/1988 (1994); 2 IHRR 12 (1995); *Blancov* v. *Nicaragua* (328/88), CCPR/C/51/D/328/1988 (1994); 2 IHRR 123 (1995); and *Bautista de Arellana* v. *Columbia* (563/93), CCPR/C/55/D/563/1993 (1995); 3 IHRR 315 (1996).

[73] *European Convention for the Protection of Human Rights and Fundamental Freedoms*, 4 November 1950, entry into force 3 September 1953, CETS No. 5, as amended by Protocol 11 CETS No. 155, 11 May 1994, entry into force 1 November 1998.

[74] American Convention on Human Rights, 22 November 1969, entry into force 18 July 1978, 114 UNTS 123.

[75] Protocol to the African Charter on Human and Peoples' Rights on the Establishment of an African Court on Human and Peoples' Rights, 9 June 1998, entry into force 25 January 2004, OAU/LEG/MIN/AFCHPR/PROT.1 rev.2 (1997).

Punishment and Reparation 31

Victims of human rights violations have been afforded the right to claim reparation before various fora of human rights mechanisms. These include, for example: the European Court of Human Rights, the recent African Court of Human and Peoples' Rights, treaty bodies, and the Inter-American Commission for Human Rights. The jurisprudence of these bodies is rich, and together, they have contributed to the formation of a meaningful human rights system, where victims' voices can be heard and claims for reparation can be instituted. While the experience of each of these institutions is undoubtedly valuable, focus is on the jurisprudence of the IACtHR due to its consolidated experience, as well as its extensive, diverse, and creative jurisprudence that may provide guidance in the architecture of reparative justice for international crimes.[76]

The Inter-American Court of Human Rights has interpreted the individual's right to a remedy stated in Article 25 of the American Convention on Human Rights as requiring states to provide reparation to individuals who have suffered a violation of the convention. Importantly, the court has held that a state which violates the convention is under a "duty to make reparation and to have the consequences of the violation remedied."[77]

Similarly to the development of reparations in international criminal law, under international human rights law, victims are the direct beneficiaries of reparations. The link between international human rights law and international criminal law has been recognized as: "The reference to human rights in the [Rome] Statute is an important recognition of victims' rights as jurisprudence on redress in international and regional human rights systems ... has significantly contributed to developing the concept of reparations."[78]

Due to some significant and systemic differences of a system based on state responsibility, and one based on individual responsibility, the principles and case law of the IACtHR cannot be directly transposed to international criminal law. Rather, it may provide some guidance as to the development of the scope of the legal duty to repair under international criminal law. Overall, it is submitted that much can be learned from a continuous dialogue among

---

[76] On the significance of the jurisprudence of the IACtHR to the development of a rich jurisprudence on reparations for human rights violations, see Philippe Weckel, "La justice internacionale en le soixantième anniversaire de la Déclaration Universelle des Droits de l'Homme," *Revue générale de Droit international public* 113 (2009), pp. 14–17.

[77] IACtHR, *Baldeón-García* v. *Peru*, Merits, Reparations and Costs, 6 April 2006, Series C No. 147, para. 147.

[78] Gilbert Bitti and Gabriela Gonzalez Rivas, "The Reparations Provisions for Victims under the Rome Statute of the International Criminal Court," in *Redressing Injustices through Mass Claims Processes, Innovative Responses to Unique Challenges*, The International Bureau of the Permanent Court of Arbitration, Oxford University Press, 2006, p. 312.

regional and international institutions committed to the promotion of international justice and the rule of law.[79]

The systems under which the IACtHR and the international criminal courts and tribunals operate share some similarities, but they are also divided by some structural and conceptual differences. For example, it has been noted that, although set up for the precise purpose of examining claims for reparation, human rights treaty bodies and human rights courts often suffer from limited budget and institutional constraints.[80] Furthermore, by their very nature, these institutions have to grapple with the individualized nature of human rights complaints when dealing with broader mass atrocities and mass victimization. The main similarity between these two systems, it can be argued, rests on the nature of the violations that underlie both systems: international crimes involve mass violations of human rights.

There are nevertheless some important distinctions between reparative justice under international human rights jurisprudence and in international criminal law. For example, human rights reparations are awarded by a state to victims (individual or collective reparation awards), rather than against individual perpetrators of international crimes. It is acknowledged that not all forms of reparation awarded on the basis of state liability can be directly transposed to international criminal proceedings, which is not aimed at state liability. This is a pivotal difference as some of the forms of reparation that have been awarded at the IACtHR which may require the participation of the state in question – for example, a change in legislation, or the building of a memorial, or the continuation of investigations – cannot be directly transposed to an international criminal law context and applied to individual perpetrators.

Furthermore, the aim of human rights systems is to examine claims of reparation against a state for its failure to prevent, punish, or protect claimant victims. Conversely, reparation within an international criminal tribunal is a direct consequence of an international crime perpetrated by an individual.

1.4.4.1 Contextual Background

The IACtHR and the Inter-American Commission of Human Rights are the main organs of the Inter-American system of human rights, which monitors

---

[79] See in this regard, Antônio Augusto Cançado Trindade, *State Responsibility in Cases of Massacres: Contemporary Advances in International Justice*, Inaugural Address as Honorary Professor to the Chair in "International and Regional Human Rights Courts," 10 November 2011 at Utrecht University, pp. 57–65.

[80] See, e.g., *Annual Report of the European Court of Human Rights*, 2006, Foreword by Jean Paul Costa, President of the European Court of Human Rights, p. 5 et seq.

the compliance of states parties with their obligations to the Inter-American Convention on Human Rights of 1979 (Pact of San José).[81] This system of human rights protection is a response to the countless atrocities that have occurred in the Americas in the past centuries, and to the struggle of peoples against their governments.[82]

Article 63(1) of the Inter-American Convention concerning reparations provides as follows:

> 1. If the Court finds that there has been a violation of a right or freedom protected by this Convention, the Court shall rule that the injured party be ensured the enjoyment of his right or freedom that was violated. It shall also rule, if appropriate, that the consequences of the measure or situation that constituted the breach of such right or freedom be remedied and that fair compensation be paid to the injured party.

The IACtHR, since its first proceedings, has cultivated a far-reaching jurisprudence on reparations which elaborates on many concepts that are omnipresent in every system of reparation and which can be taken into account for the development of reparation principles in international criminal justice.

1.4.4.2 The Concept of Victims

The IACtHR has defined "victims" as persons whose rights have been violated.[83] A main feature of the jurisprudence of the IACtHR in this context is its broad conception of persons entitled to receive reparation. The court developed the notion of "next of kin" which includes the immediate family of the victims, for example, direct descendants, ascendants, siblings, spouses, or permanent partners.[84] The development of the notion of "next of kin" as persons who may be eligible to reparation represents an enlargement of those who can receive reparation in addition to the direct victim of the violation for which reparation is awarded.[85] In this context, reparations have often been awarded to spouses and children of the direct victim since the court

---

[81] Adopted at the Inter-American Specialized Conference on Human Rights, San José, Costa Rica, 22 November 1969 ("the Inter-American Convention").

[82] For an account of civil wars and dictatorships in Latin America in the past, see e.g., Paul H. Lewis, *Authoritarian Regimes in Latin America: Dictators, Despots, and Tyrants*, Rowman & Littlefield, 2005.

[83] Cf. e.g., ICtHR, *Amparo* v. *Venezuela*, Reparations Judgment, 14 September 1996, para. 40.

[84] See IACtHR, *Garrido Baigorria* v. *Argentina*, Reparations Judgment, 27 August 1998, para. 50.

[85] IACtHR, *Juan Humberto Sanchez* v. *Honduras*, Judgment, 7 June 2003, para. 155; IACtHR, *Lopez Alvarez* v. *Honduras*, Judgment, 1 February 2006, para. 120.

considered that as a result of the violations, these persons also suffered material and moral harm.[86]

Thus, it stems clearly from the jurisprudence of the IACtHR that the award of reparation goes beyond the strict definition of who is a "direct victim" of the violation in question and also includes "indirect victims" who may have suffered harm as a consequence of the violation.[87] It goes without saying that the award of reparations is not automatic to all persons related to the victim, and the court has established some criteria on the basis of which reparation may be awarded.[88]

At this juncture, it is also worth mentioning that the court has taken a flexible approach in cases where the victim could not be found. For example, in cases of forced disappearances and massacres, surviving persons have been permitted to obtain reparation. Thus, the court considers as victims not only those who have been killed or forcefully abducted, but also those displaced as a result.[89]

Another interesting aspect of the jurisprudence of the IACtHR, which could shed some light on the development of the jurisprudence of the ICC, relates to the identity of a victim. In cases related to indigenous groups, for example, the court has established that when no identity document is available, a declaration which is made to the competent authority can be used to determine the identity of the victim.[90]

Thus, it can be seen from the jurisprudence of the IACtHR referred to herein that the court has adopted an approach concerning persons entitled to

---

[86] Ibid. See also, Elizabeth Odio Benito, "Development and Interpretation of Principles of Reparation: The Case Law of the IACHR and its Possible Contributions to the Jurisprudence of the ICC," in *Protecting Humanity: Essays in International Law and Policy in Honour of Navanethem Pillay*, ed. Chile Eboe-Osuji, Nijhoff, 2010, p. 577.

[87] IACtHR, *Garrido and Baigorria v. Argentina*, Reparations Judgment, 27 August 1998, Series C No 39, paras. 62, 63; IACtHR, *Blake* v. *Guatemala*, Judgment, 22 January 1999, para. 37; IACtHR, *Bámaca Velásquez v. Guatemala*, Reparations Judgment, 22 February 2002, paras. 33–36; IACtHR, *Aloeboetoe v. Suriname*, Reparations Judgment, 10 September 1993, para. 71; IACtHR, *Panel Banca v. Guatemala*, Reparations Judgment, 25 May 2001, para. 85, 86; IACtHR, *Case of Street Children v. Guatemala*, Reparations Judgment, 26 May 2001, para. 68; IACtHR, *Juan Humberto Sánchez v. Honduras*, Judgment, 7 June 2003, para. 152; IACtHR, *Loayza Tamayo v. Peru*, Reparations Judgment, 27 November 1998, para. 92.

[88] See IACtHR, *Aloeboetoe* v. *Suriname*, Reparations Judgment, 10 September 1993, paras. 67, 68.

[89] IACtHR, *Case of Acosta Calderon v. Ecuador*, Judgment, 24 June 2005, para. 154 and IACtHR, *Case of Mapiripan Massacre v. Colombia*, Judgment, 15 September 2005, para. 256. Cf., Elizabeth Odio Benito, "Development and Interpretation of Principles of Reparation: The Case Law of the IACHR and its Possible Contributions to the Jurisprudence of the ICC," in *Protecting Humanity: Essays in International Law and Policy in Honour of Navanethem Pillay*, ed. Chile Eboe-Osuji, Nijhoff, 2010, p. 577.

[90] IACtHR, *Case of Moiwana v. Suriname*, Judgment, 15 June 2005, paras. 117 and 178; IACtHR, *Case of Massacre of Plan de Sanchez*, Reparations Judgment, 19 November 2004, para. 62.

receive reparation which goes beyond a strict understanding of who qualifies as a victim within the system. The court has recognized the inconvenient truth: that human rights violations generally harm persons beyond the direct victim and as a consequence such individuals shall be considered victims for the purposes of claiming and potentially receiving reparations.[91]

These are important lessons which ought to be kept in mind, in spite of the inherent differences that exist between both systems of reparations, for the devising of reparation principles in international criminal law. In the context of international crimes, where the consequences thereof go beyond the direct victims of the crime,[92] affecting families and communities, it is imperative that the award of reparations does not follow a formalistic or inflexible approach as to the persons who can receive reparation.

1.4.4.3 Assessment of Harm

The IACtHR has produced a very rich jurisprudence concerning the definition and classification of damage.[93] According to the court, moral damage is the psychological impact on a victim or their family members as a consequence of the violations of the rights and freedoms guaranteed by the convention.[94] This type of damage has been considered to include changes and deterioration of the standard of living of the victims and eventual financial difficulties or family disintegration.[95]

An important remark about the jurisprudence of the IACtHR in this respect is that the court has relied on some assumptions as regards the proof of immaterial damages and has taken decisions on this basis which stem from

---

[91] IACtHR, *Case of Caracazo* v. *Venezuela*, Reparations Judgment, 29 August 2002, paras. 63–73.

[92] Rule 85 of the Rules of Procedure and Evidence of the ICC provides the following definition of victims:

> For the purposes of the Statute and the Rules of Procedure and Evidence:
> (a) "Victims" means natural persons who have suffered harm as a result of the commission of any crime within the jurisdiction of the Court;
> (b) Victims may include organizations or institutions that have sustained direct harm to any of their property which is dedicated to religion, education, art or science or charitable purposes, and to their historic monuments, hospitals and other places and objects for humanitarian purposes.

[93] Elizabeth Odio Benito, "Development and Interpretation of Principles of Reparation: The Case Law of the IACHR and its Possible Contributions to the Jurisprudence of the ICC," in *Protecting Humanity: Essays in International Law and Policy in Honour of Navanethem Pillay*, ed. Chile Eboe-Osuji, Nijhoff, 2010, p. 579.

[94] IACtHR, *Case of Velasquez-Rodriguez* v. *Honduras*, Judgment, 21 July 1989, para. 51.

[95] IACtHR, *Case of La Rochela Massacre* v. *Colombia*, Judgment, 11 May 2007, paras. 262, 263, 264.

the gravity of the violations.[96] For example, the court has found that aggression and abuses are important causes of moral suffering and that no evidence is necessary to arrive at such conclusion.[97] This is a particularly relevant consideration to be borne in mind when developing the contents of the legal duty of reparations under international criminal law. This is because it concerns the aftermath of international crimes where the gravity of the breach of international law is inherently present, but the moral harm pertaining to the consequences of conflicts and wars is often difficult to adduce.

Similarly, in relation to evidence of damage, reliance on presumptions and circumstantial evidence has been accepted "when they lead to consistent conclusions as regards the facts of the case."[98]

As to material damages, these concern the negative impact of the violations on the victim's earnings or the expenses resulting from the violations.[99] In this context, the court has also applied numerous assumptions as regards loss of future income and has made awards based on the principle of fairness.[100] The court has also found that the judgment itself can constitute a form of reparation for material damages, as it will be discussed below.[101] At this juncture, it is also worth mentioning the notion of damage to the *"proyeto de vida,"* a

---

[96] See e.g., IACtHR, *Case of Mapiripan Massacre v. Colombia*, Judgment, 15 September 2005, para. 267; IACtHR, *Case of Villagrán Morales et al v. Guatemala, Street Children Case*, Reparations Judgment, 26 May 2001, para. 79 ("in view of the lack of precise information on the real earnings of the victims, [the court] should use the minimum wage for non-agricultural activities in Guatemala as a basis"); IACtHR, *Case of Caracazo v. Venezuela*, Reparation Judgment, 29 August 2002, para. 88 (in the absence of detailed or reliable information, the reference for the court was the minimum wage in national law); IACtHR, *Case of Panel Blanca v. Guatemala*, Reparations Judgment, 25 May 2001, paras. 116–117 (in the absence of detailed or reliable information, the reference for the court was the minimum wage in national law); IACtHR, *Castillo Páez v. Peru*, Reparations Judgment, 27 November 1998, para. 75 (in the absence of detailed information, the reference for the court was the minimum wage in national law); IACtHR, *Case of Neira Alegría et al. v. Peru*, Reparations Judgment, 19 September 1996, paras. 49–52 (the court determined the loss of income "for reasons of equity and in view of the actual economic and social situation of Latin America"); IACtHR, *Case of Maritza Urrutia v. Guatemala*, Judgment, 27 November 2003, paras. 158–159 (the Court determined the loss "in fairness"); IACtHR, *Case of Suárez Rosero v. Ecuador*, Reparations Judgment, 20 January 1999, paras. 66 and 99; IACtHR, *Case of Cantoral Benavides v. Peru*, Judgment, 3 December 2001, para. 51.

[97] IACtHR, *Garrido Baigorria v. Argentina*, Reparations Judgment, 27 August 1998, para. 49; IACtHR, *Case of Loaiza Tamayo v. Peru*, Reparations Judgment, 27 November 1998, para. 138; IACtHR, *Case of La Rochela Massacre v. Colombia*, Judgment, 11 May 2007, para. 256; IACtHR, *Case of La Cantuta v. Peru*, Judgment, 29 November 2006, para. 217.

[98] IACtHR, *Gangaram Panday v. Suriname*, Merits, Reparations and Costs Judgment, 21 January 1994, para. 49.

[99] IACtHR, *Case of Acevedo Jaramillo and others v. Peru*, Judgment, 7 February 2006, para. 301.

[100] IACtHR, *Case of Molina Theissen v. Guatemala*, Reparations Judgment, 3 July 2004, para. 57.

[101] See IACtHR, *Case of La Cantuta v. Perú*, Judgment, 29 November 2006, para. 162.

Punishment and Reparation 37

concept developed by the IACtHR, which concerns a long-term reduced ability to benefit from life in light of the altered circumstances as a consequence of the violation.[102]

1.4.4.4 Collective Reparations

The IACtHR's experience with collective reparations may prove pertinent for the award of reparations in international criminal law in instances where calculating individualized reparations for victims may be a rather difficult task.

Again, the jurisprudence of the IACtHR has been a pioneer in this area.[103] While establishing that the award of collective reparation entails direct damage to individual victims,[104] in several cases, collective reparations to entire communities have been awarded. These cases deal with massacres of entire communities, as illustrated, for example, in the *Plan de Sanchez Massacre* case, which concerned the massacre of a Mayan village by the Guatemalan army that almost completely destroyed the village. During the massacre, women were raped, tortured, and assassinated; children were beaten to death.[105] The court heard the testimony of survivors of the massacre and experts about the impact of the crimes on the community as a whole. The court acknowledged in its judgment the consequences for a community of violence and extermination towards women. The court, while recognizing that it could not award reparation to victims who were not individually indicated, decided to give reparation to the communities where the victims used to live.[106] Furthermore, this case is also interesting in that the court

---

[102] See e.g., IACtHR, *Case of Cantoral Benavides v. Peru*, Reparations Judgment, 3 December 2001, para. 80; IACtHR, *Case of Loayza-Tamayo v. Peru*, Reparations and Costs Judgment, 27 November 1998, para. 147. See also Cordula Droege, "El derecho a interponer recursos y a obtener reparación por violaciones graves de los derechos humanos: guía para profesionales," 2 Serie de guías para profesionales, 2007, pp. 141–142; Sergio Garcia Ramírez, "Las reparaciones en el sistema interamericano de protección de los derechos humanos," in *El sistema interamericano de protección de los derechos humanos en el umbral del siglo XXI: tomo I*, Corte Interamericana de Derechos Humanos, 2001, pp. 150–152.

[103] Elizabeth Odio Benito, "Development and Interpretation of Principles of Reparation: The Case Law of the IACHR and its Possible Contributions to the Jurisprudence of the ICC," in *Protecting Humanity: Essays in International Law and Policy in Honour of Navanethem Pillay*, ed. Chile Eboe-Osuji, Nijhoff, 2010, p. 584.

[104] IACtHR, *Case of Aloeboetoe v. Suriname*, Reparations Judgment, 10 September 1993, para. 83.

[105] IACtHR, *Case of Massacre of Plan de Sanchez v. Guatemala*, Reparations Judgment, 19 November 2004.

[106] Ibid., para. 62.

considered the loss of traditions and cultural values (due to the death of those members of the community who transmitted such values) and it qualified such loss as grounds for the award of moral damages.[107]

The experience of the IACtHR may prove useful as to the kinds of collective reparation that can be awarded. The court has ordered various kinds of collective reparations in its jurisprudence, for example:[108] the creation of a project for the entire community to provide potable water and sanitary infra-structure[109]; establishment of a community fund for specific projects for education, health, housing, and agriculture for members of the indigenous tribe affected[110]; educational grants for the population affected by the viola-tion[111]; setting in place safety measures for displaced persons in case they decide to return to their villages[112]; public apology and acknowledgment by the state to the community where the human rights violations took place[113]; the building of memorials as a means to prevent the reoccurrence of such serious violations[114]; and setting up courses in human rights,[115] among others.

This list of collective reparations is of course not exhaustive; the jurisprudence of the IACtHR is not exhaustive either, as there are other types of collective reparations that can be awarded in cases of massacres.[116] The point to be taken from these examples of collective reparations, is the open and creative attitude of the court to award reparations that uniquely address the violation with which it is seized. The lesson to be learned is that the overwhelming task of assessing claims of reparation for massive human rights

---

[107] Ibid., paras. 12–49. See also, Julio Joe Rojas Báez, "La Jurisprudencia de la Corte Interamericana de Derechos Humanos en Materia de Reparaciones y los Criterios del Proyeto de Artículos sobre Responsabilidad del Estado por Hechos Internacionalmente Ilícitos," *American University International Law Review* 92 (2007–2008), p. 110.

[108] See in this regard, Elizabeth Odio Benito, "Development and Interpretation of Principles of Reparation: The Case Law of the IACHR and its Possible Contributions to the Jurisprudence of the ICC," in *Protecting Humanity: Essays in International Law and Policy in Honour of Navanethem Pillay*, ed. Chile Eboe-Osuji, Nijhoff, 2010, p. 586.

[109] IACtHR, *Case of Yakye Axa v. Paraguay*, Judgment, 17 June 2005, paras. 205–206.

[110] Ibid.

[111] IACtHR, *Case of Barrios Altos v. Peru*, Reparations Judgment, 30 November 2001, para. 43.

[112] IACtHR, *Case of Mapiripan Massacre v. Colombia*, Judgment, 15 September 2005, para. 313.

[113] Ibid., at para. 314.

[114] Ibid., at para. 315.

[115] Ibid., at para. 316.

[116] See e.g., Elizabeth Odio Benito, "Development and Interpretation of Principles of Reparation: the Case Law of the IACHR and its Possible Contributions to the Jurisprudence of the ICC," in *Protecting Humanity: Essays in International Law and Policy in Honour of Navanethem Pillay*, ed. Chile Eboe-Osuji, Nijhoff, 2010, p. 586, who claims that: "until now, these collective reparations do not include specific reparations for women survivors of sexual violence such as gynaecological clinics, HIV treatment programs, stigma-sharing programs, preventive campaigns on violence against women, etc."

Punishment and Reparation

violations has not stopped the court from awarding significant redress to victims.

1.4.4.5 Types of Reparation

One lesson that can be learned from the experience of the IACtHR is that reparations for mass atrocities ought to take into account the perspective of the victim and it should include a holistic approach, bearing in mind the goal and types of reparations that can be awarded.

One of the main challenges of reparations in the international criminal justice context is that the accused may not have any financial resources at the end of the trial to pay reparations to victims.[117] This criticism can be easily rebutted if one takes a broader approach of what it means to "repair" the harm caused. The aim of this section is not to be exhaustive, but rather to demonstrate that the mandate of reparations in international criminal law can be much more encompassing than equating reparations to a sum of money. This notion has guided the IACtHR in the development of its jurisprudence for human rights violations.

The IACtHR has taken a broad approach to reparations and has referred to the concept of "full reparation." In this perspective, it went beyond pecuniary reparations[118] and has awarded reparations in the form of restitution,[119] rehabilitation,[120] satisfaction and guarantee of nonrepetition,[121] reparations of symbolic or emblematic nature, going beyond individual victims and having an impact on the community in which the victim belongs.

An example of the diversity of forms of reparations ordered by the court is illustrated in the *Villagrán Morales and Others* case (*"Ninõs de la Calle"*).[122] In addition to indemnification for moral and material damage, the court ordered a change in legislation to conform with Article 19 of the American Convention,

---

[117] See e.g., Saul Levmore, "Reparations in the Wake of Atrocities: A Plan for Encouraging Participation by Governments," *Human Rights and International Criminal Law Online Forum*, invited experts on reparations question, available at http://uclalawforum.com/reparations#Levmore.

[118] See IACtHR, *Case of Loayza Tamayo v. Peru*, Reparations Judgment, 27 November 1998, para. 124.

[119] See e.g., IACtHR, *Case of Velazquez Rodriguez v. Honduras*, Reparations Judgment, 21 July 1989.

[120] See e.g., IACtHR, *Case of Barrios Altos v. Peru*, Reparations Judgment, 30 November 2001, para. 42.

[121] See e.g., IACtHR, *Case of Villagrán Morales et al., v. Guatemala*, Street Children Case, Reparations Judgment, 26 May 2001.

[122] Ibid.

the transfer of the mortal remains of one of the assassinated children and its exhumation in the place chosen by his family members, the designation of an educational center with an allusive name of the victimized children and bearing a plate naming the five victims as well as the investigation of the facts and punishment of those responsible.[123] This case demonstrates, it is submitted, the willingness of the court to take the perspective of the victim in the award of reparations, their needs and their wishes.

Moreover, the IACtHR has awarded reparations to victims consisting of sums of money and has also relied on positive obligations by the state. For example, in the *Bulacio v. Argentina* case,[124] which concerned the detention and killing of a teenager by the police, the court ordered, in addition to financial compensation, the continuation of investigation in the case and the adoption of legislative and other measures in order to ensure the nonrepetition of the violation.[125]

Significantly, the court has acknowledged that the right to truth[126] is also a form of reparation.[127] It has ordered, in this respect, *inter alia*, "the translation of the American Convention and Judgments into the language of the victims ... [and also] that these be widely disseminated among the victims of violations and ... published in official journals and newspapers with national circulation."[128] In addition to the right to truth, apology, public acknowledgement, and

---

[123] Ibid.

[124] Merits, Reparations and Costs Judgment, September 18, 2003.

[125] C.f. also, Antônio Augusto Cançado Trindade, "The Inter-American System of Protection of Human Rights (1948-2009): Evolution, Present State and Perspectives," in *Dossier Documentaires/Documentary File – XL Session d'Enseignement*, Vol. II, IIDH, 2009, p. 102.

[126] See Revised Final Report of the Special Rapporteur on the question of impunity of perpetrators of human rights violations (civil and political), 2 October 1997, E/CN.4/Sub.2/1997/20/Re v.1, para. 19, where the Inter-American Commission on Human Rights stated that: "Every society has the inalienable right to know the truth about past events, as well as the motives and circumstances in which aberrant crimes came to be committed, in order to prevent repetition of such acts in the future. Moreover, the family members of the victims are entitled to information as to what happened to their relatives ... ." See also, Report 21/00, Case 12.059, Carmen Aguiar de Lapacó (Argentina), 29 February 2000, where Argentina guaranteed "the right to truth, which involves the exhaustion of all means to obtain information on the whereabouts of the disappeared persons."

[127] IACtHR, *Case of Prison Miguel Castro Castro v. Peru*, Judgment, 25 November 2006, para. 440. In this sense, the court has ordered the translation of judgments into the language of the victims and that the judgments be disseminated among victims of violations, see IACtHR, *Case of Massacre of Plan de Sanchez v. Guatemala*, Reparations Judgment, 19 November 2004, para. 102; IACtHR, *Case of Cantoral Benavides v. Peru*, Reparations Judgment, 3 December 2001, para. 79.

[128] Elizabeth Odio Benito, "Development and Interpretation of Principles of Reparation: the Case Law of the IACHR and its Possible Contributions to the Jurisprudence of the ICC," in *Protecting Humanity: Essays in International Law and Policy in Honour of Navanethem Pillay*, ed. Chile Eboe-Osuji, Nijhoff, 2010, pp. 590–591, citing IACtHR, *Case of Massacre of Plan de Sanchez v. Guatemala*, Reparations Judgment, 19 November 2004, para. 102 and IACtHR, *Case of Cantoral Benavides v. Peru*, Reparations Judgment, 3 December 2011, para. 79.

Punishment and Reparation

acceptance of responsibility are also recognized by the court as fundamental forms of reparation.[129] The IACtHR and the Inter-American Commission have acknowledged that a judgment of the court in this respect provides a form of reparation.[130] Certainly, as the IACtHR itself has recognized, in cases of human rights violations, the judgment alone may fail to fully do justice to victims.[131]

1.4.5 International Humanitarian Law: Reparation and its Enforcement

Victims' individual right to reparation under international humanitarian law is a topic of much debate in legal doctrine.[132] It appears that there exists an

---

[129] For cases where the court ordered recognition of responsibility and public apology: IACtHR, *Case of Barrios Altos* v. *Peru*, Reparations Judgment, 30 November 2001, para. 44(e) and operative paragraph 5(e); IACtHR, *Case of Cantoral Benavides* v. *Peru*, Reparations Judgment, 3 December 2001, para. 81; IACtHR, *Case of Durand and Ugarte* v. *Peru*, Reparations Judgment, 3 December 2001, para. 39(b) and operative para. 4(b); IACtHR, *Case of Bámaca Velásquez* v. *Guatemala*, Reparations Judgment, 22 February 2002, para. 84; IACtHR, *Case of Juan Humberto Sánchez* v. *Honduras*, Judgment, 7 June 2003, para. 188; IACtHR, *Case of Plan de Sánchez Massacre*, Reparations Judgment, 19 November 2004, para. 100. Guatemala apologized publicly for the massacre: AP Guatemala Apologizes for 1982 Massacre, available at www.latinamericanstudies.org/guatemala/peten-massacre.htm. For cases where the IACtHR has ordered states to make their judgments public: IACtHR, *Case of Trujillo Oroza* v. *Bolivia*, Reparations Judgment, 27 February 2002, para. 119; IACtHR, *Case of Barrios Altos* v. *Peru*, Reparations Judgment, 30 November 2001, para. 44(d) and operative paragraph 5(d); IACtHR, *Case of Cantoral Benavides* v. *Peru*, Reparations Judgment, 3 December 2001, para. 79; IACtHR, *Case of Durand and Ugarte* v. *Peru*, Reparations Judgment, 3 December 2001, para. 39(a) and operative paragraph 3(a); IACtHR, *Case of Bámaca Velásquez* v. *Guatemala*, Reparations Judgment, 22 February 2002, para. 84; IACtHR, *Case of Caracazo* v. *Venezuela*, Reparations Judgment, 29 August 2002, para. 128; IACtHR, *Case of Juan Humberto Sánchez* v. *Honduras*, Judgment, 7 June 2003, para. 188. See also UN Human Rights Commission resolutions, Resolutions on Impunity E/CN.4/RES/2001/70, 25 April 2001, para 8; E/CN.4/RES/2002/79, para 9; E/CN.4/RES/2003/72 I, para. 8, where it is recognized that "for the victims of human rights violations, public knowledge of their suffering and the truth about the perpetrators, including their accomplices, of these violations are essential steps towards rehabilitation and reconciliation."

[130] IACtHR, *Case of Cesti Hurtado*, Reparations Judgment, 31 May 2001, para. 59, where the court found that the judgment constitutes satisfaction with regard to the reputation and honor of the victim.

[131] IACtHR, *Case of El Amparo* v. *Venezuela*, Reparations Judgment, 14 September 1996, para. 35; IACtHR, *Case of Neira Alegría et al.* v. *Peru*, Reparations Judgment, 19 September 1996, para. 56; IACtHR, *Case of Castillo Páez* v. *Peru*, Reparations Judgment, 27 November 1998, para. 84; IACtHR, *Case of Blake* v. *Guatemala*, Reparations Judgment, 22 January 1999, para. 55; *Case of Panel Blanca* v. *Guatemala*, Reparations Judgment, 25 May 2001, para. 105.

[132] See e.g., Frits Kalshoven, "State Responsibility for Warlike Acts of the Armed Forces," *International and Comparative Law Quarterly* 40 (1991), p. 827; Christopher Greenwood, "International Humanitarian Law (Laws of War)," in *The Centennial of the First International Peace Conference*, ed. Frits Kalshoven, Kluwer Law International, 2000, p. 250.

obligation to make reparations stemming from texts of international humanitarian law,[133] as will be further expanded upon below. The question of whether or not states have an obligation to pay reparation to individual victims of international humanitarian law violations is intrinsically intertwined with questions of state immunity, which is further discussed below.[134] A controversy hinges upon whether victims of international humanitarian law violations can claim reparation directly from the offender.[135]

In relation to armed conflicts, both international human rights law and international humanitarian law may be applicable, the latter being the *lex specialis*.[136] The present chapter provides an overview of the question concerning the beneficiaries of reparation for international humanitarian law violations.[137] It does not aim at an extensive analysis of reparations under international humanitarian law.[138]

---

[133] Draft Articles on State Responsibility, Article 31; Second Protocol to the Hague Convention for the Protection of Cultural Property, Article 38; First Geneva Convention, Article 51; Second Geneva Convention, Article 52; Third Geneva Convention, Article 131; Fourth Geneva Convention, Article 148; cf., Rule 150 of the ICRC Rules on Customary International Humanitarian Law: "A State responsible for violations of international humanitarian law is required to make full reparation for the loss or injury caused." As to examples of treaty provisions in international humanitarian law that establish an obligation to provide reparation for breaches, Article 3 of the Hague Convention No. IV of 1907 states that: "A belligerent party which violates the provisions of the said Regulations shall, if the case demands, be liable to pay compensation. It shall be responsible for all acts committed by persons forming part of its armed forces." Similarly, Article 91 of Additional Protocol I of 1977 states that: "A party to the conflict which violates the provisions of the Conventions or of this Protocol shall, if the case demands, be liable to pay compensation. It shall be responsible for all acts committed by persons forming part of its armed forces."

[134] See e.g., Maria Gavouneli, "War Reparation Claims and State Immunity," *Revue Hellénique de droit international* 50 (1997), pp. 595–608; Brigitte Stern, "Vers une limitation de 'l'irresponsabilité souveraine' des Etats et chefs d'Etat en cas de crime de droit international?" in *Promoting Justice, Human Rights and Conflict Resolution through International Law: Liber Amicorum Lucius Caflisch*, ed. Marcelo Kohen, Nijhoff, 2007, pp. 511–548.

[135] See e.g., Conor McCarthy, "Victim Redress and International Criminal Justice: Competing Paradigms, or Compatible Forms of Justice?" *Journal of International Criminal Justice* 10 (2012), p. 356.

[136] Cf. ICJ, Legal Consequences of the Construction of a Wall in the Occupied Palestinian Territory, Advisory Opinion, ICJ Reports 136 (2004), p. 178.

[137] See Georges Abi-Saab, "The Specificities of Humanitarian Law," in *Studies and Essays of International Humanitarian Law and the Red Cross Principles in Honour of Jean Pictet*, ed. Christophe Swinarski, Nijhoff, 1984, p. 269, where it is argued that international humanitarian law's objective goes "beyond the inter-state levels and [reaches] for the level of the real (or ultimate) beneficiaries of humanitarian protection, i.e. individuals and groups of individuals." See also, Theodor Meron, "The Humanization of Humanitarian Law," *American Journal of International Law* 94 (2000), pp. 239–278.

[138] See generally as to this question: Veronika Bílková, "Victims of War and Their Right to Reparation for Violations of International Humanitarian Law," *Miskolc Journal of International Law* 4 (2007),

Punishment and Reparation

A study by the International Law Association addressing the question of reparations for victims of armed conflict devoted some attention to the conceptualization of "victims"[139] for purposes of the application of the principles proclaimed therein:

> "1. For the purposes of this Declaration, the term 'victim' means natural or legal persons who have suffered harm as a result of a violation of the rules of international law applicable in armed conflict.
>
> 2. This provision is without prejudice to the right of other persons – in particular those in a family or civil law relationship to the victim – to submit a claim on behalf of victims provided that there is a legal interest therein. This may be the case where the victim is a minor child, incapacitated or otherwise unable to claim reparation."[140]

According to this conception of "victims," there must be (1) a violation of international law applicable in armed conflicts; (2) a harm must have been suffered; (3) there must be a link between the harm suffered and the violation of the international law applicable in the armed conflict.[141] As it has been argued, international humanitarian law ensures the protection and assistance to individuals that are victims of an armed conflict but when that same individual becomes a victim of a violation of international humanitarian law, the protection given by this field of international law does not seem sufficient.[142] Delving into the provisions that pertain to reparations for violations of international humanitarian law, as far as international armed conflicts are concerned, Article 3 of The Hague Convention IV provides that: "A

---

pp. 1–11; Christian Tomuschat, "Reparation in Favour of Individual Victims of Gross Violations of Human Rights and International Humanitarian Law," in *Promoting Justice, Human Rights and Conflict Resolution Through International Law*, ed. Marcelo G. Kohen, Nijhoff, 2007; Rainer Hofmann, "Victims of Violations of International Humanitarian Law: Do They Have an Individual Right to Reparation Against States Under International Law?" in *Common Values in International Law: Essays in Honour of Christian Tomuschat*, ed. Pierre-Marie Dupuy et al., Kehl Engel, 2006; Emanuela-Chiarra Gillard, "Reparation for Violations of International Humanitarian Law," *International Review of the Red Cross* 85 (2003), pp. 529–553.

[139] The word "victim" does not appear in all instruments of IHL. For example, the Geneva Conventions and other treaties do not mention the word "victim" in contrast with the *Additional Protocol to the Geneva Conventions of 12 August 1949, and Relating to the Protection of Victims of International Armed Conflicts*, of 8 June 1977 and the *Additional Protocol to the Geneva Conventions of 12 August 1949, and Relating to the Protection of Victims of Non-International Armed Conflicts*.

[140] International Law Association, *Remedies for Victims of Armed Conflict*, 74 International Law Association Report Conference 291, 2010, Article 4, p. 302.

[141] See commentary to International Law Association, *Remedies for Victims of Armed Conflict*, 74 International Law Association Report Conference 291, 2010, Article 4, p. 302.

[142] Liesbeth Zegveld, "Remedies for Victims of Violations of International Humanitarian Law," *International Review of the Red Cross* 85 (2003), pp. 497–526.

belligerent party which violates the provisions of the [annexed] Regulations shall, if the case demands, be liable to pay compensation. It shall be responsible for all acts committed by persons forming part of its armed forces."[143] This same obligation appears in Article 91 of Additional Protocol I to the Geneva Conventions (concerning violations of the Additional Protocol or of the Geneva Conventions of 1949).[144] The duty to make reparation for violations of international humanitarian law is also stated in Article 38 of the Second Protocol to the Hague Convention for the Protection of Cultural Property. Additionally, it is implied in the four Geneva Conventions of 1949, whereby states cannot absolve themselves for liability incurred in respect of grave breaches of international humanitarian law: First Geneva Convention, Article 51; Second Geneva Convention, Article 52; Third Geneva Convention, Article 131; Fourth Geneva Convention, Article 148.[145]

As to noninternational armed conflicts, the relevant rules are Common Article 3 to the four Geneva Conventions of 1949, Provisions of Additional Protocol II relating to Non-International Armed Conflicts,[146] Article 38 of the Second Protocol to the Hague Convention for the Protection of Cultural Property[147] (which expressly refers to the duty of states to provide reparation, and which applies in any armed conflict). Many other rules of customary international law help form the legal framework for reparations in such types of conflict.[148]

---

[143] Hague Convention (IV) Respecting the Laws and Customs of War on Land, 18 October 1907, entry into force 26 January 1910, 9 UKTS (1910).

[144] Protocol Additional to the Geneva Conventions of 12 August 1949 and Relating to the Protection of Victims of International Armed Conflicts, 8 June 1977, entry into force 7 December 1978, 1125 UNTS (1979).

[145] ICRC, Customary International Humanitarian Law, Rule 150: Reparation. 1949 Geneva Convention (I) for the Amelioration of the Condition of the Wounded and Sick in Armed Forces in the Field, 12 August 1949, entry into force 21 October 1950; 1949 Geneva Convention (II) for the Amelioration of the Condition of Wounded, Sick and Shipwrecked Members of Armed Forces at Sea, 12 August 1949, entry into force, 21 October 1950; 1949 Geneva Convention (III) Relative to the Treatment of Prisoners of War, Geneva, 12 August 1949, entry into force 21 October 1950; 1949 Geneva Convention (IV) Relative to the Protection of Civilian Persons in Time of War, 12 August 1949, entry into force 21 October 1950.

[146] Protocol II Additional to the Geneva Conventions of 12 August 1949 and Relating to the Protection of Victims of Non-International Armed Conflicts, 8 June 1977, entry into force 7 December 1978, 1125 UNTS 609.

[147] Second Protocol to the Hague Convention for the Protection of Cultural Property in the Event of Armed Conflict, 26 March 1999, entry into force 9 March 2004, 38 ILM (1999).

[148] ICRC, Customary International Humanitarian Law, Rule 150: Reparation. The ICRC concludes in its study on customary international law that a state that has violated the laws of war in relation to a noninternational armed conflict has a duty to make reparation.

1.4.6 *The Legal Duty of Reparations*

Already in 1985, the United Nations adopted the Declaration of Basic Principles of Justice for Victims of Crime and Abuse of Power,[149] within which a victim's right to obtain reparations was emphasized. The focus of this declaration was on reparation for victims of domestic crimes.[150] Subsequently, another instrument was adopted by the United Nations General Assembly: The Basic Principles and Guidelines on the Right to a Remedy and Reparation for Victims of Gross Violations of International Human Rights Law and International Humanitarian Law.[151] The right of victims of gross violations of international human rights law or serious violations of international humanitarian law to obtain reparation was enunciated in Article 15, which states: "In accordance with its domestic laws and international legal obligations, a State shall provide reparation to victims for acts or omissions which can be attributed to the State and constitute gross violations of international human rights law or serious violations of international humanitarian law." Other recent documents have also affirmed victims' right to receive reparation. For example, the *Report of the International Commission of Inquiry on Darfur to the United Nations Secretary-General* concluded that, on the basis of human rights law,

> the proposition is warranted that at present, whenever a gross breach of human rights is committed which also amounts to an international crime, customary international law not only provides for the criminal liability of the individuals who have committed that breach, but also imposes an obligation on States of which the perpetrators are nationals, or for which they acted as de jure or de facto organs, to make reparation (including compensation) for the damage made.[152]

This brief analysis demonstrates that reparations for violations is a basic tenet of international human rights law.[153] The concept of individual redress

---

[149] GA Res. 40/34, 29 November 1985.
[150] M. Cherif Bassiouni, "International Recognition of Victims' Rights," *Human Rights Law Review* 6 (2006), pp. 203–279.
[151] GA Res. A/RES/60/147, 16 December 2005. The principles distinguish between the right to a remedy and reparations. Since the focus of this book is on the latter, the right to a remedy generally will not be discussed in detail.
[152] Report of the International Commission of Inquiry on Darfur to the United Nations Secretary-General, Pursuant to Security Council Resolution 1564 of 18 September 2004, para. 598.
[153] Jurisprudence of regional human rights courts provide examples of awards of reparation in relation to violations having occurred during armed conflicts. In the European Court of Human Rights, e.g., *Khatsiyeva et al.* v. *Russia*, Merits, 17 January 2008, unreported, Application No. 5108/02, para. 139; ECtHR *Varnava et al.* v. *Turkey*, Merits, Grand Chamber, 18 September 2009, unreported, Application No. 16064/90.

for victims of armed conflict is not as alien as it used to be before the development of international human rights law.

Be that as it may, in spite of the impressive number of instruments providing for the possibility of seeking a remedy, as discussed above, there remains a large gap whereby individuals might not obtain redress through international human rights mechanisms. International human rights law is built on the premise of state responsibility for violations of rights. This explains two limitations of international human rights law for the award of reparations to individual victims of international wrongful acts. The first limitation concerns the fact that victims cannot, under international human rights mechanisms, obtain reparation directly from individual perpetrators, as a state must have been involved in the violation. As it is widely known, many international crimes are committed by armed opposition or rebel groups, and the individual victim may not be in a position to use the mechanism of the international human rights system.

The second limitation which stems from this premise is that for a human rights court (such as, for example, the European Court of Human Rights) to award reparation to victims, there needs to be a violation of the rights recognized in the basic human right instrument of that court (that is, the European Convention on Human Rights or the American Convention on Human Rights) and the state against whom reparation is sought must have acceded to the convention. Finally, the question of extraterritorial application of human rights might also restrict the ability of victims of violations of human rights during armed conflicts to seek redress under international human rights law.[154]

Thus, international human rights law has provided an important avenue for victims who have experienced human rights violations (and victims of armed conflicts) to seek redress, albeit, it cannot encompass all victims of violations. From the discussion above, it seems clear that a legal duty exists for states to provide reparations for internationally wrongful conduct, including violation of human rights norms and international crimes. This stems from the decisions of various international courts, numerous conventions imposing a specific duty to repair, and the ILC Work of State Responsibility, some of which were reviewed above.

Having established this principle, two related questions are pertinent: whether there is a legal duty for *individuals* who have committed international

---

[154] On this question, see generally, Marko Milanovic, "From Compromise to Principles: Clarifying the Concept of State Jurisdiction in Human Rights Treaties," *Human Rights Law Review* 8 (2008), p. 411.

Punishment and Reparation

crimes to pay reparations to *individual victims*. The latter concerns the beneficiaries of reparations – that is, only states, or also individual victims? The former pertains to whether individuals, just as states, can have a legal duty of reparation. These two questions will be addressed in Chapters 2 and 3.

1.4.7 The Beneficiaries of Reparations Under International Law

Having placed a positive legal duty on states to provide reparations for violations of international human rights law and international law, both in international and noninternational armed conflicts, an important question to be examined is who the intended beneficiary of such reparations should be (that is, who has the right to reparations), and whether individual victims should be allowed to directly claim reparations. In other words, who can claim reparations from states – the individual who suffered harm or solely other states?

Is it morally acceptable that the state takes over all rights of reparation from the individual victim (presumably its national) without the consent of the victim and without their participation in the reparation process, and to the exclusion of any right of reparation the victim may eventually claim? Traditionally, due to the original architecture of international law as rights and duties among sovereign states, a state's legal duty to repair was not owed directly to individuals, but rather to other states.

Importantly, however, the entire system of international human rights litigation is based on the premise of individuals claiming reparations from the state. Thus, the traditional dichotomy of an international legal order that is based upon a state vs. state relationship (as having the legal duty and being the beneficiary of reparation) is no longer the only possibility when it comes to reparation.

As discussed above, the Basic Principles provide that victims of gross violations of human rights and serious international humanitarian law violations should be provided with full and effective reparation. Article 18 provides that:

> In accordance with domestic law and international law, and taking account of individual circumstances, victims of gross violations of international human rights law and serious violations of international humanitarian law should, as appropriate and proportional to the gravity of the violation and the circumstances of each case, be provided with full and effective reparation, as laid out in principles 19 to 23, which include the following forms: restitution, compensation, rehabilitation, satisfaction and guarantees of non-repetition.[155]

---

[155] Adopted and proclaimed by General Assembly resolution 60/147 of 16 December 2005.

48 *Reparative Justice for International Crimes*

Furthermore, Article 33(2) of the International Law Commission Draft Articles on State Responsibility posits that Part II (which deals with "Content of the International Responsibility of a State") "is without prejudice to any right, arising from the international responsibility of a State, which may accrue *directly to any person or entity other than a State.*"[156] Furthermore, the commentary on Article 33 states that:

> When an obligation of reparation exists towards a State, reparation does not necessarily accrue to that State's benefit. For instance, a State's responsibility for the breach of an obligation under a treaty concerning the protection of human rights may exist towards all the other parties to the treaty, but the individuals concerned should be regarded as the ultimate beneficiaries and in that sense as the holders of the relevant rights.[157]

The International Committee of the Red Cross (ICRC) in reviewing the state of customary law regarding reparation in international humanitarian law also commented upon a trend towards enabling victims to seek reparations directly from the state. The ICRC Commentary on Customary International Humanitarian Law concerning Rule 150 (Reparations) cites various examples of individuals seeking reparations directly from states, including: (i) reparation provided on the basis of inter-state and other agreements; (ii) reparation provided on the basis of a unilateral state act; (iii) reparation sought in national courts.[158]

A few domestic courts have had to decide cases where individual victims sought reparation from a foreign state, outside the realm of international human rights law, for violations of international humanitarian law. There have been instances – in Greece[159] and Italy[160] – where individuals were successful in seeking reparations against a state (for crimes against humanity and violations of international humanitarian law). However, there is also jurisprudence which limits the ability of individuals to claim reparation directly from a state.[161]

---

[156] Emphasis added.

[157] International Law Commission, Commentary on Article 33 of the Draft Articles on State Responsibility.

[158] ICRC, Customary IHL, available at www.icrc.org/customary-ihl/eng/docs/v1_rul_rule150#r efFn_2_28, accessed in April 2016.

[159] *Prefecture Voiotia* v. *Federal Republic of Germany*, Hellenic Supreme Court, 4 May 2000, Case No. 11/2000. Note, however, that the decision was not enforced due to a lack of authorization by the Minister of Justice of Greece. See also, at the European Court of Human Rights concerning a similar factual background, ECtHR, *Kalougeropoulou and Others* v. *Greece and Germany*, Admissibility, 12 December 2002, Application No. 59021/00.

[160] *Ferrini* v. *Federal Republic of Germany*, Corte di Cassazione (Sezioni Unite), 11 March 2004, 87 *Rivista di diritto internazionale* 539.

[161] See e.g., *Bridge of Varvarin case*, Landgericht (LG) Bonn, 1 O 361/02, NJW 2004, 525, HuV-I 2/2004, 111–113, confirmed by *Oberlandesgericht* (OLG) Köln, 7 U 8/04.

Punishment and Reparation

Recently, this question was put to the International Court of Justice in the Case Concerning Jurisdictional Immunities of the State (*Germany* v. *Italy*; Greece intervening).[162] The case was concerned with the decisions of Greek and Italian courts mentioned above, which awarded reparation to individual victims against a state (Germany) for violations that occurred during the Second World War. The question of whether or not individuals have a right to reparations (enforceable against a state) under international humanitarian law was debated during the proceedings.[163] Nevertheless, based on its decision that Germany enjoyed immunity under international law, the court did not deem it necessary to dwell upon this question in the judgment.[164] Therefore, it follows that the question of state immunity places a restriction on an individual victim's ability to obtain reparations from the responsible state.

Be that as it may, it is important to keep in mind that international law in this field is tirelessly developing. On the question of reparation to victims of violations of international humanitarian law, it has been stated that

> [t]here is increasing acceptance that individuals do have a right to reparation for violations of international law of which they are victims. This is particularly well established with regard to human rights law. Not only do many of the specialized human rights tribunals have the right to award "just satisfaction" or "fair compensation", but a number of human rights treaties also expressly require States to establish a remedy for violations before national courts. ... The courts of various States have considered claims by individual victims of violations of international humanitarian law on a number of occasions and the results of such cases have been far from uniform.[165]

---

[162] Judgment of 3 February 2012 ("ICJ State Immunity Judgment").

[163] See e.g., ibid., Counter-memorial of Italy, 22 December 2009, chapter V, Section II; Reply of Germany, 5 October 2010, chapter 4, sections 37–41.

[164] See para. 108 of the ICJ State Immunity Judgment. This judgment has prompted many scholarly commentaries. Recent scholarship concerning this judgment includes: Benedetto Conforti, "The Judgment of the International Court of Justice on the Immunity of Foreign States: A Missed Opportunity," *Italian Yearbook of International Law* 21 (2011), pp. 133–142; Riccardo Pavoni, "An American Anomaly? On the ICJ's Selective Reading of United States Practice in Jurisdictional Immunities of the State," *Italian Yearbook of International Law* 21 (2011), pp. 143–159; Carlos Espósito, "Jus Cogens and Jurisdictional Immunities of States at the International Court of Justice: A Conflict Does Exist," *Italian Yearbook of International Law* 21 (2011), pp. 161–174; Mirko Sossai, "Are Italian Courts Directly Bound to Give Effect to the Jurisdictional Immunities Judgment?" *Italian Yearbook of International Law* 21 (2011), pp. 175–189.

[165] Emanuela-Chiara Gillard, "Reparation for Violations of International Humanitarian Law," *International Review of the Red Cross* 85 (2003), pp. 536–537. See also, Rudolf Dolzer, "The Settlement of War-Related Claims: Does International Law Recognize a Victim's Private Right of Action? Lessons After 1945," *Berkeley Journal of International Law* 20 (2002), p. 296.

50 *Reparative Justice for International Crimes*

In a similar vein, former President of the International Criminal Tribunal for the former Yugoslavia (ICTY), Judge Jorda, also stressed this development of international law for the benefit of individuals in saying that

> the universal recognition and acceptance of the right to an effective remedy cannot but have a bearing on the interpretation of the international provisions on State responsibility for war crimes and other international crimes. These provisions may now be construed to the effect that the obligations they enshrine are assumed by States not only towards other contracting States but also vis-à-vis the victims, i.e. the individuals who suffered from those crimes. In other words, there has now emerged in international law a right of victims of serious human rights abuses (in particular, war crimes, crimes against humanity and genocide) to reparation (including compensation) for damage resulting from those abuses.[166]

History demonstrates, however, that reparation involving states has been generally settled by other means than an individual action against a responsible state: as, for example, through claims processes and lump-sum agreements between states, especially relating to the Second World War, but also more recently.[167] Furthermore, claims commissions and arbitral tribunals have been set up to deal with reparation claims.[168] Without purporting to be exhaustive, some examples of such institutions established to settle claims of redress arising out of international armed conflicts, include, in recent years, the Eritrea-Ethiopia Claims Commission,[169] the Housing and Property Claims Commission (concerning the 1998–1999 conflict in Kosovo),[170] and the Commission for Real Property Claims of Displaced Persons and Refugees in Bosnia and Herzegovina.[171]

Thus, it can be said that under certain circumstances, states as well as individuals may be the beneficiaries of reparations claimed directly from a state.

---

[166] *Report of the International Commission of Inquiry on Darfur to the United Nations Secretary-General*, para. 597, citing a letter dated 12 October 2000 of Judge C. Jorda (the then President of the International Criminal Tribunal for the former Yugoslavia) to the United Nations Secretary General.

[167] See generally, Pierre d'Argent, *Les Réparations de Guerre en Droit International Public*, LGDJ, 2002; Jean-Marie Henckaerts and Louise Doswald-Beck, *Customary International Humanitarian Law: Volume 1: Rules*, Cambridge University Press, 2005, pp. 539 et seq.

[168] See generally, Howard Holtzmann and Edda Kristjánsdóttir, *International Mass Claims Processes: Legal and Practical Perspectives*, Oxford University Press, 2007.

[169] Agreement between the Government of the Federal Democratic Republic of Ethiopia and the Government of the State of Eritrea, 12 December 2000, 40 ILM 260 (2001). It does not grant individuals standing to submit claims.

[170] UNMIK Regulation No. 1999/23, 15 November 1999, UNMIK/REG/1999/23.

[171] Article 1, Annex 7, General Framework Agreement for Peace in Bosnia and Herzegovina, 35 ILM 75 (1996), "Dayton Agreement."

It stems from the foregoing, however, that in many instances individual victims are left without reparation outside the international human rights system. This is because, *inter alia*, of the absence of arrangements for reparations or because the reparation received does not reach the individual victims. The analysis above demonstrates that it is not ideology that is driving the development of reparation for violations of international law but rather the remnants of the historical conception of international law as inter-state relationships.

2

Reparative Justice at International and Hybrid Criminal Tribunals

International prosecutions pertaining to international crimes are not a contemporary phenomenon. Since the end of the Second World War, international prosecutions were held in Nuremberg[1] and Tokyo.[2] The suffering of victims during the war was often referred to as a justification for the creation of the tribunals and prosecution of those responsible before international fora.[3] The American Chief Prosecutor Robert Jackson stated that a finding of guilt against the defendants meant that "justice may be done to these individuals as to their countless victims,"[4] and justice was delivered through the trial and punishment of Nazi and Japanese perpetrators.[5]

Victim reparations for crimes they suffered during the Second World War were not a primary concern of the justice system which developed following the war. At its inception, international criminal justice had no space for a civil dimension that included reparations for victims. However, the building blocks of international criminal law which developed through these historical trials following the war can be credited with conceiving "justice for victims" through a criminal dimension. The trial of individual perpetrators provided victims with a symbolic sense of justice.

[1] Created by the Agreement for the Prosecution and Punishment of the Major War Criminals of the European Axis, and Charter of the International Military Tribunal, London, 8 August 1945 (London Charter).
[2] Created by the Charter for the International Military Tribunal for the Far East, Tokyo, 19 January 1946 (Tokyo Charter).
[3] Luke Moffett, *Justice for Victims before the International Criminal Court*, Routledge, 2014, p. 60.
[4] IMT Transcripts Vol. XIX, p. 434, cited in ibid.
[5] Sam Garkawe, "The Role and Rights of Victims at the Nuremberg International Military Tribunal," in *The Nuremberg Trials: International Criminal Law Since 1945*, eds. Herbert R. Reginbogin, Christoph Safferling, and Walter R. Hippel, Kluwer, 2006, pp. 86–94, p. 86, cited in Luke Moffett, *Justice for Victims before the International Criminal Court*, Routledge, 2014, p. 61.

International and Hybrid Criminal Tribunals

The focus on the prosecution of the perpetrators of international criminal acts has been reflected in the jurisprudence of the ad hoc international criminal tribunals. Other international and hybrid criminal tribunals have followed this model: they have delivered justice to victims through the trial of individual perpetrators, thus limiting international justice to a criminal dimension.

However, recent developments in international criminal law not only mean that victims have begun to play a more active role in the proceedings,[6] they have also created the possibility that a legal duty may be imposed on individual perpetrators leading to the award of reparations.

This chapter dwells upon the operationalization of the reparative dimension of international criminal justice at the international level, with a focus on the historical evolution of reparations by international criminal courts and tribunals prior to the ICC, and the reparative justice model devised by the Extraordinary Chambers in the Courts of Cambodia (ECCC). The goal of this chapter is to retrace the diverse models existing in international criminal tribunals concerning reparations, starting with a model that excludes reparations from criminal proceedings, to one that has a role for victims and encompasses reparative dimensions of justice. This chapter thus analyses in-depth the reparation regime developed at the ECCC, including the role of *parties civiles*, and the rich developing case law of the court regarding reparations. It endeavors to provide a contribution by comparing and contrasting different models and questioning the challenges of including limited reparations (that is, moral and collective) within a criminal process relating to crimes that occurred decades ago. It also analyses the *partie civile* system under which the ECCC operates.

---

[6] Concerning victim participation in criminal proceedings, see e.g., Serge Vasiliev, "Victim Participation Revisited: What the ICC is Learning About Itself," in *The Law and Practice of the International Criminal Court*, ed. Carsten Stahn, Oxford University Press, 2015; Charles P. Trumbull, "The Victims of Victim Participation in International Criminal Proceedings," *Michigan Journal of International Law* 29 (2007), p. 777; Gerard J. Mekjian and Mathew C. Varughese, "Hearing the Victim's Voice: Analysis of Victims' Advocate Participation in the Trial Proceeding of the International Criminal Court," *Pace International Law Review* 17 (2005), pp. 1–413; Brianne N. McGonigle, "Bridging the Divides in International Criminal Proceedings: An Examination into the Victim Participation Endeavor of the International Criminal Court," *Florida Journal of International Law* 21 (2009), p. 93; Christine Chung, "Victim's Participation at the International Criminal Court: Are Concessions of the Court Clouding Promise?" *Northwestern Journal of International Human Rights* 6 (2007), p. 459.

2.1 HISTORICAL ACCOUNT: REPARATIONS AND THE NUREMBERG AND TOKYO TRIALS

The Nuremberg and Tokyo trials did not envisage the possibility of reparations for the victims of international crimes committed during the Second World War.[7] Since the victims of Nazi crimes were not able to claim redress against the perpetrators during the international criminal proceedings, reparation was developed through other means, mainly through lump-sum agreements.[8]

The precedents of the Nuremberg and Tokyo trials and reparations following the Second World War regarded redress in relation to those crimes as mainly based upon state responsibility.[9] These trials did not set up a regime based upon individual responsibility at the international criminal level for reparations related to crimes committed during the Second World War. Thus, under this regime, to obtain reparation, state responsibility was a prerequisite. In such a scenario, unless a state is directly involved, redress is not an option.[10]

The objective of international criminal justice at its inception was to hold *individuals* criminally accountable for the crimes they committed, thus departing from a system based purely on state responsibility given the notion

[7] Concerning the legacy of the Nuremberg and Tokyo trials, see e.g., Yael Danieli, "Reappraising the Nuremberg Trials and Their Legacy: The Role of Victims in International Law," *Cardozo Law Review* 27 (2005), p. 1633; Christian Pross, *Paying for the Past: The Struggle over Reparations for Surviving Victims of the Nazi Terror*, Johns Hopkins University Press, 1998; Benjamin B. Ferencz, "International Criminal Courts: The Legacy of Nuremberg," *Pace International Law Review* 10 (1998), p. 203; Won Soon Park, "Japanese Reparations Policies and the 'Comfort Women' Question," *positions* 5 (1997), pp. 107–136.

[8] See Ariel Colonomos and Andrea Armstrong, "German Reparations to the Jews after World War II: A Turning Point in the History of Reparations," in *The Handbook of Reparations*, ed. Pablo de Greiff, Oxford University Press, 2006, pp. 390–419. See also, John Authers, "Making Good Again: German Compensation for Forced and Slave Laborers," in *The Handbook of Reparations*, ed. Pablo de Greiff, Oxford University Press, 2006, pp. 420–450.

[9] Ibid.

[10] For example, the attempt in Rome to include state responsibility for reparation for victims, see report on the Establishment of an International Criminal Court, Draft Statute and Draft Final Act, U.N. Doc. A/Conf.183/2/Add.1, 1998, article 73:

> b) The Court may also [make an order] [recommend] that an appropriate form of reparations to, or in respect of victims, including restitution, compensation and rehabilitation, be made by a state: [if the convicted person is unable to do so himself/herself; [and if the convicted person was, in committing the offence, acting on behalf of that state in an official capacity, and within the course and scope of his/her authority]; c) [in any case other than those referred in subparagraph b), the Court may also recommend that states grant an appropriate form of reparations to, or in respect of, victims, including restitution, compensation and rehabilitation]

cited by Thordis Ingadottir, "The Trust Fund of the ICC," in International Crimes, Peace, and Human Rights: The Role of the International Criminal Court, ed. Dinah Shelton, Transnational Publishers, 2000, p. 159.

that "crimes are committed by men, not by abstract entities."[11] However, there remained a visible reliance upon states to provide redress for the crimes at the international level.[12]

This gap between the criminal and reparative dimensions of international justice is slowly closing with new courts increasingly recognizing victims' right to reparation under international law. This new milestone in international law – where individuals are not only held criminally liable for their international crimes, but also face liability for reparations – brings about many new challenges and questions, which are examined in this chapter.

2.2 THE AD HOC TRIBUNALS FOR THE FORMER YUGOSLAVIA AND RWANDA

Sadly, the years since the Second World War and the Nuremberg and Tokyo trials have witnessed many wars, conflicts, and the mass victimization of civilians.[13] Similar to the Nuremberg and Tokyo trials, the statutes of the ad hoc tribunals of former Yugoslavia and Rwanda did not provide for a self-standing right of victims within international criminal proceedings to claim reparations from convicted persons.[14] They addressed victim redress for crimes under their jurisdiction in a limited way, through the restitution of unlawfully

---

[11] "Judgment of the Tribunal," *American Journal of International Law* 41 (1947), p. 172.

[12] Concerning the Relationship Between Individual and state responsibility: Beatrice I. Bonafè, *The Relationship Between State and Individual Responsibility for International Crimes*, Brill, 2009; Pierre-Marie Dupuy, "International Criminal Responsibility of the Individual and International Responsibility of the State," in *International Criminal Court: A Commentary*, ed. Antonio Cassese, et al., Oxford University Press, 2002; André Nollkaemper, "Concurrence Between Individual Responsibility and State Responsibility in International Law," *International and Comparative Law Quarterly* 52 (2003), p. 615–640.

[13] See M. Cherif Bassiouni, "Assessing Conflict Outcomes: Accountability and Impunity," in *The Pursuit of International Criminal Justice: A World Study on Conflicts, Victimization, and Post-Conflict Justice*, ed. M. Cherif Bassiouni, Intersentia, 2010, p. 6:

> [...] it is estimated that 92 to 101 million persons have been killed between 1945 and 2008. That does not include those who have died as a consequence of these conflicts, which a World Health Organization projection puts at twice the estimated number of persons killed during these conflicts. [...] The 313 conflicts studied in this project reveal that they involve systematic human rights violations, including genocide, crimes against humanity, torture, slavery and slave-related practices, disappearances, rape and population displacement.

[14] See Carla Ferstman and Mariana Goetz, "Reparations Before the International Criminal Court: The Early Jurisprudence on Victim Participation and its Impact on Future Reparations Proceedings," in *Reparations for Victims of Genocide, War Crimes and Crimes Against Humanity: Systems in Place and Systems in the Making*, eds. Carla Ferstman et al., Nijhoff, 2009, p. 315.

56   *Reparative Justice for International Crimes*

taken property. The ICTY's and ICTR's provisions on restitution, respectively, sections 23(3) and 24(3) which concern penalties, are very similar and read as follows: "In addition to imprisonment, the Trial Chambers may order the return of any property and proceeds acquired by criminal conduct, including by means of duress, to their rightful owners."[15] However, there are conditions that must be fulfilled before the restitution of property could be ordered. The property must have been associated with a crime pursuant to the statute and was required to be the object of a specific finding in the judgment.[16] Once these conditions were met, the Trial Chamber, at the request of the Prosecutor, or, acting *proprio motu*, was authorized to hold a special hearing for the determination of an appropriate restitution.[17]

Importantly, Rule 106 ("Compensation for Victims") of the Rules of Procedure and Evidence of the ICTY provides that:

(A) The Registrar shall transmit to the competent authorities of the States concerned the judgement finding the accused guilty of a crime which has caused injury to a victim.

(B) Pursuant to the relevant national legislation, a victim or persons claiming through the victim may bring an action in a national court or other competent body to obtain compensation.

(C) For the purposes of a claim made under Sub-rule (B) the judgement of the Tribunal shall be final and binding as to the criminal responsibility of the convicted person for such injury.[18]

It is clear from this provision that reparations for victims are not part of the Tribunal's role, nor is it one of its goals. In this regard, it is worth recalling that the United Nations Security Council, in resolution 827 of 25 May 1993, which established the ICTY, stated that: "The work of the International Tribunal

---

[15] Restitution of unlawfully taken property has been further developed in the Rules of Procedure and Evidence of the Tribunals: see Rule 98 *ter* (B), of the ICTY Rules of Evidence, adopted on 10 July 1998: "If the Trial Chamber finds the accused guilty of a crime and concludes from the evidence that unlawful taking of property by the accused was associated with it, it shall make a specific finding to that effect in its judgement. The Trial Chamber may order restitution as provided in Rule 105." Rule 88 (B) of the ICTR makes a provision to the same extent.

[16] See Susanne Malmström, "Restitution of Property and Compensation to Victims," in *Essays on ICTY Procedure and Evidence in Honour of Gabrielle Kirk McDonald*, eds. Richard May, et al., Kluwer Law International, 2001, p. 375, cited in Ilaria Bottigliero, *Redress for Victims of Crimes Under International Law*, Nijhoff, 2004, p. 198.

[17] See Rule 105 of the ICTY and the ICTR Rules of Procedure and Evidence, amended on 30 November 1999, IT/32/Rev.

[18] See Rules 106 (B) of the ICTR Rules of Procedure and Evidence, with a very minor difference in wording: "Pursuant to the relevant national legislation, a victim or persons claiming through *him* may bring an action in a national court or other competent body to obtain compensation" (emphasis added).

shall be carried out without prejudice to the right of the victims to seek, through appropriate means, compensation for damages incurred as a result of violations of international humanitarian law."[19] This resolution, on a textual reading, did not seem to exclude the possibility that victims could seek reparations through the tribunals. However, Rule 106 made it clear that although victims were not completely denied their right to receive reparations, these could not be claimed through the tribunal.

In the drafting process, the Rules Committee of the ICTY made it clear that the exclusion of victims' right to reparations from the scope of the tribunal's activities was not an oversight. It seems that the tribunal made a clear decision to avoid playing any role in relation to reparations for victims of the crimes which fall under its jurisdiction. The tribunal's focus on a sole purpose to prosecute persons who allegedly committed crimes under their jurisdiction was a deliberate decision.

In this respect, it is worth referring to a report prepared by the Rules Committee in November 2000 which dwells upon the question of reparations for victims. The report

> states that it is the view of the judges of the International Tribunal for the Former Yugoslavia that the victims of the crimes over which the International Tribunal has jurisdiction have a right in law to compensation for the injuries that they have suffered.
>
> [...] the judges have considered the possibility that the Security Council might be requested to amend the Statute of the International Tribunal in order to confer upon it the power to order the payment of compensation to the victims of the crimes that were committed by the persons whom it may convict.
>
> [...] the judges have, however, come to the conclusion that it is neither advisable nor appropriate that the Tribunal be possessed of such a power, in particular, for the reason that it would result in a significant increase in the workload of the Chambers and would further increase the length and complexity of trials. The judges doubt, moreover, whether it would be possible for the Tribunal to secure adequate resources to fund such awards as it might make. Furthermore, they consider that it would be inequitable that the victims of crimes which were committed by persons who are not prosecuted and convicted by the Tribunal would not benefit from any orders of compensation that the Tribunal might make.[20]

---

[19] See Ilaria Bottigliero, *Redress for Victims of Crimes Under International Law*, Nijhoff, 2004, p. 201.

[20] "Victims' Compensation and Participation," Appendix to a letter dated 12 October 2000 from the President of the ICTY addressed to the Secretary-General, ANNEX to UN Doc. S/2000/1063 of 3 November 2000, p. 1. The report further argued that the Security Council excluded

The foregoing does not however suggest that the tribunal deemed that reparations had no role to play in the aftermath of the mass atrocities that happened in the region. There is no question that victims of the crimes under the jurisdiction of the tribunals deserve compensation: this much does not seem to be denied. It was noted that, in order to bring about reconciliation in the former Yugoslavia and to ensure the restoration of peace, it was necessary that the victims of crimes within the jurisdiction of the tribunal receive compensation for their injuries.[21] The question is whether the way in which the tribunals dealt with the issue of reparation – that is, directing it to the appreciation of domestic courts – was satisfactory and attainable.

The interesting aspect of the 2000 report is its reference to the challenges of including a reparative dimension within international criminal trials. The challenges identified in the report provide some justification for not including victims' reparations within the mandate of the tribunal. They remain central to critiques of the ICC reparation system (which are discussed in Chapter 3). The challenges identified in the report also continue to reflect the challenges the ICC will face in the implementation of this mandate. It also fleshed out important considerations for the realization of reparations for victims.

In a nutshell, it seems that practical considerations played an important role in the decision not to have the tribunal deal with claims for reparations. The following were some of the reasons provided: the impact of reparation claims on the tribunal's daily work; the possibility of causing delays in the accused's trial; and the costs related to implementing reparation awards, among others.[22]

While these seem to be reasonable concerns, the possibility that leaving reparation matters to domestic jurisdictions may wind up providing little or no reparation at all for victims seems to have been overlooked. As it has already been pointed out, given the nature of the crimes and the system of prosecution thereof (in an international tribunal set up in The Hague), it may be very

---

the possibility of the tribunal hearing victims' claims for compensation: "Victims' Compensation and Participation," Appendix to a letter dated 12 October 2000 from the President of the ICTY addressed to the Secretary-General, ANNEX to UN Doc. S/2000/1063 of 3 November 2000, p. x. See also, in this regard, Virginia Morris and Michael P. Scharf, *An Insider's Guide to the International Criminal Tribunals for the Former Yugoslavia*, Transnational Publishers, 1995, pp. 167, 286–287, cited in UN Doc. S/2000/1063, para. 24, in support of the idea that the Security Council was aware of the issue of reparation for victims but decided not to address it.

[21] "Victims' Compensation and Participation," Appendix to a letter dated 12 October 2000 from the President of the ICTY addressed to the Secretary-General, ANNEX to UN Doc. S/2000/1063 of 3 November 2000, p. 2.

[22] "Victims' Compensation and Participation," Appendix to a letter dated 12 October 2000 from the President of the ICTY addressed to the Secretary-General, ANNEX to UN Doc. S/2000/1063 of 3 November 2000.

difficult for victims to access domestic courts in order to claim reparations. If they are able to do so, they may encounter many practical difficulties substantiating their claim.[23] Furthermore, one of the reasons in favor of creating an international tribunal with the jurisdiction to address the crimes committed in the Former Yugoslavia (and the same is true for Rwanda) was because it was not possible to prosecute the alleged perpetrators in the state of the *locus delictum*. Similar difficulties seen in criminal prosecutions may arise in relation to claims for reparations.[24]

As a matter of legal principle, it does not seem entirely equitable that victims, who have had their property taken, are eligible to receive restitution through the procedure set up by the tribunal, whereas victims of heinous crimes such as torture, rape, and sexual slavery cannot claim other forms of reparation through the tribunals. This appears to create an undue hierarchy of victimization, where some victims have rights to restitution within the proceedings but other categories of victims struggle to secure redress outside the auspices of the tribunals.

This hierarchy raises a broader concern about whether the institution has adopted a fragmented approach to justice in the aftermath of mass victimization. As the former Prosecutor of the ICTY, Ms. Carla del Ponte, stated: "A system of criminal law that does not take into account the victims of crimes is fundamentally lacking."[25] As stated above, the report concludes that "the victims of the crimes over which the Tribunal has jurisdiction are entitled to benefit from a right to compensation."[26] Nevertheless, implementing a system able to provide reparations to victims "would counter all efforts of the last few years to minimize the length of preventive detention, which is a fundamental right of the accused, by shortening the trials."[27] Importantly, the report further explained that:

> There is a clear trend in international law to recognize a right of compensation in the victim to recover from the individual who caused his or her injury. . . . There does appear to be a right to compensation for victims under international

---

[23] See Ilaria Bottigliero, *Redress for Victims of Crimes Under International Law*, Nijhoff, 2004, p. 202.

[24] Ibid.

[25] Carla del Ponte, "Compensating Victims with Guilty Money," interview with Carla del Ponte, Chief Prosecutor of the ad hoc International Criminal Tribunals for the Former Yugoslavia and Rwanda, in *Judicial Diplomacy: Chronicles and Reports on International Criminal Justice*, The Hague, 9 June 2000.

[26] "Victims' Compensation and Participation," Appendix to a letter dated 12 October 2000 from the President of the ICTY addressed to the Secretary-General, ANNEX to UN Doc. S/2000/ 1063 of 3 November 2000.

[27] Ibid., para. 32.

law. Although there is an emerging right of compensation, the law is much less developed on the mechanism by which that right can be exercised.[28]

The solution to what seems to be incongruous statements of law and principle – that is, on the one hand, a victim's right to reparation under international law, and on the other, the tribunal's lack of responsibility to implement this right – was the suggestion that "a far better approach would be for an international claims commission to be established." This solution was to be considered by the appropriate organs of the United Nations.[29] Nevertheless, such mechanism has not yet been instituted, and it is uncertain whether it will ever be.

The same result came about in the ICTR.[30] The former president of the tribunal, Judge Navanethem Pillay, on the issue of compensation, stated that:

> The Judges wholeheartedly empathize with the principle of compensation for victims, but . . . believe that the responsibility for processing and assessing claims for such compensation should not rest with the Tribunal. . . . if the Tribunals adds to its responsibilities a whole new area of law relating to compensation, then the Tribunal will not only have to develop a new jurisprudence; it will also have to expand its staffing considerably and establish new rules and procedures for assessing claims.[31]

As to the reasoning behind the rejection of implementing provisions on reparation for victims in the statutes and the work of the tribunals, the ICTR was driven by similar concerns. In the words of the then president of the tribunal:

> Research on compensation schemes presently in operation suggests that very few of the eligible victims receive the compensation to which they are entitled. Often, only victims represented by counsel achieve a satisfactory level of compensation. There are substantial overhead costs in collecting and processing documentation and the administration costs are usually very high. Victim satisfaction with compensation programmes appears to be quite low. Victims usually express considerable frustration with the complexity of compensation documentation procedures. . . . It seems likely that if the Tribunal embarks on the processing of claims for compensation, then, in addition to

---

[28] Ibid.

[29] Ibid. See also, Ilaria Bottigliero, *Redress for Victims of Crimes Under International Law*, Nijhoff, 2004, pp. 206–207.

[30] Cf. Letter of the President of the ICTR to the United Nations Secretary-General, annex to a letter of 14 December 2000 by the United Nations Secretary-General, Kofi Annan, to the United Nations Security Council, UN Doc. S/2000/1198 of 15 December 2000.

[31] Ibid.

International and Hybrid Criminal Tribunals 61

any dissatisfaction with its present progress, it can expect to add to this the frustration and disappointment of those attempting to establish claims.[32]

The judges at the ICTR, while putting forward the view that victims are entitled to compensation for international crimes, offered some suggestions about how victims of the crimes committed in Rwanda could receive reparation:

(a) A specialized agency set up by the United Nations to administer a compensation scheme or trust fund that can be based upon individual application, or community need or some group-based qualification;
(b) A scheme administered by some other agency or governmental entity on similar lines to (a);
(c) An arrangement which could operate in tandem with options (a) and (b) and which would allow the Tribunal to exercise a limited power to order payments from a trust fund for victims actually appearing before it as witnesses in a case. It is noteworthy that such a power exists in the criminal courts of the United Kingdom of Great Britain and Northern Ireland, but is especially limited to compensation issues where the issue is factually clear and where there is no dispute as to quantum before the court. In that jurisdiction, extensive inquiry into compensation issues by criminal courts is expressly abjured.[33]

While these proposals point to some possible ways of redress for victims, they are only the tip of the iceberg. For such proposals to have any effect for victims, more thought would have to go into whether they are actually feasible and desirable in practice.[34]

---

[32] Ibid., paras. 13–14. The latter refers in this regard to the work of Robert Elias, *The Politics of Victimization: Victims, Victimology and Human Rights*, Oxford University Press, 1986, especially pp. 162, 212, and 238.

[33] Ibid., para. 15.

[34] See e.g., Virginia Morris and Michael P. Scharf, *An Insider's Guide to the International Criminal Tribunal for the Former Yugoslavia*,Transnational Publishers, 1995, pp. 167, 286–287, concerning the possibility of establishing a claims commission for the victims. Concerning failed attempts by former prosecutor Carla del Ponte to amend the statute so as to compensate victims, see Anne Marie de Brouwer, *Supranational Criminal Prosecution of Sexual Violence: The ICC and the Practice of the ICTY and the ICTR*, 2005, at 406–409, cited in Anne-Marie De Brouwer, "Reparation to Victims of Sexual Violence: Possibilities at the International Criminal Court and at the Trust Fund for Victims and Their Families," *Leiden Journal of International Law* 20 (2007), p. 215. For an account that it was not the tribunals' role to provide compensation for victims, see Ralph Zacklin, "The Failings of Ad Hoc International Tribunals," *Journal of International Criminal Justice* 2 (2004), p. 544. See on the feasibility of transcending the distinction between punishment and court-ordered restitution, Marc Groenhuijsen, "Victims' Rights and Restorative Justice: Piecemeal Reform of the Criminal Justice System or a Change of Paradigm?" in *Crime, Victims and Justice: Essays on Principles and Practice*, eds. Hendrik Kaptein and Marijke Malsch, Ashgate Publishing, 2004, p. 73. In this respect, according to Van Boven, compensation during criminal proceedings can be regarded as follows: "First, it makes the criminal offender

62   *Reparative Justice for International Crimes*

To conclude, the ad hoc criminal tribunals have been successful from the perspective of retribution, trial, and punishment of the offenders; they have left a true legacy for international criminal justice.[35] However, part of this legacy is the exclusion of victim reparation[36] by focusing their efforts on the prosecution and punishment of offenders. Their legacy will always include the fact that many victims of the crimes in the former Yugoslavia and Rwanda have been, for the most part, left without redress.[37]

2.3 OTHER INTERNATIONAL OR HYBRID CRIMINAL TRIBUNALS

The chapter proceeds to overview selected ad hoc international/hybrid tribunals to draw a picture of their approach to redress for victims and focuses on

---

more aware that not only was a wrong committed against public order and public welfare but, in addition, an injury was inflicted on one or more human beings. Second, it establishes a link between punitive measures and measures of reparation. Third, it tends to facilitate and expedite the process of obtaining civil damages"; Theo van Boven, "The Perspective of the Victim," in *The Universal Declaration of Human Rights: Fifty Years and Beyond*, eds. Yael Danieli, et al., Baywood Publishing Company, 1999, p. 21.

[35] Much has been written recently about the legacy of the ICTY, from many different perspectives. See e.g., Máximo Langer and Joseph Doherty, "Managerial Judging Goes International, But Its Promise Remains Unfulfilled: An Empirical Assessment of the ICTY Reforms," *Yale Journal of International Law* 36 (2011), pp. 241–305; Giovanna M. Frisso, "The Winding Down of the ICTY: The Impact of the Completion Strategy and the Residual Mechanism on Victims," *Goettingen Journal of International Law* 3(2011), pp. 1092–1121; Michael G. Karnavas, "The ICTY Legacy: A Defense Counsel's Perspective," *Goettingen Journal of International Law* 3 (2011), pp. 1052–1092; Frédéric Mégret, "The Legacy of the ICTY as Seen Through Some of Its Actors and Observers," *Goettingen Journal of International Law* 3 (2011) pp. 1011–1052; Maria Swart, "Tadic Revisited : Some Critical Comments on the Legacy and the Legitimacy of the ICTY," *Goettingen Journal of International Law* 3 (2011), pp. 985–1009; Donald Riznik, "Completing the ICTY-Project Without Sacrificing Its Main Goals: Security Council Resolution 1966: A Good Decision," *Goettingen Journal of International Law* 3 (2011), pp. 907–922; Richard Steinberg, *Assessing the Legacy of the ICTY*, Nijhoff, 2011.

[36] See generally on retributive justice Mark A. Drumbl, "Sclerosis Retributive Justice and the Rwandan Genocide," *Punishment & Society* 2 (2000), pp. 287–307. See Irene Scharf, "Kosovo's War Victims: Civil Compensation or Criminal Justice for Identity Elimination," *Emory International Law Review* 14 (2000), p. 1423.

[37] See e.g., on the difficulties for victims to obtain compensation at the national level, Ilaria Bottigliero, *Redress for Victims of Crimes Under International Law*, Nijhoff, 2004, p. 211. See also, Jean Paul Mugiraneza, "Rwanda Genocide: Why Compensation Would Help the Healing," *Guardian*, 8 March 2014, available at http://theguardian.com/global-development-professionals-network/2014/mar/04/rwanda-genocide-victims-compensation (last accessed 11 May 2016), claiming that "the government has established a fund, Farg, to provide healthcare and tuition for survivors. But does this go far enough? Though Rwanda and the international community have valiantly pursued justice, financial compensation for genocide survivors has still not materialized."

International and Hybrid Criminal Tribunals

63

three examples which have existed for some time in order to briefly discuss their structures and experiences. These are: the Special Tribunal for Lebanon (STL), the Special Court for Sierra Leone (SCSL), and the Extraordinary Chambers in the Courts of Cambodia (ECCC).[38] Other existing international and hybrid mechanisms, which are either very unique or at early stages of functioning (e.g., the Kosovo Specialist Chambers & Specialist Prosecutor's Office) are outside the scope of this book.

2.3.1 *The Special Tribunal for Lebanon*

The STL was inaugurated in March 2009. The mandate of the STL is very specific: to bring to justice those responsible for the attack of 14 February 2005 which killed twenty-three people, including the former prime minister of Lebanon, Mr. Rafiq Hariri, and injured many others.[39]

Following the attacks that occurred in Lebanon in 2005, the Lebanese government requested that the United Nations create a tribunal of an "international character." In Resolution 1644, the United Nations Security Council acknowledged the letter of the prime minister of Lebanon in this respect.[40] In January 2007, the Lebanese government and the United Nations reached an agreement concerning the creation of the STL, which was established in 2007 by resolution 1757, adopted under chapter VII of the United Nations Charter.[41] In this resolution, the Security Council did not adopt the Statute of the Tribunal per se as it had done with the ICTY in 1993 and with the ICTR in 1994. Rather, it endowed the unratified agreement between the United Nations and Lebanon and the attached statute with legal force.[42]

---

[38] The Kosovo and East Timor mechanisms, as well as other hybrid tribunals are outside the scope of this book due to their unique structures.

[39] For an overview of the STL, and special issues facing the tribunal, see generally: Nidal Nabil Jurdi, "The Subject-Matter Jurisdiction of the Special Tribunal for Lebanon," *Journal of International Criminal Justice* 5 (2007), pp. 1125–1138; Marieke Wierda et al., "Early Reflections on Local Perceptions, Legitimacy and Legacy of the Special Tribunal for Lebanon," *Journal of International Criminal Justice* 5 (2007), pp. 1065–1081; Choucri Sader, "A Lebanese Perspective on the Special Tribunal for Lebanon Hopes and Disillusions," *Journal of International Criminal Justice* 5 (2007), pp. 1083–1089; Marko Milanović, "An Odd Couple: Domestic Crimes and International Responsibility in the Special Tribunal for Lebanon," *Journal of International Criminal Justice* 5 (2007), pp. 1139–1152.

[40] See "The Situation in the Middle East," Security Council Resolution 1644 (2005), 15 December 2005, S/RES/1644.

[41] See Security Council Resolution 1757 (2007), adopted by the Security Council at its 5685th meeting, on 30 May 2007.

[42] See Gianluca Serra, "Special Tribunal for Lebanon: A Commentary on its Major Legal Aspects," *International Criminal Justice Review* 18 (2008), pp. 344–355.

The STL thus differs from the ad hoc international criminal tribunals in that it has a connection with the national legal system of Lebanon, highlighting its hybrid nature.[43] In fact, the staff, including the judges, are a combination of internationally recruited and Lebanese nationals; the applicable law is also mixed.

This fact has in turn had an impact on provisions included for victims. Victims have a more active role during proceedings than in other ad hoc criminal tribunals. There is a special victim and witness unit. Victims also have the right to participate in proceedings[44] and can play a significant role on trial and appeal.[45] Article 17 of the STL statute states that:

> [w]here the personal interests of the victims are affected, the Special Tribunal shall permit their views and concerns to be presented and considered at stages of the proceedings determined to be appropriate by the Pre-Trial Judge or the Chamber and in a manner that is not prejudicial to or inconsistent with the rights of the accused and a fair and impartial trial.

While the STL is more progressive towards granting an active role for victims during proceedings, it stands closer in the spectrum to the ad hoc criminal tribunals in terms of providing reparations to victims. In fact, Article 25(3) of the statute, entitled "compensation to victims" states that: "Based on the decision of the Special Tribunal and pursuant to the relevant national legislation, a victim or persons claiming through the victim, whether or not such victim had been identified as such by the Tribunal under paragraph 1 of this article, may bring an action in a national court or other competent body to obtain compensation." Thus, the STL creates an interesting dichotomy in relation to victims' rights. Victims play an active role during proceedings, but have no right of redress within the auspices of the tribunal, and are directed to seek redress from national courts.

---

[43] See in general about hybrid tribunals, Kai Ambos and Mohamed Othmann, *New Approaches in International Criminal Justice: Kosovo, East Timor, Sierra Leone and Cambodia*, Max Planck Institute for International Law, 2003; Cesare P. R. Romano et al., *Internationalized Criminal Courts: Sierra Leone, East Timor, Kosovo, and Cambodia*, Oxford University Press, 2004; Taru Kuosmanen, *Bringing Justice Closer: Hybrid Courts in Post-Conflict Societies*, Erik Castrén Institute of International Law and Human Rights, 2007; Jan Erik Wetzel and Yvonne Mitri, "The Special Tribunal for Lebanon: A Court Off the Shelf for a Divided Country," *The Law and Practice of International Courts and Tribunals* 7 (2008), pp. 86–87.

[44] See arts. 17 and 25 of the STL Statute.

[45] See generally concerning victims' participation at the STL, Jérôme De Hemptinne, "Challenges Raised by Victims' Participation in the Proceedings of the Special Tribunal for Lebanon," *Journal of International Criminal Justice* 8 (2010), pp. 165–179. See also, Cécile Aptel, "Some Innovations in the Statute of the Special Tribunal for Lebanon," *Journal of International Criminal Justice* 5 (2007), pp. 1120–1121.

2.3.2 *The Special Court for Sierra Leone*

The SCSL is a product of the Civil War that devastated the country until the cessation of hostilities in 2002 following the signature of the peace agreement between the government of Sierra Leone and the Rebel United Front in 1999. The war left about 1.5 million internally displaced individuals and refugees while thousands of children were raped, killed, or conscribed as child soldiers.[46] The court was created by an agreement between the government of Sierra Leone and the United Nations in 2002.[47] In 2013 it completed its mandate and transitioned to a residual mechanism.

In many ways the SCSL has similar characteristics to the STL. It is a hybrid tribunal, with sitting judges from both Sierra Leone and the broader international community. The SCSL is supported by the government of Sierra Leone, by international human rights groups, the United Nations Security Council, the United States, and the European Union.[48] Furthermore, the SCSL was located in the country where the crimes took place.

Like the statute of the ad hoc international criminal tribunals, the statute of the SCSL does not recognize a victim's right to reparations for crimes committed under its jurisdiction. Be that as it may, pursuant to Article 19(3) the SCSL has the power to order the forfeiture of the property, proceeds, and assets of a convicted person to their rightful owner, if the property was acquired unlawfully or through criminal conduct.[49] This penalty can only be invoked after a conviction.

It must be noted, however, that the Lomé Peace Agreement foresaw reparations for victims. In this regard, one author explains that: "Under the Lomé Peace Agreement a reparations program was established to address the needs of victims of the war in Sierra Leone, with the National Commission for Social Action (NaCSA) designated in 2007 as the implementing agency. Despite some progress in community-based and capacity-building projects, the Commission has suffered from chronic under-funding."[50] In this context, on

---

[46] Celina Schocken, "The Special Court for Sierra Leone: Overview and Recommendations," *Berkeley Journal of International Law* 20 (2002), p. 436.

[47] See "Agreement Between the United Nations and the Government of Sierra Leone on the Establishment of a Special Court for Sierra Leone," available at https://treaties.un.org/Pages/showDetails.aspx?objid=0800000280086off.

[48] Celina Schocken, "The Special Court for Sierra Leone: Overview and Recommendations," *Berkeley Journal of International Law* 20 (2002), p. 436.

[49] See The Hague Justice Portal, "No Signs of Victim Compensation in Sierra Leone: Chief Prosecutor at the Special Court for Sierra Leone, Brenda Hollis Deplores the Lack of Assistance for Victims," 18 November 2010, available at http://www.rscsl.org/Clippings/2010/2010-11/pc2010-11-19.pdf.

[50] Ibid.

66 *Reparative Justice for International Crimes*

the basis of new developments at the SCSL, especially the conviction of Charles Taylor for crimes committed in Sierra Leone and the rejection of his appeal,[51] it is regretful that the statute did not contain any kind of provision concerning reparation for victims. The issue of the lack of funding, for one, could have been somewhat resolved if redress could be obtained from the convicted accused.

2.3.3 *Parting with the Trend: The Cambodian Extraordinary Chambers' (ECCC) Approach to Victims' Redress*

In May 2003, nearly three decades after the end of the 1975–1979 conflict,[52] the Cambodian government concluded an agreement with the United Nations providing for United Nations assistance with the "Extraordinary Chambers" in the domestic courts of Cambodia.[53]

The Extraordinary Chambers were created to prosecute those accused of serious violations of Cambodian Penal Law and of international humanitarian law during the Democratic Kampuchea period. This period is considered to be one of the most violent periods in modern history during which the Khmer Rouge is estimated to have killed between 1.5 and 1.7 million people.[54] The Expert Report for Cambodia pursuant to General Assembly Resolution 52/135 indicates that it was "marked by abuses of individual and group human rights on an immense and brutal

---

[51] See *Prosecutor v. Charles Ghankay Taylor*, Judgment, Special Court for Sierra Leone, 18 May 2012, SCSL, 03-01-T. See also, for the appeals judgment: *Prosecutor v. Charles Ghankay Taylor*, Appeals Judgment, Special Court for Sierra Leone, 26 September 2013, SCSL, 03-01-A.

[52] Concerning the background to the conflict that led to the creation of the ECCC, see e.g., David Chandler, *A History of Cambodia*, Westview Press, 4th ed., 2008, pp. 254–255; The Group of Experts for Cambodia, *Report of the Group of Experts for Cambodia Pursuant to General Assembly Resolution 52/135*, 1, U.N. Doc. S/1999/231, A/53/850 (16 March 1999). See also, Tessa V. Capeloto, "Reconciliation in the Wake of Tragedy: Cambodia's Extraordinary Chambers Undermines the Cambodian Constitution," *Pacific Rim Law & Policy Journal Association* 17 (2008), pp. 103–131; Padraic J. Glaspy, "Justice Delayed? Recent Developments at the Extraordinary Chambers in the Courts of Cambodia," *Harvard Human Rights Journal* 21 (2008), pp. 143–154.

[53] See Draft Agreement between the United Nations and the Royal Government of Cambodia Concerning the Prosecution under Cambodian Law of Crimes Committed During the Period of Democratic Kampuchea, 17 March 2003, approved by GA Res. 57/228B, 13 May 2003.

[54] The Group of Experts for Cambodia, *Report of the Group of Experts for Cambodia Pursuant to General Assembly Resolution 52/135*, 1, U.N. Doc. S/1999/231, A/53/850 (16 March 1999), para. 35. See also, Katheryn M. Klein, "Bringing the Khmer Rouge to Justice: The Challenges and Risks Facing the Joint Tribunal in Cambodia," *New Jersey International Human Rights* 4 (2006), pp. 549, 553–554, concerning the violations that occurred during this period.

scale."[55] Along with other initiatives, such as the Regulation 64 panels in Kosovo and Special Panels in East Timor,[56] the ECCC is an example of a hybrid criminal tribunal,[57] which involves both national and international efforts.

The court has caught the attention of many commentators, many critical of it.[58] The ECCC stands in the middle of the spectrum of examples of mechanisms providing reparation for international crimes within international criminal proceedings. It stands between the reparation system at the ICC – which is more encompassing in terms of the scope of reparations than the ECCC – and the systems embraced by other tribunals, which did not have provisions on reparation for victims.

According to their Internal Rules (as revised on 1 February 2008) – rules 10 and 11 – the chambers of the ECCC may make an award for reparations to civil parties for the moral damage they suffered. These reparations may take the following forms:

a) An order to publish the judgment in any appropriate news or other media at the convicted person's expense;
b) An order to fund any non-profit activity or service that is intended for the benefit of Victims; or
c) Other appropriate and comparable forms of reparation.

Furthermore, according to the ECCC, it is useful to note that:

[55] The Group of Experts for Cambodia, *Report of the Group of Experts for Cambodia Pursuant to General Assembly Resolution 52/135*, 1, U.N. Doc. S/1999/231, A/53/850 (16 March 1999), para. 18.

[56] These are not discussed in this book. See e.g., Suzanne Kartenstein, "Hybrid Tribunals: Searching for Justice in East Timor," *Harvard Human Rights Journal* 16 (2003), p. 245.

[57] See e.g., Laura A. Dickinson, "The Promise of Hybrid Courts," *American Journal of International Law* 97 (2003), p. 295; Suzannah Linton, "Cambodia, East Timor and Sierra Leone: Experiments in International Justice," *Criminal Law Forum* 12 (2001), p. 185.

[58] Sarah Williams, "The Cambodian Extraordinary Chambers: A Dangerous Precedent for International Justice," *International & Comparative Law Quarterly* 53 (2004), pp. 227–245; Sylvia De Bertodano, "Problems Arising from the Mixed Composition and Structure of the Cambodian Extraordinary Chambers" *Journal of International Criminal Justice* 4 (2006), pp. 285–293; Padraic J. Glaspy, "Justice Delayed? Recent Developments at the Extraordinary Chambers in the Courts of Cambodia," *Harvard Human Rights Journal* 21 (2008), p. 143; Tessa V. Capeloto, "Reconciliation in the Wake of Tragedy: Cambodia's Extraordinary Chambers Undermines the Cambodian Constitution," *Pacific Rim Law & Policy Journal* 17 (2008), p. 103; Phuong Pham, et al., "After the First Trial: A Population-Based Survey on Knowledge and Perceptions of Justice and the Extraordinary Chambers in the Courts of Cambodia," available at SSRN 1860963 (2011); Göran Sluiter, "Due Process and Criminal Procedure in the Cambodian Extraordinary Chambers," *Journal of International Criminal Justice* 4 (2006), p. 314–326; James P. Bair, "From the Numbers Who Died to Those Who Survived: Victim Participation in the Extraordinary Chambers in the Courts of Cambodia," *University of Hawaii Law Review* 31 (2008), p. 507.

Civil Parties can seek moral and collective reparation. Such reparation can only be awarded if an Accused is convicted.

Moral and collective reparations are measures that:

a) acknowledge the harm suffered by Civil Parties as a result of the commission of the crimes for which an Accused is convicted and
b) provide benefits to the Civil Parties which address this harm. These benefits shall not take the form of monetary payments to Civil Parties.

The cost of the reparations shall either be borne by the convicted person, or by external funding which has already been secured to implement a project designed by the legal representatives of the Civil Parties in cooperation with the Victims Support Section.[59]

In light of its unique nature, the reparations mandate of the ECCC has been the subject of scholarly debate.[60] It is clear from the framework of the ECCC, and the provision cited above, that only civil parties[61] are entitled to receive moral or symbolic reparation,[62] which shall be collective in form. Reparations are dependent on the conviction of the accused at the end of a criminal trial. The ECCC does not provide for the possibility of all types of reparation. When victims apply to become civil parties, the application form permits claimants to propose a type of moral or collective reparation that they wish the judges to make.

By recognizing some form of redress for victims within the proceedings before the court, the ECCC weaves a reparative dimension in the proceedings before the court. It is interesting to note that the ECCC does not recognize

---

[59] ECCC official website available at http://eccc.gov.kh/en.
[60] See e.g., Toni Holness and Jaya Ramji-Nogales, "Participation as Reparations: The ECCC and Healing in Cambodia," *Cambodia's Hidden Scars: Trauma Psychology In The Wake Of The Khmer Rouge, Documentation Center of Cambodia* (2012), pp. 2011–2029 Ruben Carranza, "Imagining the Possibilities for Reparations in Cambodia," *International Centre for Transitional Justice*, Briefing Paper (2005); Hae Duy Phan, "Reparations to Victims of Gross Human Rights Violations: The Case of Cambodia," *East Asia Law Review* 4 (2009), p. 277; Christoph Sperfeldt, "Collective Reparations at the Extraordinary Chambers in the Courts of Cambodia," *International Criminal Law Review* 12 (2012), pp. 457–490.
[61] On civil parties at the ECCC, and their rights of participation, see generally Alain Werner and Daniella Rudy, "Civil Party Representation at the ECCC: Sounding the Retreat in International Criminal Law," *Northwestern University Journal of International Human Rights* 8 (2009), p. 301; Johanna Herman, "Reaching for Justice: The Participation of Victims at the Extraordinary Chambers in the Courts of Cambodia," CHRC Policy Paper No. 5, (2010); Silke Studzinsky, "Participation Rights of Victims as Civil Parties and the Challenges of Their Implementation Before the Extraordinary Chambers in the Courts of Cambodia," in *Victims of International Crimes: An Interdisciplinary Discourse*, Thorsten Bona cker and Christoph Safferling, TMC Asser Press, 2013, pp. 175–188.
[62] See Hae Duy Phan, "Reparations to Victims of Gross Human Rights Violations: The Case of Cambodia," *East Asia Law Review* 4 (2009).

International and Hybrid Criminal Tribunals 69

monetary compensation as a form of reparation. Symbolic or moral reparations, bearing a lower cost and thus surpassing the hurdle of securing financial resources available for reparation, is the avenue provided to victims of the Cambodian conflict. This approach may be appropriate considering the specific circumstances in which the court operates, and the fact that the Cambodian conflict happened decades ago.[63]

The ECCC implemented a new scheme for victim redress which stands in contrast with other hybrid tribunals of its time, and predecessors. It differs notably from the scheme established at the ICC, which is the object of Chapter 3, both in its scope and in the manner the ECCC dealt with victim reparation in its jurisprudence. In this regard, this chapter turns attention first to a unique feature of the ECCC – the concept of civil party – and then it examines the cases at the ECCC to date which considered reparations.

2.3.3.1 Civil Parties at the ECCC

A civil party under ECCC proceedings is a victim of a crime being prosecuted at the court who applies to participate as a party in the proceedings. They are a third party to the proceedings participating alongside the defense and the prosecution. A civil party must be a natural person, or legal entity, who suffered physical, material, or psychological harm as a direct consequence of one of the crimes alleged against the accused.[64]

The civil party system created at the ECCC is unique in international criminal justice: it differs from the system at the ICC, which is reviewed in Chapter 3, and from other international or hybrid criminal tribunals. The concept of a civil party (*partie civile*) is derived from French law and grants victims full-fledged status as a legal party in proceedings. This means that, according to Rule 23 of the ECCC Internal Rules, victims have the right to "participate in criminal proceedings" with the status of civil parties and may "seek collective and moral reparations." According to Rule 23(3), civil parties are allowed to be represented as a "single, consolidated group" and present submissions on reparations in a "single claim for collective and moral reparations." Given the system's collective nature, it follows that, if the accused is convicted, civil parties will not be granted individual or material reparations.

---

[63] Ibid., pp. 290–291.

[64] For a discussion of the civil party system at the ECCC, see Alain Werner and Daniella Rudy, "Civil Party Representation at the ECCC: Sounding the Retreat in International Criminal Law?" *Northwestern Journal of International Human Rights* 8 (2009), p. 301.

70 *Reparative Justice for International Crimes*

While victims have the status of civil parties before the ECCC, the scope of their participation has been limited by the judges. In the first case (Case 001) against the Kaing Guek Eav ("Duch"), the Trial Chamber's decision of 9 October 2009 clarified that victims do not have the same standing as the prosecutor and as such could not question the accused or witnesses, nor could they present their views on sentencing.[65] In the second case (Case 002) against senior leaders of the Khmer Rouge, 4,000 victims applied to be civil parties and the Trial Chamber limited their participation through collective representatives rather than individually.

Thus, the system at the ECCC is quite distinctive in the sense that it recognizes a victim's status as a civil party, while nevertheless placing jurisprudential limits upon a victim's ability to participate and claim reparations in the proceedings.

2.3.3.2 Early Reparation Jurisprudence at the ECCC

The first case to reach a conviction, Case 001, set the course by granting modest reparations.

Civil parties in this case expressed their desire to obtain justice, which they generally conceived as a conviction of the accused, collective justice, and assistance, including poverty reduction, healthcare, education, and infrastructure.[66] Civil party groups were all conscious of the political and practical problems of financing the material reparations requested, and two groups argued that Cambodia was also responsible for reparations for human rights violations. They submitted that, according to the *Basic Principles*, when the accused is found to be indigent, the state has responsibility to provide reparations, and in more detail, that Cambodia "should take on the responsibility of aiding the court in ensuring that the victims of the Khmer Rouge are adequately compensated for their suffering, based on the collective and moral reparations they are entitled to."[67]

In the Trial Chamber's judgment, many of the arguments of the civil parties were not accepted. The Trial Chamber ordered the publication of the name of victims in the judgment and a recording of apologies by the convicted person

---

[65] ECCC, Trial Chamber, "Decision on Civil Party Co-Lawyers' Joint Request for a Ruling on the Standing of Civil Party Lawyers to Make Submissions on Sentencing and Directions Concerning the Questioning of the Accused, Experts and Witnesses Testifying on Character," Case 001: Kaing Guek Eav (001/ 18-07-2007/ECCC/TC), 9 October 2009.

[66] Renée Jeffery, "Beyond Repair? Collective and Moral Reparations at the Khmer Rouge Tribunal," *Journal of Human Rights* 13 (2014), pp. 103–119, at p. 109.

[67] Ibid., p. 114.

as a form of reparation.[68] It rejected or failed to include various other forms of reparations requested by the civil parties, including the building of memorials and pagodas, and access to health care.

On the appeal judgment of 3 February 2012, the ECCC Supreme Court Chamber accepted ten additional civil party applications. Concerning reparations, the Supreme Court denied all the civil party appeals. Some of the reparation requests were rejected "because of the lack of financial means to ensure their implementation."[69] The Supreme Court decided that "[i]t is of primary importance to limit reparations to such awards that can realistically be implemented so as to avoid the issuance of orders that, in all probability, will never be enforced and would be confusing and frustrating for the victims."[70]

The first case of the ECCC thus included minimal reparations awards which fell short of some forms of symbolic and collective reparations. It was also disappointing that both chambers did not take the opportunity to clarify and discuss in-depth the meaning, scope, and guiding principles governing reparations within the ECCC. It has been suggested that certain factors contributed to the minimalist approach by the court:

> First, and perhaps most fundamentally, from the outset the ECCC lacked a clear understanding of what "collective and moral reparations" entail. This meant that the Court was afforded a great deal of latitude in determining the sorts of measures to be included in its reparations orders and the flexibility to direct and change the reparations agenda in response to internal and external pressures as Case 001 progressed. Second, the politics of the ECCC and its complicated relationship to the government of Cambodia, borne of its history and structure, has limited the Court's ability to order reparations that appear to direct, to burden, or to place obligations on the Hun Sen government. Third, financial constraints have limited the Court's ability to award expansive reparations and have driven it to interpret the obligation to provide reparations in ways that do not place an additional financial burden on an institution that is facing substantial funding pressures. Fourth, and finally, is the fact that the original legislation setting out the Court's powers and mandate attributed responsibility for funding reparations orders to the accused.[71]

---

[68] ECCC, "Judgment," Case File/Dossier No. 001/18-07-2007/ECCC/TC, 26 July 2010.

[69] ECCC, "Appeal Judgment," Case File/Dossier No. 001/18-07-2007-ECCC/SC, 3 February 2012.

[70] ECCC, "Summary of Appeal Judgment," Case File/Dossier No. 001/18-07-2007-ECCC/SC, 3 February 2012, p. 67.

[71] Renée Jeffery, "Beyond Repair? Collective and Moral Reparations at the Khmer Rouge Tribunal," *Journal of Human Rights* 13 (2014), pp. 103–119, at p. 105.

The second case which dealt with civil parties, Case 002/01, put forward thirteen requests for reparation projects, including building memorials, designating a national remembrance day, organizing therapy groups, supporting documentation and education projects, among others. The Trial Chamber found that these projects complied with the requirements of collective and moral reparations. Two projects (relating to a Public Memorials Initiative and the construction of a memorial to Cambodian victims living in France) were not endorsed by the chamber given that it was not demonstrated that they had secured sufficient external funding.[72]

Case 002/02 concerned reparations for crimes that had an impact in the entire country. It dealt with offences such as rape within forced marriage, treatment of ethnic Vietnamese, Muslin Cham and Buddhist groups, as well as former Khmer Republic soldiers, among others. The lead co-lawyers for civil parties in the case put forward a "final claim for reparations" relating to the confirmed crimes of forced marriage and rape within forced marriage.[73] One project relates to rehabilitation, four are for the benefit of specific groups, and three concern guarantees of nonrepetition.[74] In its judgment, the chamber demonstrated support for the reparations project put forward by the lead counsels.[75]

The reparations in this case were distinctive in some respects. First, the projects were initiated before a final judgment by the chamber endorsing and supporting them. While the judgment makes the projects "official reparations" in the case, as they are institutionally recognized in a judgment of the court, it is less connected to a finding of guilt and liability of the accused, since it was planned and started being implemented before it was known whether the accused would be convicted.[76] Another particular feature of this case that results from the latter is that the reparations "cannot even symbolically be paid for by the Accused."[77] The reparations were all funded by donors.[78] Importantly, it is claimed that the civil parties have positively evaluated the reparations project.[79]

---

[72] ECCC, "Case 002/01 Judgment," Case File/ Dossier No. 002/19-09-2007/ECCC/TC, 7 August 2014.

[73] ECCC, "Civil Party Lead Co-Lawyers' Final Claim for Reparation in Case 002/02 with Confidential Annexes," Case No. 002/19-09-2007/ECCC/TC, 30 May 2017.

[74] ECCC, Case 002/02 KRT Trial Monitor Issue 80, Closing Statements, 13–23 June 2017, pp. 22–23.

[75] ECCC, "Trial Chamber Judgment," Case No. 002/19-09-2007/ECCC/TC.

[76] ECCC, Trial Chamber, "Transcript of Trial Proceedings (Public)," 13 June 2017, E1/520.1, p. 114.

[77] Ibid.

[78] See generally, ECCC, Civil Party Lead Co-Lawyers, "Civil Party Lead Co-Lawyers' Final Claim for Reparation in Case 002/02," 30 May 2017, 118 E457/6/2/1.

[79] Alina Balta, "Extraordinary Chambers in the Courts of Cambodia, Regulation of Marriage, and Reparations: Judgment in Case 002/02 Under Review," *Opinio Juris*, 20 November 2018,

In this case, reparations were far dissociated from the outcome of a criminal trial, and were more akin to an assistance given to victims of the crimes that were the object of the criminal proceedings. This case possibly stems from lessons learned from previous cases at the court, where reparations were minimal due to a finding of indigence of the accused.

From the review of the above decisions, there has already been some recorded progress in terms of reparations. However, the court shied away from developing guiding principles and has not provided additional clarity regarding the reparations scheme of the ECCC. The court thus went from rejecting requests for minimalist reparations, far from what civil parties had claimed, in the first case dealing with reparations reviewed above, to reparations completely dissociated from a finding of guilt, and solely funded by donors.

Victims' redress at the ECCC is still somewhat a work-in-progress with only three cases having dealt with reparations at this time. They have nevertheless had to grapple with some important questions such as political and financial constraints, the responsibility of the state of Cambodia, as well as victims' perception of justice and their understanding of collective and moral reparations. The court's and the civil parties' conception of redress has not always been aligned, and work still needs to be done to ensure full and effective reparations for victims. An in-depth reflection and discussion of the meaning of collective and moral reparations is still largely lacking in the jurisprudence. A more cohesive treatment of reparation requests in the future jurisprudence of the court is also to be anticipated. The ECCC will arguably be in a better position to further develop and improve the reparations mandate as it progresses by learning from its own jurisprudence and institutional knowledge.

2.4 THE DEVELOPMENT OF THE LONG ROAD TO REPARATIONS

The goal of this chapter was to review the different approaches and mechanisms that international and hybrid criminal courts and tribunals have put in place to provide redress to victims. Through a descriptive and comparative exercise, a spectrum of the different models can be perceived. At one end of the spectrum lie the Nuremberg and Tokyo Tribunals which served as precursors of modern international criminal law. The Nuremberg and Tokyo

---

available at http://opiniojuris.org/2018/11/20/extraordinary-chambers-in-the-courts-of-cambo dia-regulation-of-marriage-and-reparations-judgment-in-case-002-02-under-review/.

Tribunals were followed by the ad hoc and hybrid tribunals, with a model that did not provide an avenue for victim redress within the proceedings and focused solely on the criminal aspects of trials. Victims' roles in these courts and mechanisms are primarily that of passive spectators, other than potential witnesses to the prosecution. These tribunals did not see international criminal proceedings as the correct *fora* for dealing with victims' claims for reparation.

In the middle of the spectrum lies the model created by the ECCC. The ECCC included a reparative dimension for victims as civil parties before the court, and certain categories of victims had a possibility, albeit limited, of obtaining reparation. This model is an effort to integrate victim redress into criminal trials. Therefore, the ECCC attempted to reconcile the criminal and reparative dimensions, but not without its challenges, as discussed above.

At the other end of the spectrum, there is the model of the ICC which has created a whole system of victim reparation, still in its early stages. In the ICC's scheme, a broader range of reparations are available to victims, when compared to those available at the ECCC. An administrative mechanism, the Trust Fund for Victims, functions as part of the ICC system of reparation. Due to the significance of the system adopted at the ICC, and the innovative nature of the Trust Fund for Victims, Chapters 3 and 4 will discuss them more specifically.

There are consequences to adopting different approaches to victim redress in international criminal proceedings. According to one model, victims will be left to other mechanisms, such as domestic courts, to seek reparation for international crimes. In contrast, the model established by the ECCC and the ICC provide an avenue at the international criminal level for victims to obtain some sort of redress. Questions remain about which model is best suited to the international level in the years to come.

3

The Construction of a Reparative Dimension of International Justice Before the International Criminal Court (ICC)

The ICC was established in 2002 with the goal of ensuring accountability and ending impunity for international crimes, namely, war crimes, crimes against humanity, genocide, and the crime of aggression. One of the main innovations of the ICC, as compared to previous international criminal tribunals, has been to incorporate victims' rights, including a right to reparations,[1] within the framework of an international criminal tribunal.[2] The court has given an unprecedented role for victims, where they may request to participate in proceedings and claim reparations against a convicted person. The inclusion of victims and the possibility to obtain reparations within ICC proceedings sets the court apart from the jurisprudence of previous ad hoc international criminal tribunals, which determined that justice for victims was best attained by holding perpetrators accountable. The second preambular paragraph to the Rome Statute highlights the effects of international crimes on victims: "Mindful that during this century millions of children, women and men have been victims of unimaginable atrocities that deeply shock the conscience of humanity." Justice for victims at the ICC goes beyond retributive criminal justice, and the ICC is developing through its case law, the notion of reparative justice for victims. The Assembly of States Parties to the ICC has recognized the "reparative role of the Court" and that "assistance and reparations to victims may promote reconciliation and contribute to peace-building."[3]

---

[1] See e.g., Gioia Greco, "Victims' Rights Overview Under the ICC Legal Framework: A Jurisprudential Analysis," *International Criminal Law Review* 7 (2007), pp. 531–547.

[2] The focus of the present chapter concerns the possibility for victims to request reparations within the ICC framework. It does not review victims' right to participate in ICC proceedings.

[3] Resolution ICC-ASP/16/Res.6 "Strengthening the International Criminal Court and the Assembly of States Parties," adopted at the 13th plenary meeting, on 14 December 2017, by consensus, para. 95.

The reparative dimension of the ICC has evolved from a theoretical aspiration, during the negotiations of the statute and the first few years of the court, to a reality in the cases before the court. Since the beginning of its operations in 2002, there have been to date four cases that have reached the stage of reparations (as of mid-2019). This chapter aims to engage in a discussion of the development of reparative justice at the ICC, from a theoretical endeavor to the developing practice at the court. It provides an overview of the system developed at the ICC for reparation for victims and addresses crucial questions, such as: whether there should be a dimension of reparations for victims under international criminal law and the practical implications of adding such a dimension to the ICC. It analyses some of the key challenges that the court is facing or will likely encounter in dealing with reparative justice within the context of international criminal prosecutions and trials. It carefully analyses the numerous submissions of the parties in reparations proceedings, as well as the key decisions of the court on reparations. It addresses counterarguments to the inclusion of reparations within the ICC, the challenges it has posed thus far, and offers some views on how to deal with them.

The aim of this chapter is to provide a timely discussion of the first four cases dealing with reparations, which will pave the way and lay the foundation for the reparation system at the ICC for years to come. These cases are: the first case before the ICC (*The Prosecutor v. Thomas Lubanga Dyilo*), which established principles of reparations, and its concrete impact for the development of reparations at the court; the case of *The Prosecutor v. Germain Katanga*, which presented a unique set of issues, including individual reparations of a modest amount; the case of *The Prosecutor v. Ahmad Al Faqi Al Mahdi*, which posited original questions such as the concept of victims of cultural heritage destruction; and the case of the *The Prosecutor v. Jean-Pierre Bemba*, which posed unique challenges for the adjudication of reparations by the ICC considering the high number of victims authorized to participate in proceedings and the subsequent acquittal of the accused on appeal. The chapter proceeds with a comparison of this groundbreaking jurisprudence that will inform how the decisions of the court align and diverge on key issues, shed light on unique challenges the court is facing, and provide room for some recommendations for future development, based on concrete experiences.

3.1 THE CODIFICATION OF REPARATIONS WITHIN THE ROME STATUTE

Before analyzing the cases that have reached the reparations stage to date, and discussing some of the key challenges they have highlighted, the reparation

International Justice Before the ICC

system at the ICC is first overviewed, with a focus on the reparation provisions in the Rome Statute and an overview of beneficiaries of reparations, a notion that has been further clarified in the court's recent jurisprudence.

Reparations for international crimes are recognized within the ICC under Article 75 of the Rome Statute.[4] Reparations at the ICC are only allowed against individuals and not states, since during negotiations it was the view that the court should not have the authority to order reparations against a state.[5] The framework established is also conviction-based, that is, reparations are conditional on a finding of individual criminal responsibility of perpetrators.

Article 75 reads as follows:

1. The Court shall establish principles relating to reparations to, or in respect of, victims, including restitution, compensation and rehabilitation. On this basis, in its decision the Court may, either upon request or on its own motion in exceptional circumstances, determine the scope and extent of any damage, loss and injury to, or in respect of, victims and will state the principles on which it is acting.

2. The Court may make an order directly against a convicted person specifying appropriate reparations to, or in respect of, victims, including restitution, compensation and rehabilitation.

   Where appropriate, the Court may order that the award for reparations be made through the Trust Fund provided for in article 79.

3. Before making an order under this article, the Court may invite and shall take account of representations from or on behalf of the convicted person, victims, other interested persons or interested States.

4. In exercising its power under this article, the Court may, after a person is convicted of a crime within the jurisdiction of the Court, determine

---

4   See in this regard, e.g., Gibert Bitti and Gabriela González Rivas, "Reparations Provisions for Victims Under the Rome Statute of the International Criminal Court," in *Redressing Injustices Through Mass Claims*, International Bureau of the Permanent Court of Arbitration, 2006, pp. 299–322; Gioia Greco, "Victims' Rights Overview Under the ICC Legal Framework: A Jurisprudential Analysis," *International Criminal Law Review* 7 (2007), pp. 531–547; Carla Ferstman and Mariana Goetz, "Reparations before the International Criminal Court: The Early Jurisprudence on Victim Participation and its Impact on Future Reparations Proceedings," in *Reparations for Victims of Genocide, War Crimes and Crimes against Humanity, Systems in Place and Systems in the Making*, eds. Carla Ferstman et al., Nijhoff, 2009, pp. 313–350.

5   Luke Moffett, "Reparations for Victims at the International Criminal Court: A New Way Forward?," *The International Journal of Human Rights* 21 (2017), pp. 1204–1222, citing Fiona McKay, "Are Reparations Appropriately Addressed in the ICC Statute?" in *International Crimes, Peace, and Human Rights: The Role of the International Criminal Court*, ed. D. Shelton, Transnational Publishers, 2000, pp. 163–174, at p. 167; and Christopher Muttukumaru, "Reparations to Victims," in *The International Criminal Court: The Making of the Rome Statute; Issues, Negotiations, Results*, ed. Roy S. Lee, Kluwer, 1999, pp. 262–270.

78   *Reparative Justice for International Crimes*

whether, in order to give effect to an order which it may make under this article, it is necessary to seek measures under article 93, paragraph 1.

5. A State Party shall give effect to a decision under this article as if the provisions of article 109 were applicable to this article.

6. Nothing in this article shall be interpreted as prejudicing the rights of victims under national or international law.

Under Article 75(1), some key features of this innovative reparation system are established. First, the court is required (note the use of the word "shall") to establish principles relating to reparation. The text of Article 75(1) left some room for interpretation as to whether it would be for the plenary of the "court," or individual chambers in each case (acting as the "court") to develop such principles of reparation. The question has become purely a theoretical one, as the early jurisprudence of the court demonstrates that the establishment of such principles followed the latter approach, that is, the chambers have developed and applied principles of reparation in light of the circumstances of each case.

Article 75(1) also exemplifies some of the forms of reparation, that is, restitution, compensation, and rehabilitation, without providing an exhaustive list, and symbolic or transformative reparations, for example, can also be ordered. The precise reason for failing to mention symbolic reparations in the text of Article 75 is unknown. As Frédéric Mégret argues:

> Symbolic reparations have several uses. They may be particularly important in cases where the harm is hard to evaluate, or continuing, or where the injury cannot be repaired. Mere compensation might encourage a state to think that it can "buy its way out" of violations by simply paying the compensation but not remedying the situation ... Symbolic reparations also cater to a broader range of victim concerns, and take seriously their need for recognition, respect, dignity and hope for a safe future.[6]

Much like Frédéric Mégret suggests, it appears that material and symbolic reparations are not mutually exclusive, and may in fact complement one another. In the context of the ICC this rings true, in particular in light of the nature of international crimes which generally includes mass victimization. In the cases to date, individual awards have taken the form of compensation to individual victims, and collective awards have been symbolic and rehabilitative measures.

Article 75(2), for its part, concerns an order of reparation. Upon a textual reading of this provision, the court is not per se required to make an order of

---

[6]   Fréderic Mégret, "The International Criminal Court and the Failure to Mention Symbolic Reparations," 16(2) *International Review of Victimology* (2009), pp. 127–147.

reparation, but "may" do so. The order is made against a convicted person, making it clear that under the reparation system at the ICC, reparations are (i) dependent upon conviction, and (ii) made against the person who was found guilty, as opposed to a stand-alone order of reparation. In this latter respect, the court may decide that the reparations are paid through the Trust Fund for Victims (TFV), established under the auspices of the court.

Reparations within the ICC cannot be properly understood without examining the central role played by the TFV. The importance of this mechanism is illustrated in Chapter 4 which discusses the key features and the mandates of the TFV as well as the role played in recent cases. The TFV has an important role in the implementation of the court's reparations mandate. A five-member Board of Directors which oversees the TFV's activities was established in September 2002[7] and in 2004, a Trust Fund Secretariat was created as part of the court's registry.[8] The TFV was established by the Assembly of States Parties in accordance with Article 79 of the Rome Statue, which reads as follows:

(1) A Trust Fund shall be established by decision of the Assembly of States Parties for the benefit of victims of crimes within the jurisdiction of the Court, and of the families of such victims.
(2) The Court may order money and other property collected through fines or forfeiture to be transferred, by order of the Court, to the Trust Fund.
(3) The Trust Fund shall be managed according to criteria to be determined by the Assembly of States Parties.

The distinction between principles of reparation and an order of reparation was clarified by the Appeals Chamber. According to the chamber, principles of reparation under Article 75(1) are "general concepts that, while formulated in light of the circumstances of a specific case, can nonetheless be applied, adapted, expanded upon, or added to by future Trial Chambers," whereas a reparation order is a trial chamber's "holdings, determinations and findings based on [reparation] principles."[9]

As discussed in Chapter 2, before the adoption of the Rome Statute and the establishment of the ICC, victims had a very limited ability to claim

---

[7] Resolution ICC-ASP/1/Res.6 (9 September 2002), and Annex to same, para. 7.
[8] Resolution ICC-ASP/3/Res.7, Establishment of the Secretariat of the Trust Fund for Victims, paras. 2 and 4 (10 September 2004). The TFV is funded by the court's budget and not from the funds that the trust fund holds for the benefit of victims.
[9] ICC, *The Prosecutor* v. *Thomas Lubunga Dyilo*, ICC-01/04–01/06, Appeals Chamber, Judgment on the appeals against "Decision Establishing the Principles and Procedures to be Applied to Reparations" of 7 August 2012 with AMENDED order for reparations (Annex A) and public annexes 1 and 2, 3 March 2015, paras. 3 and 55.

reparations within international criminal proceedings. This novel feature of the permanent international criminal court bears a tremendous impact on the structure, development, and scope of international criminal justice. It will also likely influence the perception and the actual role of victims as part of the process of justice in the aftermath of international crimes.

Through the recognition of victims' rights within court proceedings, the ICC has begun developing the reparative dimension of international criminal justice. The interconnectedness of both dimensions is a feature of the system: for example, reparations can only be claimed by victims if accused person(s) are convicted (according to Article 75(2) of the Rome Statute). Beyond criminal matters, the judges decide upon the principles of reparations, the beneficiaries of reparations, the type of reparations, the proof required for purposes of reparations, among other details. At the ICC, the link between the criminal dimension and reparative dimension is such that there is the creation of a *sui generis* system.

Despite the connection of both systems within the ICC framework, the distinction between a reparative and a criminal dimension remains useful as it relates to the beneficiaries of reparation, the forms of reparation, and the role of administrative mechanisms connected to a judicial process (such as the TFV). Through the discussion of selected topics in this chapter, it will be demonstrated that we are moving towards a system that blends the two dimensions before the ICC. A system where many aspects of reparations are dependent upon, and connected to, the criminal dimension of international justice.

The purpose of this section is to provide a general overview of the system of reparation for victims at the ICC, by highlighting its main features.[10] In order to do so it is helpful to draw, first, an analysis of the reparation jurisprudence at the ICC, which is, at the time of writing, still in its infancy. This discussion will form the foundation upon which normative arguments can be made about the different models of dealing with reparations in the context of international criminal trials.

---

[10] See Eva Dwertmann, *The Reparation System of the International Criminal Court: Its Implementation, Possibilities and Limitations*, Nijhoff, 2010; Claude Jorda and Jérôme de Hemptinne, "The Status and Role of the Victim," in *The Rome Statute of the International Criminal Court: A Commentary*, eds. Antonio Cassese et al., Oxford University Press, 2002, pp. 1387–1419; Conor McCarthy, *Reparations and Victim Support in the International Criminal Court*, Cambridge University Press, 2012; Carla Ferstman, "The Reparation Regime of the International Criminal Court: Practical Considerations," *Leiden Journal of International Law* 15 (2002), p. 667; Edda Kristjánsdóttir, "International Mass Claims Processes and the ICC Trust Fund for Victims," in *Reparations for Victims of Genocide, War Crimes and Crimes Against Humanity*, eds. Carla Ferstman et al., Nijhoff, 2009, p. 167; T. Markus Funk, *Victim Rights and Advocacy at the International Criminal Court*, Oxford University Press, 2010; and Godfrey Musila, *Rethinking International Criminal Law: Restorative Justice and the Rights of Victims in the International Criminal Court*, Lambert Academic Publishing, 2010.

International Justice Before the ICC

3.2 THE SEARCH FOR VICTIMS' JUSTICE BEFORE THE ICC: RECENT CASE LAW ON REPARATIONS

Much debate has surrounded the question of reparations at the ICC and how the chambers therein would develop and apply the principles of reparations.[11] It took some time after the ICC first began its activities before one of the court's chambers had to examine requests for reparation. The first reparation decision (from a trial chamber), after a conviction, dates to 2012, that is, ten years after the ICC started its activities. To date, four cases have reached the stage of reparations. The decisions and filings of the parties and participants in these cases establish the foundation for the principles of reparation that the court will follow in future cases. They also shed light on many challenges that the reparation system devised at the ICC is facing, and will likely encounter in the future. An analysis of the cases decided to date highlights the peculiarities of developing reparative justice for international crimes, from theory to practice.

Many questions remain as to how Article 75 will continue to be interpreted and what practical effects it will have on reparation awards. At this juncture, it is worth bearing in mind that the "reparation system" within the ICC is still in its infancy with four cases having reached the reparation judgment stage. Each of the cases discussed herein presented a unique set of issues, and contributed in distinct ways to the development of principles of reparation and the establishment of reparative justice at the ICC.

3.2.1 *The Trailblazing Case of* The Prosecutor v. Thomas Lubanga Dyilo

3.2.1.1 Context of the Case

Thomas Lubanga Dyilo was the first person arrested and transferred to The Hague.[12] He is a Congolese national and was the president of the Union of

---

[11] See e.g., Carla Ferstman, "The Reparation Regime of the International Criminal Court: Practical Considerations," *Leiden Journal of International Law* 15 (2002), pp. 667–686; Liesbeth Zegveld, "Victims' Reparations Claims and International Criminal Courts," *Journal of International Criminal Justice* 8 (2010); Marc Henzelin et al., "Reparations to Victims Before the International Criminal Court: Lessons from International Mass Claims Processes," *Criminal Law Forum* 17 (2006), pp. 281–344; Gilbert Bitti and Gabriela Gonzales Rivas, "The Reparations Provisions for Victims Under the Rome Statute of the International Criminal Court," in *Redressing Injustices Through Mass Claims Processes: Innovative Responses to Unique Challenges*, The International Bureau of the Permanent Court of Arbitration, Oxford University Press, 2006, pp. 299–322.

[12] *The Prosecutor* v. *Thomas Lubanga Dyilo*, ICC-01/04-01/06 ("*Lubanga*" or "the first case on reparations").

82   *Reparative Justice for International Crimes*

Congolese Patriots (UPC), an armed group claiming to act on behalf of the ethnic Hema population in the Ituri region of northeastern Democratic Republic of the Congo (DRC). The UPC has been implicated in many serious allegations of human rights abuses, including massacres of other ethnic groups, summary executions, torture, rape, abduction and use of children as soldiers, and pillage.

The charges against Mr. Lubanga were confirmed in January 2007, and his trial began before Trial Chamber I of the ICC in January 2009. He was convicted in 2012 of committing, as coperpetrator, the war crime of enlisting and conscripting children under the age of fifteen and using them as active participants in hostilities in 2002–2003. He was sentenced to fourteen years in prison. A total of 146 persons were granted victim status and authorized to participate in the case.

While the case is precedent-setting regarding the recognition of the crime of conscripting and enlisting child soldiers, it disappointed in relation to the recognition of sexual and gender-based violence crimes, which, as evidenced during the proceedings, took place.

The *Lubanga* case was the first opportunity the court (through its trial and appeals chambers) had to tackle the establishment of the reparation principles of the ICC. It is also the largest reparations case to date, both in the amount of reparations as well the decisions and filings relating to reparations. Trial Chamber I rendered the first decision of the ICC on the question of reparations in the case against Thomas Lubanga Dyilo in 2012.[13] The Appeals Chamber rendered its subsequent judgment in 2015, further elaborating on the principles of reparation, and appending an amended reparation order to its judgment. This, however, was not the end of the road of reparations in the case. After the Appeals Judgment, there were additional filings and decisions.

3.2.1.2 First Trial Chamber Decision on Reparations: Principles of Reparations

In general terms, in its decision, Trial Chamber I established principles relating to reparations and their implementation, and emphasized that the 2012 Decision on Reparations should not affect the rights of victims in other cases. The chamber heard a number of submissions on the issue of reparations. For example, the TFV, the Women's Initiatives for Gender Justice, and

---

[13] ICC, Trial Chamber I, *The Prosecutor v. Thomas Lubanga Dyilo*, "Decision Establishing the Principles and Procedures to be Applied to Reparations," 7 August 2012, ICC-01/04-01/06 ("2012 Decision on Reparations").

the International Center for Transitional Justice were allowed to make submissions regarding reparations.[14] A common theme of these submissions was the nonlimitation of reparations to the crimes charged,[15] which ultimately did not happen, and it is established now that reparations are only available for victims of crimes for which an accused stood convicted.

The Trial Chamber held that: "the Court's reparations strategy should, in part, be directed at preventing future conflicts and raising awareness that the effective reintegration of the children requires eradicating the victimisation, discrimination and stigmatisation of young people in these circumstances."[16]

While Article 75 states that "the Court shall establish principles relating to reparations," this did not happen until this first decision on reparations. Thus, Trial Chamber I, in the context of this case, had to develop the principles of reparation for the first time. As clarified by the Appeals Chamber at a later stage, these principles could be applied, expanded upon or added to by future trial chambers in reparations proceedings,[17] which has happened in two other cases to date. The principles elaborated were informed by international instruments, national/regional/international jurisprudence and principles on reparations.[18]

The principles established by the trial chamber dealt with:

a) the applicable law; b) dignity, non-discrimination and non-stigmatization; c) the beneficiaries of reparations (including direct and indirect victims); d) accessibility and consultation with victims (including a gender-sensitive approach); e) principles relating to victims of sexual violence and child victims; f) the scope of reparations and the modalities thereof (including individual and collective reparations); g) the principle of proportional and

---

[14] ICC, Trial Chamber I, *The Prosecutor v. Thomas Lubanga Dyilo*, "Decision Granting Leave to Make Representations in the Reparations Proceedings," 20 April 2012, ICC-01/04-01/06.

[15] ICC, Trial Chamber I, *The Prosecutor v. Thomas Lubanga Dyilo*, submission on reparations issues, 10 May 2012, ICC-01/04-01/06; ICC, Trial Chamber I, *The Prosecutor v. Thomas Lubanga Dyilo*, Public Redacted Version of ICC-01/04-01/06-2803-Conf-Exp–Trust Fund for Victims' First Report on Reparations, 1 September 2011, ICC-01/04-01/06; ICC, Trial Chamber I, *The Prosecutor v. Thomas Lubanga Dyilo*, Observations of the Women's Initiatives for Gender Justice on Reparations, 10 May 2012, ICC-01/04-01/06.

[16] 2012 Decision on Reparations, para. 240.

[17] ICC, Appeals Chamber, *The Prosecutor v. Thomas Lubanga Dyilo*, "Judgment on the Appeals Against the 'Decision Establishing the Principles and Procedures to be Applied to Reparations'," 7 August 2012 with AMENDED order for reparations (Annex A) and public annexes 1 and 2, 3 March 2015 (hereinafter: "2015 Appeals Judgment on Reparations").

[18] See generally, Mariana Goetz, "Reparative Justice at the International Criminal Court: Best Practice or Tokenism?" in *Reparation for Victims of Crimes Against Humanity: The Healing Role of Reparation*, ed. Jo-Anne M. Webbers, Routledge, 2014, pp. 53–71.

84 *Reparative Justice for International Crimes*

adequate reparations; h) causation; i) standard and burden of proof; j) principles relating to the rights of the defence; k) questions relating to States and other stakeholders; l) publicity of the Principles established therein.[19]

Interestingly, the chamber indicated that the individual who had been convicted, Mr. Lubanga Dyilo, had been declared indigent. Therefore, the chamber declared that any symbolic reparation from him would need his agreement.[20] Similarly, the Trial Chamber decided not to order reparations against the accused directly given his state of indigence. Essentially, the chamber outsourced the matter of reparations to the TFV and found it unnecessary to "remain seized throughout the reparations proceedings."[21] In the operative paragraphs, the Trial Chamber authorized only collective reparations and decided not to examine individual applications for reparations; it instead instructed the Registry to transmit all the individual application forms it had received to the TFV.[22]

This first decision on reparations was groundbreaking in different respects. The Trial Chamber established principles of reparations that would be adapted and followed by future chambers. It provided the blueprint of principles for the Appeals Chamber to dwell upon and adjust to move the reparative dimension of the court forward. It is regrettable however that the Trial Chamber decision left some questions unanswered which caused delays for the implementation and realization of reparations.

3.2.1.3 The 2015 Appeals Chamber Judgment

On 3 March 2015, the Appeals Chamber reversed many of the Trial Chamber's findings in a landmark Judgment and amended order for reparations.[23] The chamber established through its judgment the principle that the convicted person is liable to remedy the harm caused. The Appeals Chamber was very clear in this regard: even if reparations are ordered through the TFV, the order is made "against a convicted person."[24] According to the chamber, reparations "oblige those responsible for serious crimes to repair the harm they caused to the victims and they enable the Court to ensure that offenders account for their acts."[25] The chamber invoked the notion of "transformative reparations"

---

[19] 2012 Decision on Reparations, pp. 64–85.
[20] Ibid., para. 269.
[21] Ibid., para. 261.
[22] Ibid., para. 289(b).
[23] 2015 Appeals Judgment on Reparations.
[24] Ibid., para. 70.
[25] Ibid., para. 2.

and stated that "[p]rogrammes that have transformative objectives, however limited, can help prevent future victimisation, and symbolic reparations, such as commemorations and tributes, may also contribute to the process of rehabilitation."[26] The chamber made it clear that the indigence of a convicted person is not a factor in their liability for reparations.[27]

The judgment is crucial to the development of reparative justice at the ICC given that the court (as the plenary of judges) had not established principles of reparation, and so this was the first time the principles were clarified by the Appeals Chamber, to be applied in this and other cases. Among its many conclusions, the Appeals Chamber established the minimum elements that are necessary in a reparations order. These are:

1) the order for reparations shall be directed against a convicted person;
2) it must establish and inform him/her of his/her liability regarding reparation;
3) it must describe and reason the type of reparation in accordance with Rules 97(1) and 98 of the Rules of Procedure and Evidence (RPE);
4) it must describe the harm caused and the modalities of reparation that are appropriate in the circumstances;
5) it shall also identify the victims or set out eligibility criteria based on the link between the harm suffered and the crimes the accused was convicted.[28]

These elements shed light on the delicate task of balancing the rights of victims and those of "convicted persons."[29] These principles were relied on and further elaborated in other cases concerning reparations.

The Appeals Chamber further confirmed that, in this case, reparations should be ordered on a collective basis rather than on an individual basis, given the number of victims involved. It rejected the general concept of "community reparations" and found that reparations are to be awarded according to the harm suffered as a consequence of the crime within the jurisdiction of the court.[30]

Another significant contribution of the Appeals Chamber judgment is its articulation of the unique reparative system at the ICC, and its focus on the conviction (the criminal dimension of international justice) of the accused: "reparation orders are intrinsically linked to the individual whose criminal

---

[26] Ibid., para. 67.
[27] Ibid., para. 104.
[28] Ibid.
[29] Ibid., para. 184.
[30] Ibid., para. 1.

86   *Reparative Justice for International Crimes*

responsibility is established in a conviction and whose culpability for these criminal acts is determined in a sentence."[31]

In light of the Appeals Chamber judgment, the essential elements set out by the chamber cannot be delegated to an administrative organ like the TFV and thus continuous monitoring by the trial chambers will be necessary. Some issues concerning reparations (including the "essential elements") are by nature legal issues and should be overseen by judicial organs.

The Appeals Chamber judgment gave a newly constituted Trial Chamber II the specific tasks of (1) determining the monetary liability of Mr. Lubanga, and (2) monitoring and overseeing the implementation of the reparations through the TFV. The number of victims who suffered harm as a result of Mr. Lubanga's crimes was not identified in the Appeals Chamber judgment and amended order.

All in all, the Appeals Chamber judgment represented a step forward as it clarified the principles of reparation at the ICC, the rights of victims and convicted persons, and the roles of chambers and the TFV. In critically assessing the judgment, Carsten Stahn has pondered that the Appeals Chamber order:

> prioritizes accountability over other societal concerns, such as well-being, security or peace. Rationales, such as relief of suffering, deterrence of future violations, societal reintegration or reconciliation, are treated as secondary objectives that should be pursued "to the extent possible" ... Critics are thus likely to remain skeptical as to whether this new liability regime will make an actual difference to the lives of victims. But the door is open for further creativity. This is the legacy of the decision – and an important turning point for future practice.[32]

3.2.1.4 After the Appeals Judgment: The Long Road to the Implementation of Reparations

The question of reparations did not end with the judgment of the Appeals Chamber. In fact, that seemed to be only the beginning of a long path to reparations. This case demonstrates how internal delays ultimately lead to delays of justice. While it is acknowledged that this was the first case of

---

[31]   2015 Appeals Judgment on Reparations, para. 65.

[32]   Carsten Stahn, "Reparative Justice after the Lubanga Appeals Judgment on Principles and Procedures of Reparation," *EJIL: Talk!* 7 April 2015, available at http://ejiltalk.org/reparative-justice-after-the-lubanga-appeals-judgment-on-principles-and-procedures-of-reparation/#more-13286.

reparations before the court, it sheds light on the complexities for the substantive realization of reparations for victims.

Once the long trial and its appeal ended, victims were caught in an exchange between the TFV and the Trial Chamber charged with monitoring the implementation of the reparation order and the determination of the amount of liability of Mr. Lubanga.[33] Since the first decision on reparations in the *Lubanga* case by Trial Chamber I in 2012, many more submissions and delays were seen regarding the implementation of the reparation plan. In fact, since the Appeals Chamber tasked a newly constituted Trial Chamber to oversee the implementation of the reparation, there have been many disagreements between the chamber and the TFV, entrusted with implementing the reparation order in the case.

The divergences between the Trial Chamber and the TFV mainly concerned their respective roles in the implementation of reparations. The Trial Chamber was of the view that it was necessary to first identify the victims that were entitled to reparations in order to determine Mr. Lubanga's liability, whereas the TFV thought that this should be done during the implementation of the order. In fact, at the end of 2015 the TFV submitted its Draft Implementation Plan for Collective Reparations to Victims ("Draft Plan"), produced after consultations in Ituri, where it addressed many issues, including victim eligibility, causality and standard of proof, and operation issues.[34] It also proposed modalities and forms of reparations, stating that psychological trauma was a cross-cutting issue. The TFV estimated that there were 3,000 potentially eligible victims.[35]

After considering the observations of parties and participants, including the defense, legal representatives of victims, the prosecution and other interested persons,[36] the Trial Chamber issued an order in February 2016 stating that the

---

[33] For a detailed account of the numerous procedural stages of the implementation of reparations in the *Lubanga* case, see the procedural history summarized in ICC, Trial Chamber II, *The Prosecutor* v. *Thomas Lubanga Dyilo*, "Order Approving the Proposed Plan of the Trust Fund for Victims in Relation to Symbolic Collective Reparations," ICC-01/04-01/06, 21 October 2016, paras. 1–10.

[34] ICC, TFV, "Draft Implementation Plan for Collective Reparations to Victims Submitted to the Amended Reparations Order of 3 March 2015 in the Case Against Thomas Lubanga Dyilo," ICC-01/04-01/06, Annex A, ICC-01/04-01/06-3177-AnxA, 3 November 2015.

[35] Ibid.

[36] ICC, "Observations du groupe de victims V01 sur le projet de plan de mis en œuvre des réparations déposé par le Fonds au profit des victimes ICC-01/04-01/06-3177," ICC-01/04-01/06-3194, 1 February 2016; ICC, "Observations de l'équipe V02 sur le projet de plan de mise en œuvre de réparations déposé par le Fonds au profit des victimes (TFV) le 3 novembre 2015 devant la Chambre d'instance II," 1 February 2016, ICC-01/04-01/06-3195; ICC, "Observations sur le Projet de mise en œuvre des réparations déposé par le Fonds au profit des victimes le 3

Draft Plan was incomplete and instructed the TFV to "begin the process of locating and identifying victims potentially eligible to benefit from the reparations."[37] The chamber also asked for more details on the reparation programs. All in all, this 2016 decision demonstrated the diverging positions of the TFV and the chamber which ultimately caused another two years of back-and-forth and delays before the final decision of the chamber on reparations. One cause of delay was the identification of victims. In other words, one of the reasons for the debate between the Trial Chamber, the TFV and other institutional actors was whether it was necessary to identify individual victims eligible to collective reparations as a prerequisite to determining the convicted person's liability (a task the Appeals Chamber entrusted to the Trial Chamber in its 2015 Judgment on Reparations).[38] Another debate centered on whether the convicted person had the right to review the potential beneficiaries of reparations, which would entail as a consequence, disclosing the identity of victims.[39] In fact, in order to assess eligibility for reparation and the harm suffered, the Trial Chamber instructed the TFV to gather interviews, copies of victim identification documents, descriptions of factual allegations, as well as the consent of victims to submit this identifying information to the defense.[40] Having been denied leave to appeal this decision,[41] the TFV asked the Trial Chamber to reconsider its position on the "individual eligibility and harm assessment" since such an exercise actually "damages and re-traumatizes victims."[42]

---

novembre 2015," 1 February 2016, ICC-01/04-01/06-3193; ICC, "Version publique expurgée des 'Observations de la Défense de M. Thomas Lubanga relatives au "Filing on Reparations and Draft Implementation Plan," daté du 3 novembre 2015', déposées le 1 février 2016 (ICC-01/04-01/06-3196-Conf)," ICC-01/04-01/06-3196- Red2; ICC, "Prosecution's Observations on the Trust Fund for Victims' Filing on Reparations and Draft Implementation Plan," 18 December 2015, ICC-01/04-01/06-3186.

[37] ICC, Trial Chamber II, "Order Instructing the Trust Fund for Victims to Supplement the Draft Implementation Plan," ICC-01/04-01/06-3198-tENG, 9 February 2016.

[38] See a discussion in this regard, Marissa R. Brodney, "Implementing International Criminal Court-Ordered Collective Reparations: Unpacking Present Debates," *Journal of the Oxford Centre for Socio-Legal Studies*, 1 November 2016, available at https://joxcsls.com/2016/11/01/i mplementing-international-criminal-court-ordered-collective-reparations-unpacking-pre sent-debates/.

[39] Ibid.

[40] ICC, Trial Chamber II, "Order Instructing the Trust Fund for Victims to Supplement the Draft Implementation Plan," ICC-01/04-01/06-3198-tENG, 9 February 2016, para. 17.

[41] ICC, Trial Chamber II, "Decision on the Request of the Trust Fund for Victims for Leave to Appeal Against the Order of 9 February 2016," ICC-01/04-01/06-3202-tENG, 4 March 2016.

[42] ICC, TFV, "First submission of victim dossiers with twelve confidential, ex parte annexes, available to the Registrar, and Legal Representatives of Victims V01 only," ICC-01/04-01/06-3208, 31 May 2016.

In a subsequent order, the Trial Chamber seemed to accept that the TFV had provided a sample of victims, and instructed the registry to assist the TFV so that the chamber "could better assess to what extent the list of victims identified is representative of all potential victims."[43] Later in October 2016, the Trial Chamber approved the TFV's proposed program regarding symbolic reparations.[44]

It was only in December 2017, that the Trial Chamber decided on Mr. Lubanga's liability. This decision did not identify all victims or assess their harm. The Trial Chamber determined, as the Appeals Chamber had tasked it to do in its 2015 judgment, the liability of the convicted person amounting to USD 10 million, the highest ICC reparations order to date. In doing so, the Trial Chamber examined whether the 472 individual victim applicants were eligible to receive reparations. It decided that 425 victims (which the chamber determined to be a "sample" of the hundreds or thousands not yet identified) had suffered an "average harm" as a result of the crimes for which Mr. Lubanga was convicted and had the right to access collective reparations. The calculation of the liability comprised: USD 8,000 "ex aequo et bono" for each of the 425 identified direct and indirect victims who suffered material, physical, and psychological harm (USD 3.4 million); and USD 6.6 million for harm suffered by victims not yet identified.[45] Given the state of indigence of Mr. Lubanga, the TFV was invited to raise additional funds with the government of the DRC. The chamber adopted the causality requirement as the accused be the proximate cause of the damages suffered. Concerning the types of damages, the chamber found that both direct and indirect victims had suffered harm, and it identified some forms of harm, such as separation from family, interruption and termination of schooling, exposure to an environment of violence and fear (direct victims); and psychological suffering from the loss of a family member, material poverty resulting from the death of a family member (indirect victims). Child soldiers, in light of their age and vulnerability, were presumed to have suffered psychological, physical, and

---

[43] ICC, Trial Chamber II, "Order Instructing the Registry to Provide Aid and Assistance to the Legal Representatives and the Trust Fund for Victims to Identify Victims Potentially Eligible for Reparations," ICC-01/04-01/06-3218-tENG, 15 July 2016, para. 8.

[44] ICC, Trial Chamber II, "Order Approving the Proposed Plan of the Trust Fund for Victims in Relation to Symbolic Collective Reparations," ICC-01/04-01/06-3251, 21 October 2016.

[45] ICC, Trial Chamber II, "Corrected Version of the 'Decision Setting the Size of the Reparations Award for Which Thomas Lubanga Dyilo Is Liable' With Corrected Version of One Public Annex (Annex I); of One Public Annex (Annex III) and One Confidential Annex, EX PARTE, Registry, Trust Fund for Victims, Legal Representatives of the V01 and V02 Groups of Victims, and Office of Public Counsel for Victims (Annex II); and Confidential Redacted Version of Annex II," ICC-01/04-01/06-3379-Red-Corr-tENG, 21 December 2017.

material damages. Concerning collective reparations, the chamber relied on the jurisprudence in the case of the *The Prosecutor v. Germain Katanga*,[46] which is discussed below, and concluded that reparations must concern a group with shared characteristics or who experienced shared harm.[47]

As expected, the decision of the Trial Chamber of December 2017 setting the amount of liability was appealed by Mr. Lubanga and the legal representatives of victims V01 and V02.[48] The issues before the Appeals Chamber included the amount of liability of the convicted person, Mr. Lubanga, as well as the Trial Chamber's decision in relation to eligible victims. The conviction of Mr. Lubanga was rendered in 2012 and only in 2019 did the court deliver a final decision concerning reparations. The Appeals Chamber rendered a unanimous decision rejecting the defense's appeal and confirming Mr. Lubanga's liability of USD 10 million for reparations to victims.[49]

The Appeals Chamber amended the Trial Chamber's decision insofar as eligible victims were concerned, making the criteria for eligibility more equitable. That is, the Trial Chamber, in the impugned decision, had decided that from the 473 victims who had submitted dossiers, only 425 were eligible to participate in the collective award, thus rejecting victims who had already been deemed eligible by the TFV. This was an unfortunate turn of events, where it appeared that the Trial Chamber had applied inconsistent approaches to identifying beneficiaries, as in an earlier decision the Trial Chamber had decided that the TFV would be screening beneficiaries of the reparation award. As it was argued before the Appeals Chamber, the Trial Chamber's decision led victims to "resent the Court because they feel they are being victimized again

---

[46] ICC, Trial Chamber II, *The Prosecutor v. Germain Katanga*, ICC-01/04-01/07, 24 March 2017.

[47] ICC, Trial Chamber II, "Corrected version of the 'Decision Setting the Size of the Reparations Award for Which Thomas Lubanga Dyilo Is Liable' With Corrected Version of One Public Annex (Annex I); of One Public Annex (Annex III) and One Confidential Annex, EX PARTE, Registry, Trust Fund for Victims, Legal Representatives of the V01 and V02 Groups of Victims, and Office of Public Counsel for Victims (Annex II); and Confidential Redacted Version of Annex II," ICC-01/04-01/06-3379-Red-Corr-tENG, 21 December 2017.

[48] ICC, "Public Redacted Version of the 'Appeal Brief of the Defence for Mr Thomas Lubanga Dyilo Against the "Décision fixant le montant des réparations auxquelles Thomas Lubanga Dyilo est tenu" handed down by Trial Chamber II on 15 December 2017 and Amended," ICC-01/04-01/06-3394-Red-tENG, 15 March 2018; ICC, "Public Version of the Corrigendum to the Appeal Brief Against the "Décision fixant le montant des réparations auxquelles Thomas Lubanga est tenu" handed Down by Trial Chamber II on 15 December 2017, ICC-01/04-01/06-3396-Conf," ICC-01/04-01/06-3396-Corr-Red-tENG, 4 April 2018.

[49] ICC, Appeals Chamber, "Judgment on the appeals against Trial Chamber II's 'Decision Setting the Size of the Reparations Award for Which Thomas Lubanga Dyilo Is Liable'," ICC-01/04-01/06-3466-Red, 18 July 2019.

International Justice Before the ICC

after so many years of waiting."[50] The Appeals Chamber decided in this regard that

> the victims whom Trial Chamber II found ineligible to receive reparations, and who consider that their failure to sufficiently substantiate their allegations, including by supporting documentation, resulted from insufficient notice of the requirements for eligibility, may seek a new assessment of their eligibility by the Trust Fund for Victims, together with other victims who may come forward in the course of the implementation stage ... any recommendations as to eligibility made by the Trust Fund for Victims shall be subject to the approval of Trial Chamber II.[51]

This is a welcome development for victims, in a case where there is much delay in "getting the law right" and realizing reparations. After the final decision on reparations in this case was rendered, it is time to turn the page, and learn lessons so that similar delays and inconsistencies do not permeate future decisions in other cases. It is time to focus on the implementation of reparations, as victims can no longer wait.

3.2.2 The Prosecutor *v.* Germain Katanga *Case: Individual Awards for the First Time*

This is the second case stemming from the conflict in the DRC. While the *Lubanga* case dealt with using child soldiers in Ituri, this case concerned an attack on the village of Bogoro in 2003. In March 2014, Mr. Katanga was found guilty as an accessory for one count of crime against humanity and four counts of war crimes. Mr. Katanga was first charged with Mr. Mathieu Ngujolo Chui, but the Trial Chamber decided to sever the cases after the evidence had been heard. The latter accused was subsequently acquitted. As a consequence, victims of the crimes allegedly committed by Mr. Ngudjolo Chui were not eligible for reparations since he was not convicted.[52]

---

[50] ICC, "Public Version of the Corrigendum to the Appeal Brief Against the 'Décision fixant le montant des réparations auxquelles Thomas Lubanga est tenu' Handed Down by Trial Chamber II on 15 December 2017, ICC-01/04-01/06-3396-Conf," ICC-01/04-01/06-3396-Corr-Red-tENG, 4 April 2018.

[51] ICC, Appeals Chamber, "Judgment on the Appeals Against Trial Chamber II's 'Decision Setting the Size of the Reparations Award for Which Thomas Lubanga Dyilo Is Liable'," ICC-01/04-01/06-3466-Red, 18 July 2019.

[52] Concerning the Trial Chamber's decision, see Juan Pablo Pérez-León-Acevedo, "The Katanga Reparation Order at the International Criminal Court: Developing the Emerging Reparations Practice of the Court," *Nordic Journal of Human Rights* 36 (2018), p. 91–102.

3.2.2.1 The 2017 Trial Chamber Decision: "Symbolic" Individual Reparations and Collective Awards

In March 2017, the Trial Chamber awarded individual and collective reparations to the victims of the crimes committed by Mr. Katanga. This is a significant case as it was the first time the court awarded individual reparations, as victims participating in the case had expressed their desire to receive financial compensation.[53] There were 345 applications for reparations for the crimes committed by Mr. Katanga. The Trial Chamber examined each application itself, without the assistance of experts, and decided that 297 were eligible for reparations. The Trial Chamber in this case adopted a different approach than in *Lubanga* concerning the beneficiaries of reparations. In this case, the Trial Chamber decided that an application-based approach would be appropriate, and no further applications could be received during the implementation of the plan.[54]

In addition to assessing each application, the Trial Chamber also decided on the monetary amount due for the harm suffered by the 297 victims at the sum of USD 3,752,620, and assessed Mr. Katanga's total liability at USD 1 million. The chamber also found that each individual victim would be awarded USD 250 as symbolic individual compensation and four collective reparations to victims: (1) support for housing, (2) income-generating activities, (3) education aid, and (4) psychological rehabilitation.[55]

The Trial Chamber requested the TFV to complement the award for reparations, considering Mr. Katanga was found indigent. In May 2017, the TFV's Board of Directors decided to provide the full amount of the reparations ordered in the case, that is, USD 1 million, including the voluntary contribution of EUR 200,000 by the government of the Netherlands, which included earmarked funding for individual awards. In July 2017, the TFV submitted a draft implementation plan for individual and collective reparations, which was the result of consultations with the Legal Representatives of Victims, the defense counsel, and the authorities in Ituri and Kinshasa in the DRC.[56]

---

[53] See Redress, "No Time to Wait: Realising Reparations for Victims Before the International Criminal Court," 2019, available at https://redress.org/wp-content/uploads/2019/02/20190221-Reparations-Report-English.pdf.

[54] ICC, *The Prosecutor* v. *Germain Katanga*, Trial Chamber II, "Order for Reparations Pursuant to Article 75 of the Statute – With One Public Annex (Annex I) and One Confidential Annex ex parte, Common Legal Representative of the Victims, Office of Public Counsel for Victims and Defence Team for Germain Katanga (Annex II)," ICC-01/04-01/07-3728-tENG, 24 March 2017 (hereinafter: "Katanga Reparations Order").

[55] Ibid.

[56] ICC, "Trust Fund for Victims Submits Draft Implementation Plan for Reparations in the Katanga Case," Press Release, 26 July 2017, available at www.icc-cpi.int/drc/katanga.

The plan submitted by the TFV regards only the 297 victims identified by the Trial Chamber.

3.2.2.2 The Appeals Chamber Judgment Largely Confirming the Katanga Reparations Order

The defense counsel, the Office of Public Counsel for Victims and the Legal Representative of Victims appealed the Katanga order for reparations. In March 2018, the Appeals Chamber rendered its judgment largely upholding the order.[57] Concerning the amount of reparations for which the convicted person is liable, the Appeals Chamber held that it is in principle irrelevant whether there are other individuals that contributed to the harm. The chamber did however express concern for the efficiency of the Trial Chamber's approach with regard to reparations. The Appeals Chamber noted the complex individual assessments that had been conducted, even though in the end each victim was awarded USD 250, and it emphasized that reparation proceedings need to be expeditious and cost effective. Interestingly, regarding the amount awarded for individual reparation, the Appeals Chamber noted that "while the Trial Chamber awarded USD 250 to each victim in this case, this should not be viewed as a precedent or indication of quantum when it comes to the determination of awards in future cases."[58]

The Appeals Chamber also dealt with the definition of "victims." It clarified that under Article 75 of the Statute and Rule 85 of the Rules of Procedure and Evidence, familial relationship is not mentioned and thus evidence demonstrating the existence of familial relationship, on a balance of probabilities is sufficient to make an individual an "indirect victim" entitled to reparations for psychological harm.[59] This finding was related to the Trial Chamber's conclusion that an applicant who had lost a family member due to the attack for which Mr. Katanga was convicted did not have to prove psychological harm; rather, it was presumed that the nature of the relationship was such that psychological harm ensued from the loss.

The Appeals Chamber also dealt with another ground of appeal concerning "transgenerational psychological harm." Five applicants alleged that they had suffered harm as a result of their parents' experience during the attack. In this

---

[57] ICC, Appeals Chamber, *The Prosecutor* v. *Germain Katanga*, "Judgement on the Appeals Against the Order of Trial Chamber II of 24 March 2017 entitled 'Order for Reparations Pursuant to Article 75 of the Statute'," ICC-01/04-01/07-3778-Red, 8 March 2018 (hereinafter: "Katanga Appeals Judgment").

[58] Ibid., para. 149.

[59] Ibid., para. 116.

94   *Reparative Justice for International Crimes*

regard, the Appeals Chamber decided to remand the issue to the Trial Chamber since no reasons had been given for rejecting the claim.[60] The Trial Chamber later reconsidered the issue but decided that the causal link between the psychological harm claimed by the applicants and the crimes committed by Mr. Katanga was missing.[61]

3.2.3 The Prosecutor *v.* Ahmad Al Faqi Al Mahdi *Case: Individual, Collective, and Symbolic Reparations*

The case of *The Prosecutor* v. *Ahmad Al Faqi Al Mahdi* has been in many respects more straightforward than previous cases concerning reparations. It has, nevertheless, presented unique sets of issues stemming from the conflict in Mali and the types of crimes perpetrated. It was, as in previous cases, also a "first" in the history of the court's developing jurisprudence on reparations: the first time the court ordered reparations in relation to crimes committed against cultural heritage.

As way of background, in September 2016, Mr. Al Mahdi plead guilty and was sentenced to nine years' imprisonment as a coperpetrator of the war crime of attacking protected objects in 2012 (Article 8[2][e][iv] of the Rome Statute) including ten religious and historical buildings (nine were UNESCO World Heritage sites in Timbuktu, Mali). In August 2017, Trial Chamber VIII delivered its reparations order.[62]

3.2.3.1 The 2017 Trial Chamber's Order: Individual, Collective, and Symbolic Reparations

In total, there were 139 applications for reparations, including two from organizations. The Trial Chamber appointed four experts to assist in the determination of reparations. The Trial Chamber decided to award individual and collective reparations for the economic and moral harm suffered by the destruction of the cultural heritage. The chamber ordered: 1) individual reparations to victims whose livelihood "exclusively depended" on the cultural heritage buildings; 2) collective reparations for the economic loss of the whole community of Timbuktu; 3) collective reparations for the moral harm suffered by the Timbuktu community and Mali; and 4) compensation for individuals' moral harm whose ancestors' burial sites were damaged. It assessed the liability of

---

[60]   Ibid.

[61]   ICC, Press Release, "Trial Chamber II Dismisses the Reparations Applications for Transgenerational Harm," 19 July 2018.

[62]   ICC, Trial Chamber VIII, *The Prosecutor* v. *Ahmad Al Faqi Al Mahdi*, "Reparations Order," ICC-01/12-01/15-236, 17 August 2017 (hereinafter: "Al Mahdi Reparations Order").

Mr. Al Mahdi to EUR 2.7 million. Similarly to previous cases, Mr. Al Mahdi was found to be indigent so it fell upon the TFV to "complement" the reparations.[63] Significantly, Mr. Al Mahdi made an apology during the trial which was video recorded and made available on the court's website (in different languages).

The Trial Chamber set out the process for the implementation of reparations: first, was the assessment of reparations in the reparations order, then it would approve the draft implementation plan to be presented by the TFV to the chamber, and then it would render a decision on the approval of projects to be proposed by the TFV. It decided that reparations should be primarily collective and that individual reparations should be prioritized. This latter aspect seems at odds with the nature of the crimes committed (destructions of World Heritage Sites and cultural property), where the harm is suffered by individuals, but also the community, and humanity at large.

It also decided that the TFV would screen the individual victims potentially entitled to receive reparations, respecting the rights of victims and the convicted person. The chamber also included guarantees of nonrepetition of war crimes against protected cultural sites. Reparations were designed, to the extent possible, to "deter future violations," language previously used in the *Lubanga* case.[64]

The Trial Chamber's order was delivered while other cases were at the reparations stage, namely, the *Lubanga* and *Katanga* cases reviewed above. This case differed from previous ones in the type of crime for which the accused stood convicted – destruction of cultural heritage property – as well as the reparations ordered, both collective and individual, with a focus on prioritizing individual reparations. As seen during the appeals proceedings, the decision of the Trial Chambers regarding individual reparations was not without some controversies, in particular with regard to the definition of the category of individual recipients. The Appeals Chamber decided to disregard the new evidence filed by the legal representatives only on appeal (without leave to admit it as additional evidence), but noted that the TFV may consider it in its screening of individuals who satisfy the group defined by the Trial Chamber.[65]

3.2.3.2 The Appeals Chamber Judgment and Beyond

The Legal Representatives of Victims appealed the reparations order. The issues on appeal were twofold. First, whether the Trial Chamber had erred in

---

[63] Ibid. See also, James Hendry, "Reparations Principles in the Al Mahdi Appeal," *PKI Global Just J* 2 (2018), 10, available at www.kirschinstitute.ca/reparations-principles-al-mahdi-appeal/.

[64] Ibid.

[65] Ibid., para. 21.

deciding to limit individual reparations to those whose livelihood "exclusively depended" on the protected buildings. They argued in this regard that the category of victims defined by the Trial Chamber was unreasonably narrow. The Legal Representatives attempted to introduce new expert evidence before the Appeals Chamber to the effect that "the category of victims eligible for individual reparations for economic loss should be understood broadly and not restricted to the custodians of the mausoleum only, as evidence shows that the income generated by the mausoleums was then re-distributed by the guardians to the members of their extended family and even more broadly."[66] The second issue raised on appeal was whether the Trial Chamber had erred in delegating its "power of adjudication" to a nonjudicial entity like the TFV.

The Appeals Chamber largely confirmed the Trial Chamber's reparations order, save for two amendments to the latter. Regarding the first issue on appeal (the definition of the category of victims for purposes of individual reparations), the Appeals Chamber noted the Trial Chamber's broad discretion to make individual and collective (or both) reparations. The Appeals Chamber concluded that the Trial Chamber did not err in its determination of the category of victims entitled to reparations for economic loss.

In its judgment, the Appeals Chamber recalled its conclusion in the *Lubanga* case concerning the standard of proof in reparations proceedings and the recognition that victims may face difficulties in obtaining evidence to support their claim due to the destruction or unavailability of evidence. It noted that, when assessing potential victims' claims, the TFV will take into account the standard applied by the Trial Chamber and its assessment of the various factors specific to the case.[67]

Regarding the second issue on appeal, that is, whether the Trial Chamber had delegated its judicial powers to the (nonjudicial) TFV, the Appeals Chamber concluded that the Trial Chamber may rely on the TFV for the administrative screening of beneficiaries when it may be "impossible or impracticable to make individual awards directly," to enhance efficiency and effectiveness of the reparations process. While it found that the Trial Chamber did not err in this respect, it amended the reparations order to the effect that applicants for individual reparations can contest the decision by the TFV concerning their eligibility for reparations, and the Trial Chamber makes a final determination in this regard. The Appeals Chamber also

---

[66] ICC, Appeals Chambers, *The Prosecutor v. Ahmad Al Faqi Al Mahdi*, "Judgment on the Appeal of the Victims Against the 'Reparations Order'," ICC-01/12-01/15-259-Red2, 8 March 2018, para. 18 ("Al Mahdi Appeals Judgment").

[67] Ibid., paras. 33–43.

found that the Trial Chamber erred in deciding that Mr. Al Mahdi should be granted access to the individual applicant's identifying information, as a condition to have their applications for reparations assessed by the TFV. The Appeals Chamber amended the reparations order to allow the TFV to assess applications from applicants who did not wish to have their identifying information disclosed to Mr. Al Mahdi, but their identities will be disclosed to the TFV for screening purposes.[68]

The judgment of the Appeals Chamber is the third concerning reparations orders by a trial chamber of the court. In this case, the Appeals Chamber had the opportunity to further clarify the powers of Trial Chambers in deciding on reparations, and more specifically, concerning individual reparations. It also expanded on the respective roles of the TFV vis-à-vis the trial chambers in the reparation process, and permissible tasks that can be delegated to an administrative mechanism such as the TFV. This is a welcome development concerning the role of the TFV which is likely in a better position to screen applications, and confirmation of the oversight by the judicial organ, the trial chambers. Through its evolving jurisprudence the chambers are painting the contours of the reparations system at the ICC.

The Trial Chamber approved an updated implementation plan proposed by the TFV in April 2019. The plan spans over three years and covers three kinds of reparations: individual, collective, and symbolic. In addition to the EUR 2.7 million awarded by the Trial Chamber, the TFV has added EUR 1.35 million to the reparations plan in the case. Concerning the collective reparations, the plan includes the rehabilitation of windows, doors, enclosures of cemetery walls, planting of trees, and a fund is set up for the customary annual maintenance. The plan also includes approved projects such as the provision of assistance for victims to return to Timbuktu; a psychological support program; the creation of safe spaces for women and girls; and the creation of an Economic Resilience Facility to support economic initiatives proposed by members of the Timbuktu community. As for symbolic reparations, there will be a ceremony where EUR 1 will be given to the authorities in Mali and the United Nations Educational, Scientific and Cultural Organization (UNESCO) to acknowledge the harm suffered by the loss of cultural heritage. Concerning individual reparation, amounts given to individuals are redacted from public documents but the TFV explained that individual reparations are provided for

---

[68] Ibid., paras. 43 et seq.

98   *Reparative Justice for International Crimes*

economic and moral harm, the latter being calculated relying on the Malian Cultural Heritage Act.[69]

3.2.4 The Prosecutor *v.* Jean-Pierre Bemba *Case: The Unfortunate Reparations Outcome*

This case presented unique challenges and an unfortunate outcome concerning reparations for victims. It highlights the challenges of conditioning reparations to a criminal conviction. It also demonstrates the detrimental effects that the outcome of proceedings at the ICC can have on victims of atrocities, due to the judicial process in place.

This is the only case in the situation in the Central African Republic (CAR), rampaged by armed conflict since 2002, and one that has left victims with no right to reparations, after fifteen years waiting for the proceedings. In March 2016 Mr. Jean-Pierre Bemba was convicted under Article 28(a) of the Rome Statute as a military commander of crimes against humanity (murder and rape) and war crimes (murder, rape, and pillage). This case was the first dealing with sexual crimes and with a high number of victims participating in the case (5,229). Victims in this case were asking for individual awards as well as awareness-raising programs to mitigate stigmatization of victims, and they were concerned about state-run projects due to rampant corruption in the CAR.[70]

In June 2018, a majority (3–2) of the Appeals Chamber reversed the Trial Chamber's decision, acquitting Mr. Bemba of all charges.[71] Mr. Bemba was ordered to be released four days later. There are many important international criminal law issues in the Appeals Chamber judgment, however, a commentary of the legal grounds for the Appeals Chamber judgment is outside the scope of this book.[72] Suffice it to state at this juncture that, given the

---

[69]   ICC, Trial Chamber VIII, *The Prosecutor* v. *Ahmad Al Faqi Al Mahdi*, "Decision on the Updated Implementation Plan from the Trust Fund for Victims," ICC-01/12-01/15-324-Red, 4 March 2019.

[70]   International Federation for Human Rights, Report, "5,000 Victims of Bemba's Crimes in Central African Republic Anxiously Await Reparation," 20 November 2017, available at www .fidh.org/en/issues/international-justice/5-000-victims-of-bemba-s-crimes-in-central-african-re public-anxiously.

[71]   ICC, Appeals Chamber, *The Prosecutor* v. *Jean-Pierre Bemba*, Judgement on the Appeal of Mr. Jean-Pierre Bemba Gombo Against Trial Chamber III's "Judgment Pursuant to Article 74 of the Statute," ICC-01/05-01/08-3636-Red, 8 June 2018.

[72]   For a commentary of the Appeals Chamber Judgment, see e.g., Alex Whiting, "Appeals Judges Turn the ICC on its Head with Bemba Decision," *Just Security*, 14 June 2018; Leila Sadat, "Fiddling While Rome Burns? The Appeals Chamber's Curious Decision in Prosecutor v. Jean-Pierre Bemba Gombo," EJIL: *Talk!* 12 June 2018.

conviction-based reparation system at the ICC, the acquittal of Mr. Bemba meant that reparations proceedings, which had commenced prior to the Appeals Chamber judgment, had to stop.

Following the Appeals Chamber judgment, Trial Chamber III invited the defense, victims' legal representatives and the prosecution to make submissions on the reparations proceedings.[73] The defense counsel submitted that "[g]iven that there is no conviction, it follows that there can be no reparations."[74] The Prosecutor stated that the Appeals Chamber had acknowledged that Mr. Bemba's Movement for the Liberation of Congo (MLC) militia had committed crimes in the 2002–2003 CAR Operation and that victims may have other possibilities of redress, including civil remedies for victims under national law. The Prosecutor also noted that the TFV could still assist the victims.[75] The Legal Representatives of Victims, while acknowledging that "the Court does not foresee any civil procedure distinct from the criminal one, it nonetheless has the duty of doing its utmost not to re-traumatize victims who have been in contact with the Court." They proposed that the chamber "read jointly paragraphs 1 and 6 of Article 75, and to interpret them as giving it the power to issue an order establishing principles relating to reparations and determining the scope and extent of victimisation of the persons who have been in contact with the Court throughout this case." They further stated that "despite the Court's efforts, it is undeniable today that victims were not given access to the justice they deserve."[76]

Following the observations of the parties and participants, the Trial Chamber issued its "Final decision on the reparations proceedings" in August 2018. The chamber held that in light of a reversal of the conviction of Mr. Bemba, under the system established by the ICC, no reparation could be ordered. In doing so, the chamber fully acknowledged the victims of the crimes committed in the CAR during 2002–2003. The chamber also appreciated the efforts during the reparations phase of the proceedings, where *amici curiae* made submissions and four experts were appointed. The

---

[73] ICC, Trial Chamber III, *The Prosecutor* v. *Jean-Pierre Bemba*, "Order Inviting Submissions Following the Appeals Decision," ICC-01/05-01/08-3639, 13 June 2018.

[74] ICC, Trial Chamber III, *The Prosecutor* v. *Jean-Pierre Bemba*, "Mr. Bemba's Response to the 'Order Inviting Submissions Following the Appeals Decision'," ICC-01/05-01/08-3645, 6 July 2018, para. 6.

[75] ICC, Trial Chamber III, *The Prosecutor* v. *Jean-Pierre Bemba*, "Prosecution's Submissions on the Reparations Proceedings Before Trial Chamber III," ICC-01/05-01/08-3646, 6 July 2018.

[76] ICC, Trial Chamber III, *The Prosecutor* v. *Jean-Pierre Bemba*, "Legal Representatives of Victims' Joint Submissions on the Consequences of the Appeals Chamber's Judgment dated 8 June 2018 on the Reparations Proceedings," ICC-01/05-01/08-3649, 12 July 2018.

100 Reparative Justice for International Crimes

chamber concluded that it would be "inappropriate" to issue principles on reparations.[77]

The TFV thus announced its "decision to accelerate the launch of a program under its assistance mandate for the benefit of victims and their families in the situation of the Central African Republic ('CAR I')." The Board of Directors of the TFV stated in this regard that:

> Activities undertaken under the Fund's assistance mandate are distinct from the judicial proceedings of the Court and do not require the conviction or even the identification of the perpetrator(s) of the harms suffered by victims. It is necessary that victims have suffered harms from crimes under the jurisdiction of the Court as defined by the "situation" under investigation by the Prosecutor. In taking its decision, the Board observed that, irrespective of the outcome of the judicial proceedings, victims who presented themselves to the Court in the context of the Bemba case are, by definition, victims of the "situation" in CAR I.[78]

The TFV's decision to accelerate the assistance program was a welcome development in the middle of the turmoil caused by the Appeals Chamber majority judgment and its consequence for victims. It does however highlight the shortcomings of a system of reparations that is conditional to a finding of conviction, especially when it is undisputed that horrific international crimes were committed (in this case by Mr. Bemba's forces).

3.2.5 A Reparative Dimension in Terminated Cases?

Another development with regard to reparations that is worth mentioning is the case against Kenya's Deputy President William Ruto and former journalist Joshua Arap Sang.[79] In light of the termination of the case against the accused (charges were vacated against the accused), the Trial Chamber was asked whether the state of Kenya had an obligation to give reparation to post-election violence victims and whether the TFV had an obligation to provide assistance to victims.[80] The court decided by majority (2–1) that it was not the right forum to rule on the reparation requested given that the case against the accused was

---

[77] ICC, Trial Chamber III, *The Prosecutor v. Jean-Pierre Bemba*, "Final Decision on the Reparations Proceedings," ICC-01/05-01/08-3653, 3 August 2018.

[78] ICC, *The Prosecutor v. Jean-Pierre Bemba*, "Communication from the Chair of the Board of Directors of the TFV to the President of the Assembly of States Parties," 13 June 2018.

[79] ICC, *The Prosecutor v. William Samoei Ruto and Joshua Arap Sang*, ICC-01/09-01/11 ("*Ruto and Sang* case").

[80] ICC, *The Prosecutor v. William Samoei Ruto and Joshua Arap Sang*, "Decision on the Requests Regarding Reparations," ICC-01/09-01/11-2038, 1 July 2016.

terminated.[81] In a Dissenting Opinion appended to this Decision, Judge Eboe-Osuji discussed at length the reparation mandate of the court and stated: "To conflate considerations of punitive justice with those of reparative justice – and say that this Court cannot entertain questions about reparation for victims when a case against the accused has been terminated – will create more confusion and anxiety about the administration of justice in this Court."[82] Judge Eboe-Osuji also added an important point regarding the role of the ICC and the role of states with regard to reparations:

> There is a critical need to recall here that the role of the ICC as an instrument of justice – including reparative justice – is only complementary. In that regard, the ICC can only be a court of last resort. The primary responsibility for the administration of justice remains with the States – also possibly augmented by other complementary regional arrangements that do not in any way jeopardise the role of the ICC as a court of last resort.
>
> That being the case, the existence of the ICC should not result in a situation in which national Governments may feel free to abdicate their responsibility to attend to the needs of justice for their own citizens. This is particularly the case as regards the responsibility for reparative justice, where the concerned Government had failed in the first place to prevent the harm that so engaged the need for reparative justice.[83]

Importantly, Judge Chile Eboe-Osuji questioned whether reparations at the ICC were necessarily conditional on the conviction of the accused person(s):

> [...] I see no convincing basis in law for the idea that an ICC Trial Chamber may not entertain questions of reparation merely because the accused they tried was not found guilty. The reasoning is [...] inimical to the 'dictates of fundamental justice [...] In my view, such formalistic approach could never supply a convincing system of reasoning that prevents an ICC Trial Chamber from entertaining questions of reparation in the absence of conviction. And this is especially so in a case, as the Ruto and Sang trial, in which there was never a question that the victims suffered harm – to the contrary, all the parties and the Government of Kenya had accepted that the victims had suffered harm.
>
> Indeed, there is a solid basis in international law to reject the no compensation without conviction thesis. International and transnational norms concerning criminal injuries compensation have completely rejected the idea. [...][84]

---

[81]   Ibid.
[82]   Ibid., Dissenting Opinion of Judge Chile Eboe-Osuji, p. 8.
[83]   Ibid., p. 9.
[84]   Ibid., p. 4.

102   *Reparative Justice for International Crimes*

In sum, while the first case of reparations before the ICC (the *Lubanga* case) clarified many questions and will pave the way for future developments, there remains many layers of complexities that are yet to be unraveled. In a very recent example, the points raised by the majority and Dissenting Opinion in the *Ruto* and *Sang* case demonstrate that there are many important questions that surround reparation proceedings at the ICC. One important issue that remains is the question surrounding the connection between the conviction of the accused person(s) and the ability of the court to pronounce on reparations. From the above discussion it is clear that the reparative dimension of international criminal justice before the ICC is still in the process of formation.

3.3 ASSESSING THE CASE LAW ON REPARATIONS TO DATE: INCONSISTENCIES, DELAYS, AND THE NEED FOR CHANGE

With four cases having reached the stage of reparations to date (with the exception of one case where reparations proceedings were discontinued after the acquittal of Mr. Bemba on appeal), the time is ripe to assess how reparations have developed from theory to practice at the ICC, and what challenges the court faces to deliver on its promise of reparative justice for victims.

This section aims to contribute to this debate by first overviewing some of the key aspects developed in the recent, yet foundational, jurisprudence of the court, the wrangles that the cases have brought to light, and some of the critical questions that have now become apparent as the court moves forward in its reparation mandate. The section proceeds as follows. First, it overviews the main characteristics of the reparation system at the ICC. It then discusses the recent case law, highlighting the main findings of different chambers of the court. Finally, it engages in a discussion of some of the important issues that have emerged from the jurisprudence.

3.3.1 *Key Features of the Reparations System at the ICC*

Before the first case reached the stage of reparations at the ICC, it was difficult to predict how the many difficult questions surrounding reparations, such as the definition of beneficiaries, the financing of reparations, the types of reparation, causation, would be resolved. The Rome Statute only set out the blueprint for reparations in Article 75, but until the first case, the court had not established principles of reparation. Against this background, an overview of the contours of the reparations system established by the court seems appropriate. The focus here will be on some key aspects dealt with by the decisions of different chambers, which highlight the difficulties and inconsistencies of realizing reparative justice at the ICC.

3.3.1.1 Defining Beneficiaries of Reparations: Beyond "Direct Victims"

Under the ICC reparation system, an individual must qualify as a victim in order to be entitled to claim reparations under the ICC scheme. According to Rule 85 of the ICC Rules of Procedure and Evidence,[85] victims are "natural persons who have suffered harm as a result of the commission of any crime within the jurisdiction of the Court." Victims may also include legal persons, such as organizations or institutions.

This Rule was interpreted by the Pre-Trial Chamber I in the Situation in the Democratic Republic of Congo[86] whereby the chamber established the criteria for determining whether individual applicants meet the definition of a victim in relation to natural persons. The four-part test developed by Pre-Trial Chamber I has been subsequently followed by other chambers and confirmed on appeal.[87] The test to identify whether an applicant could be considered a

---

[85] See, e.g., jurisprudence in relation to the definition of "victims" pursuant to Rule 85 of the Rules of Procedure and Evidence, in the context of application for victim participation, in the situation, pre-trial, and trial phases: "Decision on the Applications for Participation in the Proceedings of VPRS1, VPRS2, VPRS3, VPRS4, VPRS5, and VPRS6," 17 January 2006, ICC-01-04-101-t-ENG-Corr, para. 65 (situation phase); "Decision on Applications for Participation in Proceedings a/0004/06 to a/0009/06, a/0016/06, a/0063/06, a/0071/06 to a/0080/06 and a/0105/06," in the case of *The Prosecutor* v. *Thomas Lubanga Dyilo*, 20 October 2006, ICC-01-04-01/06-601; "Decision on the Applications for Participation in the Proceedings of Applicants a/0327/07 to a/00337/07 and a/0001/08," 2 April 2008, ICC-01/04-01/07-357; "Decision on Victims' Application for Participation a/0010/06, a/0064/06 to a/0070/06, a/0081/06, a/0082/06, a/0084/06 to a/0089/06, a/0091/06 to a/0097/06, a/0099/06, a/0100/06, a/0102/06 to a/0104/06, a/0111/06, a/0113/06 to a/0117/06, a/0120/06, a/0121/06 and a/0123/06 to a/0127/06," in the case of *The Prosecutor* v. *Joseph Kony, Vincent Otti, Okot Odhiambo, Dominic Ongwen*, 14 March 2008, ICC-02/04-01/05-282 (pre-trial phase); and "Decision on Victims' Participation," in the case of *The Prosecutor* v. *Thomas Lubanga Dyilo*, 18 January 2008, ICC-01/04-01/06-1119 (trial phase), cited in Carla Ferstman and Mariana Goetz, "Reparations before the International Criminal Court: The Early Jurisprudence on Victim Participation and its Impact on Future Reparations Proceedings," in *Reparations for Victims of Genocide, War Crimes and Crimes Against Humanity, Systems in Place and Systems in the Making*, eds. Carla Ferstman et al., Nijhoff, 2009, pp. 313 et seq.

[86] ICC, *Situation in the Democratic Republic of Congo*, "Decision on the Application for Participation in the Proceedings of VPRS1, VPRS2, VPRS3, VPRS4, VPRS5 and VPRS6," 17 January 2006, ICC-01/04-101-t-EN-Corr, para. 9.

[87] ICC, *The Prosecutor* v. *Thomas Lubanga*, "Judgment on the Appeals of the Prosecutor and The Defence Against Trial Chamber I's Decision on Victims' Participation," 18 January 2008, ICC-01/04-01/06-1432.

victim under Rule 85 of the Rules of Procedure and Evidence is based on the following:

(i) whether the identity of a natural person or legal person can be established;
(ii) whether the applicants claim to have suffered harm;
(iii) whether a crime within the jurisdiction of the Court can be established; and
(iv) whether harm was caused "as a result" of the event constituting the crime within the jurisdiction of the Court."[88]

Victim participation[89] is distinct from victim reparations within the ICC context. While this book does not deal with the details of victim participation at the ICC, it is relevant to dedicate a brief discussion to this topic.

While victim participation can happen throughout the various stages of the proceedings, reparations necessarily take place only at the end of a trial, if there is a conviction. The Appeals Chamber judgment in *Lubanga* clarified that, for purpose of reparations, victims should be treated equally and fairly "irrespective of whether they participated in the trial proceedings."[90]

Beyond the notion of a "victim" under Rule 85, in reparations proceedings, the beneficiaries that may be eligible to claim reparations is a crucial question that has been progressively defined by the court's jurisprudence. At the heart of the question of the beneficiaries of reparations is the issue of direct and indirect victims. The first decision of the court concerning reparations, the 2012 Reparations Decision in *Lubanga*, concluded that both direct victims and indirect victims, including family members of direct victims, could be beneficiaries of reparations. Legal entities under Rule 85(b) may also be entitled to reparations, as well as "anyone who attempted to prevent the commission of one or more of the crimes under consideration; and those who suffered personal harm as a result of these offences, regardless of whether they participated in the trial proceedings."[91] The Trial Chamber further held that to

---

[88] ICC, *Situation in the Democratic Republic of Congo*, "Decision on the Application for Participation in the Proceedings of VPRS1, VPRS2, VPRS3, VPRS4, VPRS5, and VPRS6," 17 January 2006, ICC-01/04-101-t-ENG-Crr, para. 79.

[89] Victim participation is outside the scope of this book. For studies of victim participation before the ICC, see Luke Moffett, "Meaningful and Effective? Considering Victims' Interests Through Participation at the International Criminal Court," *Queen's University Belfast School of Law, Research Paper* 2016–03; Sergey Vasiliev, "Article 68(3) and Personal Interests of Victims in the Emerging Practice of the ICC," in *The Emerging Practice of the International Criminal Court*, eds. Carsten Stahn and Göran Sluiter, Brill, 2008, pp. 635–690; Sergey Vasiliev, "Victim Participation Revisited: What the ICC Is Learning About Itself," in *The Law and Practice of the International Criminal Court*, ed. Carsten Stahn, Oxford University Press, 2015.

[90] 2015 Appeals Judgment, para. 12.

[91] 2012 Decision on Reparations, para. 194.

determine whether an indirect victim should be included in the reparations, "the Court should determine whether there was a close personal relationship between the indirect and direct victim." Indirect victims may also include those who suffered harm as a result of helping or intervening to help victims.[92]

Importantly, the concept of "family" has diverse cultural meaning in different communities and the court has interpreted the concept flexibly and has taken cultural and social structures into account.[93] The Appeals Chamber also had to pronounce on the question of the definition of "family" within the context of ICC reparations proceedings. In the *Katanga* case, the Defense had submitted that the Trial Chamber's definition of "family" was too far-reaching as it went beyond the nuclear family and included grandparents and grandchildren. The Appeals Chamber clarified that "family members" should be understood in a broad sense, including all persons linked by a close relationship with the direct victim. It also held that individuals can claim reparations for psychological harm suffered as a result of the loss of a family member.[94]

It is a welcome development that the court has adopted a broad approach to indirect victims and has shown cultural awareness when assessing the meaning of "family," by taking into account social and familial structures. This is a development in line with the jurisprudence of human rights courts and that follows the principle of nondiscrimination of victims.[95]

3.3.1.2 Identifying Beneficiaries and Accessing Reparations: The Ones Left Behind

A question related to the ICC's conception of those who can be eligible to claim reparation is the identification of beneficiaries of reparations, and how victims can access reparations.[96] While the definition of beneficiaries of reparations has proven by and large a positive development overall in the court's recent jurisprudence, given the broad conceptualization of "victims" for purposes of reparations, identifying beneficiaries and accessing reparations

---

[92] Ibid., paras. 195–197.

[93] Ibid., para. 195.

[94] Katanga Appeals Judgment, paras. 113–121.

[95] See IACtHR, *Case of Aloeboetoe et al. v. Suriname*, Reparations and Costs, Judgment of 10 September 1993, para. 62; IACtHR, *Case of Velasquez Rodriguez v. Honduras*, Reparations and costs. Judgment of 21 July 1989, para. 13, cited by Trial Chamber I, 2012 Decision on Reparations, para. 195.

[96] For a discussion of this theme, see Redress, "No Time to Wait: Realising Reparations for Victims Before the International Criminal Court," 2019, pp. 38–41, available at https://redress .org/wp-content/uploads/2019/02/20190221-Reparations-Report-English.pdf.

106 *Reparative Justice for International Crimes*

has proven to be a cumbersome, inconsistent exercise for the court, and frustrating for victims.

The processes in place for identifying beneficiaries and for victims to access reparations as it is currently applied in the court contributes to further delays in realizing reparations for victims. To date, the different chambers in the cases having reached the reparations stage developed two approaches to identifying victims. The first is through an individual application procedure. In this way, victims may request reparations by completing an application in writing which should include information such as: the applicant's identity, description of injury or harm suffered, location and date of the incident and person believed to be responsible for the harm, if possible, a description of the injury, among others (Rule 94 of the RPE).

The Victims Participation and Reparations Section in the Registry receives the applications and collects missing information. This process involves engaging with a representative of the court, which may create expectations of receiving reparations. Additionally, identifying victims in this manner, as it has been reported

> has benefits as well as potential drawbacks for victims. In some cases, the process of submitting a reparations' request itself may be empowering; however, the process can also potentially be very distressing, particularly in cases involving crimes of sexual violence. Victims are often unable to furnish proof of the harm they have suffered – evidence may have been destroyed or lost in the years that have elapsed since the crimes were committed. Likewise, on-going conflict, corruption, absence of government services, prohibitive costs, displacement or customary practices may also make it difficult to obtain documentation.[97]

A reparation process that involves applications by victims should ensure that affected communities are aware of the process so that potential victims are not excluded from reparations simply due to the fact they do not know that an application is required or because the application process requires evidence or information that they are unable to provide.

A second way in which victims can be identified and access reparations, under the framework developed in the ICC case law to date, is through a procedure of identification of beneficiaries done by the court, where the chamber invites the Registry, the TFV or the Office of Public Counsel for Victims (OPCV) to identify and screen other potential victim beneficiaries.

The availability of both forms of identification of victims that could benefit from reparations makes the outcome of reparations inconsistent from one case

---

[97] Ibid., p. 38.

to the next. While the court arguably has the flexibility to decide which approach to adopt for deciding the beneficiaries of reparations, a lack of uniformity causes uncertainty for victims and lack of predictability of proceedings. While flexibility is not a bad endeavor when it comes to reparations, the development of clear guidelines and predictability would favor following a singular approach in identifying beneficiaries. The jurisprudence to date has used divergent approaches without much support for using different ways to identify beneficiaries. The three cases where reparations have been awarded demonstrate the complete lack of consistency in this regard. In *Lubanga*, Trial Chamber I followed a combination of the two approaches, where it assessed the 473 applications received (and deemed that 425 applications met the requirements), and allowed other potential beneficiaries to be identified during the implementation phase. In contrast, in *Katanga*, the Trial Chamber decided to examine all the applications received itself, and no further beneficiaries could be added to the reparations at the implementation phase. Finally, the *Al Mahdi* case depicted yet another approach: the Trial Chamber decided that the TFV should screen potential beneficiaries and made sure that victims could be recognized in the implementation phase.

Considering the paramount question of expediency surrounding reparations, it would appear that the identification of beneficiaries should be left for the TFV, with support from the Registry where applicable, in order to move the reparations proceedings forward and issue a reparations order. Such an approach would provide consistency and would leave the task with the TFV, which may have a more extensive knowledge of the potential beneficiaries given its work with affected victims and communities. The chamber can establish in its order for reparations the criteria to be used to identify potential beneficiaries and overview the screening process of the TFV. Under Rule 98 (2) of the RPE, the court may order a reparations award be deposited with the TFV when at the time of the order it is "impossible or impracticable to make individual awards directly to victims."

Consistency in the approach would provide a clear message to victims and would avoid retraumatization of victims who are unsure of the process and may not trust it due to its divergent application.

A process used for identification of beneficiaries has to take into account the known as well as the unknown victims (who may be potential beneficiaries). In other words, the court shall be flexible in its approach so that victims that are unknown to the court at a given point (e.g., during the reparation proceedings) can come forward and access reparations when reparations are being implemented. In this regard, an outreach effort is of utmost importance to minimize the potential of victims being left out of reparations because they are

108   *Reparative Justice for International Crimes*

"unknown" to the court. As discussed below, as it stands, given the link to the criminal process, the court's reparation system has the effect of excluding numerous victims from accessing reparations. The identification of victims of crimes for which an accused stood convicted should not operate in a way to exclude potential beneficiaries.

3.3.1.3 Determining Harm and Causation: The Door to Reparations

Once a conviction is entered, the Trial Chamber has to start the reparation process and define the harm that victims have suffered and the amount of liability of the convicted person. The court has defined "harm" as "hurt, injury or damage," which can be material, physical, or psychological and must be personal to the victims (although not necessarily direct).[98] The definition of harm shall be included in the reparations order, but the monetary evaluation of the harm suffered can be made by the TFV (following the criteria set out by the reparations order, or by the Trial Chamber itself, or with the assistance of experts).[99] When at issue are mass atrocities, the loss of lives, of loved ones, dignity, sense of belonging, the harm is enormous, and hard to define.

The question of causation is crucial in the determination of reparation. There needs to be a link between the crime for which a person is convicted and the harm for which a victim is claiming reparations, and this causal link is determined on the basis of the specificities of a case. A standard of proof on the basis of a "balance of probabilities" is appropriate for reparations proceedings.[100] The Appeals Chamber made clear the causal link and standard of proof required in reparations proceedings:

> In the reparation proceedings, the applicant shall provide sufficient proof of the causal link between the crime and the harm suffered, based on the specific circumstances of the case. In this sense, what is the "appropriate" standard of proof and what is "sufficient" for purposes of an applicant meeting the burden of proof will depend upon the circumstances of the specific case. For purposes of determining what is sufficient, Trial Chambers should take into account any difficulties that are present from the circumstances of the case at hand.[101]

The question of causation was at the heart of the discussion regarding transgenerational harm in the *Katanga* case. In fact, as discussed above, the

---

[98]   2012 Reparations Decision, para. 228; 2015 Appeals Judgment on Reparations (Amended Order), para. 10.

[99]   2015 Appeals Judgment on Reparations, paras. 181–184.

[100]   Ibid., para. 83.

[101]   Ibid., para. 81.

victims in that case wanted to claim reparations for transgenerational harm they had suffered as a result of the harm their parents went through as a result of the attack for which Mr. Katanga was convicted. In reconsidering the matter, the Trial Chamber then decided that the applicants had not proven the causal link between the psychological harm they suffered and the crimes for which Mr. Katanga had been convicted.[102]

While there was reason to be optimistic with the conclusions on the causal link and standard of proof required in reparations proceedings, which seemed to acknowledge the difficulties of victims to obtain evidence, and recognized the differences between criminal and reparations proceedings, the decision regarding transgenerational harm was a missed opportunity. The Trial Chamber could have adopted an approach more victim-centered and relied on scientific studies on the transgenerational transmission of harm. Instead, the approach adopted was rigid concerning a type of harm (psychological suffering) that is complex to prove by material evidence. The chamber had the opportunity here to recognize a type of harm beyond that of direct victims.

The requirement of a causal link between the harm suffered and the crimes for which the accused stood convicted also resulted in the exclusion of victims of sexual and gender-based violence from reparations, despite the clear evidence that these crimes occurred. Thus, for purpose of reparations, the harm suffered is limited to those offences for which there has been a conviction, and not for all offences that occurred or for which the accused was indicted. In the *Lubanga* case, the Appeals Chamber did not consider sexual and gender-based crimes for purpose of reparations since the accused was not convicted for those crimes.[103]

3.3.1.4 Liability and the Challenge of Funding Reparations Awards

The court's jurisprudence has made it clear that the convicted person is liable for the reparations due for crimes for which they were convicted.[104] The convicted person's indigence is irrelevant for the assessment of their liability for reparations. The more controversial issues are not who is liable for reparations, but rather how this liability is assessed and how reparations are funded in practice. To date, different approaches have been followed in all cases.

---

[102] ICC, Trial Chamber II, "Decision on the Matter of the Transgenerational Harm Alleged by Some Applicants for Reparations Remanded by the Appeals Chamber in its Judgment of 8 March 2018," ICC-01/04-01/07-3804-Red-tENG, 19 July 2018. The public version is extensively redacted.

[103] 2015 Appeals Judgment on Reparations, para. 196.

[104] Ibid., para. 99.

The Appeals Chamber established that "a convicted person's liability for reparations must be proportionate to the harm caused and, *inter alia*, his or her participation in the commission of the crime for which he or she was found guilty, in the specific circumstances of the case."[105] Nevertheless, the methodology for the assessment of liability of the convicted person to date has been inconsistent and consequently unclear.[106] In the first reparations case, *Lubanga*, the reparations order was issued in 2012, and seven years later, in 2019, the question of the calculation of the convicted person's liability was still not settled.[107] The 2012 reparations order in the case did not assess the liability of the convicted person, and only in 2017 did the Trial Chamber calculate the liability of the convicted person at USD 10 million, an amount much higher than other cases, and which was calculated on the basis of the "average harm" suffered by the victims. Unsurprisingly the decision was subject to appeal. The Appeals Chamber then confirmed in July 2019, among other issues, the decision of the Trial Chamber concerning the liability of Mr. Lubanga.[108]

A different approach was used in the *Katanga* case. The Trial Chamber assessed, without the assistance of experts, the liability of the convicted person by identifying the numbers of victims having suffered harm and the totality of the harm suffered, and set the liability at USD 1 million, including individual and collective awards. In the *Al Mahdi* case, the Trial Chamber assessed his liability at EUR 2.7 million. The chamber used expert reports to "reasonably approximate" the costs of the harm, and delegated to the TFV the identification of victims.

While flexibility is natural to allow for the specificities of each case to be taken into account, the different approaches taken by chambers in the cases to date have caused delays and uncertainties in the process. Without clear guidance as to how monetary liability is calculated, all those involved in the procedure are left in the dark on how to prepare for proceedings. The inconsistency in approaches may also raise issues concerning the rights of the convicted persons and the rights of victims to adequate and prompt reparations. This is an area where a consistent approach to the calculation of monetary liability would enhance the process, by making it more efficient and transparent for all

---

[105] 2015 Appeals Judgement on Reparations, para. 18.

[106] See e.g., Marissa Brodney and Meritxell Regué, "Formal, Functional, and Intermediate Approaches to Reparations Liability: Situating the ICC's 15 December 2017 Lubanga Reparations Decision," *EJIL Talk!*, 4 January 2018.

[107] See discussion above.

[108] ICC, Appeals Chamber, "Judgment on the Appeals Against Trial Chamber II's 'Decision Setting the Size of the Reparations Award for Which Thomas Lubanga Dyilo Is Liable'," ICC-01/04-01/06-3466-Red, 18 July 2019.

stakeholders. This is a crucial question for the development of the reparations system at the ICC and one that further clarity is needed.

A related issue is the funding of reparations awards. Given that all convicted persons to date have been found indigent, the TFV has been called upon to fund the reparations awards. This is likely to remain unchanged in future cases, as even when an accused has assets when transferred to the court's custody, it is possible that such assets will be used for defense costs or will not be available after long proceedings leading to reparations. The TFV is likely to have to engage in further fundraising to sustain its reparations mandate. The funds of the TFV are limited and its capacity is also strained, given its many responsibilities (e.g., responding to filings, preparing implementation plans, outreach, assistance programs, etc.). Fundraising will likely be a major task for the TFV as its future operations will depend on it.[109] In this regard, raising awareness about the TFV's activities and diversifying donors can provide a positive way forward. Increased efforts in locating and freezing assets of convicted persons, as for example, by securing the assistance of states in the process. Furthermore, engaging states where the crimes have occurred in the reparations process will also be of utmost importance.

The role of the TFV in realizing reparative justice at the ICC is central; its potential to inspire and inform other administrative mechanisms for reparations in the aftermath of mass victimization has not been fully explored. Given its position in the reparation process, Chapter 4 overviews the TFV's mandate and activities.

3.3.2 *Tackling the Difficult Dilemmas: Reconciling Reparations Before the ICC with Conflicting Perspectives and Paradigms*

3.3.2.1 The Collective Versus the Individual: Between Victims' Requests and Court Orders

Under the terms of Rule 97 of the ICC Rules of Procedure and Evidence, the court may award reparations on an individualized basis, or where it deems it appropriate, on a collective basis, or both. Trial Chamber I in the *Lubanga* case recognized that reparations can be made both on an individual and collective basis.[110]

According to the Rules of the Court, collective awards of reparation are channeled through the TFV.[111] The TFV's job is to "set out the precise nature

---

[109]   For sources of funding, see *Regulations of the Trust Fund*, Article 21.
[110]   Decision on Reparations, paras. 217–221.
[111]   See Article 79 of the ICC Statute.

of the collective award(s), where not already specified by the Court, as well as the methods for its/their implementation."[112] It is worth noting, however, that the assessment by the Fund must be approved by the court.

In the context of mass international crimes, collective reparations[113] can play an important role in providing redress which seeks to address the collective nature of the crimes that come before the ICC. In all three reparations cases before the court, collective awards have been ordered (whether combined or not with individual awards).

A study conducted in 2015 by researchers from the Human Rights Center at the University of California, Berkeley School of Law, surveyed the attitude victims held towards individual awards. The center interviewed 622 victim participants at the ICC concerning the participation regime at the ICC. The study concluded that the participation regime needed to be reformed, but beyond that, it came to some interesting conclusions on reparations. In particular, it posited that:

> Victim participants joined ICC cases with the expectation that they would receive reparations. In Uganda and DRC, the prospect of receiving reparations was the primary motivation for the overwhelming majority of victim participants; in Kenya and Côte d'Ivoire, less than half reported that receiving reparations was their main objective. Nearly all respondents, however, reported an interest in individualized reparations for themselves and others. Their conceptions of reparations were frequently interwoven with local conceptions of justice.[114]

---

[112] Regulation 69 of the Trust Fund Regulations.

[113] For studies on collective reparations in the context of mass violations of human rights or international humanitarian law, see Friedrich Rosenfeld, "Collective Reparation for Victims of Armed Conflict," *International Review of the Red Cross* 92 (2010), pp. 731–746; see also Heidy Rombouts, *Victim Organizations and the Politics of Reparation: A Case-Study on Rwanda*, Intersentia, 2004, p. 34.

[114] Human Rights Center, University of California, Berkeley School of Law, "The Victims' Court: A Study of 622 Victim Participants at the International Criminal Court," p. 3, available at https://law.berkeley.edu/wp-content/uploads/2015/04/VP_report_2015_final_full2.pdf. The Human Rights Center interviewed ICC victim participants, in four countries where the ICC had started investigations and prosecutions: Uganda, Democratic Republic of Congo, Kenya, and Côte d'Ivoire. Individuals interviewed were either registered as victim participants or had submitted applications for consideration as victim participants. Some of the questions addressed were:

> What motivated these men and women to become victim participants? Was it to tell their story and to have it acknowledged by the court? Did they wish to see the accused punished? Or was it more important to receive reparations for the harms they suffered? What did they think of the process of becoming a victim participant? What were their perceptions of the court and how it operated? How were their interactions with court staff? And did they have security or safety concerns?

Similarly, a 2013 study on victims' rights before the ICC reported that: "As the damage to participating victims is individual, victims do not understand collective reparations and feel that individual reparations would better fulfil their expectations."[115]

A key practical advantage of collective reparations is that they can help maximize the reach of the limited resources to provide reparations to victims. In fact, many of the crimes which come before the ICC include an element of mass victimization. This in turn could potentially lead to a situation where victims may have to be triaged for reparation purposes. On the one hand, in the context of international crimes where mass atrocities are committed, individual reparations may not be the most appropriate form of redress, because by their nature, individual reparations may exclude a large number of victims of a certain crime,[116] or it may only be possible to provide a minimal, symbolic award to each individual victim, as was the case in *Katanga*, discussed above. Individual compensation may, in some instances, fail to enable victims to access services they need, if for example, those services (e.g., housing assistance) are not available in their community to repair their harm.

Another advantage of collective reparations arises out of the particular form of reparation being awarded. Collective awards may be symbolic, which in turn, may provide a measure of "moral reparation" to victims.[117] Collective reparations may also be viewed from an ontological lens. As Frédéric Mégret argues,

> the opposition between individuals and groups is also partially artificial: international crimes target the "groupness" that is in the individual, and the individual that is in the group. More than trying to offer reparation to groups and/or individuals as such, one may wonder whether a truly groundbreaking

---

[115] FIDH, "Enhancing Victims' Rights Before the ICC: A View from Situation Countries on Victims' Rights at the International Criminal Court," November 2013, pp. 27–28, available at https://fidh.org/IMG/pdf/fidh_victimsrights_621a_nov2013_ld.pdf. The Report addressed various issues relating to victims before the ICC, including reparations. FIDH selected a "group of 11 men and women, experts and representatives from local civil society from situation countries that have worked with victims of Rome Statute crimes in the field and/or have interacted with the ICC staff or have good knowledge of the Court. They came from Democratic Republic Congo (DRC), Kenya, Mali, Côte d'Ivoire, Sudan and Central African Republic".

[116] See in this regard, Naomi Roht-Arriaza "Reparations, Decisions, and Dilemmas," *Hastings International and Comparative Law Review* 27 (2004), pp. 157–219.

[117] Birte Timm, "The Legal Position of Victims in the Rule of Procedure and Evidence," in *International and National Prosecution of Crimes Under International Law*, eds. Horst Fischer et al., Arno Spitz, 2001, pp. 289 et seq., p. 304, cited in Eva Dwertmann, *The Reparation System of the International Criminal Court: Its Implementation, Possibilities and Limitations*, Nijhoff, 2010, p. 123.

theory of reparations would not try to direct itself less at mending the subjects – individual or collective – than the relations that exist between them and the rest of society. In the end, it seems, what is broken and torn apart by international crimes is not only the integrity of individuals or groups taken in isolation, as much as their place in the world and the ties that bind them. In that respect, however, looking at groups, the place of individuals within them, and the place of the group within society, is already in itself a way of focusing attention on the relational aspects of reparations.[118]

Often international crimes are not aimed at a specific individual but rather at a community, or a group of individuals. In fact, often the crime is perpetrated against individuals due to the fact that they belong to a particular group.[119] Collective reparations can potentially offer a means of redress to a large number of victims, while acknowledging their suffering and losses. Collective reparations may "address the harm the victims suffered on an individual and collective basis."[120] Collective reparations also provide a means to connect with victims.[121]

Reparation awards should be distinguished from general or humanitarian aid and shall take into account the harm suffered by victims, when the award is crafted. An obvious consideration when adjudicating and awarding reparations pertains to the nature of international crimes versus the capabilities of the institutions of international criminal justice, in particular the ICC, to fulfill its reparations mandate. This stands at the heart of the tension between individual and collective reparation.

Turning to specific examples of how individual and collective awards are reconciled in practice, victims in the *Lubanga* case requested both individual and collective reparations. Victims, their representatives, and various victim groups, advocated that reparations should take into account the needs of

---

[118] Frédéric Mégret, "The Case for Collective Reparations Before the ICC," in *Reparation for Victims of Crimes Against Humanity, ed.* Jo-Anne Wemmers, Routledge, 2014.

[119] Raphael Lemkin, "Genocide as a Crime Under International Law," *American Journal of International Law* 41 (1947), pp. 145–151, cited in Eva Dwertmann, *The Reparation System of the International Criminal Court: Its Implementation, Possibilities and Limitations*, Nijhoff, 2010, p. 122.

[120] Decision on Reparations, para. 221.

[121] Christian Tomuschat, "Darfur – Compensation for the Victims," *Journal of International Criminal Justice* 3 (2005), pp. 579–589; Paul R. Dubinsky, "Justice for the Collective – The Limits of the Human Rights Class Action," *Michigan Law Review* 102 (2004), pp. 1152–1190; Anne-Marie de Brouwer, "Reparation to Victims of Sexual Violence – Possibilities at the International Criminal Court and at the Trust Fund for Victims and Their Families," *Leiden Journal of International Law* 20 (2007), pp. 207–237.

individual victims and individual reparations should be favored.[122] Victims also claimed that individual awards should vary according to an individual victim's experience and varying needs.[123] The Trial Chamber, however, adopted a collective approach, rejecting requests for reparation on an individual basis due to the limited financial availability of funds. Since the convicted person was declared indigent, reparations would be provided through the TFV. By deciding to order collective reparations, the award could potentially benefit a greater number of victims, but it also discharged the court of crafting individual remedies and assessing each individual's claim. The choice of collective reparation, despite the requests of victims, raises the question of the true meaning of "justice for victims" before the ICC and the extent to which their voices are being heard.[124]

In contrast, in *Katanga*, victims were awarded individual symbolic compensation of a minimal amount, in addition to collective reparations. In this case, the victims had requested individual compensation awards in order to address the harm they suffered. While the decision of the Trial Chamber to award individual compensation is a testament to the acknowledgement of each individual victim's suffering, the symbolic awards can hardly provide any sort of rehabilitation, or help with harm they suffered (including physical and psychological harm, material losses, lost opportunities). Furthermore, these symbolic individual compensation awards might have the effect of trivializing the harm suffered, while excluding victims that could not have accessed the reparation proceedings in time to be included in the award.

3.3.2.2 Diverging Perceptions of the Potential for Reparative Justice at the ICC

The case law on reparations to date has demonstrated that different stakeholders involved in the reparations process have differing perceptions of the reparative system under development at the court. The goal here is not to purport that these accounts are unanimously held by all those involved in the process; rather, it is to shed light on some diverging perspectives of reparations at the ICC.

---

[122] ICC, *The Prosecutor v. Thomas Lubanga Dyilo*, "Observations on the Sentence and Reparations by Victims," (V01 Group), 18 April 2012, ICC- 01/04-01/06, paras. 24–27.

[123] ICC, *The Prosecutor v. Thomas Lubanga Dyilo*, "Observations of the V02 Group of Victims on Sentencing and Reparations," (V02 Group), 18 April 2012, ICC-01/04-01/06, para. 27.

[124] Laurel Fletcher, "Refracted Justice: The Imagined Victim and the International Criminal Court," in *Contested Justice: The Politics and Practice of International Criminal Court Interventions*, eds. Carsten Stahn, et al., Cambridge University Press, 2015, pp. 317–319.

116   *Reparative Justice for International Crimes*

While the first decision on reparations dates back to 2012, to date, victims in all cases have yet to benefit from reparations. This has led to the expression of frustration, loss of trust, and despair of victims dealing with the court. By delaying reparations, there is a potential of revictimization. Furthermore, some reparations might become moot when there is such a gap between the international crimes and the redress.

Some scholars have warned against possible detrimental effects of including a reparative dimension in international criminal justice. The operationalization of reparations within the ICC system has been criticized from various different perspectives including: the tension between the rights of victims and rights of the accused; detrimental effects on victims; and false creations of victimhood.[125] Considering these arguments, the overarching question is whether mixing criminal and reparative processes is ultimately more detrimental than beneficial, especially for victims.

A prominent argument concerning reparations is that adding a reparative dimension to international criminal trials, whose objectives are primarily to decide on the guilt or innocence of the accused, may conflict with the rights of the defense and might militate against mixing criminal and reparative dimensions of international criminal law.[126] Professor Zappalà argues that:

> Any conflict between the rights of victims and the rights of defendants has to be the object of a *delicate balancing* that must be carried out in the knowledge that the overarching purpose of criminal procedure is to reach a finding of guilt or innocence whilst protecting at the highest level the rights of those subjected to the proceedings (i.e. the suspect and the accused) … The balancing of victim participation against the rights of the accused should be inspired by some *procedural principles of an imperative nature*, which represent *the backbone of international criminal procedure*: the presumption of innocence, the right to a fair hearing in full equality, the right to an expeditious trial, the right to confront and present evidence, and so on.[127]

Where one primary consideration is the rights of the accused, the application of victims' rights in criminal contexts is not necessarily an argument against the operationalization of reparative justice for international crimes. What it does is remind us that the right to reparation shall not be to the detriment of the rights of the accused; for example, reparations shall not cause a delay in proceedings against the accused, and shall not set aside the

---

[125] See Section 3.3.2.3.

[126] Cf. Salvatore Zappalà, "The Rights of Victims v. the Rights of the Accused," *Journal of International Criminal Justice* 8 (2010), pp. 137–164.

[127] Ibid., p. 140.

presumption of innocence. The convicted person shall also have the right to submit arguments during reparations proceedings.

Reparations in the context of criminal trials raises questions as to the construction and perception of victimhood. Could including reparations within traditional criminal processes (i.e., international criminal trials) create an abstract conception of victimhood which does not always correspond to reality and is to the detriment of "real" victims? In this regard, Laurel Fletcher submits that:

> Although victims are entitled to limited participation in the trial and to seek reparations after a sentence is reached, the legal structure of the ICC prioritises retributive over restorative justice, punishment over reparations, and the conviction of perpetrators over the character of the charges they face. Looking at trial procedures, victims are framed as a consideration against which other rights and values are weighed. Thus the real victims are subordinated to the retributive justice aims of the ICC, and their desires are continually compromised despite their moral centrality to the integrated justice (retributive and restorative) mission of the Court.[128]

This dichotomy between the abstract construction of victims and the real victims of international crimes was evident in the first reparations proceedings at the ICC. While victims actually asked for individual redress (in addition to collective awards), the chamber only considered community-based reparations. It is noted that the "imagined victim worked again here to justify abstracted, collective forms of repair and obscured the particular and disparate preferences of individual victims for reparative justice."[129]

Another important consideration is the extent to which reparation is an inherently political act and whether it revictimizes vulnerable individuals by submitting them to a criminal process where they are required to be "recognized" as victims in order to be considered for reparations. In this regard, Peter Dixon argues that "provision of international criminal reparations is an inherently political act through which the ICC will necessarily become a player in local power relations" through the "politics of recognition," which is inherent in reparations.[130]

---

[128] Laurel Fletcher, "Refracted Justice: The Imagined Victim and the International Criminal Court," in *Contested Justice: The Politics and Practice of International Criminal Court Interventions*, eds. Carsten Stahn, et al., Cambridge University Press, 2015, pp. 302–325.

[129] Ibid., p. 319.

[130] Peter J. Dixon, "Reparations and the Politics of Recognition," in *Contested Justice: The Politics and Practice of International Criminal Court Interventions*, eds. Carsten Stahn et al., Cambridge University Press, 2015, p. 326–351.

Broader, institutional tensions of including reparative justice within an international *criminal* court that is traditionally conceptualized as the prosecution and punishment of offenders, have also emerged as the jurisprudence on reparations has started to develop. Two examples of recent cases illustrate these tensions. The first happened in the Kenya situation, discussed above. With the collapse of the *Ruto and Sang* case because of insufficient evidence (in the criminal standard), the question arose whether reparations could still proceed.[131] The judges were divided in this question, underpinning the diametrically opposed views within the bench on how to conceive of the reparation system at the court. Judge Fremr rejected the idea that reparations could follow despite the discontinuance of the case and stated that "[w]hile I recognise that this must be dissatisfactory to the victims, a criminal court can only address compensation for harm suffered as a result of crimes if such crimes have been found to have taken place and the person standing trial for his or her participation in those crimes is found guilty."[132] In contrast, as discussed above, Judge Eboe-Osuji took a contrary view that reparations should not be preconditioned on the conviction of the accused.[133]

In the more recent *Bemba* case, when writing separately about the effect of the acquittal of the accused on appeal, two judges of the Appeals Chambers stated their view of the role of the court in the aftermath of international crimes:

> An acquittal may mean that hundreds or perhaps thousands of potential victims see their claims for reparation evaporate. We recognise that this will generate disappointment and frustration. We are not blind to the human drama. Yet, this may not be a factor in the decision whether or not to convict an accused. It is emphatically not the responsibility of the International Criminal Court to ensure compensation for all those who suffer harm as a result of international crimes. We do not have the mandate, let alone the capacity and the resources, to provide this to all potential victims in the cases and situations within our jurisdiction. ... What we do suggest is that we stop viewing the International Criminal Court's reparation procedures as (part of) a mechanism to restore social justice and to heal the wounds of societies that have been torn apart by aggression, genocide, crimes against humanity or war crimes. Only if we do that will it be possible to manage victims' expectations

---

[131]   See for a discussion of this topic: Luke Moffett, "Reparations for Victims at the International Criminal Court: A New Way Forward?," *The International Journal of Human Rights* 21 (2017), pp. 1204–1222.

[132]   ICC, *Ruto and Sang* case, "Public redacted version of Decision on Defence Applications for Judgments of Acquittal," ICC-01/09-01/11-2027-Red 5 April 2016, para. 149.

[133]   Ibid., para. 201.

International Justice Before the ICC

and can we relieve International Criminal Court prosecutors and judges from potential pressure that is currently imposed upon them to secure convictions at all cost.[134]

3.3.2.3 Constructions of Victimhood: The Real, the Recognized, and the Invisible Victims

The reparative system being developed at the court provides an avenue for victims, who are judged eligible as beneficiaries of reparation, to eventually obtain some form of redress for the harm they have suffered, which might not have been available without the ICC. Nevertheless, at the same time, there are crucial questions pertaining to constructions of victimhood and the creation of a potential hierarchy of victims. Should certain types of victims be differentiated and prioritized when it comes to reparation?

There are some difficult yet fundamental questions that the ICC has to grapple with as it develops its reparation system. The focus here is on two main themes: 1) reparations for victims of sexual and gender-based crimes; and 2) reparations for victims who are both victims and perpetrators. These are by no means the only new paradigms or dilemmas concerning reparations for international crimes, but given their prominence in the early stages of the development of the ICC's reparations regime they merit some discussion.[135]

The first important dimension of reparations for international crimes, especially in the context of the ICC, refers to reparations for sexual and gender-based violence. Sexual crimes can be war crimes, crimes against humanity, or genocide depending on the criminal conduct and other factors.

Victims of sexual-based violence should have prompt access to reparations due to urgent needs (e.g., medical, psychological). The *United Nations Guidance Note of the Secretary General: Reparations for Conflict-Related Sexual Violence* of June 2014 recommends some principles in relation to reparation:

1. Adequate reparation for victims of conflict-related sexual violence entails a combination of different forms of reparations
2. Judicial and/or administrative reparations should be available to victims of conflict-related sexual violence as part of their right to obtain prompt, adequate and effective remedies

---

[134] ICC, Appeals Chamber, *Bemba* case, Separate opinion Judge Christine Van den Wyngaert and Judge Howard Morrison, ICC-01/05-01/08-3636-Anx2, 8 June 2018, para. 75.
[135] See references in this section for more detailed discussions of these topics.

3. Individual and collective reparations should complement and reinforce each other
4. Reparations should strive to be transformative, including in design, implementation and impact
5. Development cooperation should support States' obligation to ensure access to reparations
6. Meaningful participation and consultation of victims in the mapping, design, implementation, monitoring and evaluation of reparations should be ensured
7. Urgent interim reparations to address immediate needs and avoid irreparable harm should be made available
8. Adequate procedural rules for proceedings involving sexual violence and reparations should be in place.[136]

The report recommends that victims of sexual violence should receive "priority access to services."[137] This is due to the nature of their harm and the possible need for treatment, and thus reparation orders should take this dimension of sexual and gender-based crimes into account.

Recent conflicts have left countless victims of sexual and gender-based violence. This is compounded by criticisms concerning the ICC's reluctance to prosecute gender-based crimes.[138] When it comes to reparations, the record to date is very disappointing. Victims of sexual and gender-based violence have been left out of reparations at the ICC. The only case that dealt with sexual and gender-based crimes, the *Bemba* case, did not deliver a reparation decision given the acquittal of the accused on appeal. Nevertheless, as already stated "[t]he lack of convictions for sexual violence has not been due to lack of participation from victims, but rather insufficient evidence or narrow selection of charges."[139] For example, it is widely accepted that sexual and gender-based violence have permeated the conflicts

---

[136] *United Nations Guidance Note of the Secretary General: Reparations for Conflict-Related Sexual Violence* of June 2014, p. 2.

[137] Ibid., p. 5.

[138] Laurel Fletcher, "Refracted Justice: The Imagined Victim and the International Criminal Court," in *Contested Justice: The Politics and Practice of International Criminal Court Interventions*, eds. Carsten Stahn, et al., Cambridge University Press, 2015, pp. 302–325. See similarly Kelisiana Thynne, "The International Criminal Court: A Failure of International Justice for Victims," *Alberta Law Review*, 46 (2009), pp. 957–982, at p. 968 who claims that "[t]he fact that these charges [concerning sexual violence] were not brought in the *Lubanga* case means that the Court is excluding consideration of the major aspects of the conflict with which they are supposed to be dealing. In so doing, they are excluding the victims of all of these other crimes."

[139] Luke Moffett, "Reparations for Victims at the International Criminal Court: A New Way Forward?," *The International Journal of Human Rights* 21 (2017), pp. 1204–1222, at p. 1204.

underpinning other cases prosecuted before the ICC, but these crimes have not been charged, with the exception of the *Bemba* case.[140] Under the current framework of the reparation system, due to a lack of prosecution, no conviction was possible and no reparation could be due to victims of sexual and gender-based crimes.

For example, in the *Lubanga* case, the Office of the Prosecutor decided to limit prosecution to charges of conscripting child soldiers and did not bring any charges of sexual violence allegedly perpetrated by a rebel group. This decision instigated fierce criticism.[141] The prosecutorial decision concerning what charges to bring against the accused, Mr. Lubanga, dictated which victims could potentially ask for reparations at the appropriate stage. This sheds light on the discussion above concerning included and excluded victims for purposes of reparations. This hesitation to prosecute charges of gender-based and sexual violence effectively created, in terms of reparations, two categories of victims: the ones who were victims of a person convicted by the court (and who could benefit from the reparations regime), and the ones who suffered harm by those not convicted by the court (and could not be part of a Court's reparations order).[142] As Luke Moffett rightly notes: "victims' eligibility for reparations at the ICC is dependent on the Prosecutor's selection of charges and perpetrators, effectively a prioritisation of suffering based on evidence and expeditiousness that creates a stark hierarchy of victimhood in reparation proceedings."[143] Victims of sexual and gender-based violence have been limited to receiving assistance from the TFV.

The early jurisprudence of the court raises the question of the politics of gender justice at the ICC. Louise Chappell argues that "the failure [of the ICC] to adequately prosecute crimes of sexual and gender-based violence in its first two cases has made the Court's reparations regime appear selective and unfair to victims of these crimes, and could possibly do more harm than good in the fragile post conflict contexts in which it will be implemented."[144]

Different theories about how reparations for sexual violence should develop have emerged. Some scholars claim that reparations for victims of sexual violence should be "transformative," which includes the rebuilding of

---

[140]   Ibid.
[141]   Ibid.
[142]   Frédéric Mégret, "The Reparations Debate," 2012, *Invited Experts on Reparations Questions. ICC Forum*, available at http://iccforum.com/reparations.
[143]   Ibid., p. 1209.
[144]   Louise Chappell, *The Politics of Gender at the International Criminal Court: Legacies and Legitimacy*, Oxford University Press, 2015, pp. 156–157.

political, social, and economic relations that contributed to the exposure to the harm victims suffered.[145] A critical account claims that:

> this agenda threatens to bypass or displace reparative justice as a distinct and distinctly victim-centered ideal in favor of a different kind of justice agenda. In doing so, it threatens to efface or to demote in importance concrete forms of relief and support for individual victims as "merely" remedial or restorative, and so to demote the importance of recognizing individual victims themselves whose status as bearers of rights and subjects of justice depends crucially on their standing to claim accountability and repair for violations to their individual persons.[146]

Reparations for sexual and gender based violence is far from a straightforward issue. The ICC cannot lose sight of the fact that many of the conflicts that lead to the creation of a permanent international court have left far too many victims of sexual and gender violence.[147] It has been suggested, as a way forward, that "modifying initiatives of the ICC's Trust Fund for Victims and a greater emphasis by the ICC on the notion of member state 'reparative complementarity' may provide mechanisms for transforming conditions that trigger and perpetuate gender violence during conflict."[148]

Another dilemma in terms of reparations and constructions of victimhood concerns victim-perpetrators, and how they should be treated. Luke Moffett recently examined this question by drawing upon victimology studies and examining ways in which victim-perpetrators have been either included or

[145] See discussion and references cited in Margaret Urban Walker, "Transformative Reparations? A Critical Look at a Current Trend in Thinking About Gender-Just Reparations," *International Journal of Transitional Justice*, 10 (2016), pp. 108–125, including Colleen Duggan and Adila Abusharaf, "Reparation of Sexual Violence in Democratic Transitions: The Search for Gender Justice," in *The Handbook of Reparations*, ed. Pablo de Greiff, Oxford University Press, 2006; Ruth Rubio-Marín and Pablo de Greiff, "Women and Reparations," *International Journal of Transitional Justice* 1 (2007), pp. 318–337; Valérie Couillard, "The Nairobi Declaration: Redefining Reparations for Women Victims of Sexual Violence," *International Journal of Transitional Justice* 1 (2007), pp. 444–453; Anne Saris and Katherine Lofts, "Reparation Programmes: A Gendered Perspective," in *Reparations for Victims of Genocide, War Crimes and Crimes Against Humanity: Systems in Place and Systems in the Making*, ed. Carla Ferstman, Mariana Goetz, and Alan Stephens, Brill, 2009.

[146] Margaret Urban Walker, "Transformative Reparations? A Critical Look at a Current Trend in Thinking about Gender-Just Reparations," *International Journal of Transitional Justice*, (10) 2016, 108–125, p. 110.

[147] Cf. Louise Chappell, *The Politics of Gender at the International Criminal Court: Legacies and Legitimacy*, Oxford University Press, 2015.

[148] Andrea Durbach and Louise Chappell, "Leaving Behind the Age of Impunity: Victims of Gender Violence and the Promise of Reparations," *International Feminist Journal of Politics* 6 (2014), pp. 543–562.

excluded from reparation programs.[149] The dilemma of how to treat victims who are also (or have been) perpetrators has been explained in the author's words as: "individual identities in protracted armed conflicts and political violence can be more complex than the binary identities of victim and perpetrator, where individuals can be both victimised and victimiser over a period of time."[150]

There will be no easy answers for the ICC when it is faced with such dilemmas. Some of the questions that may arise concerning reparation for victims who also committed crimes concern their eligibility to receive reparation, whether they should be treated differently, and how the court constructs notions of victimhood. Upon a thorough analysis of the topic, Luke Moffett posits that "[b]y affirming accountability as part of reparations we can hopefully depoliticise contentions around reparations for complex victims, by neither excluding them nor equating them with innocent victims."[151]

In many different crossroads, victims that have suffered international crimes are compartmentalized, differentiated, included, or excluded by various decisions taken at the ICC: the selection of which conflict(s) to investigate, the timeframe of international crimes that may come under the jurisdiction of the court, the actual charges that are brought against perpetrators, and importantly, the conviction of the perpetrator. Then judges decide what kind of justice, in the form of reparations, to award victims.

All of these decisions give some victims (the judicially *recognized* victims) an opportunity to receive reparations while others – also victims of international crimes within the jurisdiction of the court – will fall outside the reparation scheme (the *invisible* victims).[152] This creates a hierarchy when it comes to reparations proceedings: victims of international crimes who can obtain reparation and those who are ignored. These are of course not exclusive problems of the ICC, but are necessarily issues faced by any mechanism dealing with reparations.

Nevertheless, these considerations raise the question about whether including a reparative dimension into international criminal justice, and at the ICC

---

[149] Luke Moffett, "Reparations for 'Guilty Victims': Navigating Complex Identities of Victim–Perpetrators in Reparation Mechanisms," *International Journal of Transitional Justice*, 10 (2016), pp. 146–167.

[150] Luke Moffett, "Navigating Complex Identities of Victim-Perpetrators in Reparation Mechanisms," *Queen's University Belfast, School of Law Research Paper No. 2014B13*, pp. 2–3.

[151] Ibid., p. 23.

[152] See Sara Kendall and Sarah Nouwen, "Representational Practices at the International Criminal Court: The Gap between Juridified and Abstract Victimhood," *Law and Contemporary Problems* 75 (2013), pp. 235–262.

more specifically, automatically prioritizes some victims while excluding others. It also sheds light on the disconnect between the interests of real victims, their perception of justice, when compared with the rhetoric of justice and what is actually delivered to victims. The reparative dimension of international criminal justice will undoubtedly suffer from selectivity, hierarchy, and prioritization, at one level or another. This too is a marked characteristic of international justice.

3.4 CONCLUSIONS

Building on an overview of the ICC reparation system, and an analysis of the issues highlighted by the first few cases, this chapter suggested that while the rhetoric of "justice for victims" justified the inclusion of reparations in the legal texts of the ICC, and seems to support a degree of legitimacy to the court, the operationalization of reparations demonstrates that they are still very much linked to notions of criminal accountability, and are constrained by limitations in place at the court.

The result is a system that while premised on the notion of justice for victims is struggling to move from its ideological rhetoric. The Rome Statute and its interpretation by the ICC provide a particular vision of what justice is, a vision that includes imbedded hierarchy, limitations, and exclusions of victimhood.

The court has made some progress from a time when reparative justice was only a theoretical endeavor, codified in the statute, but with no defined practical contours. The first cases before the ICC have demonstrated that the transition from reparative justice in theory to practice has presented many challenges, and reparation orders have yet to be fully implemented. Two conclusions seem appropriate at this stage. First, it is clear that the ICC cannot single-handedly advance reparative justice for international crimes. This was never supposed to be the case given its inherent limitations, starting with the crimes over which it has jurisdiction. The court faces many practical and systemic challenges which arise from reconciling reparative and criminal dimensions of international justice. It should be viewed as one piece of broader systems and efforts to deliver reparative justice, as discussed in different chapters of this book. National justice systems and other international tribunals and mechanisms must work in synergy with the ICC in order to attain the goal of providing appropriate reparations to victims of international conflicts.

Second, in light of challenges observed in the first cases analyzed, such as delays, inconsistencies in decisions, limitations, and exclusions, the reparative justice at the ICC would benefit from taking stock of the experience in the first cases and learning some lessons. Importantly, however, the court must also go beyond a lessons-learned approach, and accept that there are some inherent issues with the system as it is currently devised. It is only by acknowledging these challenges and making necessary adjustments that the court can truly deliver on the promise of reparative justice. Some recommendations for changes are discussed in Chapter 6, the conclusion of the book.

We somehow take for granted what "justice for victims" means – whose justice? Yet such assumptions leave room for raising some critical questions as to how one court can deliver justice to thousands or potentially millions of victims of international crimes.

When it is clear that international crimes have been committed, a system of reparations that is attached to and conditional upon criminal conviction of one (or more) perpetrators creates dividing notions of justice. Institutional constructions and limitations, reflecting the dominant historical paradigm governing the development of international criminal law, have excluded thousands of victims from the process. This has created a system that, although premised on the narrative of pursuing justice for victims, has yet to succeed on delivering what it was set to achieve, while creating hierarchies and limitations on victimhood.

There is a gulf between the rhetoric and the reality which stands in the way of advancing the system of "justice for victims". Then, it is the role of the court and stakeholders to tip the balance towards a meaningful effort, and develop an institution-wide understanding and international collaboration concerning the reparations mandate of the court.

4

Victims of International Crimes Within Administrative Mechanisms

The Example of the ICC Trust Fund for Victims (TFV)

With the advent of the ICC, a new mechanism for providing redress to victims of international crimes within the jurisdiction of the ICC was created under Article 79 of the Rome Statute, the Trust Fund for Victims (TFV).[1] Its inclusion in the international criminal justice scene is both unprecedented[2] and significant.

The goal was to set up a unique mechanism, within the framework of the ICC, dedicated solely to victims. The TFV was designed to assist in the

---

[1] The TFV has gained much attention in the literature in recent years. For examples of essays about the TFV, see Anne Dutton and Fionnuala D. Ni Aolain, "Between Reparations and Repair: Assessing the Work of the ICC Trust Fund for Victims Under Its Assistance Mandate" (September 24, 2018), available: https://ssrn.com/abstract=3254972 or http://dx.doi.org/10.2139/ssrn.3254972; Peter G. Fischer, "The Victims' Trust Fund of the International Criminal Court: Formation of a Functional Reparations Scheme," *Emory International Law Review* 17 (2003), p. 187; Pablo De Greiff and Marieke Wierda, "The Trust Fund for Victims of the International Criminal Court: Between Possibilities and Constraints," in *Out of the Ashes: Reparation for Victims of Gross and Systematic Violations of Human Rights*, eds. Koen de Feyter et al., Intersentia, 2005; Heidy Rombouts et al., "The Right to Reparation for Victims of Gross and Systematic Human Rights Violations of Human Rights," in *Out of the Ashes: Reparation for Victims of Gross and Systematic Violations of Human Rights*, eds. Koen de Feyter et al., Intersentia, 2005; Linda Keller, "Seeking Justice at the International Criminal Court: Victims' Reparations," *Thomas Jefferson Law Review* 29 (2007), p. 189; Tom Dannenbaum, "The International Criminal Court, Article 79, and Transitional Justice: The Case for an Independent Trust Fund for Victims," *Wisconsin International Law Journal* 28 (2010), pp. 234–298. See also on the Trust Fund, Sam Garkawe, "Victims and the International Criminal Court: Three Major Issues," *International Criminal Law Review* 3 (2003), pp. 345–367; Marc Henzelin et al., "Reparations to Victims Before the International Criminal Court: Lessons from International Mass Claims Processes," *Criminal Law Forum* 17 (2006), pp. 317–344; David Boyle, "The Rights of Victims: Participation, Representation, Protection, Reparation," *Journal of International Criminal Justice* 4 (2006), pp. 307–313.

[2] Pablo de Greiff and Marieke Wierda, "The Trust Fund for Victims of the International Criminal Court: Between Possibilities and Constraints," in *Out of the Ashes: Reparation for Victims of Gross and Systematic Violations of Human Rights*, eds. Koen de Feyter et al., Intersentia, 2005, p. 225.

The *ICC Trust Fund for Victims* 127

implementation of court-ordered reparations to victims in relation to the harm caused by the crimes within the jurisdiction of the ICC and to provide rehabilitation or material support to victims of crimes falling within the jurisdiction of the court. Its creation contributes to ensuring that victim redress is part of international criminal justice.

With a very promising purpose, nevertheless, the TFV has encountered, and is still bound to encounter, many challenges ahead. These challenges are novel since other international criminal tribunals, discussed in previous chapters, either did not provide for victim reparation, or did not create an administrative mechanism linked with a judicial procedure. In this context, much can be learned from the experience of other historical mass claims processes, and previously employed reparation mechanisms.[3]

The aim of this chapter is to examine whether, and to what extent, an administrative mechanism linked with a judicial process may provide a path to deal with the potential for mass claims of reparations following international crimes. The TFV is a unique example of such a mechanism. As such, this chapter studies the endeavor of administrative mechanisms linked with judicial processes as a possible route for civil redress for international crimes, and discusses in this light the TFV of the ICC.

After this descriptive overview, this chapter discusses the measures taken by the TFV and the impact they have had on victims of cases within the jurisdiction of the ICC. It also explores the important role the TFV has played in the reparations phase of the *Lubanga* case and critically examines how its budget has been spent so far. Finally, this chapter engages in a juxtaposition of administrative and judicial mechanisms, and discusses their positive and negative aspects. In this respect, this chapter builds upon critical scholarship examining the detrimental effects that criminal justice may have on victims.

While it is an important achievement to create an administrative mechanism that focuses on victims of the crimes under the jurisdiction of the ICC, it is also true that many victims of international crimes will necessarily be left out of the reparation scheme. Accordingly, this chapter analyzes whether linking the TFV to criminal proceedings is desirable given the potential of further victimization that criminal trials may produce for victims.[4] In this chapter,

---

[3] The International Bureau of the Permanent Court of Arbitration, *Redressing Injustices Through Mass Claims Processes: Innovative Responses to Unique Challenges*, Oxford University Press, 2006; Marc Henzelin et al., "Reparations to Victims Before the International Criminal Court: Lessons from International Mass Claims Processes," *Criminal Law Forum* 17 (2006), pp. 317–344.

[4] Concerning the creation of perceptions and constructions of victims by international criminal justice, see Laurel Fletcher, "Refracted Justice: The Imagined Victim and the International

128   *Reparative Justice for International Crimes*

the TFV will provide a lens to reflect on whether administrative mechanisms are a viable avenue for the civil redress of international crimes.

4.1 THE ROAD TO THE TFV AND ITS LEGAL FRAMEWORK

As already discussed, ordering reparations directly against perpetrators, to the benefit of individual or collective victims, is new in international law.[5] The evolution of the position of the individual in international law has led to the divide between a state and an individual's *civil* responsibility becoming blurred under international law. Crimes are committed by individuals, who, admittedly, can often operate behind the machinery of the state.[6] Now, individuals not only may be criminally responsible for their crimes, but they may also face civil liability at the international level. In this light, the ICC Statute enables an international court, for the first time in international criminal law, to order a perpetrator of an international crime to give reparation to the victims, as already discussed.

Against this context, the inclusion of reparations for victims of international crimes within the jurisdiction of the ICC was not without its controversies. One author, who studied the reparation system of the ICC in detail, has suggested that "in the formation of the Rome Statute there were widely varying views about the role of victims in the international criminal process, rooted in the different approaches varying national systems take to victims in criminal procedure."[7]

Criminal Court," in *Contested Justice: The Politics and Practice of International Criminal Court Interventions*, eds. Carsten Stahn et al., Cambridge University Press, 2015, pp. 302–325.

[5] See Eva Dwertmann, *The Reparation System of the International Criminal Court: Its Implementation, Possibilities and Limitations*, Nijhoff, 2010, pp. 22–23; Christine Evans, "Reparations for Victims in International Criminal Law," in *Festschrift in Honour of Katarina Tomaševski*, Raoul Wallenberg Institute, 2011, http://rwi.lu.se/what-we-do/academic activities/publications/tomasevski/, accessed October 2019.

[6] I subscribe, however, to the theory that individual and state responsibility for international crimes are not always disconnected, and may complement each other in cases where the state may have been involved in the international crime; see in this regard, *Jurisdictional Immunities of the State (Germany v. Italy: Greece Intervening)*, Judgment, 3 February 2012, Dissenting Opinion of Judge Cançado Trindade, paras. 57–59, and references cited therein; Antônio Augusto Cançado Trindade, "Complementarity Between State Responsibility and Individual Responsibility for Grave Violations of Human Rights: The Crime of State Revisited," in *International Responsibility Today: Essays in Memory of Oscar Schachter*, ed. Maurizio Ragazzi, Nijhoff, 2005, pp. 253–269; Pemmaraju Sreenivasa Rao, "International Crimes and State Responsibility," in *International Responsibility Today: Essays in Memory of Oscar Schachter*, ed. Maurizio Ragazzi, Nijhoff, 2005, pp. 76–77; R. Maison, *La responsabilité individuelle pour crime d'État en Droit international public*, Bruylant, Éds. de l'Université de Bruxelles, 2004, pp. 24, 85, 262–264 and 286–287.

[7] Eva Dwertmann, *The Reparation System of the International Criminal Court: Its Implementation, Possibilities and Limitations*, Nijhoff, 2010, p. 25, citing William A. Schabas,

The ICC Statute is not only innovative because it has incorporated the possibility for victims to claim reparations, but also because it has created a reparations mechanism connected to the court, the TFV. The following section provides a descriptive overview of the TFV, its legal framework, mandates, and operational matters.

4.1.1 *Relevant Legal Provisions*

The TFV was established under the auspices of the ICC. Therefore, the main legal texts governing the ICC – that is, the Rome Statute, the Rules of Procedure and Evidence, and the Regulations of the Assembly of States Parties (ASP) – also govern the operation of the TFV to some extent.

Article 75 of the Rome Statute concerns reparations to victims, and provides, in the relevant part:

1. The Court shall establish principles relating to reparations to, or in respect of, victims, including restitution, compensation and rehabilitation. On this basis, in its decision the Court may, either upon request or on its own motion in exceptional circumstances, determine the scope and extent of any damage, loss and injury to, or in respect of, victims and will state the principles on which it is acting.
2. The Court may make an order directly against a convicted person specifying appropriate reparations to, or in respect of, victims, including restitution, compensation and rehabilitation.
   Where appropriate, the Court may order that the award for reparations be made through the Trust Fund provided for in article 79. [...][8]

As for the TFV, under the terms of Article 79 of the ICC Statute,

1. A Trust Fund shall be established by decision of the Assembly of States Parties for the benefit of victims of crimes within the jurisdiction of the Court, and of the families of such victims.
2. The Court may order money and other property collected through fines or forfeiture to be transferred, by order of the Court, to the Trust Fund.

An Introduction to the International Criminal Court, Cambridge University Press, 2nd ed., 2004, p. 171 and Christopher Muttukumaru, "Reparation to Victims," in *The International Criminal Court: The Making of the Rome Statute – Issues, Negotiations, Results*, ed. Roy S. K. Lee, Kluwer Law International, 1999, p. 262 et seq.

[8] For a commentary on Article 75, see e.g., David Donat-Cattin, "Article 75: Reparations to Victims," in *Commentary on the Rome Statute of the International Criminal Court: Observers' Notes, Article by Article*, ed. Otto Triffterer, Baden-Baden, 1999; William A. Schabas, *The International Criminal Court: A Commentary on the Rome Statute*, Oxford University Press, 2010, Article 75.

130   *Reparative Justice for International Crimes*

3. The Trust Fund shall be managed according to criteria to be determined by the Assembly of States Parties.

Additionally, the Rules of Procedure and Evidence provide further guidance about the two mandates of the TFV. Rule 98(1–4) concerns reparations awarded by the court against a convicted person; Rule 98(5) concerns the TFV's assistance mandate concerning the use of "other resources" for the benefit of victims, subject to Article 79. Rule 98 reads as follows:

1. Individual awards for reparations shall be made directly against a convicted person.
2. The Court may order that an award for reparations against a convicted person be deposited with the Trust Fund where at the time of making the order it is impossible or impracticable to make individual awards directly to each victim. The award for reparations thus deposited in the Trust Fund shall be separated from other resources of the Trust Fund and shall be forwarded to each victim as soon as possible.
3. The Court may order that an award for reparations against a convicted person be made through the Trust Fund where the number of the victims and the scope, forms and modalities of reparations makes a collective award more appropriate.
4. Following consultations with interested States and the Trust Fund, the Court may order that an award for reparations be made through the Trust Fund to an intergovernmental, international or national organization approved by the Trust Fund.
5. Other resources of the Trust Fund may be used for the benefit of victims subject to the provisions of article 79.

The Regulations of the TFV were adopted by the Assembly of States Parties at the 4th plenary meeting on 3 December 2005. They were adopted to ensure the proper and effective functioning of the TFV. They regulate many areas; the TFV explains the provisions of the regulations in the following terms:

Regarding the TFV's activities and projects, the Regulations specify that all resources of the Trust Fund shall be for the benefit of victims within the jurisdiction of the Court as defined by Rule 85 of the Rules of Procedure and Evidence, and, where natural persons are concerned, their families.

The Regulations provide a detailed legal regime for the Trust Fund's two mandates:

Under the TFV's Reparation mandate, the Regulations contain detailed provisions on awards for reparations by the Court, referring to individual awards (Rule 98[2] of the Rules of Procedure and Evidence), collective awards (Rule 98[3]), and awards to an intergovernmental, international, or national organization (Rule 98[4]).

With respect to the TFV's assistance mandate, the Regulations specify that before undertaking activities to provide physical rehabilitation, psychological rehabilitation, and/or material support to victims, the Board is required to formally notify the Court of its intentions.[9]

Additionally, some of the Resolutions of the Assembly of States Parties which concern the TFV include: ICC-ASP/1/Res.6, ICC-ASP/3/Res.7, ICC-ASP/4/Res.3, ICC-ASP/4/Res.5, ICC-ASP/4/Res.7, and ICC-ASP/6/Res.3. These resolutions address some important aspects of the functioning of the TFV such as voluntary contributions, and the term of office of members of the Board of Directors, among others. These texts together govern the operation of the TFV.

At this juncture, it appears useful to recall the definition of victims contained in Rule 85 of the Rules of Procedure and Evidence of the ICC. Rule 85 (1) provides a broad definition of victims which includes "natural persons who have suffered harm as a result of the commission of any crimes within the jurisdiction of the Court." Rule 85(2) states the victims may include "organizations or institutions that have sustained direct harm to any of their property which is dedicated to religion, education, art or science or charitable purposes, and to their historic monuments, hospitals and other places and objects for humanitarian purposes."

From the above-mentioned provisions, it can be seen clearly that the TFV is not a judicial mechanism that defines beneficiaries, but rather an administrative mechanism linked to a judicial procedure. It is a complementary organ of the court, an integral part of the reparative scheme established by the ICC.[10] However, the TFV remains independent of the court.[11]

By its nature, structure, and reach of activities, the TFV has some constraints in that it is not a mechanism set up to provide reparations to *all* victims of international crimes, but rather only to "natural persons who have suffered harm as a result of the commission of crimes within the jurisdiction of the Court," pursuant to Rule 85 of the Rules of Procedure and Evidence.[12] It is also

---

[9] Available at http://trustfundforvictims.org/legal-basis.

[10] Eva Dwertmann, *The Reparation System of the International Criminal Court: Its Implementation, Possibilities and Limitations*, Nijhoff, 2010, p. 265.

[11] See Resolution of the Establishment of the Secretariat of the Trust Fund for Victims, ICC-ASP/3/Res.7 (2004).

[12] On the jurisprudential construction of the definition of victims, see ICC, Situation in the Democratic Republic of Congo, "Decision on the Applications for Participation in the Proceedings of VPRS 1, VPRS 2, VPRS 3, VPRS 4, VPRS 5 and VPRS 6," 17 January 2006, ICC-01/04-101-tEN-Corr, Pre Trial Chamber I, para. 79; ICC, *Bemba*, "Fourth Decision on

Reparative Justice for International Crimes

limited by practical considerations, such as available resources, as further discussed in Section 4.1.3.

4.1.2 The Mandates of the TFV

On the basis of the framework provided in the statute, the TFV can act in two ways: 1) as an institution through which the court can order reparation awards; or 2) it can use its "other resources" in assistance programs for the benefit of the victims pursuant to Rule 98(5). Therefore, the TFV has a double role, both of which are aimed at providing support to victims of crimes under the jurisdiction of the ICC.

The TFV pursues, on the one hand, a reparations mandate, and on the other, an assistance mandate for victims.

Concerning the *reparations mandate*, according to Rule 98, the court may order an award for reparations against a convicted person to be made through the TFV, if, at the time of making the order, it is impossible or impracticable to make individual awards directly to each victim. Reparations to victims can be individual or collective, and can include restitution, compensation, and/or rehabilitation. Reparations may be provided in collective or symbolic measures that help to promote peace and reconciliation within divided communities. Section 4.3 discusses the reparations mandate of the TFV in more detail.

The *assistance mandate* under Rule 98(5) concerns the "other resources" of the TFV. The assistance mandate is not linked to the conviction of an accused person by the ICC, and it can happen prior to the end of trial proceedings, and before, or irrespective of, a conviction. The assistance mandate provides physical and psychological rehabilitation and material support to assist victims in their recovery. The assistance mandate provides the TFV the autonomy to give support to victims outside the scope of court-ordered reparations. Section 4.2 further discusses the intricacies of the assistance mandate of the TFV.

The TFV itself has expressed the view that the two mandates are separate. It has also asserted that the assistance mandate provided for by Rule 98(5) is

---

Victims' Participation," 12 December 2008, ICC-01/05-01/08-320, Pre-Trial Chamber III, para. 30; ICC, Situation in Kenya, "Decision on Victims' Participation in Proceedings," 3 November 2010, ICC-01/09-24, Pre-Trial Chamber II, para. 19. See also, e.g., ICC, Kony, Otti, Odhiambo and Ongwen, "Decision on Victims' Applications for Participation a/0014/07 to a/0020/07 and a/0076/07 to a/0125/07," 21 November 2008, ICC 02/04-01/05-356, Pre-Trial Chamber II, para. 7. ICC, Muthaura, Kenyatta and Ali, "Decision on Victims' Participation at the Confirmation of Charges Hearing and in the Related Proceedings," 26 August 2011, ICC-01/09-02/11-267, Pre-Trial Chamber II, para. 40.

actually broader than the reparations mandate, and concerns the "provision of assistance to victims in general through the use of other resources."[13] Peter Dixon posits that "[m]orally, reparations are given to a recipient because she has been wronged, not because she is in need or is vulnerable. Politically, reparations are awarded because a recipient's rights have been violated."[14] Similarly, the distinction between reparations and assistance is "the moral and political content of the former, positing that victims are entitled to reparations because their rights have been violated."[15]

In the context of the ICC's reparations regime, how does the TFV fit within the dimensions discussed in the Chapter 1 of this book? Chapter 1 referred to the report by the United Nations Special Rapporteur on the promotion of truth, justice, reparation, and guarantees of nonrecurrence. It is relevant to mention this report again in relation to the mandate of the TFV. One significant conclusion of the report is the "scandalous" gap in the implementation of reparations.[16] In this regard, the TFV has much to contribute. The TFV can help breach this gap by designing and implementing programs for victims of crimes within the jurisdiction of the court. In the words of the report, which are worth quoting in full here:

> While well-designed reparation programmes should primarily be directed at victims of massive violations, they can have positive spillover effects for whole societies. In addition to making a positive contribution to the lives of beneficiaries and to exemplifying the observance of legal obligations, reparation programmes can help promote trust in institutions and the social reintegration of people whose rights counted for little before.[17]

4.1.3 Functioning of the TFV: Budget and Programs

As mentioned earlier, the TFV is administered by a Board of Directors, with five members originating from each region of the world. They are nominated

---

[13] ICC, *Situation in Uganda*, "Notification of the Board of Directors of the Trust Fund for Victims In Accordance With Regulation 50 of the Regulations of the Trust Fund for Victims," 25 January 2008, ICC-02/04.

[14] Peter J. Dixon, "Reparations and the Politics of Recognition" in *Contested Justice: The Politics and Practice of International Criminal Court Interventions*, eds. Carsten Stahn et al., Cambridge University Press, 2015, pp. 331–332.

[15] Naomi Roht-Arriaza and Katharine Orlovsky, "A Complementary Relationship: Reparations and Development," in *Transitional Justice and Development: Making Connections*, eds. Pablo de Greiff and Roger Duthie, Social Science Research Council, 2009, p. 179.

[16] United Nations, General Assembly, "Report of the Special Rapporteur on the promotion of truth, justice, reparation and guarantees of non-recurrence," A/69/518, 14 October 2014.

[17] Ibid., para. 82.

and elected by the Bureau of the Directors, and the Assembly of States Parties. Each member shall serve for a mandate of three years with the possibility of reelection.[18] The members serve in a *pro bono* and individual capacity.

The TFV is dependent upon contributions from states. It is reported that between 2004 and 2014 for example, the total of contributions from countries amounted to over EUR 20.4 million, with over EUR 5 million donated in 2014 alone.[19] The contributions are divided into two types: 1) earmarked contributions; and 2) general contributions. The first category serves a very specific purpose and seeks to provide redress to particular categories of victims, such as victims of sexual and gender-based violence or child soldiers, for example.[20] The conditions for the acceptance of these earmarked contributions are set out in Regulations 27–30 of the Regulations of the TFV.

In this regard, it is interesting to note that the TFV has a reserve fund which is held in order to pay reparations in case an accused appearing before the ICC is declared indigent. In 2015, the amount of the reserve was at EUR 3.6 million.[21]

Importantly, the TFV receives funds from private donors in addition to states parties. The cost of functioning is included in the budget of the court according to Regulation 16 of the Regulations of the TFV.

It is reported that the number of contributors has continuously risen since 2004, totaling thirty-four donor states in 2015. Some of the allocations found within the budget of the TFV included: EUR 1 million for current projects in Uganda and the Democratic Republic of the Congo; and EUR 600,000 for assistance mandate activities in the Central African Republic.[22]

An important question is how the budget is used for the benefit of victims. The programs in Northern Uganda and the Democratic Republic of the Congo were approved by the Pre-Trial Chamber in 2008. The programs sought to provide assistance to victims as defined under Rule 85 of the Rules of Procedure and Evidence. The TFV partnered with local organizations and provides services such as psychological rehabilitation, material support,

---

[18] See Resolution on the Establishment of a Fund for the Benefit of Victims of Crimes within the Jurisdiction of the Court, and the Families of such Victims, ICC-ASP/1/Res.6 (2002), which established the Board of Directors. See also, Resolution on the Procedure for the Nomination and Election of Members of the Board of Directors of the Trust Fund for the Benefit of Victims, ICC-ASP/1/Res.7 (2202), 9 September 2002.

[19] See http://trustfundforvictims.org/financial-information.

[20] Ibid.

[21] Ibid.

[22] The Trust Fund for Victims, "The Year 2015 in Donations," Newsletter No. 1/2016, 15 February 2016. See also, Trust Fund for Victims Board of Directors, 14th Annual Meeting, The Hague, 18–21 April 2016.

medical referrals, and physical rehabilitation.[23] In 2014, the Board of Directors approved assistance assessment missions for Kenya and Côte d'Ivoire.[24]

4.1.4 Rationales for Channeling Reparations Through the TFV

A broader question that is prompted by an analysis of the TFV mechanism is whether administrative procedures, connected to a judicial function, are an efficient way to tackle the large number of claims for reparations that are often a feature of international criminal justice. It has been argued that there are advantages to having the TFV implement reparations, and that it should have an expansive role in the fulfillment of the reparations mandate for victims. For example, it has been posited that "given the freedom of the TFV from narrowly defined legal principles – a freedom unavailable to the court itself – it will be more feasible for the TFV than for the court to design reparations programs that attain whatever goals could be attained by a reparations program at this level."[25] It can also be claimed that including an administrative mechanism such as the TFV within the ICC framework provides an efficient way to implement reparations. This may be so because the court's judges will be concerned with the trial proceedings. It will be arguably more efficient to have an administrative mechanism handle the administration of the reparation order, with the court's supervision. The question is where to draw the line between implementation of the reparations and the TFV's own ability to make decisions. This issue demonstrates the importance of having clear pronouncements about the kinds of decisions the TFV is allowed to make, and what decisions are for the court to make.

At the outset, the governing texts of the TFV established criteria that must be taken into account. For example, concerning the reparations mandate in relation to court-ordered reparations, Regulation 55 of the Regulations of the

---

[23] Some of the programs are: "Treating the Mental Health Needs of Ugandan Victims of War Crimes: A Service and Capacity Building Approach," "Capacity Building, Advocacy and Medical Rehabilitation of Northern Uganda's Victims of War," (Northern Uganda); "Accompagnement socioéconomique et psychosocial des victimes des Violences Sexuelles dans le Territoire de Beni, au Nord Kivu," "Réintégration communautaires des jeunes victimes des conflits armés en Ituri pour la lutte contre toutes formes des violences," "Accompagnement psychosocial des victimes des violences sexuelles à Bunia et 8 localités périphériques," "Projet de Réinsertion Socio-économique des victimes des violences sexuelles dues à la guerre," "A l'école de la paix" (DRC).

[24] See Record of the 11th Annual Meeting, March 2014.

[25] Pablo de Greiff and Marieke Wierda, "The Trust Fund for Victims of the International Criminal Court: Between Possibilities and Constraints," in *Out of the Ashes: Reparation for Victims of Gross and Systematic Human Rights Violations*, eds. Koen de Feyter, et al., Intersentia, 2005, p. 235.

TFV stipulates specific factors that the TFV shall take into account in determining the nature and/or size of awards when the court does not stipulate how reparations are to be distributed. These factors include: the nature of the crimes, the size and location of the beneficiary group of victims, the particular injuries to the victims, and the type of evidence to support such injuries.

In relation to the assistance mandate pursuant to Rule 98(5), the TFV enjoys more flexibility than it does with the court-ordered implementation mandate since it is not connected to the trial and guilt of the perpetrator, and the governing texts of the TFV do not set out specific factors to be taken into account.[26] Although the TFV may have wider discretion concerning its assistance mandate, Article 79(3) of the Statute states that the TFV "shall be managed according to the criteria to be determined by the Assembly of States Parties," which in practice, refers to the TFV Regulations established by the resolution ICC-ASP/4/Res.3. Of particular relevance to the TFV's assistance mandate, Regulation 48 states that "[o]ther resources of the Trust Fund shall be used to benefit victims of crimes ... who have suffered physical, psychological and/or material harm as a result of these crimes." In addition, Regulation 50(a) stipulates that the TFV shall be considered seized in relation to providing assistance to victims when "the Board of Directors consider it necessary to provide physical or psychological rehabilitation or material support for the benefit of victims and their families." Thus, the assistance mandate, while broader than court-ordered reparations, still needs to benefit victims of the situation under the jurisdiction of the court who have suffered harm as a consequence of these crimes. Therefore, the TFV was not created in order to provide general humanitarian and socioeconomic aid to victims who are not connected with said crimes.

It is argued that, because the TFV is by nature an administrative mechanism linked to a judicial body, there is a clear line of division between decision-making powers of the court and the TFV. The court is a judicial body that must have a thorough knowledge of the legal aspects of the cases it encounters. It should be for the court to make all decisions in relation to the categories of victims and the classification of victims, since they are defined in a legal text, according to legal criteria, as discussed above. The decision on what is the harm for the purposes of reparation should also be left to the court for the same reasons.

The types of reparation (e.g., symbolic reparations) should be defined in broad terms by the court, leaving the TFV with some autonomy to devise the

---

[26] Connor McCarthy, *Reparations and Victims Support in the International Criminal Court*, Cambridge University Press, 2012, pp. 232–233.

reparation programs. For instance, the court should decide in any given case whether collective reparations are allowed, and whether rehabilitation or compensation are possible forms of reparations. From this point, with the assistance of broad guidelines, the TFV should then be able to decide how it will actually implement the reparations program. While the court should still hold all judicial definitions and guide the TFV in implementing reparations, the latter should be given a large degree of autonomy to ensure that reparations are appropriate for the victims. The TFV has eyes on the ground, has experience with reparations programs, and has knowledge of the needs of victims. As such, the TFV is better placed to devise reparation programs for the full benefit of victims.

Given the nature of international crimes, it is likely that many victims will come before the court for every case, many of whom will be seeking reparations.[27] In order to fulfill such a large number of requests, the ICC reparations system has to operate differently than typical international human rights mechanisms which sometimes deal with a limited number of victims in every case. At the ICC, many victims will be eligible to participate in proceedings, and then later claim reparations. Additionally, many other victims who do not qualify to participate in court proceedings may still be real "victims of crimes within the jurisdiction of the Court," to use the language of Article 79 of the Rome Statute.

To accommodate this large number of requests, the approach used to determine the kind of reparations available should be broad. More specifically, it should not be solely focused on compensation awards to individual victims, it should also consider symbolic reparations and collective reparations.[28] These types of reparations can reach more victims and can help overcome the TFV's limited financial ability to pay compensation. As the Trial Chamber in the *Lubanga* case affirmed, "a community-based approach, using the TFV's

---

[27] For example, in the *Lubanga* case, there were 120 victims participating the case; in the *Germain Katanga/Mathieu Ngudjolo Chui* case, there were 364 victims participating, see Eleni Chaitidou, *Recent Developments in the Jurisprudence of the International Criminal Court*, available at http://zis-online.com/dat/artikel/2013_3_740.pdf.

[28] See Frédéric Mégret, "The Case for Collective Reparations Before the ICC," in *Reparation for Victims of Crimes Against Humanity*, ed. Jo-Anne Wemmers, Routledge, 2014, The author argues, *inter alia*, that

> collective reparations will in many cases be superior not only on pragmatic grounds but also because they make most sense from the point of view of transitional justice. Most importantly, collective reparations are the most faithful to a construction of most international crimes as crimes that target groups (e.g.: the Genocide Convention groups) or categories (e.g.: civilians) rather than individuals as such.

voluntary contributions, would be more beneficial and have greater utility than individual awards, given the limited funds available."[29]

Providing reparations for victims of international crimes presents unique challenges, not only due to the multiplicity of victims, but also because it is impossible to repair what is irreplaceable. Mass suffering creates an emptiness not only for victims, but for the affected society, and for humanity. A sum of money – which is likely to be modest, considering the usual lack of resources of the accused and limited sources of outside funding available[30] – to isolated, individual victims, will generally not correspond to the international law standard of *restitutio ad integrum* and will likely fall short of victims' needs. This is one of the reasons that while it may be natural to address individual claims with sums of money, this is not necessarily the best approach in the aftermath of international crimes. Compensation and the award of sums of money should be limited to attending to victims' special needs in light of the crimes they have suffered (e.g., victims of sexual crimes). This does not suggest that there should be a hierarchy of victims in the sense that some victims have greater entitlements than others. Victims should be treated equally in terms of their right to receive reparation. It is simply posited that reparation programs should take into account the needs of victims and thus should result in a sort of "custom-made" reparation. Hearing the voices of victims and attending to their needs is crucial. Designing programs that benefit a larger number of victims will ensure that redress, in the aftermath of international crimes, is dealt with more holistically, and will help reduce the risk of involuntary discrimination among victims.

Furthermore, it also makes sense to have an organ that operates within the court and that is responsible for tasks such as raising funds for reparation awards (and assistance) programs. The funds raised through the convicted individual may not be sufficient to fulfill reparation initiatives. Thus, the fundraising possibilities of an administrative reparation mechanism such as the TFV should not be overlooked.[31]

In sum, channeling reparation efforts through the TFV appears to address many concerns. Having an administrative mechanism such as the TFV is like having "eyes on the ground." In light of its role and mandate, the TFV may be

---

[29] Decision on Reparations, p. 274.

[30] Frédéric Mégret, "The Case for Collective Reparations Before the ICC," in *Reparation for Victims of Crimes Against Humanity*, ed. Jo-Anne Wemmers, Routledge, 2014, p. 7.

[31] For example, in 2013, the United Kingdom contributed £500,000 to the ICC Trust Fund for Victims as part of the G8 Initiative on Preventing Sexual Violence in Conflict, see www.icc-cpi.int/Pages/item.aspx?name=872&ln=en.

The ICC Trust Fund for Victims　139

in a position to design programs tailored to deliver reparations to a large number of victims, and organize such reparation initiatives according to the realities of victims.[32]

4.2 THE REPARATIONS MANDATE: LESSONS FROM FIRST CASES

The court and the TFV function in a kind of complementary system based upon the provisions governing reparations within the ICC. As discussed above, according to the legal texts, the court has discretion regarding whether or not to award reparations, and it has the authority to devise the principles of reparations.[33] The court is also able to decide whether an individual or collective award should be ordered (or both).[34] Finally, the court determines whether the reparation award should be made through the TFV.[35] This latter situation occurs when the court deems it "appropriate," according to the terms of Article 75(2) of the Rome Statute, or when it is "impossible or impracticable to make individual awards directly to each victim."[36] Alternatively, awards "should be made through the Trust Fund where the number of victims and the scope, forms and modalities of reparations make a collective award more appropriate."[37]

As discussed in Chapter 3, four cases have reached the stage of reparations proceedings. In the *Bemba* case, however, the TFV has had no role to play regarding reparations considering the decision of the Appeals Chamber to reverse the conviction, and its effect of halting reparations in the case, as already discussed. As a result, the TFV has triggered its assistance program in the CAR situation in light of this outcome. In the three cases where reparations were ordered to date – *Lubanga*, *Katanga*, and *Al Mahdi* – the TFV has

---

[32]　See Pablo de Greiff and Marieke Wierda, "The Trust Fund for Victims of the International Criminal Court: Between Possibilities and Constraints," in *Out of the Ashes: Reparation for Victims of Gross and Systematic Human Rights Violations*, eds. Koen de Feyter, et al., Intersentia, 2005, pp. 239–240.

[33]　See Article 75(1) of the ICC Statute.

[34]　See Article 75(2) of the Rome Statute and Rules 97(1) and 98(1)–(4) of the RPE.

[35]　Article 75(2) of the Rome Statute.

[36]　Rule 98(2) of the RPE.

[37]　Rule 98(3) of the RPE. See generally for a commentary, Eva Dwertmann, *The Reparation System of the International Criminal Court: Its Implementation, Possibilities and Limitations*, Nijhoff, 2010, pp. 265–271; Thordis Ingadottir, "The Trust Fund for Victims (Article 79 of the Rome Statute)," in *The International Criminal Court: Recommendations on Policy and Practice – Financing, Victims, Judges, and Immunities*, ed. Thordis Ingadottir, Ardsley, 2003, pp. 111 et seq.

had to step up and cover the reparations orders given the indigence of the accused.

The ICC, unlike a human rights court, does not have the power, nor the mandate, to hold states accountable for crimes committed under its jurisdiction, as already discussed. It cannot order them to pay compensation. Even when the offender may have the assets to contribute to reparation awards,[38] which has yet to happen, the TFV should still be involved in reparation process.[39] The TFV should thus focus efforts on getting states to cooperate with reparation awards, through financial contributions or assistance in locating and freezing the convicted person's assets.

In light of the cases discussed above, the court should retain a limited, supervisory, role in the management of reparation awards made to victims. Such a role would have two aspects. The first is the decision on reparation, as stated in the Rome Statute. Specific and direct guidance should be provided in relation to the role of the TFV in the realization of the reparations order. While there should be some freedom as to how the TFV will work, certain issues, such as deadlines for implementation and reporting on activities, should be detailed in the reparation order. These details will ensure that the implementation plan the TFV will provide meets the expectations of the Trial Chamber and thus avoids delays such as those seen in *Lubanga*, due to the disconnect between the information the chamber wanted and what the TFV provided in the implementation plan.

The second role should be the monitoring of the implementation of reparations. This entails judicial supervision of the reparations designed by the TFV in order to ascertain that the program meets the principles the court previously set out. It is to be recalled that the TFV is an administrative mechanism, run by a Board of Directors. It is important in this light that it remains continuously attached to the judicial arm of the ICC, the chambers. The TFV does not exist in a vacuum. The judicial role of the court in ensuring the proper design and implementation of reparation programs by the TFV should be emphasized. This approach would ensure a uniform system of reparations across cases and it would provide the "judicial" enforcement necessary in a reparation program through the court's chambers. The guidelines set by the court enable the TFV to ensure that reparations follow the

---

[38] See Pablo de Greiff and Marieke Wierda, "The Trust Fund for Victims of the International Criminal Court: Between Possibilities and Constraints," in *Out of the Ashes: Reparation for Victims of Gross and Systematic Human Rights Violations*, eds. Koen de Feyter, et al., Intersentia, 2005, p. 237, concerning the international experience recovering funds from perpetrators.

[39] Other authors have defended a more central role for the TFV, see e.g., ibid.

The ICC Trust Fund for Victims

framework of the Statute, and help the TFV remain consistent in its administration of the programs.

At the time of the writing of this book, only three reparation orders have been made. In all three cases the TFV played a central role in the reparations ordered, from the design of a plan, the funding of the awards (including fundraising) to the implementation with the selection of implementing partners on the ground (which to date the awards have yet to be fully implemented). The first case of *The Prosecutor* v. *Thomas Lubanga Dyilo* is telling of how the different roles of the court (chambers) and the TFV can be better delineated to avoid delays and improve efficiency. To illustrate the implementation of reparations by the TFV, and the role of the TFV vis-à-vis the court, some details of the reparations in this case are discussed.

In relation to the implementation of collective reparations in the *Lubanga* case, the TFV reported conducting consultations in the Ituri district between May and July 2015 in order to assess the location of direct and indirect victims. These consultations were necessary for purposes of providing reparations in accordance with the Appeals Chamber Judgment. The TFV held consultations in twenty-two localities in Ituri to assess the harm suffered and collect the views of victims concerning reparations. Despite these consultations, the TFV reported that it was

> still lacking important information required to address comprehensively the tasks set by the Appeals Chamber. In particular, the Trust Fund consider[ed] that in order to assist the Trial Chamber with establishing the liability of the convicted person and to create the draft implementation plan, it [was] necessary to have access to reliable data on the direct victims as defined by the Court currently held by third parties in the DRC.[40]

As requested, the TFV submitted a "Draft Implementation Plan" to Trial Chamber II on 3 November 2015. It outlined the TFV's plan to implement the collective reparations in the *Lubanga* case.[41] On 9 February 2016, in the exercise of its monitoring and supervisory function, Trial Chamber II, after examining the Draft Implementation Plan, decided that it was incomplete and that it could not rule on the proposed plan.[42] According to the chamber the plan did not include sufficient information on: the victims potentially

---

[40] ICC, TFV, "Assistance and Reparation: Achievements, Lessons Learned, and Transitioning – Programme Progress Report 2015," at p. 54, available at http://trustfundforvictims.org/sites/d efault/files/media_library/documents/FinalTFVPPR2015.pdf.

[41] ICC, TFV, "Filing on Reparations and Draft Implementation Plan," 3 November 2005, ICC-01/04-01/06-3177-Red, and its two annexes, ICC-01/04-01/06-3177-AnxA, and "Annex I," ICC-01/04-01/06-3177-Conf-Exp-AnxI.

[42] ICC, Trial Chamber II, "Order instructing the Trust Fund for Victims to supplement the draft implementation plan," 9 February 2016, ICC-01/04-01/06.

eligible to benefit from the reparations, including the requests for reparations and the supporting material; the extent of the harm caused to the victims; proposals regarding the modalities and forms of reparations; and the amount of the convicted person's liability. In response to the Trial Chamber's order, on 7 June 2016, the TFV provided a detailed explanation of the various issues and concerns arising from the chamber's order. In particular, the TFV: "respectfully request[ed] the Trial Chamber to accept its request for reconsideration made in the Victim Dossier Filing, to revise its current procedural approach and to instead consider approving the Draft Implementation Plan of 3 November 2015 in its entirety."[43] As explained in Chapter 3, it was only in October 2016 that the process seems to have started to move along. Fast forward to 2019, three years later, when the Appeals Chamber rendered what hopefully will be the last decision in this case concerning reparations and the plan can be fully implemented. As Luke Moffett has noted, "[t]he slowness of proceedings means that victims in this case were under the age of 15 at the time of the crimes in 2003 but are now in their thirties."[44] It is clear from the first experiences of reparation cases that much needs to be improved for efficiency and expediency of reparation proceedings, including fine-tuning the respective roles of the chambers and the TFV.

4.3 BRIDGING THE GAP: THE TFV'S ASSISTANCE MANDATE

Complementary to its reparations mandate, the TFV has an important mandate to provide assistance to victims in situations being investigated by the court. The assistance mandate is funded by voluntary contributions from donors. Three kinds of assistance are legally defined. The first is physical rehabilitation, including reconstructive and general surgery, and prosthetic and orthopedic devices. The second is psychological rehabilitation, such as trauma counseling, information sessions, and large-scale community meetings. Third, it can include material support such as vocational training, programs for income generation and training, and education grants for survivors.[45]

The assistance mandate of the TFV is not exactly of a reparative nature but more like a much-needed aid to communities affected by the crimes under the

---

[43] ICC, TFV, "Additional Programme Information Filing," 7 June 2016, ICC-01/04-01/06-3209.

[44] Luke Moffett, "Reparations at the ICC: Can it Serve as a Model?" Justiceinfo.net, 19 July 2019, available at www.justiceinfo.net/en/justiceinfo-comment-and-debate/opinion/41949-reparations-at-the-icc-can-it-really-serve-as-a-model.html (last accessed 26 July 2019).

[45] See Katharina Peschke, "The Role and Mandates of the ICC Trust Fund for Victims," in *Victims of International Crimes: An Interdisciplinary Discourse*, eds. Thorsten Bonacker and Christoph Safferling, Springer, 2013, pp. 317–327.

jurisdiction of the court. The assistance mandate reaches beyond the specific crimes being prosecuted by the Prosecutor. It is a general assistance that is not connected to a specific trial and, significantly, does not require any perpetrator to be convicted for the assistance to take place. The TFV generally discharges the assistance mandate by working with local organizations, victim survivor groups, women's associations, faith-based organizations, and international non-governmental organizations. These partnerships are crucial to enable the TFV to craft and deliver its assistance mandate to affected communities. The initial stage of the TFV's assistance mandate prioritized four areas: (a) justice and reconciliation; (b) health and well-being; (c) social support and integration; and (d) material security. Importantly, for the TFV, gender cuts across these priority areas.[46] The TFV-supported programs incorporate three common features: the activities are trauma sensitive, context sensitive, and gender sensitive.

The TFV can provide assistance to victims of the broader situations in which crimes are alleged to have occurred, and it can happen before a specific trial starts and upon the conclusion of proceedings. The TFV does need to notify the Pre-Trial Chamber of its intention to undertake an assistance program. Under Regulation 50(a)(ii) of the Regulations of the Trust Fund, the proposed activities must not violate the presumption of innocence of the accused, be inconsistent with, or prejudicial to, the rights of the accused and a fair and impartial trial.

In theory, by its nature, the assistance mandate might reach a greater number of individuals and affected communities in a more timely fashion than court-ordered reparations, since it is not connected to the cases before the court and can benefit victims of broader situations. However, both mandates aim at redressing the harm suffered due to international crimes within the jurisdiction of the court.

The assistance mandate of the TFV has received to date less attention in scholarship than its reparation mandate. The TFV has engaged in assistance programs in three situations: the DRC, Northern Uganda, and Côte d'Ivoire. In relation to the CAR, the assistance mandate was meant to be launched in 2013 but activities were canceled in light of the security situation. Following Mr. Bemba's acquittal, as discussed above, the Board of Directors of the TFV unanimously decided to accelerate the launch of its assistance program in the form of physical and psychological rehabilitation, and material support, for the benefit of victims and their families in the CAR situation.[47]

---

[46] Report of the Trust Fund for Victims, "Reviewing Rehabilitation Assistance and Preparing for Delivering Reparations," 2011, p. 2.

[47] TFV, "Following Mr Bemba's acquittal, Trust Fund for Victims at the ICC Decides to Accelerate Launch of Assistance Programme in Central African Republic," Press release, 13 June 2018, available at www.icc-cpi.int/Pages/item.aspx?name=180613-TFVPR.

In relation to the DRC, the TFV reported that 15.8 million are in need in Ituri, North Kivu, and South Kivu. It started its assistance program in the DRC in 2008, and completed five projects by 2017. Other projects are planned to continue the assistance program in the country. As for Northern Uganda, the TFV estimates that there are seven million people in need. The programs included physical and psychological rehabilitation. In the first two programs, the TFV reports that more than 350,000 victims have benefited from TFV-supported activities. In Côte d'Ivoire, the TFV calculated that there are 23.7 million in need in the entire country. The program includes medical rehabilitation, psychological rehabilitation, and socioeconomic support. The TFV initially obligated EUR 800,000 for this program and reported to aim to reserve EUR 3.6 million through 2020 for the assistance.[48]

The TFV's assistance programs currently in place demand further review. In order to fulfill its assistance mandate and provide support to victims, the TFV partners with local organizations. Therefore, it is crucial that the TFV play an active role concerning the type of support that is being provided to victims. The TFV should avoid entering into situations where contributing funds is its only role. It can do so by engaging in decision-making and maintaining control of its activities. In this regard, further reporting would be appropriate. How is the TFV ensuring that all victims are being helped by the assistance program? How are the needs of victims being met by the programs in place? What lessons can be learned from experience? These are some of the questions that are raised and for which further reporting would be beneficial.

The assistance mandate of the TFV, while different from general humanitarian or development aid, is limited by the situations in which the TFV can act. The TFV cannot provide assistance or support to all victims of all situations of conflict in the world. Nevertheless, it is important to continuously evaluate whether other situations within the jurisdiction of the court also require the TFV to act within its assistance mandate. In addition to actually implementing the assistance programs, the TFV may be advised to proactively assess situations that could fall under its assistance mandate. It is important for the TFV to set out clear guidelines on how to prioritize programs and how to attend to urgent requests. It may also be a good idea to report some best practices in order to inform future assistance programs.

The assistance mandate represents the expression of a need to bridge a gap that in many cases is left by a criminal approach to reparations. Reparations

---

[48] TFV, "Assistance Programmes," available at www.trustfundforvictims.org/en/what-we-do/assistance-programmes (last accessed 31 May 2019).

within the ICC regime, as discussed, are limited in various ways, and perpetuate exclusions and hierarchy of victims. Thus, the assistance programs of the TFV play a crucial role in recognizing that victims' harm and suffering go beyond the outcomes of criminal trials, and that community reconciliation is needed even when a perpetrator is not found guilty by a criminal standard of proof. Assistance by the TFV also ensures that victims and communities are not waiting for a long criminal trial, that must end with a conviction, in order to receive reparations.

These are crucial points that were evidenced in the *Bemba* case. As already discussed, the large number of victims, after a trial and conviction, were finally faced with the impossibility of obtaining reparations due to the acquittal of Mr. Bemba on appeal.[49] Mr. Bemba's acquittal does not, however, devictimize the individuals who were recognized as victims in the proceedings and those who suffered harm as a result of the crimes committed in the CAR. A regime that conditions reparations to a criminal conviction by criminal law standards can make a large number of victims ineligible to obtain reparations. The assistance mandate of the TFV can (and did in this case) fill in the gap, since it is not dependent upon the finding of guilt of the perpetrator(s). As the TFV has itself stated:

> Activities undertaken under the Fund's assistance mandate are distinct from the judicial proceedings of the Court and do not require the conviction or even the identification of the perpetrator(s) of the harms suffered by victims. It is necessary that victims have suffered harms from crimes under the jurisdiction of the Court as defined by the "situation" under investigation by the Prosecutor. In taking its decision, the Board observed that, irrespective of the outcome of the judicial proceedings, victims who presented themselves to the Court in the context of the Bemba case are, by definition, victims of the "situation" in CAR I.[50]

As this example illustrates, in situations of ongoing or post-conflict, the TFV can provide much-needed assistance to victims and affected communities where the outcome of criminal trials would have deprived them of any support. This case also highlights the crucial nature of this less-debated mandate of the TFV and its role in promoting restoration and reconciliation where reparations have failed. Assistance is distinct from reparation in legal and practical standpoints, but it may in some ways provide what a criminal approach to reparations does not allow.

---

[49] See ICC, Trial Chamber, "Final Decision on the Reparations Proceedings," ICC-01/05-01/08, 3 August 2018.

[50] ICC, "Communication from the Chair of the Board of Directors of the TFV to the President of the Assembly of States Parties," 13 June 2018. See also ICC-01/05-01/08-3648, para. 7.

146   *Reparative Justice for International Crimes*

Some criticisms of the exercise of the assistance mandate of the TFV is that it should be put in place sooner in certain situations. Victims need assistance in a timely manner in order to have a chance to overcome the consequences of the harm they suffered. The TFV should also put greater efforts in expanding its assistance mandate within situations, to reach more victims, as well as to other situations. These criticisms, however, all link back to a major challenge that the TFV faces regarding its limited resources, both human (the question of capacity) and financial.

4.4 THE ROAD AHEAD: THE CHALLENGES OF THE TFV AND ADMINISTRATIVE MECHANISMS IN THE AFTERMATH OF MASS VICTIMIZATION

The reparations mandate of the TFV is both noble and inspiring. As it has been noted, "[t]he challenging and ambitious mandate assigned to the International Criminal Court under article 75 to ensure reparations for victims of crimes is in stark contrast with the embryonic structure put in place to ensure the fulfillment of that mandate."[51] The fact that the TFV is an innovation in international criminal justice means that it will likely face many difficult challenges in the pursuit of its mandates.

The most obvious challenge will be the availability of sufficient funds and resources to provide redress for the large number of victims of the crimes within the jurisdiction of the ICC. The demand for assistance and the need to involve the TFV in reparations are far greater than the TFV's resources.

As explained above, the TFV may obtain funds from: 1) the voluntary contributions of governments, international organizations, individuals, corporations, and other entities in accordance with criteria established by the ASP; 2) money and property gathered through fines or forfeitures transferred to the TFV by a court order in accordance with Article 79 of the ICC Statute; 3) resources collected by awards for reparations if ordered by the court; and 4) such resources other than assessed contributions as the ASP may decide to allocate to the TFV.

The funds of the TFV are thus necessarily limited. As such, fund-raising should be an important aspect of the activities of the TFV to ensure that it has the available financial resources to fulfill its tasks.[52] In this light, the TFV

---

[51] Marc Henzelin et al., "Reparations to Victims Before the International Criminal Court: Lessons from International Mass Claims Processes," *Criminal Law Forum* 17 (2006), pp. 338–339.

[52] See Peter G. Fischer, "The Victims' Trust Fund of the International Criminal Court: Formation of a Functional Reparations Scheme," *Emory International Law Review* 17 (2003), pp. 191–192 (concerning fund-raising).

should also focus attention on gathering voluntary contributions that will ensure the fulfillment of reparation awards.

The financial limitations of the TFV do not, however, mean that the ability of the TFV to implement reparation awards will be irreversibly hampered. In this scenario, the meaning and scope of redress becomes ever more important. Indeed, financial compensation is not the only means to provide reparations to victims. Symbolic and collective reparations should be an important aspect of the TFV's programs. The financial resources of the TFV should also be managed in a way which accounts for certain victims who require specific and urgent assistance as a result of the crimes committed against them,[53] such as victims of sexual violence.

The number of victims of international crimes of the kind the ICC prosecutes will likely always be very high, and therefore, the number of potential reparation claimants will also be numerous. Another challenge refers to the practical implementation of the reparation principles elaborated by the chambers. As reviewed above, several principles were established rather abstractly. Therefore, it appears that the TFV has a significant challenge to implement reparations, while keeping in line with the principles stated by the court. In relation to reparations arising out of the *Lubanga* case, the TFV may consider taking a comprehensive approach which can inform future cases. In this sense, the TFV itself can establish principles to be followed in a transparent manner, within the limitations of the principles set out by the court and the constraints imposed by the governing texts of the ICC and the TFV. For example, the TFV may decide to set out some specific reporting guidelines and timelines governing the implementation of the court's orders which will provide some guidance for future court-ordered reparations.

Furthermore, as reviewed above, the TFV has already acquired significant experience developing programs which benefit victims of crimes under the jurisdiction of the court. These experiences have given the TFV specific knowledge about the needs of victims and the strategies that work. The TFV may consider using these experiences to inform future reparation programs. Despite the TFV's ability to learn from past experiences, it is also important that the TFV does not lose sight of the unique needs of victims which must be central to every program it devises.

The challenges and difficult questions that the court and the TFV will face, while implementing the ICC's reparations mandate, suggest that a united

---

[53] Anne-Marie De Brouwer, "Reparation to Victims of Sexual Violence: Possibilities at the International Criminal Court and at the Trust Fund for Victims and their Families," *Leiden Journal of International Law* 20 (2007), pp. 207–237.

148 *Reparative Justice for International Crimes*

effort between the court and the TFV will help create an efficient reparations mechanism.

As already discussed, the inclusion of reparation into international criminal justice is a relatively new development. Previous international criminal justice enterprises, such as the ad hoc criminal tribunals, did not have a scheme for victim reparation.[54] The ICC and the TFV represent a major step towards providing redress and assistance to victims of international crimes. An important question is whether the TFV will influence the creation outside the scope of the ICC of other similar domestic, or international, reparation initiatives for violations of international law.

Unfortunately, the ICC does not yet have jurisdiction over all international crimes that are committed worldwide. The court's limited jurisdiction[55] necessarily limits the scope of the TFV's activities to victims of crimes within the jurisdiction of the ICC. This means that many victims of international crimes and mass atrocities will remain outside the reparative dimension of international criminal justice. As Jann Kleffner and Liesbeth Zegveld argue, "while the ICC may, either upon request or on its own motion, afford reparations to victims of war crimes, these are reparations afforded within the individual responsibility framework of the ICC."[56]

Discussing specific reparations policies implemented by states to address mass human rights violations is outside the scope of this book. Nevertheless, it is hoped that the experience of the TFV as a mechanism to foster reparation for victims of crimes within the ICC, may serve as a catalyst for other similar international reparations schemes in areas where the TFV cannot act due to limits on its jurisdiction. Such efforts could be on an individual basis, for example, in relation to victims of a specific conflict. Alternatively, they could be in a more global aspect,[57] aimed at victims of international crimes or mass

---

[54] Michael Bachrach, "The Protection and Rights of Victims Under International Criminal Law," *International Lawyer* 34 (2000), pp. 7–20.

[55] On the jurisdiction of the ICC, see William A. Schabas, *An Introduction to the International Criminal Court*, Cambridge University Press, 4th ed., 2011, chapter 3.

[56] Jann K. Kleffner and Liesbeth Zegveld, "Establishing an Individual Complaints Procedure for Violations of International Humanitarian Law," *Yearbook of International Humanitarian Law* 3 (2000), p. 384.

[57] Without engaging in a detailed discussion, which is outside the scope of this book, such fund, with a global reach, could be established for the benefit of all victims of international crimes. The trust fund would receive, like the TFV, voluntary contributions from individuals, international/regional organizations, nongovernmental organizations, and States. As already discussed, the main source of funding of the TFV does not come from the accused. Such proposed trust fund could be based on the example of the TFV and could function under the auspices of the United Nations.

human rights violations, and with a view to bridging the gaps of the TFV's reparation and assistance mandates. The TFV is one piece in the fabric of international justice. The question is not whether victim reparations should be part international justice, but rather how to make it a feasible endeavor at the ICC and beyond.

5

The Role of National Courts and Mechanisms in Realizing Reparative Justice for International Crimes

There are a variety of ways to respond to international crimes. International criminal justice, in particular, stands on two pillars. It has an international dimension, performed, for example, by international courts (which can be coupled with administrative mechanisms), as discussed in previous chapters. It also has a national dimension performed by domestic courts which enforce international law.[1]

Bringing civil claims before domestic courts offers a potential for addressing international wrongs,[2] including international crimes. This chapter dwells upon whether there should be an increased role for national courts concerning reparations for victims of international crimes and whether progress in international criminal law at the international level could work as a catalyst for national claims for reparation. This chapter nevertheless also highlights the challenges that lie ahead and ponders about ways to increase the role of national courts in the quest to provide reparations for international crimes.

While the claims for reparations before domestic courts often involve questions of state immunity, such issues are outside the scope of the book, leaving out other related questions of state responsibility for international

---

[1] This chapter will focus on the role of domestic courts in the award of reparation for victims of international crimes. In relation to domestic prosecutions of international crimes, many studies have addressed this question in detail. See e.g., Robert Cryer, *Prosecuting International Crimes: Selectivity and the International Criminal Law Regime*, Cambridge University Press, 2005; Damien Vandermeersch, "Prosecuting International Crimes in Belgium," *Journal of International Criminal Justice* 3 (2005), pp. 400–421; Anthony D'Amato, "National Prosecution for International Crimes," in *International Criminal Law*, ed. M. Cherif Bassiouni, Nijhoff, 2003, pp. 217–226.

[2] Jaykumar A. Menon, "The Low Road: Promoting Civil Redress for International Wrongs," in *Realizing Utopia: The Future of International Law*, Antonio Cassese, Oxford University Press, 2012, chapter 47.

The Role of National Courts and Mechanisms   151

crimes.[3] Also outside the scope of this book are cases dealing with the responsibility or liability of corporations. The aim of this chapter is not to provide an exhaustive discussion of all cases involving reparations before domestic courts. Rather, it uses some selected examples of cases as the background to the discussion of how domestic mechanisms can play a role regarding reparations for international crimes.

5.1 DIVERGING DOMESTIC APPROACHES TO REPARATIONS WITHIN CRIMINAL LAW PROCEEDINGS

This chapter starts by providing some context for the discussion that will follow and briefly describes two leading models of adjudication of civil claims: first, where civil claims are dissociated from criminal prosecutions and processes, and another where civil claims can be brought within the criminal proceedings. The goal of this overview is to demonstrate how domestic courts may approach a claim for civil redress depending on the legal system, with limited selected examples of different jurisdictions as illustrative rather than a detailed discussion of the topic.[4]

The concept of victim participation and the adjudication of civil reparation within criminal proceedings[5] are common in many states.[6] In saying this, there is a difference within states in Europe depending on whether they come from a civil Germanic background, such as Austria and Germany, a Nordic background, such as Denmark and Norway, a civil Romanic background, such as France, Italy, and Spain, or even a mixed background, such as the

---

[3] For a review of this question and related issues, see generally: Dinah Shelton, "Righting Wrongs: Reparations in the Articles on State Responsibility," *American Journal of International Law* 96 (2002), pp. 833–856; André Nollkaemper, "Concurrence Between Individual Responsibility and State Responsibility in International Law," *International and Comparative Law Quarterly* 52 (2003), pp. 615–640; Lorna McGregor, "State Immunity and Jus Cogens," *The International and Comparative Law Quarterly* 55 (2006), pp. 437–445.

[4] For a detailed discussion see Marion E. Brienen and Ernestine Hoegen, *Victims of Crime in 22 European Criminal Justice Systems*, Wolf Legal Productions, 2000.

[5] However, as Judge Pikis has indicated, no national system has a similar provision to article 68 (3) of the Rome Statute concerning victims' participatory rights within ICC proceedings, see *The Prosecutor* v. *Thomas Lubanga Dyilo*, "Decision of the Appeals Chamber on the Joint Application of Victims a/0001/06 to a/0003/06 and a/0105/06 Concerning the Directions and Decision of the Appeals Chamber," 2 February 2007, ICC-01/04–01/06–925, Separate opinion of Judge Pikis, p. 16.

[6] See Marion E. Brienen and Ernestine Hoegen, *Victims of Crime in 22 European Criminal Justice Systems*, Wolf Legal Productions, 2000.

152   *Reparative Justice for International Crimes*

case of Greece. Nevertheless, each of these systems grants victims participatory rights as a *"partie civile."*[7]

Domestic proceedings for reparation may take dramatically different forms. The participation of victims in criminal proceedings raises the possibility that victims may claim reparations within the same criminal proceedings. However, if victims are not permitted to participate and bring claims for reparation within criminal proceedings, then often claims for reparation will be completely dissociated from the criminal prosecution of the accused.

Domestic legal systems are largely influenced by the legal tradition to which they belong. A legal system's unique approach to dealing with the civil claims of victims of international crimes will create different domestic mechanisms of reparation. Each system's features will dictate the role of domestic courts, prosecutors, and victims.

Section 5.1.1 reviews the Romano-Germanic and common law systems, not with the purpose of exhaustive analysis of the legal traditions that exist, but rather to compare and contrast different approaches to claims for reparation by victims. It will survey whether victims may, in certain instances, claim reparations within criminal proceedings. For this purpose, it provides a general overview of two main legal systems and discusses whether victims may claim reparations within criminal proceedings or whether separate civil proceedings are the only avenue available to victims.

5.1.1 *Romano-Germanic Systems*

In France,[8] victims may hold different roles within the criminal justice system. Victims may act as a *"partie civile"* (civil claimant), a complainant, or as a private prosecutor.[9] A victim who reports a crime (a "complainant") will not only inform the public authorities of the crime, but will also initiate criminal

---

[7]   Mugambi Jouet, "Reconciling the Conflicting Rights of Victims and Defendants at the International Criminal Court," *St. Louis University Public Law Review* 26 (2007), p. 3. In regards to the concept of *"partie civile,"* see in France articles 85 and 87 of the "Code de Procédure Pénale," in Belgium the *"burgerlijke partij,"* articles 63, 66, and 67 of the Belgian Criminal Procedure Code "Wetboek van Strafvordering," and in Austria the "Privatbeteiligter," para. 47 of the Austrian Criminal Procedure Code "Strafprozessordnung 7975." In Germany, victims do not act as a *partie civile* but rather as auxiliary prosecutor, see paras. 395 to 402 of the German Criminal Procedure Code "Strafprozessordnung."

[8]   See generally, Mireille Delmas-Marty and J. R. Spencer, *European Criminal Proceedings*, Cambridge University Press, 2002, pp. 218–291.

[9]   Marion E. Brienen and Ernestine Hoegen, *Victims of Crime in 22 European Criminal Justice Systems*, Wolf Legal Productions, 2000, p. 316.

The Role of National Courts and Mechanisms 153

proceedings if they are not started by the public prosecution.[10] In this sense, victims' rights are broader than the rights provided in the ICC system, since they can participate in proceedings without further conditions and begin criminal proceedings in the event that the prosecution has not yet done so. In certain cases, victims can also act as private prosecutors, which enables them to summon the accused to appear in court and start the prosecution.[11] However, once the prosecution has been initiated, the public prosecutor has to continue with the proceedings since it is the duty of the prosecution to carry on public prosecutions.[12]

As far as participating as a civil claimant, a victim has the right to demand compensation in a criminal court of justice, in addition to their rights in a civil court.[13] That being said, there are some conditions for the exercise of this right which are set out in section 2 of the French code of criminal procedure.

In Brazil, victims may act as assistants to the prosecutor throughout the criminal proceedings and no special application needs to be filed for them to be granted the status of victims in criminal proceedings.[14] Similarly, in Senegal, Articles 2 and 3 of the Code of Criminal Procedure also recognize the possibility of raising civil claims in criminal proceedings.[15]

These selected examples demonstrate that victims from countries which partake in a Romano-Germanic legal system are granted extensive participatory rights which are broader than the system established in the ICC. In this sense, if compared to Romano-Germanic legal systems, a broad

---

[10] Ibid., p. 317. This book does not analyze the case of certain crimes such as defamation in which filing a complaint is an essential condition for a public action, see for instance section 48 of the French Penal Code, cited in ibid., p. 318.

[11] See section 2, French Code of Criminal Procedure.

[12] Marion E. Brienen and Ernestine Hoegen, *Victims of Crime in 22 European Criminal Justice Systems*, Wolf Legal Productions, 2000, p. 321.

[13] Ibid., p. 318.

[14] See in general: Flaviane de Magalhães Barros Pellegrini, "Os direitos das vítimas de crimes no Estado Democrático de Direito – uma análise do Projeto de Lei n° 269/2003 – Senado Federal." The author suggests in this article that victims are lacking a few essential rights in the Brazilian criminal law system, such as the right to be informed of the initiation of proceedings, and also mentions the difficulty to effectively obtain reparation.

[15] For a discussion of Senegal and other countries, see Amnesty International, Annual Report 2012, "Universal Jurisdiction: The Scope of Universal Civil Jurisdiction," available at https://documents.law.yale.edu/sites/default/files/Amnesty%20International%20-%20Universal%20Jurisdiction_%20The%20scope%20of%20universal%20civil%20jurisdiction%20_%20Amnesty%20International.pdf.

154 *Reparative Justice for International Crimes*

interpretation of participatory rights within the ICC framework is harmonious. However, it is important to note that the large scope of participation in national systems is based on different provisions than those found in the Rome Statute which confine participatory rights to a judge-oriented system.[16]

5.1.2 *Common Law Systems*

In the common law system, victims are not granted broad participatory rights in criminal proceedings.[17] In general, victims only have the right to participate in the sentencing part of the proceedings. In Canada, victims may be given a voice during sentencing where they can express their opinion about the sentence the judge should give the convicted person.[18] In these cases, the judge is not obliged to follow the victims' suggestions. Likewise, in the American legal system, most states grant victims a participatory right at the sentencing stage.[19] Private prosecutions are banned both in federal cases, as well as in every state.[20]

In England and Wales, victims are granted no participatory rights other than that of initiating private prosecutions.[21] However, it is worth noting that in this system, victims are not granted any special status since any person can initiate a private prosecution, including nonvictims.[22]

This brief overview of the role and rights of victims in different domestic legal systems provides the backdrop for a discussion of specific case studies in the following section, and a context in which the initiatives found in each case study arose. It also provides the fabric in which proposals for the role of domestic courts in the adjudication of reparation claims for international crimes can develop.

---

[16] Article 68(3) of the Rome Statute states "where the Court considers it appropriate."

[17] Mugambi Jouet, "Reconciling the Conflicting Rights of Victims and Defendants at the International Criminal Court," *St. Louis University Public Law Review* 26 (2007), p. 4.

[18] See section 722 of the Canadian Criminal Code.

[19] Douglas E. Beloof, *Victims in Criminal Procedure*, Carolina Academic Press, 1998.

[20] Mugambi Jouet, "Reconciling the Conflicting Rights of Victims and Defendants at the International Criminal Court," *St. Louis University Public Law Review* 26 (2007), p. 5.

[21] See *inter alia*, *Queen's Bench Division R (on the application of Gladstone Pic) v. Manchester City Magistrates* [2005] All ER 56 (All England Law Reports); Divisional Court, *Jones v. Whalley* [2006] 2 Criminal Law Review 67 on appeal to the House of Lords, *Jones v. Whalley* [2006] 4 All ER 113; Cyprus: Supreme Court, *Ttofinis v. Theochandes* (1983) 2 Cyprus Law Reports 363.

[22] Mugambi Jouet, "Reconciling the Conflicting Rights of Victims and Defendants at the International Criminal Court," *St. Louis University Public Law Review* 26 (2007), p. 5.

5.2 DOMESTIC CASE STUDY: MISSED OPPORTUNITIES IN THE FORMER YUGOSLAVIA

While domestic courts can play a role in the adjudication and award of reparations for international crimes that occurred within its territory, there are many examples throughout history where mass atrocities have taken place, but domestic courts and mechanisms have failed to provide redress for victims. While it is claimed that national mechanisms have a crucial role to play in fostering reparative justice for international crimes, the shortcomings of national adjudication of reparations must also be acknowledged. In this vein, this section examines a case study of reparations in the aftermath of the Balkans war, more specifically in Bosnia and Herzegovina.

The conflict in the Balkans[23] took many lives and left hundreds of thousands of victims.[24] In addition to outrage and violence, the war was characterized by sexual violence.[25] The surviving victims not only deserve reparation but also *need* it in order to survive and cope with the

---

[23] Many pieces review efforts at the international and national levels concerning reparation for victims of international crimes committed during the wars. I rely on some accounts in detail in this section of the present chapter, see references *supra*. Other interesting works include: Dino Abazovic, "Reconciliation, Ethopolitics and Religion in Bosnia and Herzegovina," in *Post-Yugoslavia: New Cultural and Political Perspectives*, eds. Dino Abazovic and Mitja Velikonja, Palgrave Macmillan, 2014; Antoine Buyse, *Post Conflict Housing Restitution: The European Human Rights Perspective with a Case Study on Bosnia and Herzegovina*, Intersentia, 2008; Timothy Cornell and Lance Salisbury, "The Importance of Civil Law in the Transition to Peace: Lessons from the Human Rights Chamber for Bosnia and Herzegovina," *Cornell International Law Journal* 35 (2000–2001), pp. 389–426; Lara J. Nettlefield, *Courting Democracy in Bosnia and Herzegovina, The Hague Tribunal's Impact in a Postwar State*, Cambridge University Press, 2010; Linda Popic and Belma Panjeta, *Compensation, Transitional Justice and Conditional International Credit in Bosnia and Herzegovina*, Independent Research Publication, 2010, http://justice-report.com/en/file/show//Documents/Publications/Linda_Popic_ENG.pdf; Eric Rosand, "The Right to Compensation in Bosnia: An Unfulfilled Promise and Challenge to International Law," *Cornell Journal of International Law* 33 (2000), pp. 130, 131; Rodri C. Williams, *Post Conflict Property Restitution in Bosnia: Balancing Reparations and Durable Solutions in the Aftermath of Displacement*, TESEV International Symposium on "Internal Displacement in Turkey and Abroad," 5 December 2006, Istanbul, pp. 10, 11; David Yeager, "The Human Rights Chamber for Bosnia and Herzegovina: A Case Study in Transitional Justice," *International Legal Perspectives* 14 (2004), pp. 44–54.

[24] Concerning official background information of the conflict see the ICTY website: http://icty.org/sid/322.

[25] Concerning studies of sexual violence during the war, see e.g., Kelly D. Askin, "Sexual Violence in Decisions and Indictments of the Yugoslav and Rwandan Tribunals: Current Status," *American Journal of International Law* 93 (1999), pp. 97–123; Colette Donadio, "Gender Based Violence: Justice and Reparation in Bosnia and Herzegovina," *Mediterranean Journal of Social Sciences* 5 (2014), p. 692. Anne-Marie De Brouwer, *Supranational Criminal Prosecution of Sexual Violence*, Intersentia, 2005; Courtney Ginn, "Ensuring the Effective Prosecution of Sexually Violent Crimes in the Bosnian War Crimes Chamber: Applying Lessons from the ICTY," *Emory International*

156 *Reparative Justice for International Crimes*

consequences of rapes and sexual violence.[26] They have been left with unwanted pregnancies, internal injuries and mutilations, and sexually transmitted infections such as HIV, which require ongoing medical care. In countries like Bosnia and Herzegovina which have been devastated by war, the harm caused can never be fully repaired. Yet, efforts towards reconciliation and reparation contribute to a sense of justice for victims and may help create lasting peace.[27]

5.2.1 *International Mechanisms*

The war in the former Yugoslavia witnessed hundreds of thousands of international crimes perpetrated on a massive scale, creating widespread victimization. The armed conflict and atrocities committed prompted the establishment, by the Security Council acting under its chapter VII powers,[28] of the International Criminal Tribunal for the former Yugoslavia (ICTY). The legacy of the ICTY is long-lasting insofar as it pertains to criminal accountability for the crimes perpetrated during the war. The question of reparations for victims, however, has not been fully addressed by the tribunal.[29]

Judge Jorda, then President of the Tribunal, expressed his concern about the need to develop necessary mechanisms to award reparations to victims.[30] However, as already discussed in Chapter 2,[31] the ICTY did not award

---

Law Review 27 (2013), pp. 565–601. See also reports by Amnesty International concerning sexual violence during the conflict: "Bosnia-Herzegovina: Rape and Sexual Abuse by Armed Forces," 1993; "'Whose Justice?' – The Women of Bosnia and Herzegovina Are Still Waiting," 2009; "Public Statement – Bosnia and Herzegovina: Amnesty International Calls for Justice and Reparation for Survivors of War Crimes of Sexual Violence," 2010; "Old Crimes, Same Suffering: No justice for Survivors of Wartime Rape in North-East Bosnia and Herzegovina," 2012.

[26] Concerning sexual violence crimes and rapes during the war in Bosnia, see Helsinki Watch, Human Rights Watch, "War Crimes in Bosnia-Herzegovina," 1992; *Report on the Situation of Human Rights in the Territory of the Former Yugoslavia Submitted by Tadeusz Mazowiecki, Special Rapporteur of the Commission on Human Rights*, U.N. ESCOR, 49th Sess., Annex, Agenda Item 27, U.N. Doc. E/CN.4/1993/50 (1993); see also Yolanda S. Wu, "Genocidal Rape in Bosnia: Redress in United States Courts Under the Alien Tort Claims Act," *UCLA Women's Law Journal* 4 (1993), pp. 101–111.

[27] Manfred Nowak, "Reparation by the Human Rights Chamber for Bosnia and Herzegovina," in *Out of the Ashes: Reparations for Victims of Gross and Systematic Human Rights Violations*, Koen de Feyter et al., Intersentia, 2005, p. 245.

[28] See Chapter 2 for details.

[29] See Chapter 2, and references cited therein.

[30] Cf. UN Doc./S/ 2000/1063, 3 November 2000. See also discussion in Carla Ferstman and Sheri P. Rosenberg, "Reparations in Dayton's Bosnia and Herzegovina," in *Reparations for Victims of Genocide, War Crimes and Crimes Against Humanity: Systems in Place and Systems in the Making*, eds. Carla Ferstman et al., Nijhoff, 2009, p. 484.

[31] See Chapter 2.

reparation to victims of the Balkans wars. The issue of redress for victims was highlighted by the tribunal as an important one. According to Rule 106 of the Rules of Procedure and Evidence of the Tribunal, a judgment condemning an accused is final and binding as to the criminal responsibility of the perpetrator concerning claims of compensation, which may be brought by victims in a national court. Thus, compensation for victims was left for national courts and domestic mechanisms.

Another development at the international level pertaining to reparations for victims of the Balkans wars arose out of the *Bosnia Genocide* case before the International Court of Justice. This case concerned claims by Bosnia and Herzegovina seeking reparations from Serbia for alleged acts of genocide.[32] Although this is a case involving questions of state responsibility, it is relevant because it is an attempt at the international level to obtain reparations for international crimes committed during a war.

The ruling of the court was to the effect that Serbia had not committed genocide in Bosnia, nor was it an accomplice. Although the court did find that Serbia could be held responsible for its failure to prevent and punish the genocide that occurred in Srebrenica, it was held that the genocide could not be attributed to Serbia. In this sense, the court held that compensation would not be an appropriate remedy for Serbia's breach of the obligation to prevent the genocide in Srebrenica:

> The question is whether there is a sufficiently direct and certain causal nexus between the wrongful act, the Respondent's breach of the obligation to prevent genocide, and the injury suffered by the Applicant, consisting of all damage of any type, material or moral, caused by the acts of genocide. Such a nexus could be considered established only if the Court were able to conclude from the case as a whole and with a sufficient degree of certainty that the genocide at Srebrenica would in fact have been averted if the Respondent had acted in compliance with its legal obligations. However, the Court clearly cannot do so.[33]

In particular, the ICJ held that: "the Court's findings [...] constitute appropriate satisfaction, and [...] the case is not one in which an order for payment of compensation, or, in respect of the violation referred to in subparagraph (5)

---

[32] ICJ, *Application of the Convention on the Prevention and Punishment of the Crime of Genocide (Bosnia and Herzegovina v. Serbia and Montenegro)*, Judgment, 26 February 2007.

[33] Ibid., at para. 462.

[failure to prevent genocide], a direction to provide assurances and guarantees of non-repetition, would be appropriate."[34]

Another case concerning the application of the Convention on the Prevention and Punishment of the Crime of Genocide, between Croatia and Serbia, was recently adjudicated by the court. This case refers to a claim by Croatia, and a counterclaim by Serbia, for reparations for allegations of genocide committed by Serbia in Croatia, and by Croatia in Serbia (during "Operation Storm"). This case represented another missed opportunity for the court to address the question of reparations. The court looked at the crimes alleged to have occurred in each of the municipalities put forward by Croatia, and although it found that the *actus reus* of the crime of genocide was proven in many localities addressed by Croatia, it could not find that the specific intent, or the *mens rea*, was proven by either Party in their respective claim and counterclaim. As a consequence of this finding, the claims for reparations were not entertained by the court.[35]

An analysis of the reasoning of the court, and a discussion of the merits of these cases, in particular the allegations of breaches of the Genocide Convention from a state responsibility perspective, are beyond the scope of this book.[36] The conclusion that can be drawn from the judgment of the ICJ is that victims have yet again been left without reparations for international crimes that were committed during the wars in the Balkans.[37]

---

[34]   ICJ, Judgment, 26 February 2007, p. 239.

[35]   See ICJ, *Application of the Convention on the Prevention and Punishment of the Crime of Genocide (Croatia v. Serbia)*, Judgment, 5 February 2015. For an in-depth discussion of the question of reparations, see the Dissenting Opinion of Judge Cançado Trindade.

[36]   See in this regard a commentary on the case: Monica Moyo, "ICJ Delivers Decision on the Application of the Genocide Convention," *AJIL International Law in Brief*, 3 February 2015.

[37]   See criticisms of the court's treatment of the question of reparations: Marko Milanović, "State Responsibility for Genocide: A Follow-Up," *European Journal of International Law* 18 (2007), pp. 669–694; see also Christian Tomuschat, "Reparation in Cases of Genocide," *Journal of International Criminal Justice* 5 (2007), pp. 905–912, at p. 911, who states, in regard to the court's treatment of the question of reparation:

> in the human rights field the judges take into account the degree of pain and suffering endured by the victims. It is hard to understand why the international judge at The Hague dismisses any such considerations, without even addressing the issue. The praetorian statement – one sentence! – that a simple declaration indicating the occurrence of a breach constitutes appropriate satisfaction fails to comply with the duty of any judge to support his or her decision by explicit reasons. This is all the more deplorable since the proceedings in the case had been going on for 14 years. There was ample time to assess every facet of the relevant facts. Instead, the Court rushes through the issue of satisfaction as if it intended to avoid giving it due consideration.

The Role of National Courts and Mechanisms 159

In both cases, the jurisdictional basis for the court was the Genocide Convention, and thus, the legal claims of the Applicant States were circumscribed by the legal framework of that convention. More importantly, they had to prove a breach of the convention by the Respondent State (Serbia in both cases). This was an important point since the court could not adjudicate claims of war crimes or crimes against humanity.[38] Thus, the treatment of the question of reparation was, in both cases, limited by the finding of a breach of an obligation of the Genocide Convention (or otherwise). As already discussed, given the court's finding in the *Bosnia Genocide* case of Serbia's failure to prevent genocide, reparation in the form of compensation could have been ordered. Instead, the court limited itself when dealing with the request for reparation in a cursory manner by stating that its finding was appropriate reparation.[39]

The other question that needs to be answered is: if reparations were to be ordered by the court, would they have reached the individual victims themselves? The ICJ deals with questions of state responsibility rather than individual criminal responsibility,[40] and one of the consequences thereof is that individual victims have no role to play in the proceedings, including for purposes of reparation. Thus, even if the court were to order reparation in the form of compensation, it is not clear whether individual victims would have directly benefited from the compensation awarded, other than the obviously important symbolic meaning of such a decision.

5.2.2 *Seeking Redress Domestically: Mechanisms in Bosnia and Herzegovina*

In addition to the international efforts concerning the crimes committed during the wars, there have also been initiatives undertaken at the domestic level. As Frederiek de Vlaming and Kate Clark have reviewed with great detail, victims have claimed reparations in relation to the wars in various different fora.[41]

---

[38] There is currently no universal Convention on Crimes Against Humanity on which the Applicant State could have based its claims.

[39] See ICJ, Application of the Convention on the Prevention and Punishment of the Crime of Genocide (*Bosnia and Herzegovina v. Serbia and Montenegro*), Judgment, 26 February 2007, p. 239.

[40] On the question of state responsibility and individual criminal responsibility relating to the proceedings before the Court and the Court's decision see: Richard J. Goldstone and Rebecca J. Hamilton, "Bosnia v. Serbia: Lessons from the Encounter of the International Court of Justice with the International Criminal Tribunal for the Former Yugoslavia," *Leiden Journal of International Law* 21 (2008), pp. 95–112.

[41] Frederiek de Vlaming and Kate Clark, "War Reparations in Bosnia and Herzegovina: Individual Stories and Collective Interests," in *Narratives of Justice In and Out of the*

160   *Reparative Justice for International Crimes*

In December 1995, the Dayton Peace Agreement was signed which put a formal end to the conflict. Annex 6 of the Agreement provided for the establishment of a Commission on Human Rights and a Human Rights Chamber.[42] The Dayton Peace Agreement provided for two fora in order to deal with reparations for victims. Annex 7 established a Commission for Real Property Claims of Displaced Persons and Refugees (CRPC). The study of these two mechanisms demonstrate that they are *sui generis*, quasi-international mechanisms set up by a peace agreement.

According to chapter 2 of Annex 6 of the Dayton Peace Agreement, the Human Rights Chamber was modeled on the basis of the European Court of Human Rights, and was set up to examine allegations of human rights violations of one of the parties to the Dayton Peace Agreement (that is, the state of Bosnia and Herzegovina, the Federation of Bosnia and Herzegovina and the *Republika Srpska*).[43] The chamber could only hear claims that had occurred after the entry into force of the Dayton Peace Agreement dated 14 December 1995.[44]

The chamber was comprised of fourteen members and heard hundreds of cases concerning human rights abuses during the war in Bosnia and Herzegovina. It was set up to be a court of last instance.[45] Naturally, given the number of victims devastated by the conflict, the chamber had a busy docket and established some practices which aided in dealing with the high volume of cases, such as, for example, relying on ICTY cases to set the historical record of a given case.[46] The chamber entertained applications

---

     Courtroom, eds. Zarkov Dubravka and Glasius Marlies, Springer International Publishing, 2014, pp. 163–185.

[42]   See concerning the work of the Human Rights Chamber, David Yeager, "The Human Rights Chamber for Bosnia and Herzegovina: A Case Study in Transitional Justice," *International Legal Perspectives* 14 (2004), pp. 44–54.

[43]   Carla Ferstman and Sheri P. Rosenberg, "Reparations in Dayton's Bosnia and Herzegovina," in *Reparations for Victims of Genocide, War Crimes and Crimes Against Humanity: Systems in Place and Systems in the Making*, eds. Carla Ferstman et al., Nijhoff, 2009, p. 486.

[44]   Ibid.

[45]   Ibid., at pp. 487–488.

[46]   See e.g., *Ferida Selimović et al. v. the Republika Srpska*, Decision on Admissibility and Merits, 7 March 2003, where the Human Rights Chamber applied the trial chamber decision of the ICTY in the case of *The Prosecutor v. Radislav Krstić*, [IT-98-33-T], to provide the overall context for the events at Srebrenica: "As the *Krstić* judgment contains a comprehensive description of the historical context and underlying facts of the Srebrenica events, established after long adversarial proceedings conducted by a reputable international court, the Chamber will utilise this judgment to set forth the historical context and underlying facts important for a full understanding of the applications considered in the present decision," cited in Carla Ferstman and Sheri P. Rosenberg, "Reparations in Dayton's Bosnia and Herzegovina," in *Reparations for Victims of Genocide, War Crimes and Crimes against Humanity: Systems in Place and Systems in the Making*, eds. Carla Ferstman et al., Nijhoff, 2009, p. 489.

The Role of National Courts and Mechanisms 161

from victims or legal entities in relation to allegations of human rights violations by the state of Bosnia and Herzegovina, the Federation of Bosnia and Herzegovina and the *Republika Sprska.*

The cases decided by the Human Rights Chamber were wide-ranging. It is worth mentioning that the chamber ordered innovative and varied reparation awards for international crimes committed during the war, and had a major impact on victims.[47] The chamber dealt with important issues including cases concerning enforced disappearances, which was a major problem during the war[48] and repossession of property. In this regard, the case law of the Human Rights Chamber played a role in reviewing the laws, policies, and practices which related to the return of property.[49]

The Commission for Real Property Claims of Refugees and Displaced Persons (CRPC), was established pursuant to Article XI of Annex 7 of the Dayton Peace Agreement. The CRPC was a quasi-judicial entity, whose task was described as encompassing "hundreds of thousands of claims in a short period of time" where "the Commission developed a stream-lined approach aimed at maximizing efficiency, and its operating procedures bore greater resemblance to a mass arbitration or claims process."[50]

The CRPC faced a few challenges[51] in dealing with property claims, but together with the Human Rights Chamber, provided a domestic mechanism where victims could claim a variety of reparations.[52] Many of the challenges the CRPC faced were connected to the poor state of property books, and the

---

[47] Carla Ferstman and Sheri P. Rosenberg, "Reparations in Dayton's Bosnia and Herzegovina," in *Reparations for Victims of Genocide, War Crimes and Crimes Against Humanity: Systems in Place and Systems in the Making*, eds. Carla Ferstman et al., Nijhoff, 2009, p. 491.

[48] To the extent that the Chamber deemed that the violation of enforced disappearance was a continuous violation after the entry into force of the Dayton Peace Agreements, such cases were admissible, see: *Palic v. Republika Srpska*, Decision on Admissibility and Merits, 11 January 2001, Case No. CH/99/3196; *Unkovic v. Federation of Bosnia and Herzogovina*, Decision on Admissibility and Merits, 9 November 2001, Case No. CH/99/2150; *Josip, Bozana and Tomislav Matanovic v. the Republika Srpska*, Decision on Admissibility, 13 September 1996, Decision on the Merits, 6 August 1997, Decisions on Admissibility and Merits, March 1996–December 1997, Case No. CH/96/01; *Ferida Selimović et al. v. the Republika Srpska*, Decision on Admissibility and the Merits, 7 March 2003, CH/01/8365 et. al.

[49] Examples of such cases relating to repossession of property: *Rasim Jusufović v. the Republika Srpska*, Decision on Admissibility and Merits, 9 June 2000, Case No. CH/98/698; *Ivica Kevesevic v. the Federation of Bosnia and Herzegovina*, 10 September 1998, Case No. CH/97/46.

[50] Carla Ferstman and Sheri P. Rosenberg, "Reparations in Dayton's Bosnia and Herzegovina," in *Reparations for Victims of Genocide, War Crimes and Crimes against Humanity: Systems in Place and Systems in the Making*, eds. Carla Ferstman et al., Nijhoff, 2009, p. 502.

[51] Ibid., pp. 507–511.

[52] Ibid.

162   *Reparative Justice for International Crimes*

impact of this on deciding property claims which included the handling of property transfers, and the enforcement of commission decisions. It is reported that, at the end of the mandate of the commission, local authorities in Bosnia and Herzegovina had decided approximately ninety-three percent of all claims.[53]

It can be said that alongside court proceedings, which are reviewed in Section 5.2.3, there can be other domestic mechanisms that deal with the question of reparations. Interestingly, these domestic mechanisms served not only to provide an avenue for victims to seek redress domestically for international crimes they suffered, but they also inspired other institutions. In this sense, it has been argued that: "In many ways, therefore, the Human Rights Chamber was a training ground for the Entities of *Republika Srpska* and the Federation of Bosnia and Herzegovina and state level institutions to bring their laws and practices in line with the European Convention."[54] In terms of national laws and proceedings, currently in Bosnia and Herzegovina there does not exist a governmental reparation system for victims of crimes committed during the Balkans war. As Popic and Panjeta rightly summarize, in terms of a domestic reparation scheme, Bosnia and Herzegovina operates "a complex array of on-going payments to people who suffered war-related personal harms."[55]

5.2.3 *Proceedings Before Domestic Courts in Bosnia and Herzegovina*

As far as reparations for international crimes are concerned, it is important to bear in mind the broader context regarding reparations. At the international level, the ICTY (dealing with international criminal responsibility) and the ICJ (dealing with the state responsibility of Serbia) have left victims without any significant form of redress. At the national level, the mechanisms devised by the Dayton Peace Agreement (the Human Rights Chamber and the CRPC) halted activities in 2004.

---

[53]   UNDP Access to Justice, 2009–2011, unknown year of publication; Carla Ferstman and Sheri P. Rosenberg, "Reparations in Dayton's Bosnia and Herzegovina," in *Reparations for Victims of Genocide, War Crimes and Crimes Against Humanity: Systems in Place and Systems in the Making*, eds. Carla Ferstman et al., Nijhoff, 2009, p. 511.

[54]   Carla Ferstman and Sheri P. Rosenberg, "Reparations in Dayton's Bosnia and Herzegovina," in *Reparations for Victims of Genocide, War Crimes and Crimes Against Humanity: Systems in Place and Systems in the Making*, eds. Carla Ferstman et al., Nijhoff, 2009, p. 511.

[55]   Linda Popic and Belma Panjeta, *Compensation, Transitional Justice and Conditional International Credit in Bosnia and Herzegovina*, Independent Research Publication 2010, http://www.nuhanovicfoundation.org/en/reports/independent-research-paper-compensation-transitional-justice-and-conditional-credit-in-bosnia-and-herzegovina-attempts-to-reform-gov ernment-payments-to-victims-and-veterans-of-the-1992-1995-war-by-l-popic-and-b-panjeta/.

As a result, numerous victims have initiated lawsuits in order to try to obtain reparations, or a civil remedy, for international crimes.[56] Most court cases were filed on behalf of collectives of victims, such as former detainees. Because many victims were unsuccessful in obtaining compensation from the state authorities, as they did not fall under the scope of the domestic governmental war victims' reparation scheme, many former detainees filed suits before national courts in Bosnia.[57] Usually, the overall goal was to achieve a change of behavior from authorities, to encourage a recognition of the harm that was caused, and reestablish the rule of law.

Bosnian courts have awarded compensation in a limited number of cases. However, the cases weren't uniform in terms of the amount, and it is reported that the actual reparations have not yet been paid to victims.[58]

While some claims for reparation were brought before national courts in Bosnia and Herzegovina, it is suggested that the gaps left by the international courts (ICTY and ICJ), as well as the scheme set up by the Dayton Peace Accords, could have been ultimately filled by domestic courts. Bosnian courts could have played (and could still play) a more active role in postwar reparation and contributing in the process of healing and reconciliation of the communities involved.

In addition to cases brought before national courts and mechanisms in Bosnia and Herzegovina, there were also cases brought before the courts of foreign states for reparations for the crimes committed during the war. These cases demonstrate that often, when victims cannot find relief in the courts of their own countries, they end up relying on courts of foreign states by bringing suits based on heads of jurisdiction other than territoriality. This idea, and the associated cases, will be explored in Section 5.5, which examines universal civil jurisdiction.

---

[56] For a detailed analysis of case studies, see Frederiek de Vlaming and Kate Clark, "War Reparations in Bosnia and Herzegovina: Individual Stories and Collective Interests," in *Narratives of Justice In and Out of the Courtroom*, eds. Zarkov Dubravka and Glasius Marlies, Springer International Publishing, 2014, pp. 179–182.

[57] UNDP, "Access to Justice, Facing the Past and Building Confidence for the Future (2009–2011)," p. 10–12; Selma Boracic, "Bosnia War Victims' Compensation Struggle" (International War and Peace Reporting [IWPR]) 3 August 2011, cited in Frederiek de Vlaming and Kate Clark, "War Reparations in Bosnia and Herzegovina: Individual Stories and Collective Interests," in *Narratives of Justice In and Out of the Courtroom*, Zarkov Dubravka and Glasius Marlies, Springer International Publishing, 2014, p. 182.

[58] Denis Dzidic, "Bosnian Ex-Camp Detainees Join Forces," 2012 *Balkan Transitional Justice*, https://balkaninsight.com/2012/06/13/bosnian-ex-camp-detainees-coming-together/; see also, Selma Boracic, "Bosnia War Victims' Compensation Struggle," cited in Frederiek de Vlaming and Kate Clark, ibid., p. 182.

5.3 REPARATIONS FOR VICTIMS OF HISSÈNE HABRÉ AND BEYOND: BREAKING NEW GROUND?

Another interesting example of a mechanism which includes reparations for mass atrocities is the case against Mr. Hissène Habré, a former Chadian president, who has been living in Senegal for decades. This is yet another instance where delays and difficulties are seen with the implementation of reparations, and alternative ways must be sought to realize reparative justice for victims.[59]

The Extraordinary African Chamber (EAC) was established upon an agreement between the African Union and Senegal, where Mr. Habré had been living free for a long time, in spite of the allegation of mass crimes committed by him. The EAC was set up to try those most responsible for international crimes committed in Chad between 1982 and 1990. The EAC followed its own statute (complemented by the Senegalese Code of Criminal Procedure), and some of its funding was external. In addition to criminal prosecution, the EAC could also award reparations (restitution, rehabilitation, and compensation) to victims.[60]

After much delay, in 2017 the Appeals Chamber confirmed the conviction and life imprisonment of Mr. Habré for torture, crimes against humanity, and war crimes.[61] A reparations award against Mr. Habré recognized his civil liability towards victims, alongside his criminal responsibility, within the same proceedings. The Appeals Chamber of the EAC also dealt with the question of reparations, which had been decided by the first instance chamber in 2016. The Appeals Chamber judgment filled in the gaps left by the first decision on reparation, and decided on the question of implementation of the reparation award and the role of the trust fund that had been set up by the African Union. Cognizant of the challenge of the insufficiency of assets from Mr. Habré to cover the reparations,[62] the Appeals Chamber ordered the trust fund to provide the reparations awarded to the 7,396 civil parties and to identify and recover any additional assets from Mr. Habré. As it has been noted, recovering further assets from Mr. Habré (who was reported to have fled

---

[59] For a discussion of the case against Mr. Habré see Nader Iskandar Diab, "Challenges in the Implementation of the Reparation Award Against Hissein Habré: Can the Spell of Unenforceable Awards Across the Globe be Broken?," *Journal of International Criminal Justice* 16 (2018), pp. 141–163.

[60] Ibid.

[61] Ibid.

[62] His frozen assets were estimated at EUR 1 million whereas the award was set to approximately EUR 124 million, see ibid.

Chad with approximately EUR 11.8 million)[63] could be a difficult task given, *inter alia*, the time elapsed between the award of reparations and when he fled Chad.[64] It further directed the trust fund to "work for the establishment of collective and moral reparations."[65]

While this case provided an innovative precedent for claiming reparations for international crimes, at the time of writing, the same story repeated itself: victims were left with a judgment awarding them significant reparations, which they have yet to receive.[66]

5.4 FOSTERING CIVIL REDRESS FOR INTERNATIONAL CRIMES IN DOMESTIC COURTS: RATIONALES AND CHALLENGES

The review of different initiatives and mechanisms that were put in place after the war in Bosnia and Herzegovina demonstrates that there are both advantages and disadvantages to requesting reparations for international crimes through domestic proceedings. This is especially so when these proceedings take place in war-torn countries. This section addresses the rationales for fostering a more active role of domestic courts in the award of reparations for international crimes. It will also discuss some of the challenges to the domestic adjudication of such claims by painting the larger picture of some important hurdles victims may face in domestic court proceedings.

The main rationale for fostering a greater role for domestic courts relates to the scarcity of appropriate international mechanisms and their limited authority (due to jurisdiction or temporal limitations). National courts are already in place – that is, they do not need to be devised to deal specifically with cases of reparations for victims of international crimes. The judicial machinery for potentially claiming civil redress for wrongful conduct already exists in some form under domestic laws, sparing the time and resources required to create a special apparatus to deal with reparation claims.

---

[63] Aida Grovestins, "Victims' Lawyers Start Battle to Seize Habré's millions," Justice Hub, 4 August 2016, available at https://justicehub.org/article/victims-lawyers-start-battle-to-seize-ha bres-millions/.

[64] Nader Iskandar Diab, "Challenges in the Implementation of the Reparation Award Against Hissein Habré: Can the Spell of Unenforceable Awards Across the Globe be Broken?," *Journal of International Criminal Justice* 16 (2018), pp. 141–163.

[65] Ibid., citing Hissein Habré case, Appeals Judgment on Reparations, Appeals Chamber of the Extraordinary African Chamber, 27 April 2017.

[66] Setondji R. Adjovi, "Can the Victims of the Habré Regime Still Get Reparations?" Justiceinfo .Net, available at www.justiceinfo.net/en/justiceinfo-comment-and-debate/opinion/41572-can-the-victims-of-the-habre-regime-still-get-reparations.html (accessed 10 July 2019).

166   *Reparative Justice for International Crimes*

Another advantage of domestic courts, as opposed to international mechanisms, is their proximity to the witnesses and the evidence. These logistical considerations affect the conduct of proceedings. National courts in the areas where international crimes were committed could, *in theory*, be in a privileged position to deal with claims for reparations: they are the closest forum for victims.

Be that as it may, it is not always straightforward for victims to rely upon national courts for the purposes of seeking reparations for international crimes. The first important challenge relates to the lack of political will and the lack of functioning judicial institutions capable of entertaining reparation claims. The lack of political will may be connected, among other things, to the involvement of political authorities in the criminal conduct which is the object of the proceedings. For example, in the Bosnian case study above, many victims often requested reparations directly from official authorities. Only after these avenues were exhausted would they seek redress in national courts.

Finally, in postwar societies, the judicial machinery is often broken, making not only prosecutions, but also civil proceedings, difficult, if not impossible, to be pursued in domestic courts. Without domestic institutions able to address the (international) criminal conduct and the corresponding civil liability, victims are left with no domestic avenue to pursue. Even if a victim is successful in a domestic forum, they are confronted with the practical difficulties of enforcing domestic decisions against an accused, especially when they are outside the county where the crimes were committed, or when their assets are outside the country.

Thus, while it may initially seem that national courts are the most natural path for reparation, in practice, there are many challenges which victims may face in order to settle their grief domestically.

Civil claims in national courts may provide an avenue for victims to obtain redress for the crimes they have suffered. Additionally, in cases where bringing a civil suit is not possible or desirable, in many civil law countries, victims may participate in prosecutions as *parties civiles* and seek reparation within the criminal proceedings, if the defendant is convicted.[67] Nevertheless, more

---

[67] See in general, Mireille Delmas-Martry and John Spencer, *European Criminal Procedures*, Cambridge University Press, 2002. Victims may also in some cases seek reparation from a civil fund, as for example in France, where victims of some violent crimes may obtain compensation from the state through a solidarity fund where offenders do not have the necessary funds, Criminal Code of France, Arts. 706-3.

The Role of National Courts and Mechanisms

needs to be done for victims to be able to truly benefit from national claims and domestic proceedings in countries torn apart by war.

International criminal mechanisms should promote the role of national courts and civil mechanisms of redress for victims. International criminal justice should not be fragmented in the sense that international and national proceedings and mechanisms operate in a dissociated and parallel manner. They should feed off each other, and work in conjunction. As Professor Nollkaemper theorized,

> For one thing, international institutions can develop creative incentives for domestic actors to provide for reparation schemes; for instance, by the prospect that absence of proper domestic reparation will lead to top-down obligations by human rights courts. International institutions also can provide critical knowledge to attorneys, who will have the prime responsibility to raise such issues before the courts and other actors. They also may help to provide financial and material means to actually deliver reparation.[68]

One manner in which international mechanisms can foster domestic initiatives is by adopting appropriate legislation. For example, states parties to the ICC, in implementing the ICC Statute, may legislate their own avenues for victims to seek redress for international crimes. This would counter the practical difficulty experienced by victims who cannot turn to their own domestic courts for civil claims because victims' redress is not available due to a lack of legislation, legal tools, or political will.

5.5 UNIVERSAL CIVIL JURISDICTION AS AN ALTERNATIVE AVENUE TO SEEK REDRESS FOR INTERNATIONAL CRIMES?

As already discussed,[69] some jurisdictions combine both the criminal and civil dimensions in the same proceedings, allowing for a claim of reparation to be made in the context of criminal prosecutions.[70]

---

[68] André Nollkaemper, "The Contribution of International Institutions to Domestic Reparation for International Crimes," *Proceedings of the Annual Meeting (American Society of International Law)* 103 (2009), pp. 203–207.

[69] See Section 5.1.

[70] See references in Section 5.1. See also, Marion E. Brienen and Ernestine Hoegen, *Victims of Crime in 22 European Criminal Justice Systems: The Implementation of Recommendation (85) 11 of the Council of Europe on the Position of the Victim in the Framework of Criminal Law and Procedure*, Wolf Legal Publisher, 2000.

168 *Reparative Justice for International Crimes*

While in theory, civil redress can be claimed in domestic courts (either separately or combined within criminal proceedings), a challenge can arise, as it has been discussed, when crimes are committed in a jurisdiction where access to the courts is difficult due to, for example, collapsed justice mechanisms, or undue political interference. The flight of the accused from the jurisdiction and the location of assets overseas are important challenges to bringing reparation claims in a state where the crimes were committed.

With this in mind, this chapter will now explore the possibilities and challenges of reverting to a system of universal jurisdiction as a means to claim reparations from perpetrators[71] for international crimes committed outside the jurisdiction of the forum state. This section proceeds as follows: first, it discusses the concept of universal jurisdiction. Then it examines whether under the current state of international law, a civil dimension is permitted. It also discusses the scope of this dimension – whether civil claims are connected with criminal trials or are completely separate civil proceedings – and how universal civil jurisdiction should develop. In this perspective, the discussion of universal civil jurisdiction considers developments in the field and examines whether universal jurisdiction may assist in establishing new possibilities for reparation claims for international crimes in national courts.

5.5.1 *The Doctrine of Universal Criminal Jurisdiction*

In a time of global concern about impunity for grave human rights atrocities that amount to international crimes, universal criminal jurisdiction has received much scholarly attention.[72] In recent years, many authors,

---

[71] As already explained, procedures to obtain reparation from states are largely outside the scope of the book. In any event, the examination of universal jurisdiction for claims of reparation does not concern claims against states.

[72] In the past decades, scholarly literature and a great number of human rights defenders dedicated attention to the topic of universal jurisdiction. Some of the prominent efforts to describe the theory and practice of universal jurisdiction in modern international law are: Mitsue Inazumi, *Universal Jurisdiction in Modern International Law: Expansion of National Jurisdiction for Prosecuting Serious Crimes Under International Law*, adapted version of dissertation defended at Utrecht University on 27 October 2004, Oxford University Press, 2005; Stephen Macedo, *Universal Jurisdiction: National Courts and the Prosecution of Serious Crimes Under International Law*, University of Pennsylvania Press, 2003; and Luc Reydams, *Universal Jurisdiction: International and Municipal Legal Perspectives*, Oxford University Press, 2003 (in this book, the author not only addresses a comprehensive analysis of universal jurisdiction in international law but also provides an insightful account for the approach of national legal systems to universal jurisdiction). Among the nongovernmental efforts to

The Role of National Courts and Mechanisms 169

governments and nongovernmental organizations have expressed growing concern about human rights violations that happen within borders and across frontiers, and the need to end impunity and to achieve justice. Especially in an era where "never again" is not a mirror image of reality when it comes to genocide and crimes against humanity, great efforts have been deployed to make the case for expanding national jurisdiction to prosecute serious human rights offenses. In the Annex to the question of the Impunity of Perpetrators of Human Rights Violations (civil and political) revised final report prepared by Mr. Joinet, impunity is "the impossibility, *de jure* or *de facto*, of bringing the perpetrators of human rights violations to account – whether in criminal, civil, administrative or disciplinary proceedings – since they are not subject to any inquiry that might lead to their being accused, arrested, tried and, if found guilty, sentenced to appropriate penalties, and to make reparation to their victims."[73] The exercise of criminal jurisdiction over nonnationals is by no means a new phenomenon.[74] Yet in the past few decades, discussions over the doctrine have reemerged.[75]

The exercise of jurisdiction is generally limited by dictates of the sovereign equality of states and the principle of noninterference.[76] International law

---

promote universal jurisdiction for human rights atrocities, some studies have proved insightful in the description and analysis of the principle: Amnesty International, *Universal Jurisdiction: The Duty of States to Enact and Implement Legislation* (September 2001), AI Index: IOR 53/002/2001 and Amnesty International, *Universal Jurisdiction: 14 Principles on Effective Exercise of Universal Jurisdiction* (1999); International Council on Human Rights Policy, *Hard Cases: Bringing Human Rights Violators to Justice Abroad – A Guide to Universal Jurisdiction* (1999); Redress, *Universal Jurisdiction in Europe: Criminal Prosecutions in Europe since 1990 for War Crimes, Crimes Against Humanity, Torture and Genocide* (1999); International Law Association, *Final Report on the Exercise of Universal Jurisdiction in Respect of Gross Human Rights Offences*, Committee on International Human Rights Law and Practice, London Conference (2000).

[73] Set of Principles for the Protection and Promotion of Human Rights Through Action to Combat Impunity, UN Doc. E/CN.4/Sub.2/1997/20/Rev.1.

[74] Universal jurisdiction was the subject of various studies in the beginning of the past century: see e.g., Eric Beckett, "Criminal Jurisdiction over Foreigners. The Francofonìa and the Lotus," *British Yearbook of International Law* 8 (1927), pp. 108–128. Universal jurisdiction was originally used as a means to prosecute piracy and slave trade.

[75] See e.g., Princeton Project on Universal Jurisdiction, *The Princeton Principles on Universal Jurisdiction* (2001). Scholarly collective initiatives have also created materials concerning universal jurisdiction: cf. TMC Asser Institute for International Law, *Universal Jurisdiction in Theory and Practice*; Princeton University Program in Law and Public Affairs, *The Princeton Principles on Universal Jurisdiction*.

[76] See Donald Donovan and Anthea Roberts, "The Emerging Recognition of Universal Civil Jurisdiction," *American Journal of International Law* 100 (2006), p. 142.

170   *Reparative Justice for International Crimes*

generally requires some connection or link for the exercise of jurisdiction.[77] Such a link is often found in territory,[78] the nationality of the offender[79] (or the victim),[80] or the need to protect the national security interests of the state.[81]

By contrast, universal jurisdiction is based upon the premise that certain crimes are so grave that they should become universally abolished. As such, any state is entitled to prosecute the offender of said crimes regardless of the nationality of the accused or the victim, or the territory where the crime occurred.[82] The universality principle is not based upon a direct nexus between the offender and the forum. The reasoning behind the principle's existence is rooted in law, morality, fundamental ethical values,[83] and the "conscience of humankind."[84]

As one author puts it, universal jurisdiction holds the potential for a global system of accountability.[85] From a time where universal jurisdiction played a

---

[77] Ibid., pp. 142–143.

[78] This principle stands for the proposition that acts committed within the limits of a state are subject to the laws of that state. The most interesting point to underscore about the territoriality principle relates to acts that have not been committed entirely in the territory of a certain state. The conduct of states varies with regards to the application of the territoriality principle. Thus, if part of an act occurred within the boundaries of the forum state, this is an exercise of the territoriality principle and not the universality principle.

[79] This principle concerns the jurisdiction of a state in relation to its nationals abroad. In this case, the nexus between the state exercising jurisdiction and the conduct is the nationality of the alleged criminal. States have competence to extend the application of their laws to nationals even when they are outside the territory. State practice under this principle varies greatly depending on the legal system.

[80] According to this principle, the national state of the victim of a crime committed abroad can assert prescriptive jurisdiction over the offender. This principle is intimately connected to certain offenses, often targeted at nationals of certain countries, such as the offense of terrorism. See generally Geoffrey R. Watson, "The Passive Personality Principle," *Texas International Law Journal* 28 (1993), p. 1.

[81] According to this principle, a state can exercise prescriptive jurisdiction over aliens for acts done abroad which affect certain "vital" interests of the state. This principle is often justified by reference to a state's right of self-defense. Common offenses for a claim of the protective principle are treason, espionage, and attacks against embassies, see Manuel R. Garcia-Mora, "Criminal Jurisdiction over Foreigners for Treason and Offences Against the Safety of the State Committed upon Foreign Territory," *University of Pittsburgh Law Review* 19 (1958), p. 567.

[82] See M. Cherif Bassiouni, "The History of Universal Jurisdiction and Its Place in International Law," in *Universal Jurisdiction: National Courts and the Prosecution of Serious Crimes Under International Law*, ed. Stephen Macedo, University of Pennsylvania Press, 2004.

[83] See Christopher Keith Hall, "Universal Jurisdiction: New Uses for an Old Tool," in *Justice for Crimes Against Humanity*, eds. Mark Lattimer and Philipe Sands, Hart, 2007, pp. 55–56.

[84] Antoine Bailleux, *La compétence universelle au carrefour de la pyramide et du réseau*, Bruylant, 2005, p. 137, cited in Antônio Augusto Cançado Trindade, *International Law for Humankind: Towards a New Jus Gentium*, Nijhoff, 2010, p. 386.

[85] Stephen Macedo, *Universal Jurisdiction: National Courts and the Prosecution of Serious Crimes Under International Law*, University of Pennsylvania Press, 2003, Introduction, p. 4.

The Role of National Courts and Mechanisms

role in the prosecution of piracy and slave trade,[86] to an era of grave human rights atrocities, universal jurisdiction has been instrumental in addressing human rights violations and providing an important tool to combat impunity and enforce accountability.[87]

5.5.1.1 Conceptualizing Universal Jurisdiction: Legal Basis and Conditions for Its Exercise

There are two main forms of jurisdiction within international law: prescribing jurisdiction and enforcement jurisdiction. Universal jurisdiction is an additional principle for exercising jurisdiction alongside other heads of jurisdiction in international law (i.e., territoriality principle, nationality principle, passive personality principle, and protective principle). As Professor Cryer explains, universal jurisdiction "refers to jurisdiction established over a crime without reference to the place of perpetration, the nationality of the suspect or the victim or any other recognized linking point between the crime and the prosecuting state. It is a principle of jurisdiction limited to specific crimes."[88] For the purposes of this book, I refer to universal jurisdiction, in its criminal dimension, as a state having jurisdiction over foreigners for crimes committed abroad, when foreigners (alleged perpetrators) are present in their territory.

Legal Basis for Exercising Universal Jurisdiction: Permissibility and the Lotus Principle.[89]

There are two main sources of law that may provide for the exercise of universal jurisdiction: customary international law and treaty

---

[86] See M. Cherif Bassiouni, "The History of Universal Jurisdiction and Its Place in International Law," in *Universal Jurisdiction: National Courts and the Prosecution of Serious Crimes Under International Law*, ed. Stephen Macedo, University of Pennsylvania Press, 2004.

[87] Nongovernmental organizations and human rights activists advocate for a broader use of universal jurisdiction for perpetrators of mass human rights violations. See also generally, Henry Steiner, "Three Cheers for Universal Jurisdiction: Or Is It Only Two?" *Theoretical Inquiries in Law* 6 (2004), p. 200. See also, Kenneth Roth, "The Case for Universal Jurisdiction," *Foreign Affairs* 80 (2001), pp. 150–154. See Menno T. Kamminga, "Lessons Learned from the Exercise of Universal Jurisdiction in Respect of Gross Human Rights Offenses," *Human Rights Quarterly* 23 (2003), pp. 940–974.

[88] Robert Cryer et al., *An Introduction to International Criminal and Procedure*, Cambridge University Press, 2007, p. 44. See also, Luc Reydams, *Universal Jurisdiction: International and Municipal Legal Perspectives*, Oxford University Press, 2003, p. 220.

[89] The *Lotus* principle refers to the judgment of the PCIJ in the case of *The S.S. Lotus Case* PCIJ Ser. A, No. 10, p. 4 (1927) ("*Lotus* case"). The principle per se will be explained in the following section of this chapter.

law.[90] At this juncture, it is important to address the question of whether it is necessary under international law to have a legal basis to exercise universal jurisdiction, or whether the absence of prohibition is enough to allow a state to exercise the principle. To address this question, it is important to understand the so-called *Lotus* principle.

The *Lotus* case involved a collision between a French ship (the S.S. *Lotus*) and a Turkish ship, leading to the death of Turkish sailors. France claimed before the Permanent Court of International Justice (PCIJ) that Turkey did not have *jurisdiction* to try the French officers, because they were on a French boat in international waters at the time of the accident. The court essentially decided that: "Restrictions upon the independence of States cannot ... be presumed" as international law accords to states "a wide measure of discretion which is only limited in certain cases by prohibitive rules."[91]

Applying the *Lotus* principle, in the absence of express prohibition, are states permitted to exercise universal jurisdiction? In this sense, Professor Scharf posited that:

> In the setting of international criminal law, the contemporary logic of the *Lotus* Principle is supported by the nature of State sovereignty and the embryonic status of international law relative to domestic law. The continued growth and evolution of international criminal law requires a permissive legal culture, which encourages the collective expansion of extraterritorial jurisdiction over international crimes.[92]

Thus, the lawful exercise of universal jurisdiction can be traced back to the *Lotus* principle,[93] which may operate to permit the exercise of universal jurisdiction in the absence of a prohibition.

---

[90] In this chapter, I will not focus on whether, as a matter of treaty or customary international law, a specific international crime is subject to universal jurisdiction. See Luc Reydams, *Universal Jurisdiction: International and Municipal Legal Perspectives*, Oxford University Press, 2003 (for a thorough study of treaties and state practice regarding universal jurisdiction). See also, Jon B. Jordan, "Universal Jurisdiction in a Dangerous World: A Weapon for All Nations Against International Crimes," *Michigan State University – DCL Journal of International Law* 9 (2000) (noting that treaties themselves can become customary international law; if they are accepted by a great number of countries, the treaty will become customary international law and will be binding upon all nations, even nonsignatories).

[91] *Lotus* case, p. 18.

[92] Michael P. Scharf, "Application of Treaty-Based Universal Jurisdiction on Nationals of Non-Party States," *New England Law Review* 35 (2000), p. 368.

[93] Cedric Ryngaert, *Jurisdiction Under International Law*, Oxford University Press, 2nd ed., 2015, p. 128.

The Role of National Courts and Mechanisms | 173

Be that as it may, under customary international law, jurisdiction is primarily territorial.[94] The *Lotus* principle is not widely used as a justification for the exercise of universal jurisdiction. Ryngaert, upon providing a detailed study of jurisdiction under international law, has succinctly summarized the state of the law: "[A] jurisdictional assertion is lawful if it is justified under a generally accepted principle authorizing the exercise of jurisdiction. Only to the extent that there is uniformity of state practice as to the *lawfulness* of the exercise of universal criminal jurisdiction over core crimes could a state establish such jurisdiction."[95] Thus, universal jurisdiction under international law is either treaty-based (i.e., it is recognized as a basis for the exercise of jurisdiction under a treaty regime) or it is based upon customary international law.[96] Some scholars claim that universal jurisdiction for a core international crime (i.e., war crimes, crimes against humanity, genocide) is lawful under customary international law.[97] At this print of international law, a number of treaties recognize universal jurisdiction.[98] To assert universal jurisdiction over a certain crime, it is necessary an applicable treaty or rule under customary international law.

The Presence of the Accused as a Precondition for the Exercise of Universal Jurisdiction?

Universal jurisdiction involves two subcategories[99]: the jurisdiction over offenses when the accused is present in the territory of the state asserting jurisdiction; and the jurisdiction of a state to try offenses regardless of the offender's whereabouts. The latter is often called "pure universal

---

[94] Ibid., p. 35.

[95] Ibid., p. 129.

[96] Michael P. Scharf, "Application of Treaty-Based Universal Jurisdiction on Nationals of Non-Party States," *New England Law Review* 35 (2000), p. 363. See also, Lee A. Steven, "Genocide and the Duty to Extradite or Prosecute: Why the United States is in Breach of Its International Obligations," *Virginia Journal of International Law* 39 (1999), pp. 425–466; see also M. Cherif Bassiouni and Edward M. Wise, *Aut Dedere Aut Judicare: The Duty to Extradite or Prosecute in International Law*, Martinus Nijhoff, 1995 (according to whom under international law, nations may agree through treaties to exercise universal jurisdiction over offenses that might not otherwise allow such exercise of jurisdiction).

[97] Cedric Ryngaert, *Jurisdiction Under International Law*, Oxford University Press, 2nd ed., 2015, pp. 3–60.

[98] See Michael P. Scharf, "Application of Treaty-Based Universal Jurisdiction on Nationals of Non-Party States," *New England Law Review* 35 (2000), pp. 363–382 for full references and comments on each treaty.

[99] Robert Cryer et al., *An Introduction to International Criminal and Procedure*, Cambridge University Press (2007), at p. 45. See also, Antonio Cassese, "Is the Bell Tolling for Universality? A Plea for a Sensible Notion of Universal Jurisdiction," 1 *Journal of International Criminal Justice* 1 (2003), pp. 589–595 (for a discussion of this distinction).

174   *Reparative Justice for International Crimes*

jurisdiction"[100] or universal jurisdiction *in absentia*.[101] The manner in which universal jurisdiction is enforced according to the latter sub-category depends upon the cooperation of states. Only through this cooperation can the accused be brought to trial in the territory of the forum state,[102] since the forum state does not have custody of the offender.

In this sense, the prescribing state issues an international arrest warrant and requests that any state with custody of the alleged offender surrender them. The controversies that universal jurisdiction *in absentia* raise are complex and have been explored by many scholars.[103] In the traditional conception of universal jurisdiction, states exercise jurisdiction over offenders present in their territory.[104] It may be argued that the presence of the accused is a criterion that justifies the interest of the prosecuting state to exercise jurisdiction over individuals present in its territory.[105] None of the treaties that recognize universal criminal jurisdiction provide an express legal basis for the application of universal jurisdiction *in absentia*.[106] The complexities and controversies of universal criminal jurisdiction *in absentia* are numerous and outside the scope of this book.

[100]   See Robert Cryer et al., ibid.

[101]   For an analysis of the exercise of universal jurisdiction *in absentia*, see Ryan Rabinovitch, "Universal Jurisdiction *in Absentia*," *Fordham Int'l Law Journal* 28 (2004–2005), pp. 500–530; Luc Reydams, "Belgium's First Application of Universal Jurisdiction: The Butare Four Case," *Journal of International Criminal Justice* 1 (2003), pp. 428–436; Anthony J. Colangelo, "The New Universal Jurisdiction: In Absentia Signaling over Clearly Defined Crimes," *Georgetown Journal of International Law* 36 (2004–2005), pp. 537–603.

[102]   See Stephen Ratner, "Belgium's War Crimes Statute: A Postmortem," *American Journal of International Law* 97 (2003) (narrating the saga of Belgium concerning the exercise of universal jurisdiction over foreigners that are found outside of Belgium).

[103]   For an example of some of the controversies raised by the exercise of universal jurisdiction *in absentia* relate, see Luc Reydams, *Universal Jurisdiction: International and Municipal Legal Perspectives*, Oxford University Press (2003). See also, *Arrest Warrant Case (Democratic Republic of Congo v. Belgium)*, ICJ Reports 3 (2002), p. 43, Opinions of Judges Guillaume and Rezek.

[104]   See Mitsue Inazumi, *Universal Jurisdiction in Modern International Law: Expansion of National Jurisdiction for Prosecuting Serious Crimes Under International Law*, adapted version of dissertation defended at Utrecht University on 27 October 2004, Oxford University Press (2005), p. 103, cited in Cedric Ryngaert, *Jurisdiction Under International Law*, Oxford University Press, 2nd ed., 2015, p. 133.

[105]   In the Netherlands, for example, there have been prosecutions on the basis of universal jurisdiction involving suspects who were residing in the Netherlands when the proceedings started. Under Dutch law, presence on the territory is a necessary precondition for the exercise of jurisdiction of national courts, see Liesbeth Zegveld and Jeff Handmaker (eds.), "Universal Jurisdiction: State of Affairs and Ways Ahead: A Policy Paper," January 2012, p. 6.

[106]   Cedric Ryngaert, *Jurisdiction Under International Law*, Oxford University Press, 2nd ed., 2015, p. 133.

Some Technical Legal Aspects

In analyzing universal jurisdiction, some technical legal aspects need to be briefly discussed in light of some previous examples of state practice in this area. These legal aspects may also be transposed to the civil dimension of universal jurisdiction, which will be examined later in the section.

The first aspect arises out of national statutes of limitations relating to international crimes which may bar prosecution. The United Nations Convention on the Non-Applicability of Statutes of Limitations for War Crimes and Crimes Against Humanity[107] and the more recent European Convention on Non-Applicability of Statutes of Limitations for Crimes against Humanity and War Crimes (Inter-European)[108] have not been widely ratified.

Another relevant question relates to the collection of evidence. Given that criminal prosecutions based on universal jurisdiction refer to conduct that happened outside of the forum state, the process of gathering evidence is of utmost importance. The complexity involved in collecting evidence is well-illustrated by a case involving Guus Kouwenhoven, a Dutch businessman charged with having committed war crimes in Liberia in early 2000. In this case, there was great difficulty obtaining the cooperation of local officials and collecting evidence.[109]

5.5.1.2 The Evolution of Theoretical Rationales for Universal Jurisdiction: From Piracy to Crimes of Universal Concern

Piracy was the "traditional" crime which attracted the application of the universal jurisdiction principle.[110] However, universal jurisdiction has since grown from its traditional application to piracy.[111] Because of its central

---

[107]   26 November 1968, 754 UNTS 73.

[108]   Europ. T.S. No. 82.

[109]   See a discussion of this case at: Liesbeth Zegveld and Jeff Handmaker (eds.), "Universal Jurisdiction: State of Affairs and Ways Ahead: A Policy Paper," January 2012, p. 6.

[110]   See e.g., Mark Janis, *An Introduction to International Law*, Aspen, 4th ed., 2003 (explaining universal jurisdiction as the jurisdiction of every state traditionally over pirates); see also, Eugene Kontorovich, "International Legal Responses to Piracy off the Coast of Somalia," *American Society of International Law* 13 (2009), available at www.asil.org/insights090206.cfm ("Piracy is the original universal jurisdiction crime") and Eugene Kontorovich, "The Piracy Analogy: Modern Universal Jurisdiction's Hollow Foundation," *Harvard International Law Journal* 45 (2004), pp. 183–237 (the author criticizes the analogy between piracy and human rights violations for the purposes of applying universal jurisdiction).

[111]   See Mitsue Inazumi, *Universal Jurisdiction in Modern International Law: Expansion of National Jurisdiction for Prosecuting Serious Crimes Under International Law*, adapted version of dissertation defended at Utrecht University on 27 October 2004, Oxford University Press (2005), at pp. 45–60 (discussing the two main rationales for the development of universal jurisdiction).

176   *Reparative Justice for International Crimes*

relevance to the foundation and development of universal jurisdiction, Section 5.5.2 outlines the rationales used to justify the exercise of universal jurisdiction in relation to piracy.[112] This discussion will lay the foundations for an argument on the civil dimension of the doctrine.[113]

Piracy is ancient[114] and, as one author states, it is the oldest offense that invokes the assertion of universal jurisdiction.[115] Piracy has been an ongoing historical concern: "even before International Law in the modern sense of the term was in existence, a pirate was already considered an outlaw, a *'hostis humani generis'.*"[116] The United Nations Convention on the Law of the Sea establishes universal jurisdiction over piracy in Article 105:

> On the high seas, or in any other place outside the jurisdiction of any State, every State may seize a pirate ship or aircraft, or a ship or aircraft taken by piracy and under the control of pirates, and arrest the persons and seize the property on board. The courts of the State which carried out the seizure may decide upon the penalties to be imposed, and may also determine the action to be taken with regard to the ship, aircraft or property, subject to the rights of third parties acting in good faith.[117]

---

[112] Understanding the crime of piracy in international law is not only important because it was the precursor of the doctrine of universality, see M. Cherif Bassiouni, "Universal Jurisdiction for International Crimes: Historical Perspectives and Contemporary Practice," *Virginia Journal of International Law* 42 (2000–2001) (for an analysis of the evolution of universal jurisdiction). The importance of discussing piracy relies also on the premise that piracy is the precursor of the conception of international crimes. However important the study of the crime of piracy may be to understanding the broad scope of universal jurisdiction in contemporary international law, the majority of the literature concerning universal jurisdiction deals very superficially with the crime of piracy. The analogy between piracy and other crimes is done in a very subtle manner in scholarly writings and very few studies have been devoted to an in-depth analysis of this analogy.

[113] The focus on the crime of piracy in this section is because this is the genesis of universal jurisdiction and it provides an adequate framework to discuss the rationales underpinning universal jurisdiction.

[114] See Joshua Michael Goodwin, "Universal Jurisdiction and the Pirate: Time for an Old Couple to Part," *Vanderbilt Journal Transnational l Law* 39 (2006), pp. 987–1002; see Willard Cowles, "Universality of Jurisdiction over War Crimes," *California Law Review* 33 (1945), at pp. 181–194 (noting that jurisdiction over piracy has occurred since the sixteenth century).

[115] See generally, Edwin D. Dickinson, "Is the Crime of Piracy Obsolete?," *Harvard Law Review* 38 (1925), 334, 337–339, cited in Kenneth C. Randall, "Universal Jurisdiction Under International Law," *Texas Law Review* 66 (1988), at p. 791.

[116] Lassa Oppenheim, Robert Yewdall Jennings, and Arthur Desmond Watts, *Oppenheim's International Law: Peace*, Longman, 9th ed., 1992, at 609.

[117] 1982 United Nations Convention on the Law of the Sea, 21 ILM 1261 (1982), article 105. This provision states the right, but not the obligation, to assert universal jurisdiction over acts of piracy, see Kenneth C. Randall, "Universal Jurisdiction Under International Law," *Texas Law Review* 66 (1988), p. 792.

The Role of National Courts and Mechanisms

177

Piracy involves acts of robbery and violence.[118] An important feature of the definition of piracy is the fact that it happens on the high seas, "a global common," outside the jurisdiction of any state.[119] Every state has an equal right to navigate the high seas. This characteristic of the high seas is sometimes argued to one rationale for the exercise of universal jurisdiction since other traditional principles of jurisdiction would be inapplicable.[120]

As it can be perceived from the previous discussion, universal jurisdiction is not a recent phenomenon.[121] The principle that states can punish foreigners for crimes committed outside their territorial boundaries is a concept that has existed for a long time in international law.[122] Without purporting to provide a thorough analysis of the formation of the principle of universality, this chapter analyses a few basic points in the evolution of this doctrine.

As already discussed, universal jurisdiction was developed to combat the crime of piracy based on the rationale that because the crime occurred on the high seas,[123] no state could have jurisdiction over pirates unless they claimed

---

[118] See *Fitfield* v. *Ins. Co. of Pa.*, 47 Pa. 166, 187 (1864) (concluding that pirates are sea robbers); see also, Alfred Rubin, *The Law of Piracy*, University Press of the Pacific, 2nd ed., 2006, p. 213 (noting that states can define statutorily what constitutes acts of piracy).

[119] Eugene Kontorovich, "The Piracy Analogy: Modern Universal Jurisdiction's Hollow Foundation," *Harvard International Law Journal* 45 (2004), at p. 190. One interesting note is that universal jurisdiction, by definition, is exercised regardless of where the offense occurs, see Luc Reydams, "Universal Criminal Jurisdiction: The Belgian State of Affairs," *Criminal Law Forum* 11 (2000), pp. 183–216.

[120] See generally, *Sosa* v. *Alvarez-Machain*, 124 US 2739, 2775 (2004) (Scalia, J., concurring in part and dissenting in part) (suggesting that the norm for piracy was developed because pirates were "beyond all ... territorial jurisdictions"); Lee A. Casey, "The Case Against the International Criminal Court," *Fordham International Law Journal* 25 (2002), pp. 840–872 (contending that universal jurisdiction for piracy has been accepted since it takes place "on the high seas, beyond the territorial jurisdiction of any single State"), cited in Eugene Kontorovich, "Implementing *Sosa* v. *Alvarez-Machain*: What Piracy Reveals About the Limits of the Alien Tort Statute," *Notre Dame Law Review* 80 (2004), at p. 151.

[121] See Antônio Augusto Cançado Trindade, *International Law for Humankind: Towards a New Jus Gentium*, Nijhoff, 2010, p. 383 (affirming that universal jurisdiction "has a long history, which dates back to the thinking of the founding fathers of the law of nations").

[122] See generally, Harvard Research in International Law, "Draft Convention on Jurisdiction with Respect to Crime," *American Journal of International Law* 29 (1935), pp. 439–442; Kenneth C. Randall, "Universal Jurisdiction Under International Law," *Texas Law Review* 66 (1988), pp. 785–841.

[123] It is often argued that the heinous nature of piracy is the basis for universal jurisdiction, see Kenneth C. Randall, "Universal Jurisdiction Under International Law," *Texas Law Review* 66 (1988), pp. 785–841. This rationale has been criticized, see Eugene Kontorovich, "The Piracy Analogy: Modern Universal Jurisdiction's Hollow Foundation," *Harvard International Law Journal* 45 (2004), pp. 183–238.

178 — *Reparative Justice for International Crimes*

the universality of jurisdiction.[124] The doctrine changed with time and the basis for a claim of universal jurisdiction shifted to the grave nature of the crime and the need to combat impunity for such conduct.[125] Thus, the underlying principles justifying the application of universal jurisdiction over certain crimes arise out of the location where the offense occurred (i.e., outside the jurisdiction of any state) or the grave nature of the crime.[126]

In the case of universal jurisdiction over grave offenses, "because a state exercising universal jurisdiction does so on behalf of the international community, it must place the overall interests of the international community above its own."[127] In its criminal dimensions, universal jurisdiction is mostly acclaimed to be an effective tool to fight impunity and to fill in the gaps of international criminal tribunals' proceedings.[128] In addition to being a resource for prosecuting serious human rights violations, universal jurisdiction is also viewed as a tool for global justice, especially when countries are unwilling or unable to prosecute criminals within their jurisdiction.[129]

Universal jurisdiction is premised upon the idea that, contrary to other principles of international jurisdiction, the heinous nature of the crime justifies the exercise of jurisdiction by any state.[130] In this sense, the seriousness

---

[124] See Kenneth C. Randall, "Universal Jurisdiction Under International Law," 66 *Texas Law Review* (1988), pp. 785–841; M. Cherif Bassiouni, "Universal Jurisdiction for International Crimes: Historical Perspectives and Contemporary Practice," 42 *Virginia Journal of International Law* 81 (2000–2001), pp. 153–199.

[125] Ibid. The authors claim that the modern basis for universal jurisdiction is the grave nature of the crime and the need to combat impunity for those crimes.

[126] See Mitsue Inazumi, *Universal Jurisdiction in Modern International Law: Expansion of National Jurisdiction for Prosecuting Serious Crimes Under International Law*, adapted version of dissertation defended at Utrecht University on 27 October 2004, Oxford University Press, 2005; Chandra Lekha Sriram, *Globalizing Justice for Mass Atrocities*, Routledge, 2005.

[127] M. Cherif Bassiouni, "Universal Jurisdiction for International Crimes: Historical Perspectives and Contemporary Practice," *Virginia Journal of International Law* 42 (2000–2001), pp. 153–199.

[128] See Hays Butler, "Universal Jurisdiction: A Review of the Literature," *Criminal Law Forum* 11 (2000), pp. 353–373, citing Daniel T. Ntanda Nsereko, "The International Criminal Court: Jurisdictional and Related Issues," *Criminal Law Forum* 10 (1999), pp. 87–120 (concerning the limited scope of the Court's jurisdiction and arguing for an increased role of universal jurisdiction of national courts to complete the gaps of international institutions in prosecuting egregious crimes).

[129] Anne Geraghty, "Universal Jurisdiction and Drug Trafficking: A Tool for Fighting One of the World's Most Pervasive Problems," *Florida Journal of International Law* 16 (2004), pp. 371–403.

[130] M. Cherif Bassiouni, "The History of Universal Jurisdiction and Its Place in International Law," in *Universal Jurisdiction: National Courts and the Prosecution of Serious Crimes Under International Law*, University of Pennsylvania Press, 2004, pp. 39–63.

of the crime allows any state to prosecute an offender.[131] Due to the gravity of certain crimes, their consequences extend beyond victims and their communities, and affect the international community as a whole.[132]

There thus seem to be three main points which provide a theoretical foundation for the development of universal jurisdiction in relation to the (original) crime of piracy. The first rationale is the fact that pirates are "stateless" and therefore no country can have jurisdiction over them based on the nationality principle. The second rationale is the idea that crimes of piracy happen on the high seas where no state has jurisdiction based on the territoriality principle. Under these two rationales, states are not acting in violation of each other's sovereignty, but rather for a common objective, a sort of "mutual interest" to combat a crime that potentially affects all nations.

The third rationale for universal jurisdiction is based on the claim that some crimes are so heinous that they are perpetrated against the international community and not only individual states.[133] Under this rationale, in exercising universal jurisdiction, states are acting on behalf of the interests of the international community as a whole, for the pursuit of the ultimate goal of justice. This last rationale provided the basis for the expansion of universal jurisdiction from the crime of piracy to crimes of universal concern.

Currently, universal jurisdiction arises from the concept that some kinds of crimes are so heinous that they shock all humankind and thus preclude any claims against extraterritoriality. In this regard, it has been asserted that:

> universal jurisdiction [is] founded on the sheer heinousness of certain crimes, such as genocide and torture, which are universally condemned and which every state has an interest in repressing even in the absence of traditional connecting factors… . [T]hough subject to evolution, the roster of crimes presently covered by universal jurisdiction includes … genocide, torture, some war crimes, and crimes against humanity.[134]

Thus, universal criminal jurisdiction as it is currently conceived has gone beyond piracy and the slave trade to include international crimes such as

---

[131] Ibid., pp. 41–44.

[132] Ibid., pp. 42–43.

[133] See Moussounga Itsouhou Mbadinga, "Le recours à la compétence universelle pour la répression des crimes internationaux: étude de quelques cas," *Revue de droit international et de sciences diplomatiques et politiques* 81 (2003), pp. 285–305.

[134] Donald Francis Donovan and Anthea Roberts, "The Emerging Recognition of Universal Civil Jurisdiction," *American Journal of International Law* 100 (2006), p. 143.

180   *Reparative Justice for International Crimes*

genocide, torture, war crimes, and crimes against humanity that shock the conscience of humankind.[135]

Concerns based on comity and international relations between states are often cited against the human rights enforcement benefits of universal jurisdiction. In looking ahead at the development, or rather retreat of universal jurisdiction, it may be wise, rather than balancing the pros and cons, to actually focus on a reasonable exercise and development of the doctrine.[136] That would mean that states making use of universal jurisdiction would follow certain principles regarding, for example, comity, requests for extradition, and the ability and willingness of the state having stronger grounds of jurisdiction (e.g., based on nationality or territoriality) to assert jurisdiction over the offender.

5.5.2 *Towards a Victim-Orientated Approach: A Civil Dimension of Universal Jurisdiction?*

This part of the chapter discusses whether the doctrine of universal jurisdiction can be used to enforce a victim's right to reparations. The key question as it pertains to the further development of universal *civil* jurisdiction is whether the foundation of the doctrine, in its criminal dimension, can be expanded to include a civil dimension.

5.5.2.1 Defining the Civil Dimension of Universal Jurisdiction

Universal civil jurisdiction, often also called universal tort jurisdiction,[137] similar to that of universal criminal jurisdiction, does not require any jurisdictional link between the forum and the wrongful act.[138] It has been defined "as the principle under which civil proceedings may be brought in a domestic court irrespective of the location of the unlawful conduct and irrespective of the nationality of the perpetrator or the victim, on the grounds that the unlawful conduct is a matter of international concern."[139]

---

[135]   See e.g., ICTY, *Prosecutor v. Furundžija*, Trial Chamber, Judgment of 10 December 1998 (no. IT-95-17/1-T).

[136]   See on this point also, Cedric Ryngaert, *Jurisdiction in International Law*, Cambridge University Press, 2nd ed., 2015.

[137]   See Cedric Ryngaert, *Jurisdiction in International Law*, Cambridge University Press, 2015, 2nd ed., pp. 135ff. In this chapter, I will use the terms "universal civil jurisdiction" and "universal tort jurisdiction" interchangeably.

[138]   Donald Donovan, "Universal Jurisdiction: The Next Frontier?," *American Society of International Law Proceedings* 99 (2005), p. 117–128.

[139]   Menno T. Kamminga, "Universal Civil Jurisdiction: Is it Legal? Is it Desirable?" *American Society of International Law Proceedings* 99 (2005), p. 123.

The concept of universal civil or tort jurisdiction is less known than its counterpart, universal criminal jurisdiction. In short, as the other side of the coin, universal tort jurisdiction refers to civil action taken against perpetrators of international crimes, in any forum, irrespective of where the crime was committed and the nationality of the offender or the victim.[140] While universal criminal jurisdiction is reserved primarily for international crimes (as discussed), universal civil jurisdiction has been claimed for gross human rights violations, wherever they may have occurred.[141] Thus, at the current print of international law, it is not possible to refer to a clearly circumscribed list of criminal conduct that may be subject to universal civil jurisdiction.

Concerning the presence requirement, beyond questioning whether it is permissible under international law, it does not seem that universal civil jurisdiction *in absentia* is desirable. In order to obtain enforcement of civil awards of reparations, a minimal territorial connection such as the mere presence of the perpetrator in the forum state during the proceedings[142] may be necessary, without the need for formal links such as residence or nationality.[143]

As to the scope and reach of universal civil jurisdiction, state practice, as discussed below, demonstrates that victims have claimed reparation under this doctrine against individual perpetrators – as it is shown by cases against individuals alleged to be guilty of war crimes during the former Yugoslavia wars; against corporations – as it is shown by diverse cases brought before United States courts[144]; and (with more difficulty due to claims of state immunity) against states – as it is illustrated in the recent cases against Germany.[145]

5.5.2.2 Lawfulness of Universal Civil Jurisdiction

A question exists, however, as to the lawfulness of universal civil jurisdiction and whether such an exercise is permitted by international law. It has been

---

[140] See generally on the concept of universal tort jurisdiction, Cedric Ryngaert, *Jurisdiction in International Law*, Cambridge University Press, 2nd ed., 2015, pp. 135 et seq. and Donald Donovan, "Universal Jurisdiction: The Next Frontier?" *American Society of International Law Proceedings* 99 (2005), pp. 117–128.

[141] Ibid., p. 135.

[142] Ibid., p. 135, n. 216.

[143] Ibid.

[144] See discussion of cases and references in Section 5.5.2.4.

[145] See the Case Concerning Jurisdictional Immunities of the State (*Germany* v. *Italy*, Greece intervening), Judgment, *ICJ Reports* 2011 and related national proceedings in Italy and Greece.

182 *Reparative Justice for International Crimes*

rightly observed that there is no general international treaty allowing for universal civil jurisdiction.[146] Unlike universal criminal jurisdiction, there is not yet enough state practice and *opinio juris* to ground unequivocally the argument that customary international law allows for the exercise of universal civil jurisdiction for the same crimes as those allowing universal criminal jurisdiction.

International law has not yet reached a stage where universal civil jurisdiction is recognized under customary international law. Nevertheless, an argument has been made that: "It would make sense to assume that the exercise of universal civil jurisdiction is permitted in respect of the same unlawful conduct as universal criminal jurisdiction and that similar conditions apply"[147]; and that "[i]nternational law authorizes universal civil jurisdiction, in part because it operates as a less intrusive form of jurisdiction than universal criminal jurisdiction."[148] In a similar vein, in a concurring opinion to the United States Supreme Court Decision in *Sosa v. Alvarez-Machain*, Justice Breyer stated that "universal criminal jurisdiction necessarily contemplates a significant degree of civil tort recovery as well" and that the exercise of universal civil jurisdiction is no more threatening than that of universal criminal jurisdiction.[149]

In discussing the lawfulness of universal civil jurisdiction, Professor Ryngaert posits that: "the fact that only a limited number of states allow the exercise of universal tort jurisdiction is not fatal to the lawfulness of such jurisdiction under international law." He goes on to claim that "[t]hese states may not provide for universal tort jurisdiction because they prefer criminal justice solutions, rather than because they consider such jurisdiction to be internationally unlawful."[150] With regards to whether universal jurisdiction is actually permissible under international law, although only a few states have actually exercised universal civil jurisdiction, there is no crystallized customary rule that prohibits its application.[151]

In contrast, it does not seem that universal civil jurisdiction (in relation to international crimes) is uniformly accepted under international law. Some

---

[146] Luc Reydams, "Universal Jurisdiction in Context," *American Society of International Law Proceedings* 99 (2005), pp. 118–120.

[147] Menno T. Kamminga, "Universal Civil Jurisdiction: Is it Legal? Is it Desirable?" *American Society of International Law Proceedings* 99 (2005), pp. 123–125.

[148] Beth Van Schaack, "Justice Without Borders: Universal Civil Jurisdiction," *American Society of International Law Proceedings* 99 (2005), pp. 120–122.

[149] 542 U.S. 692 (2004), p. 763.

[150] Cedric Ryngaert, "Universal Tort Jurisdiction over Gross Human Rights Violations," *Netherlands Yearbook of International Law* 38 (2007), pp. 3–60.

[151] Ibid.

The Role of National Courts and Mechanisms 183

states have expressed the view that, although international law recognizes universal criminal jurisdiction, it does not "recognize universal civil jurisdiction for any category of cases at all, unless the relevant states have consented to it in a treaty or it has been accepted in customary international law."[152]

In any event, at this early stage of the development of the doctrine under international law, the examination of individual states' practice is not of much help when attempting to define the contours of universal civil jurisdiction. Instead, universal civil jurisdiction should be justified through reliance upon principles of international law, such as the right of victims to receive reparation, which transcends the realm of international human rights law. It is in this perspective that attention is now turned to recent state practice and possible *rationales* that may justify adding a civil dimension to universal jurisdiction, as well as potential challenges.

5.5.2.3 Rationales for Adding a Civil Dimension to Universal Jurisdiction

It is appropriate at this juncture to examine state practice and legal rationales that could eventually underpin universal civil jurisdiction. Universal jurisdiction (in its criminal dimension) has strengthened its foundation pursuant to the principle of combating impunity and providing accountability for serious violations of international law.[153] It has done so by allowing any state to prosecute crimes such as piracy, slave trade, genocide, war crimes, and torture, which typically defy the traditional boundaries of criminal justice and which shock the conscience of humankind.[154] Hence, at first sight, inserting a civil dimension into the doctrine of universal jurisdiction may seem inappropriate.[155]

However, universal jurisdiction for international crimes has developed pursuant to the rationale that some crimes are so heinous that any state can

---

[152] Brief of the Governments of the Commonwealth of Australia, the Swiss Confederation and the United Kingdom of Great Britain and Northern Ireland as *Amici Curiae*, *Sosa* v. *Alvarez-Machain*, 542 U.S. 692 (2004) (No. 03-339).

[153] Cf. Kenneth C. Randall, "Universal Jurisdiction Under International Law," *Texas Law Review* 66 (1988), pp. 785–841; Princeton Project on Universal Jurisdiction, *The Princeton Principles on Universal Jurisdiction* 28–29 (2001); Mitsue Inazumi, *Universal Jurisdiction in Modern International Law: Expansion of National Jurisdiction for Prosecuting Serious Crimes Under International Law*, adapted version of dissertation defended at Utrecht University on 27 October 2004, Oxford University Press, 2005.

[154] American Law Institute, Restatement (Third), *The Foreign Relations Law of the United States* (1987), section 404; see also *Sosa* v. *Alvarez-Machain*, 542 U.S. 692 (2004) (No. 03-339), Concurring Opinion of Justice Breyer.

[155] See Beth Van Schaack, "Justice Without Borders: Universal Civil Jurisdiction," *American Society of International Law Proceedings* 99 (2005), pp. 120–122.

184 *Reparative Justice for International Crimes*

prosecute the perpetrator, no matter where they may be found.[156] This rationale provides a foundation for the development of the civil dimension of universal jurisdiction. The same rationale that supported the expansion of universal jurisdiction for "crimes of universal concern" could potentially justify the exercise of universal civil jurisdiction.[157] Thus, victims of crimes subject to universal jurisdiction would be able to claim reparation in any forum, without necessarily a jurisdictional link to the offender or the place where the heinous conduct took place.

As for the theoretical perspective, the link between the criminal and civil dimensions of universal jurisdiction is the heinous nature of the criminal conduct and the gravity of the crime, which exclude a territorial nexus.[158] In its civil dimension, universal jurisdiction can serve as an alternative for victims of international crimes to seek and obtain reparations. Furthermore, civil proceedings provide victims a chance to tell their stories and have their day in court. It is also important to bear in mind that civil remedies may serve as an independent means of enforcing international norms proscribing defined criminal conduct, and as a means to give victims access to international criminal justice pertaining to international crimes.[159]

The civil dimension of universal jurisdiction is also a way to end impunity which may help to create a culture of accountability, a goal which was one of the driving forces behind the modern expansion of universal jurisdiction. Civil judgments have an important declarative function as identifying conduct which is condemned by the international community.

These considerations are necessarily abstract and there certainly remain some questions and challenges about how universal civil jurisdiction will work in practice and how it will further develop in international law. At this stage, however, courts exercising (universal) jurisdiction over civil claims for reparations will usually have to follow their domestic laws and rules of procedure. This may mean that some technical legal aspects of domestic

---

[156] See discussion in Section 5.5.1.

[157] Donald Donovan, "Universal Jurisdiction: The Next Frontier?" *American Society of International Law Proceedings* 99 (2005), pp. 117–128.

[158] Cedric Ryngaert, *Jurisdiction in International Law*, Cambridge University Press, 2015, 2nd ed., p. 135.

[159] See Linda Malone, "Enforcing International Criminal Law Violations with Civil Remedies: The US Alien Tort Claims Act," in *International Criminal Law*, Brill, 3rd ed., Vol. III, 2008, pp. 421–455.

The Role of National Courts and Mechanisms   185

legal systems, such as statutes of limitations, may also apply to civil claims in relation to international crimes, depending on the laws of the forum state.

Other relevant concerns about the implementation of universal civil jurisdiction include, for example, the impact of claims of state or official immunity on the exercise of universal jurisdiction for international crimes and breaches of *jus cogens* norms, the grants of amnesties, and the enforcement of judgments based on universal jurisdiction. While a detailed analysis of such questions is outside the scope of the present chapter, the review of state practice that follows will shed some light on how these questions have been treated in practice.

5.5.2.4 State Practice and Possible Rationales for a Civil Dimension of Universal Jurisdiction

Universal jurisdiction in its civil dimension has developed in the case law of some states. The main country where something akin to a civil dimension of universal jurisdiction has developed is the United States. This is because in the United States, there are two statutes that have been interpreted to allow for the exercise of a sort of universal civil jurisdiction. The *Alien Tort Claims Act* (ATCA),[160] from 1789, states that "[t]he district courts shall have original jurisdiction of any civil action by an alien for a tort only, committed in violation of the law of nations or a treaty of the United States." Additionally, the *Torture Victims Protection Act* (TVPA) provides a cause of action for any victim of torture and extrajudicial killing, wherever the crime was committed.[161]

Most cases that relied on the ATCA concern corporate liability rather than individual civil liability.[162] While in the past decades there has been a great number of cases concerning torts committed outside the United States which relied on the ATCA,[163] a notable case before the Supreme Court of the United States has somewhat changed the panorama of ATCA litigation. In 2013, the United States Supreme Court decided the case *Kiobel v. Royal Dutch Petroleum*[164] which dealt with allegations that Shell entities planned, conspired, and facilitated extrajudicial executions, torture, and crimes against

---

[160] 28 U.S.C. § 1350 (2006) (ATCA).

[161] Pub. L. 102-256, 12 March 1992, 106 Stat. 73, in particular Section 2(a) of the TVPA.

[162] For a list of ATCA cases concerning corporations, see Michael D. Goldhaber, "Corporate Human Rights Litigation in Non-U.S. Courts: A Comparative Scorecard," *UC Irvine Law Review* 3 (2013), Appendix A (list of cases compiled by Jonathan Drimmer concerning corporate cases).

[163] See ibid.

[164] 133 S. Ct. 1659 (2013). Not long after the Judgment of the Supreme Court was rendered, many scholars commented on it, see e.g., Janine M. Stanisz, "The Expansion of Limited Liability Protection in the Corporate Form: The Aftermath of *Kiobel* v. *Royal Dutch Petroleum Co.*,"

186   *Reparative Justice for International Crimes*

humanity by Nigeria in the Niger Delta between 1992 and 1995. The case was based on the ATCA. While not dealing with individual civil liability for international crimes (which is the paradigm of the present book), this case is worth discussing due to the impact it has had on the development of the concept of universal civil jurisdiction before US courts.

One of the main issues in the *Royal Dutch Petroleum* case revolved around the extraterritorial nature of the ATCA. More specifically, whether the United States courts could rely on the ATCA to hear civil claims concerning human rights violations that had no connection to the United States, that is, violations that were not committed on United States soil, or by an American national, or against an American victim.[165] Thus, under these parameters, this case fell

---

Brook. J. Corp. Fin. & Com. L. 5 (2010), pp. 573–600 (for a commentary before the Supreme Court Judgment); Frank Cruz-Alvarez and Laura E. Wade, "The Second Circuit Correctly Interprets the Alien Tort Statute: *Kiobel v. Royal Dutch*," *University of Miami Law Review* 65 (2010), pp. 1109–1132 (for a piece before the Supreme Court Judgment). For commentary on the Supreme Court Judgment, see e.g., Ingrid Wuerth, "The Supreme Court and the Alien Tort Statute: *Kiobel v. Royal Dutch Petroleum Co.*," *American Journal of International Law* 107 (2013), pp. 601–621; Anthony J. Colangelo, "The Alien Tort Statute and the Law of Nations in Kiobel and Beyond," *Georgetown Journal of International Law* 44 (2013), pp. 1329–1346; Vivian G. Curran, "Extraterritoriality, Universal Jurisdiction, and the Challenge of *Kiobel v. Royal Dutch Petroleum Co.*," *Maryland Journal of International Law* 28 (2013), pp. 76–89, available at http://digitalcom mons.law.umaryland.edu/mjil/vol28/iss1/6; Humberto Fernando Cantú Rivera, "Recent Developments in *Kiobel vs. Royal Dutch Petroleum*: An Important Human Rights Forum In Peril?" *Cuestiones Constitucionales* 28 (2013), pp. 243–254; Angelica Bonfanti, "No Extraterritorial Jurisdiction Under the Alien Tort Statute: Which Forum for Disputes on Overseas Corporate Human Rights Violations After Kiobel?" *Diritti umani e diritto internazionale* (2013), pp. 377–398.

[165]   The questions presented to the Supreme Court of the United States, on appeal from the Second Circuit, were:

    1. Whether the issue of corporate civil tort liability under the Alien Tort treated by all other courts prior to the decision below, or an issue of subject matter jurisdiction, as the court of appeals held for the first time.

    2. Whether corporations are immune from tort liability for violations of the law of nations such as torture, extrajudicial executions or genocide, as the court of appeals decision provides, or if corporations may be sued in the same manner as any other private party defendant under the ATS for such egregious violations, as the Eleventh Circuit has explicitly held.

Petition for Writ of Certiorari, Kiobel, 133 S. Ct. 1659 (No. 10-1491).

    In the oral arguments phase, the Court ordered the Parties to argue the following point: "Whether and under what circumstances the Alien Tort Statute, 28 U.S.C. § 1350, allows courts to recognize a cause of action for violations of the law of nations occurring within the territory of a sovereign other than the United States." *Kiobel v. Royal Dutch Petroleum Co.*, 132 S. Ct. 1738 (2012) (mem.). See on this question: Vivian G. Curran, "Extraterritoriality, Universal Jurisdiction, and the Challenge of *Kiobel v. Royal Dutch Petroleum Co.*," 28 *Maryland Journal of International Law* 76 (2013), available at http://digitalcommons.law.u maryland.edu/mjil/vol28/iss1/6.

squarely within the conception of universal civil jurisdiction. Although this case centered on *corporate* civil liability, it also has implications for the development of universal civil jurisdiction concerning international crimes committed by individuals.

The Supreme Court took a decision that has a negative impact on the potential development of universal civil jurisdiction claims under the ATCA. The Supreme Court decided that the ATCA could not be applied in civil suit cases for acts committed outside of the United States. Claims under the ATCA cannot be brought before federal courts in the United States for violations of the law of nations occurring within the territory of a sovereign state other than the United States.[166]

It may be argued, based on the focused questions before the court,[167] that this interpretation of the ATCA applies only to cases concerning torts for violations of the law of nations, and not to a treaty of the United States, as the second prong for the application of the ATCA. It has also been argued that the "Court's misunderstanding has not completely erased the possibility of future claims involving foreign elements from being brought under the [ATCA]. The Court left the door open to claims that sufficiently 'touch and concern' the United States."[168]

Another recent case concerning corporate liability under ATCA further limited the potential for using this law for universal jurisdiction cases. In *Jesner et al. v. Arab Bank, PLC*,[169] the Supreme Court of the United States further limited the scope of the ATCA for human rights litigation and the potential use of universal civil jurisdiction. This case concerned foreign nationals who were allegedly killed or injured by terrorist attacks abroad (i.e., outside the United States) and sued a Jordan-based bank for allegedly helping finance terrorist groups through a conduct that took place in the United States. The court decided ultimately that foreign corporations cannot be sued as defendants under ATCA.[170]

---

[166] See *Kiobel v. Royal Dutch Petroleum*, 133 S. Ct. 1659 (2013).

[167] See "2. Whether corporations are immune from tort liability for violations of the law of nations such as torture, extrajudicial executions or genocide, as the court of appeals decision provides, or if corporations may be sued in the same manner as any other private party defendant under the ATS for such egregious violations, as the Eleventh Circuit has explicitly held." Petition for Writ of Certiorari at, Kiobel, 133 S. Ct. 1659 (No. 10-1491).

[168] Anthony J. Colangelo, "The Alien Tort Statute and the Law of Nations in Kiobel and Beyond," *Georgetown Journal of International Law* 44 (2013), pp. 1329–1346.

[169] 584 U. S. (2018).

[170] For a commentary, see 132 *Harvard Law Review* 397, 9 November 2018, available at https://harvardlawreview.org/2018/11/jesner-v-arab-bank-plc/.

188   *Reparative Justice for International Crimes*

As regretful as these precedents may seem for the development of the jurisprudence supporting universal civil jurisdiction, it cannot be said that universal civil jurisdiction is a dead doctrine. Another case may be cited as an example in the development of universal civil jurisdiction. In 2012, a Dutch court in The Hague awarded reparations in the form of compensation to a Palestinian doctor who was imprisoned in Libya for allegedly infecting children with HIV/Aids. The claimant alleged that he was unjustly detained and tortured by the defendants. The claimant, born in Egypt, who resided in the Netherlands, sued twelve Libyan officials pursuant to a Dutch law extending universal jurisdiction.[171] The plaintiff sought both material and nonmaterial damages.[172]

This case, decided by a first instance court in The Hague, proceeded on the basis that, as the case was of an international character, it had to be determined whether the Dutch court had jurisdiction. The alleged basis for jurisdiction was Article 9(c) of the Code of Civil Procedure. This provision states that jurisdiction is found when the case is "sufficiently connected with the Dutch legal order" and when "it would be unacceptable to ask of the plaintiff that he bring the case before a foreign court." The court found jurisdiction on the basis that it was unacceptable to require the claimant to take the case before a court in Libya, considering the circumstances in Libya at the time of the initial filing of the case (in July 2011), and considering the fact that the claimant was a resident in the Netherlands.[173]

While this decision was a judgment of a first instance court without much substantive analysis, it is a recent and insightful example of the use of universal civil jurisdiction using domestic laws and procedures – in this case, the crimes were committed abroad, the victim and alleged perpetrators were not nationals of the forum state. The Dutch court looked at two important aspects to base its jurisdiction: the first was the fact that the claimant was a resident in the Netherlands, providing an important link with the forum state and a procedural basis for jurisdiction. The second important aspect of this case is the fact that the court found that it was "unacceptable to ask the claimant to bring the case in a foreign court," therefore the necessary criterion was met. These aspects point to two potential

[171] *El-Hojouj* v. *Amer Derbas* et al., 21 March 2012, Case No. 400882/HA ZA 11-2252. See also, "Dutch Court Compensates Palestinian for Libya Jail," BBC news, 28 March 2012, available at http://bbc.co.uk/news/world-middle-east-17537597. For a commentary, see Eugene Kontorovich, "Kiobel (IV): Precedent-Setting Dutch Civil Universal Jurisdiction Case," *Opinio Juris*, 28 March 2012, available at http://opiniojuris.org/2012/03/28/precedent-setting-dutch-civil-universal-jurisdiction-case/.

[172] The analysis of this case is based on an unofficial translation of the Judgment (original in Dutch).

[173] *El-Hojouj* v. *Amer Derbas* et al., 21 March 2012, Case No. 400882/HA ZA 11-2252.

guiding principles for the development of universal civil jurisdiction in a sensible manner and with respect for certain international legal principles such as international comity. The first is the existence of a sufficient link with the forum state (e.g. a residency requirement); the second is the notion of "forum of necessity," where a claimant's case cannot be heard in another jurisdiction.

On this latter point, the *Institut de Droit International* published a report in 2015 concerning universal civil jurisdiction for international crimes in which it provided a detailed review of state practice (concerning claims against individuals, corporations, and states), and posited that

> the evolution of European international law is sensitive to the desirability of a certain opening of the courts to disputes concerning serious violations of fundamental rights even in the absence of a forum based on ordinary rules. The existence of a safeguarding forum as a "forum of necessity" is a tradition in many European countries. However, if public opinion is rather favorable to such a forum, political positions are more reserved.[174]

In reviewing the practice of states in Europe, including France and the Netherlands, as well as Canada, on the question of the applicability of the "forum of necessity," the report noted that:

> The question is not, therefore, whether national interests are at stake to the point that the jurisdictional power must be available to provide a remedy for crimes against humanity committed by the "enemies of humanity". The question is whether the interests of the international community argue that such a remedy should be provided by an appropriate jurisdiction in such a way that no "safe haven" subsists that could ultimately operate as a screen protector against the legitimate demands of victims of torture, genocide and other such atrocities. In order to avoid such an outcome, international law should ensure the existence and proper functioning of courts capable of judging them in order to protect victims from a denial of justice. The few

---

[174] *Institut de droit international, Commission I,* "La compétence universelle civile en matière de réparation pour crimes internationaux – Universal civil jurisdiction with regard to reparation for international crimes," Report by Andreas Bucher, p. 22, available on the site of the *Institut* (session of 2015, Tallinn) at http://www.idi-iil.org/app/uploads/2017/06/01-Bucher-Compete nce_universel.pdf (last accessed 10 July 2019). Author's translation, original text:

> *l'évolution du droit international européen est sensible à l'opportunité d'une certaine ouverture des tribunaux aux litiges portant sur des graves violations des droits fondamen-taux même en l'absence d'un for fondé sur les règles ordinaires. L'existence d'un for de sauvegarde en tant que "for de nécessité" est de tradition dans plusieurs pays européens. Cependant, si l'opinion publique est plutôt favorable à un tel for, les positions politiques sont plus reservées.*

190   *Reparative Justice for International Crimes*

trials that have been conducted have, because of their disastrous effects on the image of the targeted societies, caused an awareness leading to a prevention approach in relation to human rights.[175]

In addition to cases brought before domestic courts in the Balkans, domestic courts *outside* of Bosnia and Herzegovina[176] have heard reparation claims from victims of the crimes perpetrated during the war.[177] Interestingly, such suits were mainly filed in United States courts.[178] Two of these cases were brought against Radovan Karadžić, both of which concluded in default judgments in the 1990s.[179]

These cases concerned civil suits brought by two individuals who claimed to be victims of the crimes allegedly perpetrated by Mr. Karadžić. The alleged

---

[175]   Ibid., p. 26. Author's translation, original text:

> *La question n'est pas, dès lors, de savoir si des intérêts nationaux sont en jeu au point que le pouvoir juridictionnel doit être à disposition afin de fournir un remède à des crimes contre l'humanité commis par les "ennemis de l'humanité". La question est plutôt de savoir si les intérêts de la communauté internationale militent pour qu'un tel remède soit fourni par une juridiction appropriée de telle manière à ce qu'aucun "havre sûr" ne subsiste qui pourrait en fin de compte opérer comme un écran protecteur à l'encontre des demandes légitimes des victimes de torture, de génocide et d'autres atrocités de ce genre. Afin d'éviter une telle issue, le droit international devrait assurer l'existence et le bon fonctionnement de tribunaux aptes à en juger afin de protéger les victimes face à un déni de justice. Les quelques procès qui ont été menés ont permis, en raison de leurs effets désastreux sur l'image des sociétés visées, de provoquer une prise de conscience débouchant sur une approche de prévention par rapport aux droits de l'homme.*

[176]   These cases are detailed in the chapter by Frederiek de Vlaming and Kate Clark, "War Reparations in Bosnia and Herzegovina: Individual Stories and Collective Interests," *Narratives of Justice In and Out of the Courtroom*, Springer International Publishing, 2014, pp. 167–175.

[177]   See Carla Ferstman and Sheri P. Rosenberg, "Reparations in Dayton's Bosnia and Herzegovina," in *Reparations for Victims of Genocide, War Crimes and Crimes Against Humanity: Systems in Place and Systems in the Making*, Nijhoff, 2009, pp. 483–513.

[178]   Commentators have affirmed that "[it] appears these cases, when taken together with other anti-impunity efforts around the world, are also helping to create a climate of deterrence and [to] catalyze efforts in several countries to prosecute their own human rights abusers": Sandra Coliver, Jennie Green, and Paul Hoffman, "Holding human rights violators accountable by using international law in U.S. courts: Advocacy efforts and complementary strategies," *Emory International Law Review* 19 (2005), pp. 174–175. For a commentary from the representative of some of the victims, see Catherine MacKinnon, "Remedies for War Crimes at the National Level," *The Journal of the International Institute* 6 (1998).

[179]   *Kadic v. Karadžić*, 70 F.3d 232 (2d. Circ. 1995), cert. denied, 518 US 1005 (1996). For a commentary, see David P. Kunstle, "Kadic v. Karadžić: Do Private Individuals Have Enforceable Rights and Obligations Under the Alien Tort Claims Act?" *Duke Journal of Comparative & International Law* 6 (1996), pp. 319–346.

The Role of National Courts and Mechanisms   191

crimes for which compensation was being sought included: "genocide, rape, forced prostitution and impregnation, torture and other cruel, inhuman, and degrading treatment, assault and battery, sex and ethnic inequality, summary execution, and wrongful death."[180] In the first instance District Court, the claims were dismissed on the basis of lack of jurisdiction under the ATCA (which the plaintiffs used as a basis of their action).

Nevertheless, the Second Circuit Court reversed the decision of the first instance court and found that there was subject-matter jurisdiction under the ATCA for a violation of the law of nations committed by a nonstate actor, such as the defendant, Mr. Karadžić. The court thus decided that individual nonstate actors could be held liable for crimes such as genocide and war crimes[181] and that individuals could bring a suit against the perpetrator claiming redress for such violation. Given the decision of the court, the jury awarded a total of USD 745 million to the fourteen plaintiffs (USD 265 million compensatory damages and USD 480 million punitive damages).[182]

Similarly, in 1998, a case was brought before a United States court by four Bosnian Muslim plaintiffs against Nikola Vucković, a Bosnian Serb soldier.[183] The claimants sought compensation and punitive damages for allegations of crimes committed against them during the conflict. The claimants alleged they were victims of arbitrary detention, torture, and abuse allegedly committed against Bosnian Muslims and Croats, and the forced relocation of Bosnian Muslim and Croat families living in the municipality of Bosanski Šamac in Bosnia and Herzegovina. The court found for the claimants and awarded USD 10 million each in compensatory damages, and USD 25 million each in punitive damages.[184]

These cases were remarkable as they had been filed with domestic courts even before the ICTY had custody of the accused. As one of the claimants against Mr. Karadžić stated, the "verdict was not about monetary damages, but about gaining recognition of the acts committed by Bosnian Serb ultra-nationalists."[185] The question then is whether the symbolic value of the judgment is sufficient when the enforcement of the award does not follow.

---

[180] Cf. *Kadic v. Karadžić*, 70 F.3d, 232.

[181] *Kadic v. Karadžić*, 70 F.3d, 241–43.

[182] *Kadic v. Karadžić*, No. 93 Civ. 1163, judgment (S.D.N. August 16, 2000).

[183] *Mehinovic, Kemal, et al.* 2009 v. *Nikola Vuckovic*, Civil Section 1:98-cv-2470-MHS US District Court, Northern District of Georgia, 29 July 2009.

[184] *Mehinovic, Kemal, et al.* 2009 v. *Nikola Vuckovic*, Civil Section 1:98-cv-2470-MHS US District Court, Northern District of Georgia, 29 July 2009.

[185] David Rohde, "A Jury in New York Orders Bosnian Serb to Pay Billions," *New York Times*, 26 September 2000, available at http://nytimes.com/2000/09/26/world/jury-in-new-york-orders-bosnian-serb-to-pay-billions.html.

192   *Reparative Justice for International Crimes*

There were many other perpetrators in the Balkan wars but there were not as many civil suits brought in domestic courts – why was this precedent not followed? There are certainly many hurdles when bringing cases of this magnitude. In the end, when examining civil suits before domestic courts, it is important to bear in mind that the ultimate success may be symbolic since monetary damages are difficult to enforce.

In addition to cases brought before the United States courts, there have also been other cases brought before European courts, including in Serbia. The first case in Europe in relation to the Balkan wars, in courts outside the region, took place in France, before the Tribunal de Grande Instance. The case concerned allegations of crimes committed during the Bosnian war by Bosnian Serb defendants Radovan Karadžić and Biljana Plavsić. The court ordered Karadžić and Plavsić to pay EUR 200,000 to the victims as reparation.[186]

Another case was brought before Norwegian courts. A series of decisions from the District Court of Oslo (lower court) culminated with the 2010 decision of Norway's Supreme Court against a former member of the Croatian Armed Forces, Mirsad Repak. Repak was a guard in the Dretelj detention camp in Bosnia and Herzegovina, and had been allegedly involved in the arrest, unlawful detention, and torture of civilian noncombatants. The defendant was found guilty and sentenced to imprisonment, and the victims were awarded reparations awards valued between EUR 4,000 and EUR 12,000.[187]

Commenting on the series of decisions in Norway, Frederiek de Vlaming, and Kate Clark rightly posited that:

> The case against Repak was the first of its kind in Norway. It demonstrates how judicial reasoning succeeded in weaving together domestic and international legal provisions that came into being at different times but were nonetheless aimed at protecting the same interests. Moreover, the extensive

---

[186] See Ann Riley, "France Court Awards Bosnia Civil War Victims Damages for Injuries," *Jurist*, 14 March 2011, http://jurist.org/paperchase/2011/03/france-court-awards-bosnia-civil-w ar-victimsdamages-for-injuries.php, and Rachel Irwin, *Civil Actions Offer Some Closure for Bosnia Victims*, Institute for War and Peace Reporting (IWPR), 26 April 2011, http://iwpr.net/ report-news/civil-actions-offersome-closure-bosnia-victims, cited in Frederiek de Vlaming and Kate Clark, "War Reparations in Bosnia and Herzegovina: Individual Stories and Collective Interests," *Narratives of Justice In and Out of the Courtroom*, Springer International Publishing, 2014, pp. 163–185.

[187] For all judgments, see *The Public Prosecuting Authority v. Mirsad Repak*, Oslo District Court case no: 08-018985MEDOTIR/08, 2 December 2008; Borgarting Lagmannsretten, Court of Appeal, Judgement of 12 April 2010 (case summary at International Red Cross database on Humanitarian Law available at http://icrc.org/customaryihl/eng/docs/v2_cou_no_rule99, Supreme Court of Norway Judgement, case no. 2010/934, 3 December 2010).

investigations that led to the indictment were done by the Norwegian prosecutor in cooperation with the Serbian war crimes prosecutor, and they involved the statements of at least 211 former detainees of the Dretelj camp, almost all the prisoners who were detained in the camp at the time. The above points taken together show once again that the criminal prosecution of individual war crimes perpetrators can bring benefits to more than the small group of witnesses/victims involved in the case: They can help facilitate the intermeshing of national and international law to achieve broader jurisdiction over war criminals, and such cooperation between national and foreign prosecutors signals that crossing a border may no longer be enough to save a war criminal from prosecution.[188]

In Sweden, like Norway, a district court in Stockholm convicted another Dretelj camp officer, Mr. Ahmet Makitan, for participating in the abuse of twenty-one Serb civilian prisoners. He was sentenced to five years in prison. In addition to the prison sentence, the defendant was also ordered to pay 1.5 million Krona (approximately EUR 170,000) in the form of compensation to victims.[189]

These examples of cases across the United States and Europe demonstrate that domestic courts, even in States outside the region where the crimes occurred, have indeed played a role in the adjudication and award of reparations to victims of international crimes. It is also interesting to note that victims often turned to foreign courts after it had become clear that they would not be able to settle their case with the authorities.[190] This is an important example of the argument that state and individual responsibility for reparation for international crimes are not mutually exclusive.

5.5.2.5 Desirability, Advantages, and Criticism of a Civil Dimension for Universal Jurisdiction

Having discussed the scope and lawfulness of universal civil jurisdiction under international law, based on state practice, it is important to turn attention to

---

[188] Frederiek de Vlaming and Kate Clark, "War Reparations in Bosnia and Herzegovina: Individual Stories and Collective Interests," *Narratives of Justice In and Out of the Courtroom*, Springer International Publishing, 2014, pp. 163–185.

[189] Stockholms Tingsrätt (Stockholm District Court), case no. B 382-10, 8 April 2011. See also, International Review of the Red Cross, Volume 93, Number 883, September 2011, English language summary, available at http://icrc.org/eng/assets/files/review/2011/irrc-883-reportsdo cuments.pdf.

[190] Frederiek de Vlaming and Kate Clark, "War Reparations in Bosnia and Herzegovina: Individual Stories and Collective Interests," *Narratives of Justice In and Out of the Courtroom*, Springer International Publishing, 2014, pp. 163–185.

the advantages and disadvantages of the civil dimension of the doctrine. The question to be asked is why might states wish to assert civil jurisdiction for crimes committed abroad to nonnationals? This section highlights many of the questions underlying the act of adding a civil dimension to international justice, such as: what features make it "civil"? What precisely is the difference from "criminal"? These questions have been dealt with in detail by Ryngaert in his exhaustive analysis which balanced the advantages and issues raised by universal tort jurisdiction.[191] The present section briefly weighs these advantages and challenges in order to discuss the desirability of using universal civil jurisdiction as a means of claiming reparations for international crimes.

Arguments in favor of universal tort litigation include the fact that it is a victim-oriented approach in the aftermath of mass atrocities. This means that victims may initiate proceedings (rather than prosecutorial bodies). It also gives victims control over the proceedings, they have their day in court, and their voices and stories are heard (which can be a form of healing). Civil actions controlled by victim plaintiffs could also be effective in preserving the collective memory.[192]

Another advantage is the limited involvement of the state in civil suits. This might work to preserve foreign relations concerning extraterritorial litigation, since "the greater involvement of the State in criminal prosecutions appears to be more likely to produce adverse effects on the conduct of foreign relations than the adjudicatory practice of civil judges."[193]

It may also be argued that universal civil jurisdiction complements the goals of international criminal justice, of which universal criminal jurisdiction is a tool. Civil awards may also bear a sanctioning effect, especially with the award of punitive damages, which, in addition to repairing, may also foster punitive goals. As to the deterrent effect which universal criminal jurisdiction (and international criminal justice in general) seek to attain, universal civil jurisdiction, through the award of reparations to victims, may also contribute to this goal. The threat of a lawsuit and the possibility that an individual might lose their assets, may provide a significant deterrent effect.[194]

---

[191] Cedric Ryngaert, "Universal Tort Jurisdiction over Gross Human Rights Violations," *Netherlands Yearbook of International Law* 38 (2007), pp. 6–17.

[192] See Jose E. Alvarez, "Rush to Closure: Lessons of the *Tadić* Judgment," *Michigan Law Review* 96 (1998), pp. 2101–2102.

[193] Cedric Ryngaert, "Universal Tort Jurisdiction over Gross Human Rights Violations," *Netherlands Yearbook of International Law* 38 (2007), pp. 7–8.

[194] See, however, ibid., pp. 11–12 stating that "it is no doubt true that universal tort litigation may hardly deter future human rights violations."

As to criticisms and challenges of universal jurisdiction, the first one to be mentioned is the difficulties victims may encounter when attempting to enforce a judgment. Freezing assets and obtaining compensation from the accused is not always straightforward.

Another challenge is that gathering evidence for crimes committed elsewhere might lengthen proceedings or make it difficult for victims to make use of universal civil jurisdiction, even though the burden of proof is less stringent in civil prosecutions. Referencing the civil suits brought against Mr. Karadžić in the United States, and more recently in France, the Institute for War and Peace Reporting states that while victims are unlikely to ever receive the payments, this "does not diminish the enormous symbolic significance of these decisions"; such cases "contribute to the growing body of State practice relevant to the implementation of the right to reparation for violations of International Humanitarian Law."[195]

Another criticism is related to the private nature of civil suits and the community condemnation that international crimes call for. It may be argued that because universal civil jurisdiction does not involve prosecution and punishment, only private interests are pursued rather than community interests.

Finally, it has also been claimed, especially as it relates to corporations, that the exercise of universal civil jurisdiction could impinge on a foreign nation's prerogative to "regulate its own commercial affairs" and could "affect much needed foreign investment in host countries."[196]

5.5.3 Assessing Universal Civil Jurisdiction as a Way to Seek Redress for Victims of International Crimes

Certain criminal conduct is so heinous that it shocks the universal conscience of humankind and it affects the international community as a whole, which in turn requires it to respond. However, despite this response, heinous conduct often leaves the victim(s) to suffer with the consequences. Their grievances are rooted in the same conduct that prompted the juridical

---

[195] Rachel Irwin, "Civil Actions Offer Some Closure for Bosnia Victims: Huge Damages Demanded of Perpetrators Unlikely to be Recovered, but the Judgements do Provide a Degree of Justice for the Victims," cited in Nuhanovic Foundation, Center for War Reparations, available at http://nuhanovicfoundation.org/en/reparations-cases/france-tribu nal-de-grande-instance-kovac-vs-karadzic-march-2011/ (accessed 10 May 2016).

[196] See Supplemental Brief of the Governments of the Kingdom of the Netherlands and the United Kingdoms of Great Britain and Northern Ireland as *Amici Curiae* in support of neither party, *Kiobel* v. *Royal Dutch Petroleum Co.*, 133 S. Ct. 1659 (2013) (No 10-1491).

conscience of humankind to punish the offenders. Universal civil jurisdiction, on a normative level, offers the possibility that justice for international crimes will not only focus on the trial and punishment of the perpetrators, but will also take into account the internationally recognized right of victims to receive reparation.

While universal civil jurisdiction may provide an alternative avenue on a normative level, at the current point in the development of international law, it is still not widely accepted. Customary international law has not crystallized towards a rule of universal civil jurisdiction for all international crimes. Nevertheless, some of the state practice reviewed above demonstrates that there is an emerging recognition of some form of universal civil jurisdiction, despite the recent retreat in the United States.

In the wake of heinous conduct, the international community should, in addition to efforts to punish the offender, have victims' rights in mind. In this sense, the criminal and civil dimensions in the aftermath of an international crime cannot be completely dissociated. In its civil dimensions, universal jurisdiction can prove to be an effective alternative avenue that victims can use to enforce their right to receive reparations. This avenue is necessary because claiming reparation in domestic courts where the crime occurred can often prove to be difficult, if not impossible. This is particularly true in post-conflict situations where the judicial system of the concerned state has fallen, or when an offender is no longer in the territory where the crimes were committed. Nevertheless, the time is not yet ripe for affirming that universal jurisdiction can be exercised to pursue claims of civil redress, despite the progress in this direction.

As some states have demonstrated, universal civil jurisdiction in relation to international crimes could be further developed by considering the doctrine of "forum of necessity." This doctrine can be used to ensure that victims have an avenue to claim a right to reparation from perpetrators, while requiring some link exist between the alleged perpetrator and the forum state.

5.6 CONCLUSIONS

This chapter reviewed the role of domestic courts in the realization of reparative justice for international crimes, through case studies and an examination of the doctrine of universal jurisdiction for victim reparations. The discussion in this chapter fits within the position that reparative justice for international crimes should not be only internationalized and dealt with by international courts or mechanisms, such as the ICC. Domestic courts have an important role to play in the realization of reparative justice for international crimes. Relying completely on international courts or mechanisms to deliver reparations would be a mistake, given the limitations discussed in this book. In an ideal scenario, national and international systems work in synergy to deliver redress for victims. Nevertheless, often victims cannot turn to national courts where the crimes occurred due to reasons such as corruption of the judicial system or procedural difficulties in bringing cases to the court. Universal civil jurisdiction may be one way forward to counter some of the obstacles of local litigation for civil claims, however not without its controversies.

One common denominator in domestic litigation of reparation claims is the total (or very significant) lack of implementation of awards. When victims do manage to take their case to court, the judgment ends up having only symbolic value since, in spite of (often rich) awards, victims do not manage to obtain reparations. One reason for the lack of actual reparations (even despite a court-ordered award) is the indigence of the perpetrator. Another obstacle is the enforcement of the awards when assets are not available or cannot be traced. This reality sheds light on the fact that to realize reparative justice, the award of reparations in court orders must be followed by the implementation of such awards, otherwise reparative justice is not fully realized.

Domestic mechanisms beyond claims for reparations in domestic courts should be envisioned. These could include the creation of special chambers (as the case of Senegal) with jurisdiction to adjudicate on reparations, (no-fault) state-sponsored reparations programs, and national claims commissions.

6

Conclusions

Millions of persons have been victims of unimaginable atrocities in the past centuries. Yet only recently have there been many developments with regards to reparations. The notion of justice for victims of international crimes has evolved from its historical roots. From its inception, justice for victims meant solely the criminal accountability of perpetrators. The contemporary notion of justice for victims includes a more active role for victims in the proceedings against the accused, and the possibility in certain circumstances to claim reparations directly from the perpetrator. From the inclusion of the right to reparation in international criminal tribunals, to the creation of administrative mechanisms, to domestic cases concerning reparations for international crimes, international justice has been moving away from a purely criminal dimension, focused on retribution, towards the inclusion of a reparative dimension. This emerging new dimension of international justice raises many questions, including whether the realization of reparation for victims should be one of its goals. This book overviewed the development of reparative justice for international crimes, and examined how it has evolved from theory to its practical application in different frameworks. This conclusion aims to bring together the key themes discussed in this book as well as to offer some recommendations.

6.1 THE THEORY AND PRACTICE OF REPARATIVE JUSTICE FOR INTERNATIONAL CRIMES

A theory of international justice should not be oblivious of victims. A purely criminal outlook and accused-centric approach is not sufficient to respond to the complexities of international crimes. As discussed in the book, the inclusion of reparations in international criminal justice has met with difficulties. From a normative, almost utopian perspective, it is argued that international criminal justice ought to provide a reparative dimension for victims. Nevertheless, much still needs to be done before reparations can be said to be fully integrated in international criminal justice.

Reparations for victims of international crimes should develop in a holistic manner. National and international mechanisms and initiatives are interconnected and feed off each other. The individualized approach to reparations for international crimes is not necessarily better than other mechanisms such as state-based reparations. It is complementary, and not mutually exclusive.

By contrasting different judicial mechanisms, both at the national and international levels, some conclusions can be drawn. Justice, in the aftermath of mass international crimes, is evolving towards a broader meaning, one that encompasses accountability of the offender, and reparation for their victims. Trial and punishment without reparations is an incomplete conception of justice; reparations without accountability of offenders is unsatisfactory, as illustrated by some examples discussed in the book. Retributive and reparative justice are complementary in the realization of international justice. Similar to the manner in which international law evolved in order to bring *individual* perpetrators to justice to be tried for their crimes, the way is being paved (albeit slowly) to provide victim redress for international crimes both at national and international levels.

Be that as it may, there are still some inconsistencies and uncertainties across the board. At the current point in the development of international criminal justice, the spectrum of how international courts and mechanisms treat victims and reparations is still wide-ranging. Some provide no possibilities of claiming reparations, while others provide systems of reparation that have the potential (not yet fully developed) to deliver a meaningful result. The same is true about national court proceedings and mechanisms.

Limiting reparations claims to the realm of state responsibility, international human rights law, international humanitarian law, and domestic law perpetuates a gap where victims of international crimes may be left without a forum to make their claim. While international human rights law can inform the development of international criminal justice as it pertains to reparations for victims, human rights law and state responsibility mechanisms cannot be directly transposed to international criminal justice.

The analysis in this book has also demonstrated that when reparations are put into practice, many challenges become apparent. The reminiscence of historical dichotomies and dogmas, and a clear-cut division of theories of justice dictated the development of international criminal justice from its inception. While some systems in place take an approach to international criminal justice that excludes victim redress, such as the ad hoc international criminal tribunals (ICTY and ICTR), more recent examples such as the ICC have changed the traditional vision, with the development of a reparations system.

The system developed at the ICC is on the one hand ground-breaking, and on the other, still immature. Efforts should be made to develop it to its full potential, making sure there is legal certainty concerning principles of reparation and their practical application. In addition, it is important to recognize that the ICC is but one mechanism that exists; it cannot be the sole avenue for victims' redress.

When reparations for international crimes start to be unpacked at the ICC, many practical, moral, ethical, and political challenges arise. It is important to dwell upon and engage with these critical accounts, always bearing in mind the broader picture: the ICC (and the reparation system developed therein), is one of many alternative systems for victim redress for international crimes. The system that is now developing through practice is not without its flaws, and this is apparent when looked at through the lens of the Court's recent jurisprudence. As reparations proceedings at the Court advance, and the Court's principles of reparations are further developed, new lessons will be learned from past practice. The condition of a criminal conviction and the link with the entire criminal process is limiting and excludes many victims from obtaining reparations due to decisions (e.g., which charges to bring and against which accused) that they were not a part of. Additionally, there should be an emphasis on understanding the real experiences of victims.

In relation to national courts, there are many challenges that victims face in obtaining reparations in countries where the international crime took place. In the case of Bosnia, there were mechanisms set up by the Dayton Agreements which filled the role of national courts for a period of time. Using the case study of the aftermath of the Bosnian wars, and the mechanisms instituted to provide victims with a forum to claim reparations, this book has illustrated that, often times, national courts do not provide a perfect road to redress and restoration.

Seeing some of the challenges of obtaining reparation in the courts where the crimes took place, the emerging doctrine of universal jurisdiction as applied in cases of reparation was addressed. The book analyzed the scope of universal civil jurisdiction under international law, how it can be further developed and how it can work to overcome some of the challenges of bringing cases before national courts where the international crimes were committed. While it is not yet widely recognized, and some difficulties remain, universal civil jurisdiction, within certain circumscribed parameters, could provide an avenue for victims to claim reparations.[1]

6.2 KEY THEMES: THE EMERGING REPARATIVE DIMENSION OF INTERNATIONAL JUSTICE AND NEW PARADIGMS

In this journey of discovery and improvement, it is important to remember the symbolic gain that including a reparative dimension to international criminal law represents.

The theoretical justifications supporting reparative justice include empowerment of victims and the notion of justice for victims. The question whether it is a desirable model to respond to international crimes hinges on how the reparative dimension will continue to develop and be implemented in international criminal justice. The system of reparations at the ICC could be a catalyst for the further development of domestic systems of reparation for international crimes.

A victim-centered approach to international justice is not limited to questions of reparations, and includes, for example, victim participation in the criminal proceedings. The report of the Special Rapporteur on the promotion of truth, justice, reparation, and guarantees of nonrecurrence is enlightening in this regard.[2] Including a reparative dimension to international criminal justice also brings about new paradigms which may differ from the criminal dimension: the required expertise of judges dealing with reparation requests, the enforcement of reparation awards, the standard of proof, hierarchy as well as exclusion of victims, and challenges when reparation is connected to a conviction.

6.2.1 *Reparation Is Only One Facet of the Broader Goal of Delivering "Justice for Victims" of International Crimes*

Reparations for international crimes do not stand in a vacuum. There are important dimensions that accompany and are crucial to any reparation initiative, and that contribute in delivering justice for victims of international crimes. As the Special Rapporteur on the promotion of truth, justice,

---

[1] See discussion in Chapter 5.
[2] United Nations, General Assembly, "Report of the Special Rapporteur on the Promotion of Truth, Justice, Reparation and Guarantees of Non-recurrence," A/69/518, 14 October 2014.

reparation, and guarantees of nonrecurrence concluded, to be seen as a true mechanism of justice, reparations must be "accompanied by an acknowledgment of responsibility and needs to be linked with other justice initiatives such as efforts aimed at achieving truth, criminal prosecutions and guarantees of non-recurrence."[3] This calls for two related propositions. The first is that *symbolic* forms of reparation such as acknowledgement of responsibility, as well as guarantees of nonrepetition, have important roles to play in restoration and reconciliation, and should not be discarded automatically. An effort should be made by the different actors involved in reparations proceedings to accommodate these approaches, bearing in mind seemingly conflicting rationales such as the human rights of the accused.

The second proposition, that stems from the different dimensions of justice for victims, is that reparations are distinct from humanitarian assistance or development aid; they may complement one another but they are distinct responses in the aftermath of international crimes.

6.2.2 Individual Perpetrators Have a Legal Duty to Provide Reparations to Victims of International Crimes, in Certain Circumstances, and Victims Have a Corollary Right to Receive Reparations

Over the years, international law has seen an evolution with regard to reparations in general, and in particular in relation to international crimes. Traditionally, reparations were owed from one state to another state. In human rights law, individuals began to be recognized as potential beneficiaries of reparations owed by the state. Since then a third paradigm has developed: the construction of a legal duty owed by the individual (perpetrator/convicted person) to the individual victim (who is the direct beneficiary). Still in its infancy, the contours of this legal duty are in process of formation. The legal duty to pay reparations to victims under modern international criminal law is a corollary of the criminal accountability of perpetrators. Imposing a legal duty on perpetrators to pay reparations to victims serves symbolic purposes, contributes to the overall goal of international justice to deliver justice for victims, and assists in the path to reconciliation. This legal duty imposed on individuals must move from rhetoric to implementation; it has yet to be fully realized. The legal duty of perpetrators and the right of victims are two sides of the same coin: an international crime gives rise both to the accountability of perpetrators and to the right of victims to receive reparation.

[3] Ibid.

6.2.3 The Contents of the Legal Duty to Repair Imposed on Individual Perpetrators are Still Under Formation in International Criminal Justice and Lessons Can Be Learned from Other Reparations Initiatives

Principles of reparation in other fields, such as in the human rights field, may inform the content of the legal duty to repair under international criminal law, while bearing in mind some systemic differences that exist across different fields. Importantly, international human rights law can inform matters such as the form and types of reparation (collective or individual, rehabilitation, apology, compensation, etc.). Other difficult questions related to including a reparative dimension in international criminal justice are: the identification of beneficiaries, known and unknown victims, implementation of reparations, and the balancing of different rights at stake. This book reviewed the jurisprudence of the ICC and ECCC, as well as of national courts. The operationalization of reparations for international crimes before international courts and tribunals is in the process of development and, in this process, it is important to devise clear and fair principles of reparation and keep striving to apply them consistently and meet the challenges required.

6.2.4 An Individualized Approach to Reparations Remains Complementary to State Responsibility for Reparations for International Crimes

An individualized approach to reparations is not meant to exclude a state-based approach. The emphasis is different. Some forms of reparation, such as guarantees of nonrepetition might make more sense within state-based reparations schemes – where the state will continue in power. One rationale for seeking reparations directly from individual perpetrators is to empower victims, by connecting the criminal and civil liabilities of the perpetrators. Nevertheless, in order to fully achieve justice for victims of international crimes, the potential responsibility of states has still to be borne in mind. The nature of international crimes is such that individual accountability should not automatically exclude state responsibility. Where state responsibility for international crimes is also involved, states should be jointly liable to pay reparations in order to fully achieve the objective of realizing justice for victims. It should also be questioned whether a state has the right to negotiate and enter into agreements relating to reparation for harm that individual victims suffered, without any form of consultation, participation, or assignment of rights.

There are diverse avenues where victims can claim, and possibly obtain, reparations for international crimes. Much will depend on some specific circumstances, such as whether a state is involved, and thus, whether reparations can be claimed against a state. In many instances, however, the state is not involved in the atrocities committed. Relying solely on the responsibility of states, and excluding reparative justice within international criminal law, might leave victims without any form of redress, which explains the importance of analyzing individual responsibility as it relates to redress for victims of international crimes.

Individual liability for reparations should not be to the exclusion of any other right victims might have against the state. A victim's right to reparation against the individual perpetrator might be complemented by a right to reparation against the state. The state can be involved in the fulfillment of reparations awards, even if it is found that individual perpetrators are liable. Such an approach should be preferred so as to afford the best chance for reparations to be implemented.

6.2.5 Disconnect Between the Rhetoric that Included Reparations in International Criminal Justice, Supported by the Idea of Justice for Victims, and the Substantive Realization of Reparations

The goal of delivering justice for victims of international crimes may theoretically justify including reparations as part of international criminal justice. As Luke Moffett argues:

> Attaching responsibility for reparations to perpetrators, whether individual, state, or organisational, can provide an important psychological function for victims in appropriately directing blame at those who committed the atrocity against them and to relieve their guilt. Reparations made by the responsible perpetrator can also help to symbolise their commitment to remedying the past and to be held to account for their actions.[4]

The reparative dimension of international criminal justice needs to equate to the realization of justice for victims. The time for reparations is now. In the example of the first case before the ICC, after many years since the crimes were committed, victims have yet to receive reparations. Once the long trial ended, victims were caught in a back and forth between the TFV and the Trial Chamber charged with monitoring the

---

[4] Luke Moffett, *Justice for Victims Before the International Criminal Court*, Routledge, 2014, p. 147.

Conclusions

implementation of reparations.[5] While it is acknowledged that this was the first case of reparations before the Court, this example sheds light on the delays and complexities for the substantive realization of reparations for victims. It is hoped that lessons can be learned from this first case and the process can be streamlined in the future.

6.2.6 A Reparative Dimension of International Criminal Justice, Including Reparations for Victims of International Crimes, Is Not Limited to the ICC

The ICC cannot single-handedly be responsible for reparations for victims of international crimes. Its possibilities are limited by numerous factors. For example, temporal jurisdiction and subject-matter jurisdiction mean that some international crimes, as well as other serious human rights violations that do not amount to international crimes, will fall outside its scope and the victims of those atrocities will not be able to turn to the ICC. Furthermore, the ICC is limited by its resources, both human and financial. Systemic limitations such as the inherent selectivity of international prosecutions, and the connection between a conviction of the accused and adjudication of reparation claims are additional barriers to reparations for victims.

Administrative mechanisms such as trust funds connected to judicial mechanisms could play an important role in the adjudication of reparations particularly in light of the massive nature of international crimes and the complexities of planning and implementing reparation awards. The TFV is the primary example in this regard.

In the same vein, national courts have an important (and not yet fully developed) role to play in relation to reparations. The ICC is a court of last resort. This is true in relation to criminal proceedings as well as regarding reparations. Thus, positive complementarity should also include reparations – national courts should play an important role in cases of reparations for international crimes.[6] More efforts have to be put towards the implementation and enforcement of reparation awards. Rich reparations are often awarded but not always implemented, thus bearing only the symbolic benefit of the reparation award.

---

[5] For a detailed account of the numerous procedural stages of the implementation of reparations in the *Lubanga* case, see the procedural history summarized in ICC, Trial Chamber II, *The Prosecutor v. Thomas Lubanga Dyilo*, "Order approving the proposed plan of the Trust Fund for Victims in relation to symbolic collective reparations," ICC-01/04-01/06, 21 October 2016, paras. 1–10.

[6] See in this regard, Luke Moffett, *Justice for Victims Before the International Criminal Court*, Routledge, 2014.

6.2.7 In the ICC Context, Expectations with Regards to Reparations Have to Be Measured

The potential for the ICC to provide reparations for victims of international crimes is limited. While this was true when reparations were only recognized in the ICC Statute, the review of recent jurisprudence makes it undeniable that in the Court serious constraints exist. Reparative justice at the ICC is limited by the system itself, which links reparations to a conviction, and thus only the victims of crimes whose perpetrator was prosecuted and convicted by the ICC can potentially receive reparations. As discussed, this limited reach of the ICC is not always in line with victim expectations.[7] Part of the journey of the Court in regard to its reparation mandate will be to manage victim expectations. This can be done through a coherent and connected effort of all organs of the Court to inform affected communities of the Court's inherent limitations and explain its multifaceted mandates (i.e., accountability, reparation, etc.). The study conducted by the Human Rights Center at the University of California, Berkeley School of Law indicates that many victims see the Court as a venue where they can get reparations for the harm they have suffered, and many joined the ICC proceedings with the expectation they would individually receive reparation.[8] Outreach to affected communities should include information about the possibilities as well as limitations of reparations through the ICC. Filling in this informational and knowledge gap about what the Court can realistically achieve in terms of reparation can indeed help avoid false expectations and limit further victimization.

6.2.8 Victims' Provisions at the ICC Have a Significant Symbolic Value and Could Be a Catalyst for the Implementation of Reparations in Other Fora

Including a reparative dimension in international criminal justice and the ICC in particular, provides theoretical justification for the Court, which was instituted as a Court to seek justice for victims. It also adds a degree of legitimacy to the Court, in that victims are part of the international criminal justice project. The symbolic meaning of recognizing victims' suffering and

---

[7] See a discussion on this topic: Sharon Nakandha, "ICC Court Ruling on Reparation for Kenyan Victims: Does the ICC Oversell Its Mandate or Are Victims Simply Expecting Too Much?" *International Justice Monitor*, 25 July 2016, available at https://ijmonitor.org/2016/07/icc-court-ruling-on-reparation-for-kenyan-victims-does-the-icc-oversell-its-mandate-or-are-victims-simply-expecting-too-much/.

[8] Human Rights Center, University of California, Berkeley School of Law, "The Victims' Court: A Study of 622 Victim Participants at the International Criminal Court," p. 3, available at https://law.berkeley.edu/wp-content/uploads/2015/04/VP_report_2015_final_full2.pdf.

Conclusions 207

giving them rights is empowering, and can have a ripple effect. But after almost two decades of existence, the Court has to capitalize on this and endeavor to become a catalyst for the implementation of reparations in other fora, including before domestic courts and mechanisms. As Luke Moffett argues, "the Court will need to encourage states to implement justice for victims to overcome its structural limitations and to move beyond the rhetoric of realizing justice for victims of international crimes."[9]

6.2.9 *Adding a Civil Dimension to Universal Jurisdiction May Provide an Avenue for Victims' Claims for Reparation*

Using the doctrine of universal jurisdiction to allow victims to bring civil claims against individual perpetrators before domestic courts of foreign states is a way to counter some of the challenges of domestic civil litigation in the state where the crime occurred (e.g., lack of legislation supporting civil claims in relation to international crimes, political interference, or the collapse of judicial institutions). As discussed in Chapter 5, universal jurisdiction in its criminal dimension has been gaining support in recent decades as a strong tool against impunity; a civil dimension, despite all the hurdles it may encounter, could be the next frontier.

This book examined the difficulties with universal civil jurisdiction and concluded that there isn't any customary international law rule prohibiting the exercise of universal civil jurisdiction (with some exceptions, such as in cases of state immunity). States could thus envision the adoption of legislation that allows for a civil claim to be brought against individual perpetrators for crimes for which universal jurisdiction is already recognized (in its criminal dimension) under domestic law.

*

Having reviewed some general themes of the book, the way is paved to provide some recommendations and to dwell upon the road ahead.

6.3 REALIZING REPARATIVE JUSTICE: THE ROAD AHEAD

The road ahead for reparations in international criminal justice looks like a steep uphill. Nevertheless, progress is being made. In terms of international tribunals, only the ICC and ECCC provide the possibility for victims to obtain

---

[9] Luke Moffett, *Justice for Victims Before the International Criminal Court*, Routledge, 2014, p. 283.

some meaningful form of reparation, and many challenges lie within. In terms of administrative mechanisms, the TFV provides an interesting model, but it is still in the process of defining its contours and overcoming some challenges. At the national level, much still needs to be done, and national courts have to start playing a more significant role in the adjudication of reparations. Other domestic mechanisms, such as trust funds or domestic claims commissions, should be envisaged. With these remarks in mind, this section turns to some recommendations.

6.3.1 A New Phase of International Justice: The Need to Move Reparative Justice Forward

Considering the examples of the ICC, the ECCC, and the trial of Hissène Habré, it can be seen that a conception of justice for international crimes which completely excludes victims is no longer mainstream. If seen from an evolutive perspective, one can say that international justice has entered a new phase, one that strives to reconcile competing goals, from accountability and end of impunity, to retribution, reconciliation, and victim redress. This new phase is not yet perfect but the turn has been made from a conception of justice in the aftermath of international crimes that is purely retributive, to one that encompasses a degree of victims redress. It is now necessary to keep on pushing the reparative dimension forward and make systems work in synergy to deliver justice for victims. Perhaps the main achievements of the system developed at the ICC to date are to include reparations in the international justice discourse, to provide a forum to develop reparations from theory to practice, to foster a shift in the conception of justice in the aftermath of mass atrocities.

6.3.2 Realizing Reparative Justice for International Crimes Requires Global Efforts

The individualized approach to reparations in respect of international crimes is inherently selective. It is also limited, as international crimes do not encompass all kinds of human rights violations and mass atrocities. It further suffers from other practical restrictions such as lack of resources, especially when the perpetrator is indigent. Thus, it is important that it is seen for what it is: another avenue where victims may claim and obtain reparations, that coexists with other avenues and mechanisms. To effectively realize reparations for victims, it is important to take a global perspective and engage international and domestic mechanisms. States have to step up and join in realizing reparative justice for victims, beyond the rhetoric, and actually contribute to or collaborate with existing systems, or devise domestic reparations schemes. This can include, for example, making contributions to the TFV, assisting in the implementation of reparations, and setting up reparations funds for victims of crimes occurring within their territory.

Victims of international crimes outside the jurisdiction of the ICC should also receive redress. As already stated, the ICC reparative mandate is limited. Too many victims are left outside the scope of existing reparations mechanisms. Limiting reparative justice to the system being developed at the ICC will inevitably fail. More needs to be done at a global level. For example, international courts and tribunals such as the ICTY and ICTR did not have provisions on reparations. History has now shown that victims of those conflicts have been left without reparations. A claims commission or trust fund could be set up by the UN to deal with reparations for victims of those conflicts who could not turn to the tribunals for claims of assistance or reparation and for victims of international crimes outside the jurisdiction of the ICC.

6.3.3 To Be Effective, Reparative Justice Needs to Be Expeditious

Victims of international crimes and mass atrocities, have rights. They have desires and needs. They cannot wait – their harm needs to be repaired in an expeditious manner so as to be meaningful. The cases studied in this book have demonstrated that while reparations are now part of many justice processes in the aftermath of international crimes, even after favorable decisions, victims still have to wait too long to potentially receive reparations. Proceedings need to be expedited, and reparations implementation plans need to be devised from the beginning of the process.

Expediting proceedings can be achieved in different ways, taking into account some particularities of the forum. A timeline for reparations could be anticipated from the beginning of the process, so as to provide clarity and transparency to victims. Given that there is now an existing jurisprudence at the ICC and beyond, establishing timelines should not be completely unchartered ground, and the experience of previous cases can be illuminating in this respect. Having a clear structure of how reparations proceedings should be carried out also assists with expediency. Victims and their claims for reparations should not be an afterthought once there is a conviction. Planning for a potential reparations phase is crucial.

6.3.4 Seeing the Victims, Not the Perpetrators: Reparations Unconditioned to Convictions

The reparative system developed at the ICC is at a crossroad. The first cases that have reached the reparations stage have demonstrated that the system developed at the ICC where reparations can only take place when there is a conviction is problematic. When reparations only existed in theory at the ICC, it might have been thought that conceptually, because reparations are provided within a criminal court, it could be premised on a criminal conviction. The early jurisprudence of the Court has proven that this model is selective, overly limiting, unsatisfactory, and ultimately leads to unfair outcomes for victims. The Court is only beginning to develop its jurisprudence on reparations. There are two obvious options: to continue on the path paved by the pioneering cases, or adjust the system.

It is time for the Court to take stock and admit that it can do better in relation to delivering reparative justice for victims. The point of start is to recognize that a theory of reparations conditioned on a conviction is doomed to fail in practice. While some victims, after a long criminal process, and (possibly) even longer reparation proceedings, might receive reparations, the delays, the lack of resources, the exclusions of many, cannot be an accepted part of the outcome.

Moreover, criminal convictions are judged on the basis of criminal processes and standards of proof. When it is clear on the evidence that international crimes were committed, the fact that these crimes were not charged (e. g., sexual crimes in *Lubanga*), or that an accused (who was selected to be prosecuted by the Office of the Prosecutor on the basis of evidence for a criminal trial) is not convicted by the standard required for a *criminal* conviction (e.g., Mr. Jean-Pierre Bemba), should reparations be denied to victims?

A regime of victim redress not conditioned on a criminal conviction would address some of the issues that a criminal process approach to reparations exacerbates. Victim redress should not be viewed in a shallow box where a conviction equals the possibility of reparations and an acquital means no reparation can be obtained. An alternative system can be more effective in realizing reparative justice for international crimes.

The TFV is a key player in the reparations scheme at the Court. It has two mandates: to implement reparations orders of the Court, and, importantly, to provide assistance to the victims of crimes where an investigation has started. This latter mandate, while different from general development aid, is not linked to a conviction, does not have the same limitations as a reparations order, is implemented sooner, and has a greater potential to foster reconciliation.

There are important distinctions between the reparations ordered by the Court against a convicted person and the assistance mandate of the TFV. With regard to reparations, the form and extent of an award is judicially determined within the confines of a criminal trial. Whereas even though assistance is provided due to harm caused by a crime within the jurisdiction of the Court, it is provided through an administrative mechanism outside the confines of the judicial process and regardless of the conviction of the accused person. When there is a conviction, symbolic and moral reparations can be ordered against the accused. These can include a recorded apology and the recognition of victims' harm in the judgment, but these forms of reparation should not exclude a broader form of redress unconditioned to a conviction, that can take place as a result of the evidence that international crimes within the jurisdiction of the Court have been committed. The perpetrator(s) of these crimes will likely be many, beyond those prosecuted before the Court.

The early jurisprudence of the Court has also made another point clear. While the reparations are made against a convicted person, those convicted to date have been found indigent. This is likely to happen in many other cases, which will inevitably place reparations in the hands of the TFV. This is yet another reason to divorce reparations from a conviction. While going through a complex process of determining the liability of a convicted person provides the hope that the latter will pay for reparations, the reality is that it is uncertain whether convicted persons will repay reparations awards provided by the TFV.

The limited financial capacity of the TFV is not to be ignored. It is a reality that the TFV cannot act in all situations before the Court, and that fundraising is a challenge. Focusing on developing and strengthening the assistance mandate of the TFV, the Court would begin to fill the gaps left by a criminal process approach to reparations. In this regard, the assistance mandate should be seen as a form of redress to victims, that when deployed, recognizes that individuals were victimized by the conduct of international crimes within the jurisdiction of the Court. Starting assistance programs should not be a response to frustrated reparations outcome, but rather should be put in place as soon as possible when there is evidence that international crimes within the jurisdiction of the Court were committed.

In this context, the outcome of the *Bemba* case is a failure in the pursuit of realizing reparative justice. This is so not because the accused was set free on appeal (by a majority of three judges, with two judges dissenting). It failed the victims, who after a lengthy process, were denied reparations which they desperately needed, simply because of how the system is devised. It is clear from the record that international crimes were committed in the CAR. The

TFV promptly announced that assistance programs would be undertaken in the CAR, but this does not erase the fact that the outcome of a *criminal* process, where the conviction of Mr. Bemba was not upheld on appeal, dictated the outcome of reparative justice. This case demonstrates that it is time for the Court to move away from a theoretical conception of how the reparative and criminal dimensions of justice can be reconciled. The way forward in the realization of reparative justice is to start seeing the victims who are left with the consequences of crimes, but with no reparations if there is no conviction. It is not a path that is easy: it would require moving away from the early jurisprudence of the Court and getting the Assembly of States Parties onboard. But the reparations system at the ICC is in its infancy, no more time and resources should be spent on maintaining inherent exclusions, limitations, delays, and a sense of injustice among victims that the current model inevitably carries.[10]

6.3.5 At the ICC, There Should Be a Collaborative Effort Towards Realizing the Reparations Mandate

Developing an effective and responsive reparative dimension of international justice means empowering victims. Including reparations as a response to international crimes ultimately acknowledges victims' suffering, and gives them a stake in the justice process.

All organs and stakeholders of the Court have to work towards realizing the reparations mandate of the Court. This includes limiting any influence of internal or external politics. The delay observed at the stage of reparations in the first cases before the Court can no longer be justified. The Court must learn from its own mistakes. The review of the jurisprudence of the Court demonstrates diverging perceptions from different stakeholders within the Court as to the role of reparative justice in the overall mandate of the ICC, as well as how effectively to deliver reparations. More efforts should be made towards a cohesive understanding of the reparative mandate of the Court.

The early jurisprudence of the Court illustrated a disconnect between the requests and interests of victims on the one hand, and the decision of the judges. This disconnect can create an impression among victims that their voices are not being heard. When making decisions on reparations, judges should bear in mind the impact that such decisions might have on victims and

---

[10] See discussion and references in Chapter 4.

Conclusions

affected communities. After all, victims and reparative justice are part of the Court's endeavor.

Moving towards the realization of reparative justice may include a process of selection of the composition of the Court (or at least some Judges) who have expertise and sensibility concerning victims' rights and victimology. Judicial training on victimology might also fill potential gaps of the criminal and reparative dimensions of international justice from the judicial perspective.

6.3.6 More Efforts Have to Be Put into Bridging Informational Gaps and Managing Victims' Understanding and Expectations of the Mandate and Limitations of the ICC

The first decade of the Court's operation has demonstrated a disconnect between what the Court can realistically do, and what victims expect it to do. In interactions with victims and affected communities, more efforts have to be put into educating them about the role of the Court, its different mandates (including reparations, and the prosecution of the offender), and its inherent limitations. Victims should also be informed of the role of the TFV and other potential avenues to obtain redress. An educational approach to the role of the Court can avoid secondary victimization and a general sense of dissatisfaction on the part of victims and affected communities, especially when the outcome of proceedings is dissatisfactory to them. This outreach process must be a priority for the Court in order to truly connect with victims and manage their expectations. Informing victims is empowering them.

It cannot be denied that the dangerous security situations in many of the countries where victims are located make the outreach capacities limited. Efforts have to be placed in developing trusting local partnerships which can assist in the outreach task of the Court and the TFV.

6.3.7 States Parties Should Engage in Realizing Reparations

In the international plane, states should consider making contributions towards the TFV. Furthermore, with the recognition of reparations for international crimes at the ICC, and the Court's developing jurisprudence on the principles of reparations, the Assembly of States Parties can advance the mandate of the ICC by ensuring there is a meaningful approach to reparations domestically. This can be accomplished through concrete reports and resolutions advocating an active role for states parties to implement provisions on reparations for victims of international crimes, and the building of national trust funds for reparations for victims of international crimes (that fall within the jurisdiction of the Court).[11]

All States Parties, and especially those where mass international crimes have been committed, should be proactive in removing any barriers allowing victims to claim reparations through domestic courts. Setting up claims commissions or administrative mechanisms for the benefit of victims of the conflict might also provide an avenue for victims to obtain redress. Seeing the limitations of the ICC, and other international ad hoc mechanisms, it might well be that getting states onboard to allocate a budget for reparations, just as there is a budget for international courts and tribunals, might be a meaningful way forward. This budget can be provided to the TFV or used to set trust funds or reparations programs.

States parties have to act on their duty to complement the ICC's criminal and reparative dimensions of international justice, including reparations. This is in line with the Basic Principles, which provide in Article 16 that: "States should endeavour to establish national programmes for reparation and other assistance to victims in the event that the parties liable for the harm suffered are unable or unwilling to meet their obligations." Article 17 posits that: "States shall, with respect to claims by victims, enforce domestic judgements for reparation against individuals or entities liable for the harm suffered and endeavour to enforce valid foreign legal judgements for reparation in accordance with domestic law and international legal obligations. To that end, States should provide under their domestic laws effective mechanisms for the enforcement of reparation judgements."

6.3.8 The Context in Which Reparation Is Sought Is Important

Another important consideration is the context in which reparation is claimed: whether a post-conflict/peacetime context, or an armed conflict context. While a conflict is still ongoing, avenues are more limited in international criminal law. At the ICC, even when the broader conflict has not ceased, there may be a possibility for reparation if individual perpetrators are brought to trial and convicted of crime(s) within the jurisdiction of the Court.

---

[11] See in a similar vein, Luke Moffett, "Elaborating Justice for Victims at the International Criminal Court: Beyond Rhetoric and The Hague," *Journal of International Criminal Justice* 13 (2015), pp. 281–311, who claims that the Assembly of States Parties and states parties should play a greater role in implementing justice for victims domestically.

Conclusions 215

Reparation in an armed conflict situation, where the conflict has not completely ceased, should take into account the difficulties imposed by the armed conflict and the particular needs of victims in those situations.

In post-conflict situations, one alternative model is that adopted in Rwanda in 1998[12], where the Rwandan government established a fund (FARG) which counts on a percentage of the government's annual fund, grants by foreign governments, individual donations, and damages payable by those convicted of participating in the genocide.[13] Moving forward, however, there are a number of lessons that ought to be learned from this experience, especially the fact that many victims have not been able to claim reparations.[14]

One avenue, that was briefly mentioned but is nevertheless crucial, concerns the inclusion of claims in peace treaties. When peace is achieved, and a peace treaty is signed, one way to ensure reparations are provided to victims is to include reparation provisions in the peace treaty. The issue, however, is that, as history demonstrates, if peace treaties are accorded between states, reparations are often provided to the injured state, rather than directly to individual victims. Reparation may be for injury suffered by states or their nationals, but the payment (usually in lump sums) is provided to the injured state, who is responsible for its distribution.[15] One example to be noted is Article 16 of the 1951 Treaty of Peace between the Allied Powers and Japan where it was provided that the lump sum awarded was a final settlement of all claims precluding individual claims by victims.[16]

In post-conflict situations and peacetime contexts, the focus might be different, such as in rebuilding communities and providing programs of rehabilitation and community stability. In the case of peace agreements with rebel groups, one way forward would be the inclusion of claims of reparation for victims. There is also the possibility of including claims commissions such as the one adopted in the peace agreement between

---

[12] Law No. 69/2008 of 30/12/2008, Law relating to the establishment of the Fund for the support and assistance to the survivors of the Tutsi genocide and other crimes against humanity committed between 1st October 1990 and 31st December 1994, and determining its organisation, powers and functioning, Article 26.

[13] See ibid., Article 22.

[14] Heidy Rombouts and Stef Vandeginste, "Reparations for Victims in Rwanda: Caught Between Theory and Practice," in *Out of the Ashes: Reparation for Victims of Gross and Systematic Human Rights Violations* eds. K. De Feyter, et al., Intersentia, 2005, p. 310.

[15] Emanuela-Chiara Gillard, "Reparation for Violations of International Humanitarian Law," *IRRC* 85 (2003), pp. 535–536.

[16] Ibid., p. 536.

216 *Reparative Justice for International Crimes*

Eritrea and Ethiopia.[17] It is worth mentioning that, in a 2001 decision, the Commission established that the appropriate form of reparation was in principle compensation, but it did not exclude that other forms of reparation could be given if in accordance with the principles of international law.[18] This Commission is tasked with deciding through binding arbitration all claims between the two states and private entities for losses and damages during the conflict (violations of international humanitarian law and other violations of international law). Another example, which was not explored or discussed in the book, is mixed claims commissions (arbitral tribunals established by treaty), where individuals may be able to assert claims against states. One such commission is the Iran-US Claims Tribunal established by the so-called Algiers Accords between Iran and the United States in 1981. The tribunal can hear claims of nationals of one state against the other state (and also claims of one state against the other). A further possibility is to set up quasi-judicial institutions, either by peace treaties or the Security Council, to hear claims for reparations. One notable example is the United Nations Compensation Commission, established by the Security Council in 1991, which has jurisdiction over claims against Iraq for "any direct loss, damage – including environmental damage and the depletion of natural resources – or injury to foreign governments, nationals and corporations as a result of its unlawful invasion and occupation of Kuwait."[19]

6.4 FINAL REMARKS

The analysis of this book sought to demonstrate that while different forms of reparations for international crimes (i.e., reparations obtained from individuals, reparations obtained from states) present some systemic differences, they all form part of a broader system of reparative justice for mass atrocities. This book aimed at exploring a piece of this puzzle: the development and operationalization of reparative justice in the context of international crimes. This dimension is still in its infancy, it needs to be nurtured in order to thrive. The rhetoric of (reparative) justice for victims

---

[17] Agreement between the Government of the Federal Democratic Republic of Ethiopia and the Government of the State of Eritrea, 12 December 2000, Article 5, International Legal Materials, Vol. 40, 2001, p. 260.

[18] Eritrea-Ethiopia Claims Commission, *Decision Number 3: Remedies*, 24 July 2001. See Emanuela-Chiara Gillard, "Reparation for Violations of International Humanitarian Law," *IRRC* 85 (2003), pp. 542–543.

[19] UN Security Council resolution 687, 3 April 1991, para. 16. Technically, individuals do not bring claims directly to the Commission but rather do it through their state, that acts in an administrative function rather than espousing the claims in diplomatic protection.

is past; the time has come to make concrete actions to realize reparations for victims of international crimes. Reparative justice for international crimes should be international, national, and hybrid; judicial, quasi-judicial, or administrative. Realizing international justice for international crimes is after all a mosaic of different systems and mechanisms that aim at repairing humanity's most egregious conduct.

Bibliography

BOOKS

Abel, Charles F., and Marsh, Frank H., *Punishment and Restitution: A Restitutionary Approach to Crime and the Criminal*, Greenwood Press, 1984.

Ambos, Kai, and Othmann, Mohamed, *New Approaches in International Criminal Justice: Kosovo, East Timor, Sierra Leone and Cambodia*, Max Planck Institute for International Law, 2003.

Bailleux, Antoine, *La compétence universelle au carrefour de la pyramide et du réseau*, Bruylant, 2005.

Bassiouni, M. Cherif, and Wise, Edward M., *"Aut dedere aut judicare": The Duty to Extradite or Prosecute in International Law*, Nijhoff, 1995.

Beloof, Douglas E., *Victims in Criminal Procedure*, Carolina Academic Press, 1998.

Beristain, Carlos M., *Diálogos sobre la Reparación: Experiencias en el Sistema Interamericano de Derechos Humanos*, Universidad Santo Tomas, 2008.

Bigger, Nigel, *Burying the Past: Making Peace and Doing Justice After Civil Conflict*, Georgetown University Press, 2003.

Boister, Neil, and Currie, Robert J., *Routledge Handbook of Transnational Criminal Law*, Routledge, 2014.

Bonacker, Thorsten, and Safferling, Christoph, *Victims of International Crimes: An Interdisciplinary Discourse*, Intersentia, 2013.

Bonafè, Beatrice I., *The Relationship Between State and Individual Responsibility for International Crimes*, Brill, 2009.

Borchard, Edwin, *Diplomatic Protection of Citizens Abroad of the Law of International Claims*, Banks Law Publishing, 1919.

Bottigliero, Ilaria, *Redress for Victims of Crimes under International Law*, Nijhoff, 2004.

Bourdon, William, Duverger, Emmanuelle, and Badinter, Robert, *La Cour Pénale Internationale: Le Statut de Rome* (Commentary on the Rome Statute), Olivier Duhamel, 2000.

Brienen, Marion E., and Hoegen, Ernestine H., *Victims of Crime in 22 European Criminal Justice Systems*, Wolf Legal Productions, 2000.

Buyse, Antoine, *Post Conflict Housing Restitution: The European Human Rights Perspective with a Case Study on Bosnia and Herzegovina*, Intersentia, 2008.

Cesare, Beccaria, *Dei Delliti e Delle Pene*, 1974, translation available at www .constitution.org/cb/crim_pun.htm.

Chandler, David, *A History of Cambodia*, Westview Press, 4th ed., 2008.

Chappell, Louise, *The Politics of Gender at the International Criminal Court: Legacies and Legitimacy*, Oxford University Press, 2015.

Crawford, James, *The International Law Commission's Articles on State Responsibility: Introduction, Text and Commentaries*, Cambridge University Press, 2002.

Cryer, Robert, *Prosecuting International Crimes: Selectivity and the International Criminal Law Regime*, Cambridge University Press, 2005.

Cryer, Robert, Friman, Håkan, Robinson, Darryl, and Wilmshurst, Elizabeth, *An Introduction to International Criminal Law and Procedure*, Cambridge University Press, 2007.

d'Argent, Pierre, *Les Réparations de Guerre en Droit International Public*, LGDJ, 2002.

de Brouwer, Anne-Marie, *Supranational Criminal Prosecution of Sexual Violence: The ICC and the Practice of the ICTY and the ICTR*, Intersentia, 2005.

Delmas-Marty, Mireille, and Spencer, John, *European Criminal Proceedings*, Cambridge University Press, 2002.

Dominicé, Christian, *Observations sur les droits de l'Etat victime d'un fait internationalement illicite*, in *Droit international 2*, edited by C. Dominicé et al., Pedone, 1982.

Driscoll, William, Zompetti, Joseph P., and Zompetti, Suzette, *The International Criminal Court: Global Politics and the Quest for Justice*, International Debate Education Association, 2004.

Droege, Cordula, *Guía para profesionales N°2: El derecho a interponer recursos y a obtener reparación por violaciones graves de los derechos humanos*, International Commission of Jurists, 2007.

Drumbl, Mark A., *Atrocity, Punishment, and International Law*, Cambridge University Press, 2007.

Dwertmann, Eva, *The Reparation System of the International Criminal Court: Its Implementation, Possibilities and Limitations*, Nijhoff, 2010.

Elias, Robert, *The Politics of Victimization: Victims, Victimology and Human Rights*, Oxford University Press, 1986.

Eyh, Brianne McGonigle, *Procedural Justice? Victims Participation in International Criminal Proceedings*, Intersentia, 2011.

Fauchille, Paul, *Traité de Droit international public*, vol. I, Part I, Libr. A. Rousseau Éd., 1922.

Ferstman, Carla, Goetz, Mariana, and Stephens, Alan, *Reparations for Victims of Genocide, Crimes Against Humanity and War Crimes: Systems in Place and Systems in the Making*, Nijhoff, 2009.

Funk, Markus, *Victims' Rights and Advocacy at the International Criminal Court*, Oxford University Press, 2010.

García-Amador, Francisco V., *Principios de derecho internacional que rigen la responsabilidad: análisis crítico de la concepción tradicional*, Escuela de funcionarios internacionales, 1963.

García-Amador, Francisco V., *The Changing Law of International Claims*, Oceana, 1984.

Grotius, Hugo, *The Law of War and Peace*, translation by Francis W. Kelsey, Clarendon Press, 1925.

Hart, Herbert L. A., *Punishment and Responsibility*, Clarendon Press, 1968.

Henckaerts, Jean-Marie, and Doswald-Beck, Louise, *Customary International Humanitarian Law: Volume 1: Rules*, Cambridge University Press, 2005.

Holtzmann, Howard, and Kristjánsdóttir, Edda, *International Mass Claims Processes: Legal and Practical Perspectives*, Oxford University Press, 2007.

Inazumi, Mitsue, *Universal Jurisdiction in Modern International Law: Expansion of National Jurisdiction for Prosecuting Serious Crimes Under International Law*, adapted version of dissertation defended at Utrecht University on 27 October 2004, Oxford University Press, 2005.

Jackson, Robert, *The Case Against the Nazi War Criminals*, Alfred A. Knopf, 1946.

Janis, Mark Weston, *An Introduction to International Law*, Aspen Publishers, 4th ed., 2003.

Johnstone, Gerry, *Restorative Justice: Ideas, Values, Debates*, Willan, 2002.

International Bureau of the Permanent Court of Arbitration, *Redressing Injustices Through Mass Claims Processes: Innovative Responses to Unique Challenges*, Oxford University Press, 2006.

International Council on Human Rights Policy, *Hard Cases: Bringing Human Rights Violators to Justice Abroad - A Guide to Universal Jurisdiction*, International Council on Human Rights Policy, 1999.

Kant, Immanuel, *The Metaphysics of Morals*, translation by Mary Gregor, Cambridge University Press, 1996.

Kiza, Ernesto, Rathgeber, Corene, and Rohne, Holger, *Victims of War: War-Victimization and Victims' Attitudes towards Addressing Atrocities*, Hamburger Edition, 2006.

Kuosmanen, Taru, *Bringing Justice Closer: Hybrid Courts in Post-Conflict Societies*, Erik Castrén Institute of International Law and Human Rights, 2007.

Lebigre, Arlette, *Quelques Aspects de la Responsabilité Pénale en Droit Romain Classique*, Presses Universitaires de France, 1967.

Lewis, Paul H., *Authoritarian Regimes in Latin America: Dictators, Despots, and Tyrants*, Rowman & Littlefield, 2005.

Lillich, Richard, Weston, Burns, and Bederman, David, *International Claims: Their Settlement by Lump-Sum Agreement*, University Press of Virginia, vol. 1, 1975.

Macedo, Stephen, *Universal Jurisdiction: National Courts and the Prosecution of Serious Crimes Under International Law*, University of Pennsylvania Press, 2003.

Maison, Rafaëlle, *La responsabilité individuelle pour crime d'État en Droit international public*, Bruylant/Éds. de l'Université de Bruxelles, 2004.

McCarthy, Conor, *Reparations and Victim Support in the International Criminal Court*, Cambridge University Press, 2012.

Minow, Martha, *Between Vengeance and Forgiveness: Facing History After Genocide and Mass Violence*, Beacon Press, 1998.

Moffett, Luke, *Justice for Victims before the International Criminal Court*, Routledge, 2014.

Morris, Virginia, and Scharf, Michael P., *An Insider's Guide to the International Criminal Tribunals for the Former Yugoslavia*, Transnational Publishers, 1995.

Musila, Godfrey, *Rethinking International Criminal Law: Restorative Justice and the Rights of Victims in the International Criminal Court*, Lambert Academic Publishing, 2010.

Nettlefield, Lara J., *Courting Democracy in Bosnia and Herzegovina, The Hague Tribunal's Impact in a Postwar State*, Cambridge University Press, 2010.

Oppenheim, Lassa, *International Law: A Treatise*, Longmans, Green, 2nd ed., 1912.

Oppenheim, Lassa, Jennings, Robert Y., and Watts, Arthur D., *Oppenheim's International Law: Peace*, Longman, 9th ed., 1992.

Patton, George Whitecross, *A Textbook of Jurisprudence*, Clarendon Press, 4th ed., 1972.

Personnaz, Jean, *La réparation du préjudice en Droit international public*, Libr. Rec. Sirey, 1939.

Pross, Christian, *Paying for the Past: The Struggle over Reparations for Surviving Victims of the Nazi Terror*, Johns Hopkins University Press, 1998.

Randelzhofer, Albrecht, and Tomuschat, Christian, *State Responsibility and the Individual: Reparation in Instances of Grave Violations of Human Rights*, Nijhoff, 1999.

Raphael, David D., *Concepts of Justice*, Clarendon Press, 2003.

Ratner, Steven R., Abrams, Jason, and Bischoff, James, *Accountability for Human Rights Atrocities in International Law*, Oxford University Press, 1997.

Rawls, John, *A Theory of Justice*, Harvard University Press, 1971.

Reichel, Philip, and Albanese, Jay S., *Handbook of Transnational Crime and Justice*, Sage Publications, 2nd ed., 2014.

Reitzer, Ladislas, *La réparation comme conséquence de l'acte illicite en Droit international*, Libr. Rec. Sirey, 1938.

Reydams, Luc, *Universal Jurisdiction: International and Municipal Legal Perspectives*, Oxford University Press, 2003.

Romano, Cesare P. R., Nollkaemper, André, and Kleffner, Jann K., *Internationalized Criminal Courts – Sierra Leone, East Timor, Kosovo, and Cambodia*, Oxford University Press, 2004.

Rombouts, Heidy, *Victim Organizations and the Politics of Reparation: A Case-Study on Rwanda*, Intersentia, 2004.

Rubin, Alfred P., *The Law of Piracy*, Transnational Publishers, 1998.

Ryngaert, Cedric, *Jurisdiction in International Law*, Oxford University Press, 2nd ed., 2015.

Schabas, William A., *An Introduction to the International Criminal Court*, Cambridge University Press, 2nd ed., 2004.

Schabas, William A., *An Introduction to the International Criminal Court*, Cambridge University Press, 4th ed., 2011.

Schabas, William A., *The International Criminal Court: A Commentary on the Rome Statute*, Oxford University Press, 2010.

Shelton, Dinah, *Remedies in International Human Rights Law*, Oxford University Press, 3rd ed., 2015.

Shklar, Judith N., *The Faces of Injustice*, Yale University Press, 1992.

Sriram, Chandra Lekha, *Globalizing Justice for Mass Atrocities*, Routledge, 2005.

Stahn, Carsten, and El Zeidy, Mohamed M., *The International Criminal Court and Complementarity: From Theory to Practice*, Cambridge University Press, 2011.

Steinberg, Richard H., *Assessing the Legacy of the ICTY*, Nijhoff, 2011.

Strang, Heather, and Braithwaite, John, *Restorative Justice and Civil Society*, Cambridge University Press, 2001.

Trindade, Antônio Augusto Cançado, *International Law for Humankind: Towards a New* Jus Gentium, Nijhoff, 2010. Harvard Research in International Law.

van Ness, Daniel W., and Strong, Karen Heetderks, *Restoring Justice*, Routledge, 2nd ed., 2002.

von Mehren, Arthur T., and Murray, Peter L., *Law in the United States*, Cambridge University Press, 2nd ed., 2007.

Wemmers, Jo-Anne M., *Reparation and the International Criminal Court: Meeting the Needs of Victims*, International Centre for Comparative Criminology, University of Montreal, 2006.

Westlake, John, *The Collected Papers of John Westlake on Public International Law*, ed. Lassa Oppenheim, Cambridge University Press, 1914.

Yamamoto, Eric K., *Interracial Justice: Conflict and Reconciliation in Post-Civil Rights America*, New York University Press, 1999.

ARTICLES

Accioly, Hidelbrando, "Principes généraux de la responsabilité internationale d'après la doctrine et la jurisprudence," *Recueil des Cours de l'Académie de Droit International de La Haye* 96 (1953), pp. 349–441.

Akhavan, Payam, "Beyond Impunity: Can International Criminal Justice Prevent Future Atrocities?" *American Journal of International Law* 95 (2001), pp. 7–31.

Amezcua-Noriega, Octavio, "Reparation Principles under International Law and their Possible Application by the International Criminal Court: Some Reflections," *Reparations Unit, Briefing Paper No.1*, Dr. Clara Sandoval, University of Essex, 2011, pp. 1–12.

Antkowiak, Thomas, "An Emerging Mandate for International Courts: Victim-Centered Remedies and Restorative Justice," *Stanford Journal of International Law* 47 (2011), pp. 279–332.

Antkowiak, Thomas M., "Remedial Approaches to Human Rights Violations: The Inter-American Court of Human Rights and Beyond," *Columbia Journal of Transnational Law* 46 (2008), pp. 351–419.

Anzilotti, Dionisio, "La responsabilité internationale des États a raison des dommages soufferts par des étrangers," *Revue générale de droit international public* 13 (1906), pp. 5–29.

Aptel, Cécile, "Some Innovations in the Statute of the Special Tribunal for Lebanon," *Journal of International Criminal Justice* 5 (2007), pp. 1107–1124.

Arajärvi, Noora, "Looking Back from Nowhere: Is There a Future for Universal Jurisdiction over International Crimes?," *Tilburg Law Review* 16 (2011), pp. 5–29.

Arsanjani, Mahnoush H., "The Rome Statute of the International Criminal Court," *American Journal of International Law* 93 (1999), pp. 22–43.

Askin, Kelly D., "Sexual Violence in Decisions and Indictments of the Yugoslav and Rwandan Tribunals: Current Status," *American Journal of International Law* 93 (1999), pp. 97–123.

Bachrach, Michael, "The Protection of Rights and Victims Under International Criminal Law," *International Law* 34 (2000), pp. 7–20.

Bibliography

Bair, James P., "From the Numbers Who Died to Those Who Survived: Victim Participation in the Extraordinary Chambers in the Courts of Cambodia," *University of Hawaii Law Review* 31 (2008), pp. 507–552.

Beckett, W. Eric, "Criminal Jurisdiction Over Foreigners," *British Yearbook of International Law* 8 (1927), pp. 108–128.

Bílková, Veronika, "Victims of War and Their Right to Reparation for Violations of International Humanitarian Law," *Mickolc Journal of International Law* 4 (2007), pp. 1–11.

Bittner, Egon, and Platt, Anthony, "The Meaning of Punishment," *Issues in Criminology* 2 (1966), pp. 79–99.

Boracic, Selma, "Bosnia War Victims' Compensation Struggle," *International War and Peace Reporting* (IWPR), 3 August 2011, available at https://iwpr.net/global-voices/bosnia-war-victims-compensation-struggle.

Boyle, David, "The Rights of Victims Participation, Representation, Protection, Reparation," *Journal of International Criminal Justice* 4 (2006), pp. 307–313.

Braithwaite, John, "A Future Where Punishment Is Marginalized: Realistic or Utopian?," *UCLA Law Review* 46 (1999), pp. 1727–1750.

Braithwaite, John, "Restorative Justice and De-Professionalization," *The Good Society* 13 (2004), pp. 28–31.

Butler, Hays, "The Doctrine of Universal Jurisdiction: A Review of the Literature," *Criminal Law Forum* 11 (2000), pp. 353–373.

Capeloto, Tessa V., "Reconciliation in the Wake of Tragedy: Cambodia's Extraordinary Chambers Undermines the Cambodian Constitution," *Pacific Rim Law & Policy Journal Association* 17 (2008), pp. 103–132.

Carranza, Ruben, "Imagining the Possibilities for Reparations in Cambodia," *International Centre for Transitional Justice*, Briefing Paper (2005), pp. 1–3.

Casey, Lee A., "The Case Against the International Criminal Court," *Fordham International Law Journal* 25 (2002), pp. 840–872.

Cassese, Antonio, "Is the Bell Tolling for Universality? A Plea for a Sensible Notion of Universal Jurisdiction," *Journal of International Criminal Justice* 1 (2003), pp. 589–595.

Cassese, Antonio, "On the Current Trends Towards Criminal Prosecution and Punishment of Breaches of International Humanitarian Law," *European Journal of International Law* 9 (1998), pp. 2–17.

Chaitidou, Eleni, "Recent Developments in the Jurisprudence of the International Criminal Court," *Zeitschrift für Internationale Strafrechtsdogmatik* 8 (2013), pp. 130–160.

Chung, Christine H., "Victim's Participation at the International Criminal Court: Are Concessions of the Court Clouding the Promise?" *Northwestern Journal of International Human Rights* 6 (2007), pp. 459–545.

Colangelo, Anthony J., "The New Universal Jurisdiction: In Absentia Signaling over Clearly Defined Crimes," *Georgetown Journal of International Law* 36 (2004–2005), pp. 537–603.

Conforti, Benedetto, "The Judgment of the International Court of Justice on the Immunity of Foreign States: A Missed Opportunity," *Italian Yearbook of International Law* 21 (2011), pp. 135–142.

Cornell, Timothy, and Salisbury, Lance, "The Importance of Civil Law in the Transition to Peace: Lessons from the Human Rights Chamber for Bosnia and Herzegovina," *Cornell International Law Journal* 35 (2000–2001), pp. 389–426.

Couillard, Valérie, "The Nairobi Declaration: Redefining Reparations for Women Victims of Sexual Violence," *International Journal of Transitional Justice* 1 (2007), pp. 444–453.

Cowles, Willard, "Universality of Jurisdiction over War Crimes," *California Law Review* 33 (1945), pp. 177–218.

d'Argent, Pierre, "Le Fonds et la Commission de Compensation des Nations Unies," *Revue Belge de Droit International* 25 (1992), pp. 485–518.

Danieli, Yael, "Reappraising the Nuremberg Trials and Their Legacy: The Role of Victims in International Law," *Cardozo Law Review* 27 (2006), pp. 1633–1650.

Dannenbaum, Tom, "The International Criminal Court, Article 79, and Transitional Justice: The Case for an Independent Trust Fund for Victims," *Wisconsin International Law Journal* 28 (2010), pp. 235–298.

David, Eric, "Le Tribunal International Pénal pour l'Ex-Yougoslavie," *Revue Belge de Droit International* 25 (1992), pp. 565–598.

De Bertodano, Sylvia, "Problems Arising from the Mixed Composition and Structure of the Cambodian Extraordinary Chambers," *Journal of International Criminal Justice* 4 (2006), pp. 285–293.

De Brouwer, Anne-Marie, "Reparation to Victims of Sexual Violence: Possibilities at the International Criminal Court and at the Trust Fund for Victims and Their Families," *Leiden Journal of International Law* 20 (2007), pp. 207–237.

De Hemptinne, Jérôme, "Challenges Raised by Victims' Participation in the Proceedings of the Special Tribunal for Lebanon," *Journal of International Criminal Justice* 8 (2010), pp. 165–179.

De Hemptinne, Jérôme, "The Creation of Investigating Chambers at the International Criminal Court," *Journal of International Criminal Justice* 5 (2007), pp. 402–418.

Diab, Nader Iskandar, "Challenges in the Implementation of the Reparation Award Against Hissein Habré: Can the Spell of Unenforceable Awards Across the Globe be Broken?" *Journal of International Criminal Justice* 16 (2018), pp. 141–163.

Dickinson, Edwin D., "Is the Crime of Piracy Obsolete?" *Harvard Law Review* 38 (1925), pp. 334–360.

Dickinson, Laura A., "The Promise of Hybrid Courts," *American Journal of International Law* 97 (2003), pp. 295–310.

Dolzer, Rudolf, "The Settlement of War-Related Claims: Does International Law Recognize a Victim's Private Right of Action? Lessons After 1945," *Berkeley Journal of International Law* 20 (2002), pp. 296–341.

Donadio, Colette, "Gender Based Violence: Justice and Reparation in Bosnia and Herzegovina," *Mediterranean Journal of Social Sciences* 5 (2014), pp. 692–702.

Donovan, Donald Francis, "Universal Jurisdiction – The Next Frontier?," *American Society of International Law Proceedings* 99 (2005), pp. 117–128.

Bibliography

Donovan, Donald Francis, and Roberts, Anthea, "The Emerging Recognition of Universal Civil Jurisdiction," *American Journal of International Law* 100 (2006), pp. 142–163.

Drumbl, Mark A., "Sclerosis: Retributive Justice and the Rwandan Genocide," *Punishment & Society* 2 (2000), pp. 287–307.

Dubinsky, Paul R., "Justice for the Collective: The Limits of the Human Rights Class Action," *Michigan Law Review* 102 (2004), pp. 1152–1190.

Durbach, Andrea, and Chappell, Louise, "Leaving Behind the Age of Impunity: Victims of Gender Violence and the Promise of Reparations," *International Feminist Journal of Politics* 8 (2014), pp. 1–22.

Espósito, Carlos, "*Jus Cogens* and Jurisdictional Immunities of States at the International Court of Justice: A Conflict Does Exist," *Italian Yearbook of International Law* 21 (2011), pp. 161–174.

Evans, Christine, "Reparations for Victims in International Criminal Law," *Raoul Wallenberg Institute of Human Rights and Humanitarian Law*, online, 2012.

Ferencz, Benjamin B., "International Criminal Courts: The Legacy of Nuremberg," *Pace International Law Review* 10 (1998), pp. 203–235.

Ferstman, Carla, "The Reparation Regime of the International Criminal Court: Practical Considerations," *Leiden Journal of International Law* 15 (2002), pp. 667–686.

Fischer, Peter G., "The Victims' Trust Fund of the International Criminal Court: Formation of a Functional Reparations Scheme," *Emory International Law Review* 17 (2003), pp. 187–240.

Frisso, Giovanna M., "The Winding Down of the ICTY: The Impact of the Completion Strategy and the Residual Mechanism on Victims," *Goettingen Journal of International Law* 3 (2011), pp. 1092–1121.

Garcia-Mora, Manuel R., "Criminal Jurisdiction over Foreigners for Treason and Offences Against the Safety of the State Committed Upon Foreign Territory," *University of Pittsburgh Law Review* 19 (1958), pp. 567–590.

Garkawe, Sam, "Victims and the International Criminal Court: Three Major Issues," *International Criminal Law Review* 3 (2003), pp. 345–367.

Gavouneli, Maria, "War Reparation Claims and State Immunity," *Revue Hellénique de droit international* 50 (1997), pp. 595–608.

Geraghty, Anne H., "Universal Jurisdiction and Drug Trafficking: A Tool for Fighting one of the World's Most Pervasive Problems," *Florida Journal of International Law* 16 (2004), pp. 371–403.

Gillard, Emanuela-Chiarra, "Reparation for Violations of International Humanitarian Law," *International Review of the Red Cross* 85 (2003), pp. 529–553.

Ginn, Courtney, "Ensuring the Effective Prosecution of Sexually Violent Crimes in the Bosnian War Crimes Chamber: Applying Lessons from the ICTY," *Emory International Law Review* 27 (2013), pp. 565–601.

Glaspy, Padraic J., "Justice Delayed? Recent Developments at the Extraordinary Chambers in the Courts of Cambodia," *Harvard Human Rights Journal* 21 (2008), pp. 143–154.

Goldstone, Richard J., and Hamilton, Rebecca J., "Bosnia v. Serbia: Lessons from the Encounter of the International Court of Justice with the International Criminal

Tribunal for the Former Yugoslavia," *Leiden Journal of International Law* 21 (2008), pp. 95–112.

Goodwin, Joshua Michael, "Universal Jurisdiction and the Pirate: Time for an Old Couple to Part," *Vanderbilt Journal of Transnational Law* 39 (2006), pp. 973–1011.

Greco, Gioia, "Victims' Rights Overview under the ICC Legal Framework: A Jurisprudential Analysis," *International Criminal Law Review* 7 (2007), pp. 531–547.

Grovestins, Aida, "Victims' Lawyers Start Battle to Seize Habré's Millions," Justice Hub, 4 August 2016, available at https://justicehub.org/article/victims-lawyers-start-battle-to-seize-habres-millions/.

Hall, Jerome, "Interrelations of Criminal Law and Torts," *Columbia Law Review* 43 (1943), pp. 753–779.

Harvard Research in International Law, "Draft Convention on Jurisdiction with Respect to Crime," *American Journal of International Law* 29 (1935), pp. 439–442.

Hassan, Farooq, "The Theoretical Basis of Punishment in International Criminal Law," *Case Western Reserve Journal of International Law* 15 (1983), pp. 39–60.

Henzelin, Marc, Heiskanen, Veijo, and Mettraux, Guénaël, "Reparations to Victims Before the International Criminal Court: Lessons From International Mass Claims Processes," *Criminal Law Forum* 17 (2006), pp. 281–344.

Herman, Johanna, "Reaching for Justice: The Participation of Victims at the Extraordinary Chambers in the Courts of Cambodia," *CHRC Policy Paper* No. 5, (2010), pp. 1–8.

Ingadottir, Thordis, "The International Criminal Court: The Trust Fund for Victims (Article 79 of the Rome Statute), A Discussion Paper," ICC Discussion Paper No. 3, PICT, February 2001.

"International Military Tribunal Nuremberg, Judgment and Sentences," *American Journal of International Law* 41 (1947), pp. 172–333.

Jordan, Jon B., "Universal Jurisdiction in a Dangerous World: A Weapon for All Nations Against International Crimes," *Michigan State University-DCL Journal of International Law* 9 (2000), pp. 1–31.

Jouet, Mugambi, "Reconciling the Conflicting Rights of Victims and Defendants at the International Criminal Court," *St. Louis University Public Law Review* 26 (2007), pp. 249–308.

Jurdi, Nidal Nabil, "The Subject-Matter Jurisdiction of the Special Tribunal for Lebanon," *Journal of International Criminal Justice* 5 (2007), pp. 1125–1138.

Kalshoven, Frits, "State Responsibility for Warlike Acts of the Armed Forces," *International and Comparative Law Quarterly* 40 (1991), pp. 827–858.

Kamminga, Menno T., "Lessons Learned from the Exercise of Universal Jurisdiction in Respect of Gross Human Rights Offenses," *Human Rights Quarterly* 23 (2001), pp. 940–974.

Kamminga, Menno T., "Universal Civil Jurisdiction: Is it Legal? Is it Desirable?" *American Society of International Law Proceedings* 99 (2005) pp. 123–125.

Karnavas, Michael G., "The ICTY Legacy: A Defense Counsel's Perspective," *Goettingen Journal of International Law* 3 (2011), pp. 1052–1092.

Kartenstein, Suzanne, "Hybrid Tribunals: Searching for Justice in East Timor," *Harvard Human Rights Journal* 16 (2003), pp. 245–278.

Keller, Linda M., "Seeking Justice at the International Criminal Court: Victims' Reparations," *Thomas Jefferson Law Review* 29 (2007), pp. 189–217.

Kelsen, Hans, "Collective and Individual Responsibility in International Law with Particular Regard to the Punishment of War Criminals," *California Law Review* 31 (1943), pp. 530–571.

Kendall, Sara, and Nouwen, Sarah, "Representational Practices at the International Criminal Court: The Gap Between Juridified and Abstract Victimhood," *Law and Contemporary Problems* 75 (2013), pp. 235–262.

Kleffner, Jann K., and Zegveld, Liesbeth, "Establishing an Individual Complaints Procedure for Violations of International Humanitarian Law," *Yearbook of International Humanitarian Law* 3 (2000), pp. 384–401.

Klein, Katheryn M., "Bringing the Khmer Rouge to Justice: The Challenges and Risks Facing the Joint Tribunal in Cambodia," *New Jersey International Human Rights* 4 (2006), pp. 549–566.

Kleinhaus, Brian, "Serving Two Masters: Evaluating the Criminal or Civil Nature of VWPA and MVRA Through the Lens of the Ex Post Facto Clause, the Abatement Doctrine and the Sixth Amendment," *Fordham Law Review* 73 (2005), pp. 2711–2768.

Kontorovich, Eugene, "Implementing *Sosa v. Alvarez-Machain*: What Piracy Reveals About the Limits of the Alien Tort Statute," *Notre Dame Law Review* 80 (2004), pp. 111–162.

Kontorovich, Eugene, "International Legal Responses to Piracy," *American Society of International Law* 13 (2009), available at https://asil.org/insights/volume/13/issue/2/international-legal-responses-piracy-coast-somalia.

Kontorovich, Eugene, "The Piracy Analogy: Modern Universal Jurisdiction's Hollow Foundation," *Harvard International Law Journal* 45 (2004), pp. 183–238.

Langer, Máximo, and Doherty, Joseph W., "Managerial Judging Goes International, but Its Promise Remains Unfulfilled: An Empirical Assessment of the ICTY Reforms," *Yale Journal of International Law* 36 (2011), pp. 241–305.

Lauterpacht, Hersch, "Règles générales du droit de la paix," *Recueil des Cours* 62 (1937) (translation), pp. 95–422.

Lauterpacht, Hersch, "The Law of Nations and the Punishment of War Crimes," *British Yearbook of International Law* 21 (1944), pp. 58–95.

Lemkin, Raphael, "Genocide as a Crime under International Law," *American Journal of International Law* 41 (1947), pp. 145–151.

Levmore, Saul, "Reparations in the Wake of Atrocities: A Plan for Encouraging Participation by Governments," *Human Rights and International Criminal Law Online Forum*, available at https://doi.org/10.1163/9789004304451_029, pp. 249–251.

Linton, Suzannah, "Cambodia, East Timor and Sierra Leone: Experiments in International Justice," *Criminal Law Forum* 12 (2001), pp. 185–246.

Mbadinga, M. Itsouhou, "Le recours à la compétence universelle pour la répression des crimes internationaux: étude de quelques cas," *Revue de Droit International et de Sciences Diplomatiques et Politiques* 81(2003), pp. 285–305.

McCarthy, Conor, "Reparations under the Rome Statute of the International Criminal Court and Reparative Justice Theory," *International Journal of Transitional Justice* 3 (2009), pp. 250–271.

McCarthy, Conor, "Victim Redress and International Criminal Justice: Competing Paradigms, or Compatible Forms of Justice?" *Journal of International Criminal Justice* 10 (2012), pp. 325–372.

McGonigle, Brianne N., "Bridging the Divides in International Criminal Proceedings: An Examination into the Victim Participation Endeavor of the International Criminal Court," *Florida Journal of International Law* 21 (2009), pp. 93–151.

McGonigle, Brianne N., "Two for the Price of One: Attempts by the Extraordinary Chambers in the Courts of Cambodia to Combine Retributive and Restorative Justice Principles," *Leiden Journal of International Law* 22 (2009), pp. 127–149.

McGregor, Lorna, "State Immunity and *Jus Cogens*," *The International and Comparative Law Quarterly* 55 (2006), pp. 437–445.

Mégret, Frédéric, "Justifying Compensation by the International Criminal Court's Victims Trust Fund: Lessons from Domestic Compensation Schemes," *Brooklyn Journal of International Law* 36 (2010–2011), pp. 123–204.

Mégret, Frédéric, "The Case for Collective Reparations Before the ICC" (November 15, 2012), pp. 1–18, available at SSRN: http://ssrn.com/abstract=2196911.

Mégret, Frédéric, "The International Criminal Court Statute and the Failure to Mention Symbolic Reparation," *International Review of Victimology* 16 (2009), pp. 127–147.

Mégret, Frédéric, "The Legacy of the ICTY as Seen Through Some of Its Actors and Observers," *Goettingen Journal of International Law* 3 (2011), pp. 1011–1052.

Mekjian, Gerard J., and Varughese, Mathew C., "Hearing the Victim's Voice: Analysis of Victims' Advocate Participation in the Trial Proceeding of the International Criminal Court," *Pace International Law Review* 17 (2005), pp. 1–46.

Meron, Theodor, "The Humanization of Humanitarian Law," *American Journal of International Law* 94 (2000), pp. 239–278.

Milanović, Marko, "An Odd Couple: Domestic Crimes and International Responsibility in the Special Tribunal for Lebanon," *Journal of International Criminal Justice* 5 (2007), pp. 1139–1152.

Milanović, Marko, "From Compromise to Principles: Clarifying the Concept of State Jurisdiction in Human Rights Treaties," *Human Rights Law Review* 8 (2008), pp. 411–448.

Milanović, Marko, "State Responsibility for Genocide: A Follow-Up," *European Journal of International Law* 18 (2007), pp. 669–694.

Moffett, Luke, "Elaborating Justice for Victims at the International Criminal Court: Beyond Rhetoric and The Hague," *Journal of International Criminal Justice* 13 (2015), pp. 281–311.

Moffett, Luke, "Meaningful and Effective? Considering Victims Interests Through Participation at the International Criminal Court," *Criminal Law Forum* 26 (2015), pp. 255–289.

Moffett, Luke, "Navigating Complex Identities of Victim-Perpetrators in Reparation Mechanisms," Queen's University Belfast, School of Law Research Paper No. 2014B13, pp. 1–23, available at https://ecpr.eu/filestore/paperproposal/14d84c59-1767-467b-814c-0d57e7404655.pdf.

Moffett, Luke, "Realising Justice for Victims Before the International Criminal Court," *International Crimes Database* (2014).

Bibliography

Moffett, Luke, "Reparations at the ICC: Can It Really Serve as a Model?" Justiceinfo .net, 19 July 2019, available at www.justiceinfo.net/en/justiceinfo-comment-and-debate/opinion/41949-reparations-at-the-icc-can-it-really-serve-as-a-model.html (last accessed 26 July 2019).

Moffett, Luke, "Reparations for 'Guilty Victims': Navigating Complex Identities of Victim–Perpetrators in Reparation Mechanisms," *International Journal of Transitional Justice* 10 (2016), pp. 146–167.

Moffett, Luke, "Reparative Complementarity: Ensuring an Effective Remedy for Victims in the Reparation Regime of the International Criminal Court," *International Journal of Human Rights* 17 (2013), pp. 368–390.

Monachesi, Elio, "Pioneers in Criminology IX: Cesare Beccaria (1738–1794)," *Journal of Criminal Law, Criminology & Political Science* 46 (1955), pp. 439–449.

Moyo, Monica, "ICJ Delivers Decision on the Application of the Genocide Convention," *AJIL International Law in Brief*, 3 February 2015, available at www .asil.org/blogs/icj-delivers-decision-application-genocide-convention-february-3-2015.

Mugiraneza, Jean Paul, "Rwanda Genocide: Why Compensation Would Help the Healing," *Guardian*, 8 March 2014, available at www.theguardian.com/global-development-professionals-network/2014/mar/04/rwanda-genocide-victims-compensation.

Nollkaemper, André, "Concurrence Between Individual Responsibility and State Responsibility in International Law," *International and Comparative Law Quarterly* 52 (2003), pp. 615–640.

Nollkaemper, André, "The Contribution of International Institutions to Domestic Reparation for International Crimes," *Proceedings of the Annual Meeting (American Society of International Law)* 103 (2009), pp. 203–207.

Nsereko, Daniel Ntanda, "The International Criminal Court: Jurisdictional and Related Issues," *Criminal Law Forum* 10 (1999), pp. 87–120.

Park, Won Soon, "Japanese Reparations Policies and the 'Comfort Women' Question," *positions* 5 (1997), pp. 107–134.

Pavoni, Riccardo, "An American Anomaly? On the ICJ's Selective Reading of United States Practice in Jurisdictional Immunities of the State," *Italian Yearbook of International Law* 21 (2011), pp. 143–159.

Pellegrini, Flaviane de Magalhães Barros, "Os direitos das vítimas de crimes no Estado Democrático de Direito – uma análise do Projeto de Lei n° 269/2003 – Senado Federal," *Virtuajus: Revista da Faculdade de Direito da PUC-MG*.

Pellet, Alain, "Le Tribunal Criminel International pour l'Ex-Yougoslavie," *Revue Générale de Droit International Public* 98 (1994), pp. 7–60.

Pham, Phuong, Vinck, Patrick, Balthazard, Mychelle, and Hean, Sokhom, "After the First Trial: A Population-Based Survey on Knowledge and Perceptions of Justice and the Extraordinary Chambers in the Courts of Cambodia," available at SSRN 1860963 (2011).

Phan, Hae Duy, "Reparations to Victims of Gross Human Rights Violations: The Case of Cambodia," *East Asia Law Review* 4 (2009), pp. 277–298.

Rabinovitch, Ryan, "Universal Jurisdiction *in Absentia*," *Fordham International Law Journal* 28 (2004–2005), pp. 500–530.

Randall, Kenneth C., "Universal Jurisdiction Under International Law," *Texas Law Review* 66 (1988), pp. 785–841.

Ratner, Stephen, "Belgium's War Crimes Statute: A Postmortem," *American Journal of International Law* 97 (2003), pp. 888–897.

Reydams, Luc, "Belgium's First Application of Universal Jurisdiction: The Butare Four Case," *Journal of International Criminal Justice* 1(2003), pp. 428–436.

Reydams, Luc, "Universal Criminal Jurisdiction: The Belgian State of Affairs," *Criminal Law Forum* 11 (2000), pp. 183–216.

Reydams, Luc, "Universal Jurisdiction in Context," *American Society of International Law Proceedings* 99 (2005), pp. 118–120.

Riznik, Donald, "Completing the ICTY-Project Without Sacrificing Its Main Goals: Security Council Resolution 1966: A Good Decision," *Goettingen Journal of International Law* 3 (2011), pp. 907–922.

Robinson, Darryl, "Serving the Interests of Justice: Amnesties, Truth Commissions, and the International Criminal Court," *European Journal of International Law* 14 (2003), pp. 481–505.

Roht-Arriaza, Naomi, "Reparations, Decisions, and Dilemmas," *Hastings International and Comparative Law Review* 27 (2004), pp. 157–219.

Rojas Báez, Julio Joe, "La Jurisprudencia de la Corte Interamericana de Derechos Humanos en Materia de Reparaciones y los Criterios del Proyeto de Artículos sobre Responsabilidad del Estado por Hechos Internacionalmente Ilícitos," *American University International Law Review* 92 (2007–2008), pp. 91–126.

Rosand, Eric, "The Right to Compensation in Bosnia: An Unfulfilled Promise and Challenge to International Law," *Cornell Journal of International Law* 33 (2000), pp. 113–158.

Rosenfeld, Friedrich, "Collective Reparation for Victims of Armed Conflict," *International Review of the Red Cross* 92 (2010), pp. 731–746.

Roth, Kenneth, "The Case for Universal Jurisdiction," *Foreign Affairs* 80 (2001), pp. 150–154.

Rubio-Marín, Ruth, and de Greiff, Pablo, "Women and Reparations," *International Journal of Transitional Justice* 1 (2007), pp. 318–337.

Ryngaert, Cedric, "Universal Tort Jurisdiction over Gross Human Rights Violations," *Netherlands Yearbook of International Law* 38 (2007), pp. 3–60.

Sader, Choucri, "A Lebanese Perspective on the Special Tribunal for Lebanon: Hopes and Disillusions," *Journal of International Criminal Justice* 5 (2007), pp. 1083–1089.

Scharf, Irene, "Kosovo's War Victims: Civil Compensation or Criminal Justice for Identity Elimination," *Emory International Law Review* 14 (2000), pp. 1415–1449.

Scharf, Michael P., "Application of Treaty-Based Universal Jurisdiction on Nationals of Non-Party States," *New England Law Review* 35 (2001), pp. 363–382.

Schimmel, Naom, "A UN Trust Fund," Huffington Post, 25 May 2012, available at www.huffingtonpost.co.uk/noam-785/a-un-trust-fund-for-rwand_b_1542340.html?guccounter=1.

Schocken, Celina, "The Special Court for Sierra Leone: Overview and Recommendations," *Berkeley Journal of International Law* 20 (2002), pp. 436–461.

Serra, Gianluca, "Special Tribunal for Lebanon:A Commentary on its Major Legal Aspects," *International Criminal Justice Review* 18 (2008), pp. 344–355.

Shelton, Dinah, "Righting Wrongs: Reparations in the Articles on State Responsibility," *American Journal of International Law* 96 (2002), pp. 833–856.

Shelton, Dinah L., and Ingadottir, Thordis, "The International Criminal Court Reparations to Victims of Crimes (Article 75 of the Rome Statute) and the Trust Fund (Article 79): Recommendations for the Court Rules of Procedure and Evidence," Center on International Cooperation, New York University, Meeting of the Preparatory Commission for the International Criminal Court (26 July–13 August 1999), available at www.vrwg.org/downloads/reparations.pdf.

Sluiter, Göran, "Due Process and Criminal Procedure in the Cambodian Extraordinary Chambers," *Journal of International Criminal Justice* 4 (2006), pp. 314–326.

Sossai, Mirko, "Are Italian Courts Directly Bound to Give Effect to the Jurisdictional Immunities Judgment?" *Italian Yearbook of International Law* 21 (2011), pp. 175–189.

Sperfeldt, Christoph, "Collective Reparations at the Extraordinary Chambers in the Courts of Cambodia," *International Criminal Law Review* 12 (2012), pp. 457–489.

Spinedi, Marina, "State Responsibility *v* Individual Responsibility for International Crimes: *Tertium Non Datu*," *European Journal of International Law* 13 (2002), pp. 895–899.

Stahn, Carsten, "Reparative Justice after the Lubanga Appeal Judgment: New Prospects for Expressivism and Participatory Justice or 'Juridified Victimhood' by Other Means?" *Journal of International Criminal Justice* 13 (2015), pp. 801–813.

Stahn, Carsten, "Reparative Justice after the Lubanga Appeals Judgment on Principles and Procedures of Reparation," *Ejil: Talk!*, 7 April 2015, available at http://ejiltalk.org/reparative-justice-after-the-lubanga-appeals-judgment-on-principles-and-procedures-of-reparation/#more-13286.

Steiner, Henry, "Three Cheers for Universal Jurisdiction: Or Is it Only Two?" *Theoretical Inquiries in Law* 6 (2004), pp. 199–236.

Stephens, Beth, "Conceptualizing Violence Under International Law: Do Tort Remedies Fit the Crime?" *Albany Law Review* 60 (1996–1997), pp. 579–606.

Stephens, Beth, "Translating Filartiga: A Comparative and International Law Analysis of Domestic Remedies for International Human Rights Violations," *Yale Journal of International Law* 27 (2002), pp. 1–58.

Steven, Lee A., "Genocide and the Duty to Extradite or Prosecute: Why the United States Is in Breach of Its International Obligations," *Virginia Journal of International Law* 39 (1999), pp. 425–466.

Swart, Maria, "Tadic Revisited: Some Critical Comments on the Legacy and the Legitimacy of the ICTY," *Goettingen Journal of International Law* 3 (2011), pp. 985–1009.

The Hague Justice Portal, "No signs of victim compensation in Sierra Leone: Chief Prosecutor at the Special Court for Sierra Leone, Brenda Hollis deplores the lack of assistance for victims," 18 November 2010, available at www.haguejusticeportal.net/index.php?id=12284.

Thynne, Kelisiana, "The International Criminal Court: A Failure of International Justice for Victims," *Alberta Law Review* 46 (2009), pp. 957–982.

Tomuschat, Christian, "Darfur: Compensation for the Victims," *Journal of International Criminal Justice* 3 (2005), pp. 579–589.

Tomuschat, Christian, "Reparation for Victims of Grave Human Rights Violations," *Tulane Journal of International and Comparative Law* 10 (2002), pp. 157–184.

Tomuschat, Christian, "Reparation in Cases of Genocide," *Journal of International Criminal Justice* 5 (2007), pp. 905–912.

Triffterer, Otto, "Prosecution of States for Crimes of State," *Revue Internationale de Droit Penal* 67 (1996), pp. 345–364.

Trumbull, Charles P., "The Victims of Victim Participation in International Criminal Proceedings," *Michigan Journal of International Law* 29 (2008), pp. 777–826.

Van Schaack, Beth, "In Defence of Civil Redress: The Domestic Enforcement of Human Rights Norms in the Context of the Proposed Hague Judgments Convention," *Harvard International Law Journal* 42 (2001), pp. 141–200.

Van Schaack, Beth, "Justice Without Borders: Universal Civil Jurisdiction," *American Society of International Law Proceedings* 99 (2005), pp. 120–122.

Vandermeersch, Damien, "Prosecuting International Crimes in Belgium," *Journal of International Criminal Justice* 3 (2005), pp. 400–421.

Villa-Vicencio, Charles, "Why Perpetrators Should Not Always Be Prosecuted: Where the International Criminal Court and Truth Commissions Meet," *Emory Law Journal* 49 (2000), pp. 205–222.

Walker, Margaret Urban, "Transformative Reparations? A Critical Look at a Current Trend in Thinking about Gender-Just Reparations," *International Journal of Transitional Justice* 10 (2016), pp. 108–125.

Walleyn, Luc, "Victimes et Témoins de Crimes Internationaux: du droit à une Protection au Droit à la Parole," *Revue Internationale de la Croix Rouge* 84 (2002), pp. 51–78.

Watson, Geoffrey R., "The Passive Personality Principle," *Texas International Law Journal* 28 (1993), pp. 1–46.

Weckel, Philippe, "La justice internationale en le soixantième anniversaire de la Déclaration Universelle des Droits de l'Homme," *Revue générale de Droit international public* 113 (2009), pp. 5–18.

Wemmers, Jo-Anne M., "Victim Reparation and the International Criminal Court," *International Review of Victimology* 16 (2009), pp. 123–126.

Werner, Alain, and Rudy, Daniella, "Civil Party Representation at the ECCC: Sounding the Retreat in International Criminal Law," *Northwestern University Journal of International Human Rights* 8 (2010), pp. 301–309.

Wetzel, Jan Erik, and Mitri, Yvonne, "The Special Tribunal for Lebanon: A Court Off the Shelf for a Divided Country," *The Law and Practice of International Courts and Tribunals* 7 (2008), pp. 81–114.

White, Brent T., "Say You're Sorry: Court-Ordered Apologies as a Civil Rights Remedy," *Cornell Law Review* 91 (2006), pp. 1261–1312.

Wierda, Marieke, Nassar, Habib, and Maalouf, Lynn, "Early Reflections on Local Perceptions, Legitimacy and Legacy of the Special Tribunal for Lebanon," *Journal of International Criminal Justice* 5 (2007), pp. 1065–1081.

Wiersing, Anja, "*Lubanga* and its Implications for Victims Seeking Reparations at the International Criminal Court," *Amsterdam Law Forum* 4 (2012), pp. 21–39.

Williams, Sarah, "The Cambodian Extraordinary Chambers: A Dangerous Precedent for International Justice," *International & Comparative Law Quarterly* 53 (2004), pp. 227–245.

Wippman, David, "Atrocities, Deterrence, and the Limits of International Justice," *Fordham International Law Journal* 23 (1999), pp. 473–488.

Wringe, Bill, "Why Punish War Crimes? Victor's Justice and Expressive Justifications of Punishment," *Law and Philosophy* 25 (2006), pp. 159–191.

Wu, Yolanda S., "Genocidal Rape in Bosnia: Redress in United States Courts Under the Alien Tort Claims Act," *UCLA Women's Law Journal* 4 (1993), pp. 101–112.

Yeager, David, "The Human Rights Chamber for Bosnia and Herzegovina: A Case Study in Transitional Justice," *International Legal Perspectives* 14 (2004), pp. 44–55.

Zacklin, Ralph, "The Failings of Ad Hoc International Tribunals," *Journal of International Criminal Justice* 2 (2004), pp. 541–545.

Zapallà, Salvatore, "The Rights of Victims v. the Rights of the Accused," *Journal of International Criminal Justice* 8 (2010), pp. 137–164.

Zedner, Lucia, "Reparation and Retribution: Are they Reconcilable?" *The Modern Law Review* 57 (1994), pp. 228–250.

Zegveld, Liesbeth, "Remedies for Victims of Violations of International Humanitarian Law," *International Review of the Red Cross* 85 (2003), pp. 497–527.

Zegveld, Liesbeth, "Victims' Reparations Claims and International Criminal Courts, Incompatible Values?," *Journal of International Criminal Justice* 8 (2010), pp. 79–111.

CHAPTERS IN BOOKS

Abazovic, Dino, "Reconciliation, Ethopolitics and Religion in Bosnia and Herzegovina," in *Post-Yugoslavia: New Cultural and Political Perspectives*, edited by Dino Abazovic and Mitja Velikonja, Palgrave Macmillan, 2014, pp. 35–56.

Abi-Saab, Georges, "The Specificities of Humanitarian Law," in *Studies and Essays of International Humanitarian Law and the Red Cross Principles in Honour of Jean Pictet*, edited by Christophe Swinarski, Nijhoff, 1984, pp. 265–280.

Authers, John, "Making Good Again: German Compensation for Forced and Slave Laborers," in *The Handbook of Reparations*, edited by Pablo de Greiff, Oxford University Press, 2006, pp. 420–448.

Bassiouni, Cherif, "Assessing Conflict Outcomes: Accountability and Impunity," in *The Pursuit of International Criminal Justice: A World Study on Conflicts, Victimization, and Post-Conflict Justice*, edited by M. Cherif Bassiouni, Intersentia, 2010, pp. 3–39.

Benito, Elizabeth Odio, "Development and Interpretation of Principles of Reparation: The Case Law of the IACHR and its Possible Contributions to the Jurisprudence of the ICC," in *Protecting Humanity: Essays in International Law and Policy in Honour of Navanethem Pillay*, edited by Chile Eboe-Osuji, Nijhoff, 2010, pp. 571–594.

Benito, Elizabeth Odio, "Foreword," in *Reparations for Victims of Genocide, War Crimes and Crimes Against Humanity: Systems in Place and Systems in the Making*, edited by Carla Ferstman, Mariana Goetz, and Alan Stephens, Nijhoff, 2009, pp. 1–3.

Bassiouni, Cherif, "The History of Universal Jurisdiction and Its Place in International Law," in *Universal Jurisdiction: National Courts and the Prosecution of Serious Crimes Under International Law*, edited by Stephen Macedo, University of Pennsylvania Press, 2004, pp. 39–63.

Bassiouni, Cherif, "The Sources and Content of International Criminal Law: A Theoretical Framework," in *International Criminal Law*, edited by Cherif Bassiouni (2nd rev. ed., vol. 1), Transnational Publishers, 1999, pp. 3–127.

Bitti, Gilbert, "Article 21 of the International Criminal Law Statute and the Treatment of Sources of Law in the Jurisprudence of the ICC," in *The Emerging Practice of the*

International Criminal Court, edited by Carsten Stahn and Göran Sluiter, Nijhoff, 2008, pp. 285–304.

Bitti, Gilbert, and Rivas, Gabriela Gonzalez, "The Reparations Provisions for Victims under the Rome Statute of the International Criminal Court," in *Redressing Injustices through Mass Claims Processes, Innovative Responses to Unique Challenges*, The International Bureau of the Permanent Court of Arbitration, Oxford University Press, 2006, pp. 299–322.

Buti, Antonio, "The Notion of Reparations as a Restorative Justice Measure," in *One Country, Two Systems, Three Legal Orders – Perspectives of Evolution: Essays on Macau's Autonomy after the Resumption of Sovereignty by China*, edited by Jorge Costa Oliveira and Paulo Cardinal, Springer, 2009, pp. 191–206.

Chifflet, Pascale, "The Roles and Status of the Victims," in *International Criminal Law and Developments in the Case Law of the ICTY*, edited by Gideon Boas and William A. Schabas, Nijhoff, 2003, pp. 75–111.

Colonomos, Ariel, and Armstrong, Andrea, "German Reparations to the Jews after World War II: A Turning Point in the History of Reparations," in *Handbook of Reparations*, edited by Pablo de Greiff, Oxford University Press, 2006, pp. 390–419.

D'Amato, Anthony, "National Prosecution for International Crimes," in *International Criminal Law*, edited by M. Cherif Bassiouni, Nijhoff, 2008. 3rd edn, Vol. III, 1987, pp. 285–295.

de Greiff, Pablo, and Wierda, Marieke, "The Trust Fund for Victims of the International Criminal Court: Between Possibilities and Constraints," in *Out of the Ashes: Reparation for Victims of Gross and Systematic Violations of Human Rights*, edited by Koen de Feyter et al., Intersentia, 2005, pp. 225–243.

de Vlaming, Frederiek, and Clark, Kate, "War Reparations in Bosnia and Herzegovina: Individual Stories and Collective Interests," in *Narratives of Justice In and Out of the Courtroom*, edited by Zarkov Dubravka and Glasius Marlies, Springer International Publishing, 2014, pp. 163–185.

del Ponte, Carla, "Compensating Victims with Guilty Money," interview with Carla del Ponte, Chief Prosecutor of the ad hoc international criminal tribunals for the former Yugoslavia and Rwanda, in *Judicial Diplomacy: Chronicles and Reports on International Criminal Justice*, The Hague, 9 June 2000.

Dixon, Peter J., "Reparations and the Politics of Recognition," in *Contested Justice: The Politics and Practice of International Criminal Court Interventions*, edited by Carsten Stahn et al., Cambridge University Press, 2015, pp. 326–351.

Dolinko, David, "Punishment," in *The Oxford Handbook of Philosophy of Criminal Law*, edited by John Deigh and David Dolinko, Oxford University Press, 2011, pp. 403–440.

Donat-Cattin, David, "Article 75 – Reparations to Victims," in *Commentary on the Rome Statute of the International Criminal Court: Observers' Notes, Article by Article*, edited by Otto Triffterer, Baden-Baden, 1999, pp. 1399–1412.

Duff, Anthony, "Authority and Responsibility in International Criminal Law," in *The Philosophy of International Law*, edited by Samantha Besson and John Tasioulas, Oxford University Press, 2010, pp. 589–604.

Duggan, Colleen, and Abusharaf, Adila, "Reparation of Sexual Violence in Democratic Transitions: The Search for Gender Justice," in *The Handbook of Reparations*, edited by, pablo de Greiff, Oxford University Press, 2006, pp. 623–649.

Bibliography

Dupuy, Pierre-Marie, "International Criminal Responsibility of the Individual and International Responsibility of the State," in *The Rome Statute of the International Criminal Court: A Commentary*, edited by Antonio Cassese et al., Oxford University Press, 2002, pp. 1085–1099.

Evans, Malcolm, "International Wrongs and National Jurisdiction," in *Remedies in International Law: The Institutional Dilemma*, edited by Malcolm Evans, Hart Publishing, 1998, pp. 173–190.

Fattah, Ezzat A., "From a Guilt Orientation to a Consequence Orientation: A Proposed New Paradigm for the Criminal Law in the 21st Century," in *Beitraege zur Rechtswissenschaft*, edited by Wilfried Küper and Jürgen Welp, C. F. Mueller Juristischer Verlag, 1993, pp. 771–792.

Ferstman, Carla, and Goetz, Mariana, "Reparations Before the International Criminal Court: The Early Jurisprudence on Victim Participation and its Impact on Future Reparations Proceedings," in *Reparations for Victims of Genocide, War Crimes and Crimes Against Humanity: Systems in Place and Systems in the Making*, edited by Carla Ferstman et al., Nijhoff, 2009, pp. 313–350.

Ferstman, Carla, and Rosenberg, Sheri P., "Reparations in Dayton's Bosnia and Herzegovina," in *Reparations for Victims of Genocide, War Crimes and Crimes against Humanity: Systems in Place and Systems in the Making*, edited by Carla Ferstman et al., Nijhoff, 2009, pp. 483–513.

Fletcher, Laurel, "Refracted Justice: The Imagined Victim and the International Criminal Court," in *Contested Justice: The Politics and Practice of International Criminal Court Interventions*, edited by Carsten Stahn et al., Cambridge University Press, 2015, pp. 302–325.

Fox, Hazel, "The International Court of Justice's Treatment of Acts of the State and in Particular the Attribution of Acts of Individuals to States," in *Liber Amicorum Judge Shigeru Oda*, edited by Nisuke Ando et al., Kluwer Law International, 2002, pp. 147–163.

Garkawe, Sam, "The Role and Rights of Victims at the Nuremberg International Military Tribunal," in *The Nuremberg Trials: International Criminal Law since 1945*, edited by Herbert R. Reginbogin, Christoph J. Safferling, and Walter R. Hippel, Kluwer, 2006, pp. 86–94.

Goetz, Mariana, "Reparative Justice at the International Criminal Court: Best Practice or Tokenism?," in *Reparation for Victims of Crimes against Humanity: The Healing Role of Reparation*, edited by Jo-Anne M. Webbers, Routledge, 2014, pp. 53–71.

Greenwood, Christopher, "International Humanitarian Law (Laws of War)," in *The Centennial of the First International Peace Conference*, edited by Frits Kalshoven, Kluwer Law International, 2000, pp. 161–260.

Groenhuijsen, Marc, "Victims' Rights and Restorative Justice: Piecemeal Reform of the Criminal Justice System or a Change of Paradigm?," in *Crime, Victims and Justice: Essays on Principles and Practice*, edited by Hendrik Kaptein and Marijke Malsch, Ashgate Publishing, 2004, pp. 63–79.

Hall, Christopher Keith, "Universal Jurisdiction: New Uses for an Old Tool," in *Justice for Crimes Against Humanity*, edited by Mark Lattimer and Philipe Sands, Hart, 2007, pp. 47–71.

Haslam, Emily, "Victim Participation at the International Criminal Court: A Triumph of Hope Over Experience," in *The Permanent International Criminal Court*, edited by D. McGoldrick, Hart, 2004, pp. 315–334.

Hofmann, Rainer, "Victims of Violations of International Humanitarian Law: Do They Have an Individual Right to Reparation Against States Under International Law?" in *Common Values in International Law: Essays in Honour of Christian Tomuschat*, edited by Pierre-Marie Dupuy et al., Kehl Engel, 2006, pp. 341–359.

Holness, Toni, and Ramji-Nogales, Jaya, "Participation as Reparations: The ECCC and Healing in Cambodia," in *Cambodia's Hidden Scars: Trauma Psychology in the Wake of the Khmer Rouge*, Documentation Center of Cambodia, 2012, pp. 172–188.

Ingadottir, Thordis, "The Trust Fund of the ICC," in *International Crimes, Peace, and Human Rights: The Role of the International Criminal Court*, edited by Dinah Shelton, Transnational, 2000, pp. 149–174.

Ingadottir, Thordis, "The Trust Fund for Victims (Article 79 of the Rome Statute)," in *The International Criminal Court: Recommendations on Policy and Practice – Financing, Victims, Judges, and Immunities*, edited by Thordis Ingadottir, Ardsley, 2003, pp. 111–144.

Jorda, Claude, and de Hamptinne, Jerome, "The Status and Role of the Victims," in *The Rome Statute of the International Criminal Court: A Commentary*, edited by Antonio Cassese et al., Oxford University Press, 2002, pp. 1387–1419.

Kristjánsdóttir, Edda, "International Mass Claims Processes and the ICC Trust Fund for Victims," in *Reparations for Victims of Genocide, War Crimes and Crimes against Humanity*, edited by Carla Ferstman et al., Nijhoff, 2009, pp. 167–195.

Malmström, Susanne, "Restitution of Property and Compensation to Victims," in *Essays on ICTY Procedure and Evidence in Honour of Gabrielle Kirk McDonald*, edited by Richard May et al., Kluwer Law International, 2001, pp. 373–384.

Malone, Linda, "Enforcing International Criminal Law Violations with Civil Remedies: The U.S. Alien Tort Claims Act," in *International Criminal Law*, edited by Cherif Bassiouni, Brill, 2008, pp. 421–455.

Mazzeschi, Riccardo Pisillo, "International Obligations to Provide for Reparation Claims," in *State Responsibility and the Individual – Reparations in Instances of Grave Violations of Human Rights*, edited by Albrecht Randelzhofer and Christian Tomuschat, Kluwer Law International, 1999, pp. 149–172.

Menon, Jaykumar A., "The Low Road: Promoting Civil Redress for International Wrongs," in *Realizing Utopia: The Future of International Law*, edited by Antonio Cassese, Oxford University Press, 2012, pp. 626–642.

Muttukumaru, Christopher, "Reparations to Victims," in *The International Criminal Court: The Making of the Rome Statute, Issues, Negotiations, Results*, edited by Roy S. K. Lee, Kluwer Law International, 1999, pp. 262–293.

Nowak, Manfred, "Reparation by the Human Rights Chamber for Bosnia and Herzegovina," in *Out of the Ashes: Reparations for Victims of Gross and Systematic Human Rights Violations*, edited by Koen de Feyter et al., Intersentia, 2005, pp. 245–288.

Peschke, Katharina, "The Role and Mandates of the ICC Trust Fund for Victims," in *Victims of International Crimes: An Interdisciplinary Discourse*, edited by Thorsten Bonacker and Christoph Safferling, Springer, 2013, pp. 317–327.

Plato, "Protagoras," in *Works of Plato*, edited by Irwin Edman, The Modern Library, 1956, pp. 71–116.

Posner, Eric A., "A Minimalist Reparations Regime for the International Criminal Court," in *Human Rights and International Criminal Law Online Forum*, February 1, 2012, pp. 264–270, available at https://brill.com/view/title/32363.

Ramírez, Sergio Garcia, "Las reparaciones en el sistema interamericano de protección de los derechos humanos," in *El sistema interamericano de protección de los derechos humanos en el umbral del siglo XXI: tomo I*, Corte Interamericana de Derechos Humanos, 2001, pp. 129–158.

Rao, Pemmaraju Sreenivasa, "International Crimes and State Responsibility," in *International Responsibility Today: Essays in Memory of Oscar Schachter*, edited by Maurizio Ragazzi, Nijhoff, 2005, pp. 63–80.

Roht-Arriaza, Naomi, and Orlovsky, Katharine, "A Complementary Relationship: Reparations and Development," in *Transitional Justice and Development: Making Connections*, edited by Pablo de Greiff and Roger Duthie, Social Science Research Council, 2009, pp. 170–213.

Rombouts, Heidy et al., "The Right to Reparation for Victims of Gross and Systematic Human Rights Violations," in *Out of the Ashes: Reparation for Victims of Gross and Systematic Violations of Human Rights*, edited by Koen de Feyter et al., Intersentia, 2005, pp. 345–503.

Scomparin, Laura, "La Victime du Crime et la Juridiction Pénale Internationale," in *La Justice Pénale Internationale entre Passé et Avenir*, edited by M. Chiavario, Giuffrè, 2003, pp. 335–352.

Sen, Amartya, "Global Justice: Beyond International Equity," in *Global Public Goods: International Cooperation in the 21st Century*, edited by I. Kaul, UNDP, 1999, pp. 116–125.

Stern, Brigitte, "Vers une limitation de 'l'irresponsabilité souveraine' des Etats et chefs d'Etat en cas de crime de droit international?," in *Promoting Justice, Human Rights and Conflict Resolution through International Law: Liber Amicorum Lucius Caflisch*, edited by Marcelo Kohen, Nijhoff, 2007, pp. 511–548.

Studzinsky, Silke, "Participation Rights of Victims as Civil Parties and the Challenges of Their Implementation Before the Extraordinary Chambers in the Courts of Cambodia," in *Victims of International Crimes: An Interdisciplinary Discourse*, edited by Thorsten Bonacker and Christoph Safferling, TMC Asser Press, 2013, pp. 175–188.

Timm, Birte, "The Legal Position of Victims in the Rule of Procedure and Evidence," in *International and National Prosecution of Crimes under International Law*, edited by Horst Fischer, Claus Kress, and Sascha Rolf Lüder, Berlin Verlag, 2001.

Tomuschat, Christian, "Reparation in Favour of Individual Victims of Gross Violations of Human Rights and International Humanitarian Law," in *Promoting Justice, Human Rights and Conflict Resolution through International Law*, edited by Marcelo G. Kohen, Nijhoff, 2007, pp. 569–590.

Trindade, Antônio Augusto Cançado, "Complementarity Between State Responsibility and Individual Responsibility for Grave Violations of Human Rights: The Crime of State Revisited," in *International Responsibility Today: Essays in Memory of Oscar Schachter*, edited by Maurizio Ragazzi, Nijhoff, 2005, pp. 253–269.

Trindade, Antônio Augusto Cançado, "State Responsibility in Cases of Massacres: Contemporary Advances in International Justice," Inaugural Address as Honorary Professor to the Chair in International and Regional Human Rights Courts, 10 November 2011 at Utrecht University.

Trindade, Antônio Augusto Cançado, "The Inter-American System of Protection of Human Rights (1948–2009): Evolution, Present State and Perspectives," in *Dossier Documentaires/Documentary File- XL Session d'Enseignement*, Vol. 2, IIDH, 2009.

van Boven, Theo, "The Perspective of the Victim," in *The Universal Declaration of Human Rights: Fifty Years and Beyond*, edited by Yael Danieli and Elsa Stamatopoulou, Baywood, 1999, pp. 13–26.

van Boven, Theo, "The Position of the Victim in the Statute of the International Criminal Court," in *Reflections on the International Criminal Court: Essays in Honour of Adrian Bos*, edited by Herman A. M. von Hebel, Johan G. Lammers, and Jolien Schukking, Asser Press, 1999, pp. 77–90.

Vasiliev, Sergey, "Article 68(3) and Personal Interests of Victims in the Emerging Practice of the ICC," in *The Emerging Practice of the International Criminal Court*, edited by Carsten Stahn and Göran Sluiter, Brill, 2008, pp. 635–690.

Vasiliev, Sergey, "Victim Participation Revisited: What the ICC Is Learning About Itself," in *The Law and Practice of the International Criminal Court*, edited by Carsten Stahn, Oxford University Press, 2015, pp. 1133–1202.

Vasiliev, Sergey, "Trial Process at the ECCC: The Rise and Fall of the Inquisitorial Paradigm in International Criminal Law" in *The Extraordinary Chambers in the Courts of Cambodia: Assessing their Contribution to International Criminal Law*, edited by Simon Meisenberg and Ignaz Stegmiller, Asser Press, 2016, pp. 389–433.

Watson, David, Boucherat, J., and Davis, G., "Reparation for Retributivists," in *Mediation and Criminal Justice: Victims, Offenders and Community*, edited by Martin Wright and Burt Galaway, Sage, 1989, pp. 212–228.

Zedner, Lucia, "England," in *Reparation in Criminal Law: International Perspectives*, edited by Albin Eser and Susanne Walther (vol. 1), Iuscrim, Max-Planck Institute Für Ausländisches und International Strafrecht, 1996.

CASES

ADC Affiliate Limited and ADC & ADMC Management Limited v. *Republic of Hungary*, Case No. ARB/03/16, Award of 2 October 2006, ICSID.

Amoco International Finance Corporation v. *The Islamic Republic of Iran et al.*, Partial Award No. 310–56-3 of 14 July 1987, 15 Iran-United States Claims Tribunal Reports.

Aydin v. *Turkey*, Merits, Grand Chamber, 25 September 1997, 25 EHRR 251.

Baldeón-García v. *Peru*, Merits, Reparations and Costs, 6 April 2006, Series C No. 147.

Bautista de Arellana v. *Columbia* (563/93), CCPR/C/55/D/563/1993 (1995); 3 IHRR 315 (1996).

Blancov v. *Nicaragua* (328/88), CCPR/C/51/D/328/1988 (1994); 2 IHRR 123 (1995).

Bridge of Varvarin case, Landgericht (LG) Bonn, 1 O 361/02, NJW 2004, 525, HuV-I 2/2004, 111–113, confirmed by *Oberlandesgericht* (OLG) Köln, 7 U 8/04.

ECtHR *Kalougeropoulou and Others* v. *Greece and Germany*, Admissibility, 12 December 2002, Application No. 59021/00.

ECtHR *Khatsiyeva et al.* v. *Russia*, Merits, 17 January 2008, Unreported, Application No. 5108/02.

ECtHR *Papamichalopoulos and Others* v. *Greece*, Judgment, 31 October 1995, Application No. 14556/89, Series A, No. 330-B.

ECtHR *Varnava et al.* v. *Turkey*, Merits, Grand Chamber, 18 September 2009, Unreported, Application No. 16064/90.

Factory at Chorzów, Jurisdiction, Judgment No. 8, 1927, *PCIJ*, Series A, no. 17.

Ferida Selimović et al. v. *the Republika Srpska*, Decision on Admissibility and the Merits, 7 March 2003, CH/01/8365 et al.

Ferrini v. *Federal Republic of Germany*, Corte di Cassazione (Sezioni Unite), 11 March 2004, 87 Rivista di diritto internazionale 539.

Final Award, *Eritrea's Damages Claims Between the State of Eritrea and the Federal Democratic Republic of Ethiopia*, 17 August 2009, Eritrea-Ethiopia Claims Commission.

Fitfield v. *Ins. Co. of Pa.*, 47 Pa. 166, 187 (1864).

Hissène Habré case, Appeals Judgment on Reparations, Appeals Chamber of the Extraordinary African Chamber, 27 April 2017.

Human Rights Chamber, *Ferida Selimović et al.* v. *the Republika Srpska*, Decision on Admissibility and Merits, 7 March 2003.

IACtHR, *Aloeboetoe* v. *Suriname*, Reparations Judgment, 10 September 1993.

IACtHR, *Amparo* v. *Venezuela*, Reparations Judgment, 14 September 1996.

IACtHR, *Bámaca Velásquez* v. *Guatemala*, Reparations Judgment, 22 February 2002.

IACtHR, *Blake* v. *Guatemala*, Reparations Judgment, 22 January 1999.

IACtHR, *Bulacio* v. *Argentina*, Merits, Reparations and Costs Judgment, 18 September 2003.

IACtHR, *Case of Acevedo Jaramillo and others* v. *Peru*, Judgment, 7 February 2006.

IACtHR, *Case of Acosta Calderon* v. *Ecuador*, Judgment, 24 June 2005.

IACtHR, *Case of Bámaca Velásquez* v. *Guatemala*, Judgment, 25 November 2000.

IACtHR, *Case of Barrios Alto* v. *Peru*, Judgment, 14 March 2001.

IACtHR, *Case of Barrios Altos* v. *Peru*, Reparations Judgment, 30 November 2001.

IACtHR, *Case of Cantoral Benavides* v. *Peru*, Reparations Judgment, 3 December 2001.

IACtHR, *Case of Caracazo* v. *Venezuela*, Reparations Judgment, 29 August 2002.

IACtHR, *Case of Cesti Hurtado Case*, Reparations Judgment, 31 May 2001.

IACtHR, *Case of Durand and Ugarte* v. *Peru*, Reparations Judgment, 3 December 2001.

IACtHR, *Case of El Amparo* v. *Venezuela*, Reparations Judgment, 14 September 1996.

IACtHR, *Case of Goiburú* et al. v. *Paraguay*, Merits, Reparations and Costs Judgment, 22 September 2006.

IACtHR, *Case of Ituango Massacre* v. *Colombia*, Merits, Reparations and Costs Judgment, 1 July 2006.

IACtHR, *Case of La Cantuta* v. *Peru*, Judgment, 29 November 2006.

IACtHR, *Case of La Rochela Massacre* v. *Colombia*, Judgment, 11 May 2007.

IACtHR, *Case of Mapiripan Massacre* v. *Colombia*, Judgment, 15 September 2005.

IACtHR, *Case of Maritza Urrutia* v. *Guatemala*, Judgment, 27 November 2003.

IACtHR, *Case of Massacre of Plan de Sanchez* v. *Guatemala*, Reparations Judgment, 19 November 2004.

IACtHR, *Case of Miguel Castro Castro Prison* v. *Peru*, Judgment, 25 November 2006.

IACtHR, *Case of Moiwana* v. *Suriname*, Judgment, 15 June 2005.

IACtHR, *Case of Molina Theissen* v. *Guatemala*, Reparations Judgment, 3 July 2004.

IACtHR, *Case of Neira Alegría et al.* v. *Peru*, Reparations Judgment, 19 September 1996.

IACtHR, *Case of Plan de Sánchez Massacre*, Reparations Judgment, 19 November 2004.

IACtHR, *Case of Prison Miguel Castro-Castro* v. *Peru*, Judgment, 25 November 2006.

IACtHR, *Case of Street Children* v. *Guatemala*, Reparations Judgment, 26 May 2001.

IACtHR, *Case of Suárez Rosero* v. *Ecuador*, Reparations Judgment, 20 January 1999.

IACtHR, *Case of Trujillo Oroza* v. *Bolivia*, Reparations Judgment, 27 February 2002.

IACtHR, *Case of Velazquez Rodriguez* v. *Honduras*, Reparations Judgment, 21 July 1989.

IACtHR, *Case of Villagrán Morales et al.* v. *Guatemala, Street Children Case*, Reparations Judgment, 26 May 2001.

IACtHR, *Case of Villagrán Morales et al.* v. *Guatemala, Street Children Case*, Reparations Judgment, 26 May 2001, Separate Opinion of Judge Cançado Trindade.

IACtHR, *Case of Yakye Axa* v. *Paraguay*, Judgment, 17 June 2005.

IACtHR, *Case of Yvon Neptune* v. *Haiti*, Judgment, 6 May 2008.

IACtHR, *Castillo Páez* v. *Peru*, Reparations Judgment, 27 November 1998.

IACtHR, *Gangaram Panday* v. *Suriname*, Merits, Reparations and Costs Judgment, 21 January 1994.

IACtHR, *Garrido Baigorria* v. *Argentina*, Reparations Judgment, 27 August 1998.

IACtHR, *Juan Humberto* Sanchez v. *Honduras*, Judgment, 7 June 2003.

IACtHR, *Loayza Tamayo* v. *Peru*, Reparations Judgment, 27 November 1998.

IACtHR, *Lopez Alvarez* v. *Honduras*, Judgment, 1 February 2006.

IACtHR, *Panel Banca* v. *Guatemala*, Reparations Judgment, 25 May 2001.

IACtHR, *Velásquez-Rodríguez* v. *Honduras*, Merits Judgment, 29 July 1988.

ICC, Appeals Chamber, Judgment on the appeals against the "Decision establishing the Principles and Procedures to be applied to Reparations," 7 August 2012 with AMENDED order for reparations (Annex A) and public annexes 1 and 2, 3 March 2015.

ICC, "Fourth Decision on Victims' Participation," 12 December 2008, ICC-01/05–01/08–320, Pre-Trial Chamber III.

ICC, "Decision on the Applications for Participation in the Proceedings of Applicants a/0327/07 to a/00337/07 and a/0001/08," 2 April 2008, ICC-01/04–01/07–357.

ICC, "Decision on the Applications for Participation in the Proceedings of VPRS1, VPRS2, VPRS3, VPRS4, VPRS5, and VPRS6," 17 January 2006, ICC-01–04-101-t-ENG-Corr (situation phase).

ICC, "Decision on Applications for Participation in Proceedings a/0004/06 to a/0009/06, a/001606, a/0063/06, a/0071/06 to a/0080/06 and a/01/05/06," in the case of *The Prosecutor* v. *Thomas Lubanga Dyilo*, 20 October 2006, ICC-01/04–01/06–601.

ICC, "Decision on Victims' Application for Participation a/0010/06, a/0064/06 to a/0/0070/06, a/0081/06, a/0082/06, a/0084/06 to a/0089/06, a/0091/06 to a/0097/06, a/0099/06, a/0100/06, a/0102/06 to a/0104/06, a/0111/06, a/0113/06 to a/0117/06, a/0120/06, a/0121/06 and a/0123/06 to a/0127/06," in the case of *The Prosecutor* v. *Joseph*

Kony, Vincent Otti, Okot Odhiambo, Dominic Ongwen, 14 March 2008, ICC-02/04–01/05–282, Pre-Trial Phase.

ICC, "Decision on Victims' Participation," in the case of *The Prosecutor* v. *Thomas Lubanga Dyilo,* 18 January 2008, ICC-01/04–01/06–1119.

ICC, *Kony, Otti, Odhiambo & Ongwen,* "Decision on Victims' Applications for Participation a/0014/07 to a/0020/07 and a/0076/07 to a/0125/07," 21 November 2008, ICC 02/04–01/05–356, Pre-Trial Chamber II.

ICC, *Muthaura, Kenyatta and Ali,* "Decision on Victims' Participation at the Confirmation of Charges Hearing and in the Related Proceedings," 26 August 2011, ICC-01/09–02/11–267, Pre-Trial Chamber II.

ICC, "Corrigendum of Decision on the Prosecutor's Application for a Warrant of Arrest, Article 58," 10 February 2006, ICC-01/04–01/06-l-US-Exp-Con, Pre-Trial Chamber I.

ICC, *The Prosecutor* v. *Lubanga,* "Observations on the Sentence and Reparations by Victims," ('V01 Group'), 18 April 2012, ICC- 01/04–01/06.

ICC, *The Prosecutor* v. *Lubanga,* "Observations of the V02 Group of Victims on Sentencing and Reparations," ('V02 Group'), 18 April 2012, ICC-01/04–01/06.

ICC, *The Prosecutor* v. *Thomas Lubanga Dyilo,* "Decision of the Appeals Chamber on the Joint Application of Victims a/0001/06 to a/0003/06 and a/0105/06 Concerning the Directions and Decision of the Appeals Chamber," 2 February 2007, ICC-01/04–01/06–925, Separate opinion of Judge Pikis.

ICC, *The Prosecutor* v. *Thomas Lubanga Dyilo,* "Judgment on the Appeal of Mr. Thomas Lubanga Dyilo Against the Decision on the Defence Challenge to the Jurisdiction of the Court pursuant to article 19 (2) (a) of the Statute of 3 October 2006," 14 December 2006, ICC-01/04–01/06–772.

ICC, *The Prosecutor* v. *Thomas Lubanga,* "Judgment on the Appeals of the Prosecutor and the Defence against Trial Chamber I's Decision on Victims' Participation," 18 January 2008, ICC-01/04–01/06–1432.

ICC, *The Prosecutor* v. *Thomas Lubanga Dyilo,* "Scheduling Order Concerning Timetable for Sentencing and Reparations," 14 March 2012, ICC-01/04–01/06–2844.

ICC, *The Prosecutor* v. *Thomas Lubanga Dyilo,* "Decision Establishing the Principles and Procedures to Be Applied to Reparations," 7 August 2012, ICC-01/04–01/06.

ICC, *Situation in the Democratic Republic of Congo,* "Decision on the Application for Participation in the Proceedings of VPRS1, VPRS2, VPRS3, VPRS4, VPRS5 and VPRS6," 17 January 2006, ICC-01/04–101-tEN-Corr.

ICC, *Situation in the Democratic Republic of the Congo,* "Judgment on the Prosecutor's Application for Extraordinary Review of Pre-Trial Chamber I's 31 March 2006 Decision Denying Leave to Appeal," 13 July 2006, ICC-01/04–168.

ICC, *Situation in Kenya,* "Decision on Victims' Participation in Proceedings," 3 November 2010, ICC-01/09–24.

ICC, *Statement of the ICC Deputy Prosecutor in the opening of the Prosecutor's case in Katanga and Chui,* "ICC Cases and Opportunity for Communities in

Ituri to Come Together and Move Forward," ICC-OTP-20080627-PR332, 27 June 2008.

ICC, *The Prosecutor v. Thomas Lubanga Dyilo*, "Order Approving the Proposed Plan of the Trust Fund for Victims in Relation to Symbolic Collective Reparations," ICC-01/04–01/06, 21 October 2016.

ICC, *The Prosecutor v. Germain Katanga*, "Order Instructing the Parties and Participants to File Observations in Respect of the Reparations Proceedings," 1 October 2015, ICC-01/04–01/07–3532-tENG.

ICC, *The Prosecutor v. William Samoei Ruto and Joshua Arap Sang*, "Decision on the Requests Regarding Reparations" ICC-01/09–01/11, 1 July 2016.

ICJ, *Application of the Convention on the Prevention and Punishment of the Crime of Genocide (Croatia v. Serbia)*, Judgment, 5 February 2015.

ICJ, *Application of the Convention on the Prevention and Punishment of the Crime of Genocide (Bosnia and Herzegovina v. Serbia and Montenegro)*, Judgment, 26 February 2007.

ICJ, *Arrest Warrant Case (Democratic Republic of Congo v. Belgium)*, ICJ Reports 3 (2002), Opinions of Judges Guillaume and Rezek.

ICJ, *Case Concerning Ahmadou Sadio Diallo (Republic of Guinea v. Democratic Republic of the Congo)*, Judgment, 30 November 2010.

ICJ, *Case Concerning Ahmadou Sadio Diallo (Republic of Guinea v. Democratic Republic of the Congo)*, Judgment, 30 November 2010, Separate Opinion of Judge Cançado Trindade.

ICJ, *Case Concerning Application of the Convention on the Prevention and Punishment of the Crime of Genocide (Bosnia and Herzegovina v. Serbia and Montenegro)*, Judgment, ICJ Reports 2007.

ICJ, *Case Concerning Armed Activities on the Territory of the Congo (Democratic Republic of the Congo v. Uganda)*, Judgment, ICJ Reports 2005.

ICJ, *Case Concerning Avena and Other Mexican Nationals (Mexico v. United States of America)*, Judgment, 31 March 2004.

ICJ, *Case Concerning Gabčíkovo-Nagymaros Project (Hungary v. Slovakia)*, Judgment, ICJ Reports 1997.

ICJ, *Case Concerning the Jurisdictional Immunities of the State (Germany v. Italy: Greece intervening)*, Judgment, 3 February 2012.

ICJ, *Case Concerning the Jurisdictional Immunities of the State (Germany v. Italy: Greece intervening)*, Judgment, 3 February 2012, Dissenting Opinion of Judge Cançado Trindade.

ICJ, *Case Concerning Legal Consequences of the Construction of a Wall in the Occupied Palestinian Territory*, Advisory Opinion, ICJ Reports 136, 2004.

ICJ, *Case Concerning Pulp Mills on the River Uruguay (Argentina v. Uruguay)*, Judgment, 20 April 2010.

ICJ, *Reparation for Injuries Suffered in the Service of the United Nations*, Advisory Opinion, ICJ Reports 1949.

ICTR, *The Prosecutor v. Jean-Paul Akayesu*, Judgment, 2 September 1998, Case No. ICTR-96–4-T.

Bibliography

ICTY, Trial Chamber, *The Prosecutor* v. *Furundžija*, Judgment, 10 December 1998, IT-95–17/1-T.

ICTY, Trial Chamber, *The Prosecutor* v. *Obrenović*, "Sentencing Judgment," 10 December 2003, IT-02–60/2-S.

ICTY, *The Prosecutor* v. *Radislav Krstić*, IT-98–33-T.

Ivica Kevesevic v. the *Federation of Bosnia and Herzegovina*, 10 September 1998, Case No. CH/97/46.

Jones v. Whalley [2006] 2 Criminal Law Review 67, Divisional Court, on appeal to the House of Lords, *Jones v. Whalley* [2006] 4 All ER 11.

Josip, Bozana and Tomislav Matanovic v. *the Republika Srpska*, Decision on Admissibility, 13 September 1996, Decision on the Merits, 6 August 1997, Decisions on Admissibility and Merits, March 1996–December 1997, Case No. CH/96/01.

LG&E Energy Corp., LG&E Capital Corp., LG&E International Inc. v. *Argentine Republic*, Case No. ARB/02/1, Award of 25 July 2007, ICSID.

M/V "Saiga" (No. 2) (Saint Vincent and the Grenadines v. *Guinea)*, Judgment, ITLOS Reports 1999.

Palic v. Republika Srpska, Decision on Admissibility and Merits, 11 January 2001, Case No. CH/99/3196.

PCIJ, The S.S. *Lotus Case*, PCIJ Ser. A, No. 10, p. 4 (1927).

Prefecture Voiotia v. *Federal Republic of Germany*, Hellenic Supreme Court, 4 May 2000, Case No. 11/2000.

The Prosecutor v. *Charles Ghankay Taylor*, Judgment, Special Court for Sierra Leone, 18 May 2012, SCSL, 03–01-T.

The Prosecutor v. *Charles Ghankay Taylor*, Appeals Judgment, Special Court for Sierra Leone, 26 September 2013, SCSL, 03–01-A.

Rasim Jusufović v. *the Republika Srpska*, Decision on Admissibility and Merits, 9 June 2000, Case No. CH/98/698.

R (on the application of Gladstone Pic) v. *Manchester City Magistrates* [2005] All ER 56, Queen's Bench Division.

Rodriquez v. Uruguay (322/88), CCPR/C/51/D/322/1988 (1994); 2 IHRR 12 (1995).

Sosa v. Alvarez-Machain, 124 U.S. 2739, 2775 (2004).

Sosa v. Alvarez-Machain, Supreme Court, 542 U.S. 692 (2004).

Trial of Major War Criminals before the International Military Tribunal, Nuremberg, 14 November 1945–1 October 1946 (Nuremberg: International Military Tribunal, 1947).

Ttofinis v. Theochandes (1983) 2 Cyprus Law Reports, 363, Cyprus Supreme Court.

Unkovic v. *Federation of Bosnia and Herzogovina*, Decision on Admissibility and Merits, 9 November 2001, Case No. CH/99/2150.

REPORTS

Africa Legal Aid, *The Cairo-Arusha Principles on Universal Jurisdiction in Respect of Gross Human Rights Offences* (2002).

Amnesty International, *Bosnia-Herzegovina: Rape and Sexual Abuse by Armed Forces* (1993).

Bibliography

Amnesty International, *International Criminal Court: Ensuring an Effective Trust Fund for Victims*, IOR 40/005/2001 (1 September 2001).

Amnesty International, *Old Crimes, Same Suffering: No Justice for Survivors of Wartime Rape in North-East Bosnia and Herzegovina* (2012).

Amnesty International, *Public Statement – Bosnia and Herzegovina: Amnesty International Calls for Justice and Reparation for Survivors of War Crimes of Sexual Violence* (2010).

Amnesty International, *Universal Jurisdiction: The Duty of States to Enact and Implement Legislation* (September 2001).

Amnesty International, *Universal Jurisdiction: 14 Principles on Effective Exercise of Universal Jurisdiction* (1999).

Amnesty International, *"Whose Justice?" – The Women of Bosnia and Herzegovina Are Still Waiting* (2009).

Annual Report of the European Court of Human Rights, Foreword by Jean Paul Costa, President of the European Court of Human Rights (2006).

Basic Principles and Guidelines on the Right to Remedy and Reparation for Victims of Gross Violations of International Human Rights Law and Serious Violations of International Humanitarian Law, General Assembly Resolution 60/147 U.N. Doc. A/RES/60/147 (21 March 2006).

FIDH, "Enhancing Victims' Rights Before the ICC: A View from Situation Countries on Victims' Rights at the International Criminal Court," November 2013, pp. 27–28, available at https://fidh.org/IMG/pdf/fidh_victims rights_621a_nov2013_ld.pdf.

Forman, Shepard, "The International Criminal Court Reparations to Victims of Crimes (Article 75 of the Rome Statute) and the Trust Fund (Article 79): Recommendations for the Court Rules of Procedure and Evidence," Prologue, prepared by the Center for International Cooperation, New York University, for the 26 July–13 August 1999 Meeting of the Preparatory Commission for the International Criminal Court.

Helsinki Watch, Human Rights Watch, *War Crimes in Bosnia-Herzegovina* (1992).

Human Rights Center, University of California, Berkeley School of Law, "The Victims' Court: A Study of 622 Victim Participants at the International Criminal Court," p. 3, available at https://law.berkeley.edu/wp-content/uploads/2015/04/V P_report_2015_final_full2.pdf.

International Council on Human Rights Policy, *Hard Cases: Bringing Human Rights Violators to Justice Abroad: A Guide to Universal Jurisdiction* (1999).

International Law Association, *Final Report on the Exercise of Universal Jurisdiction in Respect of Gross Human Rights Offences*, Committee on International Human Rights Law and Practice, London Conference (2000).

International Law Association, *Remedies for Victims of Armed Conflict*, 74 International Law Association Report Conference 291 (2010).

Letter of the President of the ICTR to the United Nations Secretary-General, annex to a letter of 14 December 2000 by the United Nations Secretary-General, Kofi Annan, to the United Nations Security Council, UN Doc. S/2000/1198 (15 December 2000).

Liesbeth Zegveld, and Jeff Handmaker, *Universal Jurisdiction: State of Affairs and Ways Ahead: A Policy Paper*, International Institute of Social Studies Working Paper 532 (January 2012).

Linda Popic, and Belma Panjeta, *Compensation, Transitional Justice and Conditional International Credit in Bosnia and Herzegovina*, Independent Research Publication (2010).

Mohamad Suma and Cristián Correa, *Report and Proposals for the Implementation of Reparations in Sierra Leone*, International Center for Transitional Justice (December 2009).

Princeton Project on Universal Jurisdiction, *The Princeton Principles on Universal Jurisdiction* (2001).

Redress, *The International Criminal Court's Trust Fund for Victims Analysis and Options for the Development of Further Criteria for the Operation of the Trust Fund for Victims*, Discussion Document (December 2003).

Redress, *Universal Jurisdiction in Europe: Criminal Prosecutions in Europe Since 1990 for War Crimes, Crimes Against Humanity, Torture and Genocide* (1999).

Reparations Before the International Criminal Court: Issues and Challenges, Conference Report, Peace Palace, The Hague (12 May 2011).

Report of the International Commission of Inquiry on Darfur to the United Nations Secretary-General, 25 January 2005, Pursuant to Security Council Resolution 1564 of 18 September 2004.

Report of the International Commission of Inquiry on Darfur to the United Nations Secretary-General, citing a letter dated 12 October 2000 of Judge C. Jorda to the United Nations Secretary General.

Report of the Working Group on Procedural Matters of 13 July 1998 (UN Doc. A/CONF.183/C.1/WGPM/L2/Add.7).

Report on the Establishment of an International Criminal Court, Draft Statute and Draft Final Act, U.N. Doc. A/Conf.183/2/Add.1 (1998).

Report on the Situation of Human Rights in the Territory of the Former Yugoslavia Submitted by Tadeusz Mazowiecki, Special Rapporteur of the Commission on Human Rights, U.N. ESCOR, 49th Sess., Annex, Agenda Item 27, U.N. Doc. E/CN.4/1993/50 (1993).

Report 21/00, Case 12.059, Carmen Aguiar de Lapacó (Argentina) (29 February 2000).

Report to the President by Mr. Justice Jackson, International Conference on Military Trials (6 June 1945).

Revised final report of the Special Rapporteur on the question of impunity of perpetrators of human rights violations (civil and political), E/CN.4/Sub.2/1997/20/Re v.1 (2 October 1997).

Rodri C. Williams, *Post Conflict Property Restitution in Bosnia: Balancing Reparations and Durable Solutions in the Aftermath of Displacement*, TESEV International Symposium on "Internal Displacement in Turkey and Abroad," Istanbul (5 December 2006).

The Group of Experts for Cambodia, *Report of the Group of Experts for Cambodia Pursuant to General Assembly Resolution 52/135*, 1, U.N. Doc. S/1999/231, A/53/850 (16 March 1999).

246   *Bibliography*

Victims' Compensation and Participation, Appendix to a letter dated 12 October 2000 from the President of the ICTY addressed to the Secretary-General, ANNEX to UN Doc. S/2000/1063 (3 November 2000).

RESOLUTIONS

Basic Principles and Guidelines on the Right to a Remedy and Reparation for Victims of Gross Violations of International Human Rights Law and International Humanitarian Law, General Assembly Resolution A/RES/60/147 (December 16, 2005).

Resolution ICC-ASP/1/Res.6 and Annex to same (9 September 2002).

Resolution ICC-ASP/3/Res.7, Establishment of the Secretariat of the Trust Fund for Victims (10 September 2004).

Resolution on the Establishment of a Fund for the Benefit of Victims of Crimes Within the Jurisdiction of the Court, and the Families of such Victims, ICC-ASP /1/Res.6 (2002).

Resolution of the Establishment of the Secretariat of the Trust Fund for Victims, ICC-ASP/3/Res.7 (2004).

Resolution on the Procedure for the Nomination and Election of Members of the Board of Directors of the Trust Fund for the Benefit of Victims, ICC-ASP/1/Res.7 (2202) (9 September 2002).

Security Council Resolution 1757 (2007), Adopted by the Security Council at its 5685th meeting, on 30 May 2007.

Situation in Uganda, Notification of the Board of Directors of the Trust Fund for Victims in accordance with Regulation 50 of the Regulations of the Trust Fund for Victims, 25 January 2008, ICC-02/04.

"The Situation in the Middle East," Security Council Resolution 1644 (2005), 15 December 2005, S/RES/1644.

United Nations Guidance Note of the Secretary General: Reparations for Conflict-Related Sexual Violence of June, 2014.

United Nations Voluntary Fund for Victims of Torture, G.A. Res 36/151, U.N. Doc A/RES/36/151 (16 December 1981).

United Nations Voluntary Trust Fund on Contemporary Forms of Slavery, G.A. Res. 46/122, U.N. Doc A/RES/46/122 (17 December 1991).

TREATIES AND DOMESTIC LEGISLATION

Agreement between the Government of the Federal Democratic Republic of Ethiopia and the Government of the State of Eritrea, 12 December 2000, 40 ILM 260 (2001).

Agreement for the Prosecution and Punishment of the Major War Criminals of the European Axis, and Charter of the International Military Tribunal, London, 8 August 1945 (London Charter).

American Convention on Human Rights, 22 November 1969, entry into force 18 July 1978, 114 UNTS 123.

American Law Institute, Restatement (Third), *The Foreign Relations Law of the United States* (1987).

Charter for the International Military Tribunal for the Far East, Tokyo, 19 January 1946 (Tokyo Charter).

Convention against Torture and Other Cruel, Inhuman or Degrading Treatment or Punishment, United Nations, Treaty Series, vol. 1465.

Declaration of Basic Principles of Justice for Victims of Crime and Abuse of Power, General Assembly Resolution 40/34, 29 November 1985.

Draft Agreement between the United Nations and the Royal Government of Cambodia Concerning the Prosecution under Cambodian Law of Crimes Committed During the Period of Democratic Kampuchea, 17 March 2003, approved by GA Res. 57/228B, 13 May 2003.

European Convention for the Protection of Human Rights and Fundamental Freedoms, 4 November 1950, entry into force 3 September 1953, CETS No. 5, as amended by Protocol 11 CETS No. 155, 11 May 1994, entry into force 1 November 1998.

European Convention on the Compensation of Victims of Violent Crimes, European Treaty Series, European Treaty Series No. 116, Strasbourg, 24. XI.1983.

European Convention on Non-Applicability of Statutes of Limitations for Crimes against Humanity and War Crimes (Inter-European), Europe. T.S. No. 82.

French Code of Criminal Procedure, entered into force 2 March 1959. General Framework Agreement for Peace in Bosnia and Herzegovina, 35 ILM 75 (1996), "Dayton Agreement."

Hague Convention (IV) Respecting the Laws and Customs of War on Land, 18 October 1907, entry into force 26 January 1910, 9 UKTS (1910).

Inter-American Convention on Human Rights of 1979 (Pact of San José), adopted at the Inter-American Specialized Conference on Human Rights, San José, Costa Rica, 22 November 1969.

Protocol Additional to the Geneva Conventions of 12 August 1949 and Relating to the Protection of Victims of International Armed Conflicts, 8 June 1977, entry into force 7 December 1978, 1125 UNTS (1979).

Protocol to the African Charter on Human and Peoples' Rights on the Establishment of an African Court on Human and Peoples' Rights, 9 June 1998, entry into force, 25 January 2004, OAU/LEG/MIN/AFCHPR/PROT.1 rev.2 (1997).

Rome Statute of the International Criminal Court, U.N. Doc. A/CONF.183/9.

Second Protocol to the Hague Convention for the Protection of Cultural Property in the Event of Armed Conflict, 26 March 1999, entry into force 9 March 2004, 38 ILM (1999).

United Nations Convention on the Non-Applicability of Statutes of Limitations for War Crimes and Crimes Against Humanity, 26 November 1968, 754 U.N.T. S. 73.

Universal Declaration of Human Rights, General Assembly Resolution 217A (III), 10 December 1948.

UN Transitional Administration in East Timor (UNTAET): Reg. 2000/15, *On the Establishment of Panels with Exclusive Jurisdiction over Serious Criminal Offences*, 6 June 2000.

United Nations Trust Fund for Chile, G.A. Res. 33/174, U.N. Doc A/RES/33/174 (20 December 1978).

United Nations, Vienna Convention on the Law of Treaties, 23 May 1969, United Nations, Treaty Series, vol. 1155.

Victims of Terrorism Compensation Act, Title VIII of the Omnibus Diplomatic Security and Antiterrorism Act, 22 U.S.C. 4801 (1986).

Index

access to justice, 8, 99
accountability, 2, 171, 183, 208
accused, 73
accused-centric approach, 198
Acosta Calderon v. Ecuador, Judgment, 34
acquittal, 76, 120
actus reus, 158
Additional Protocol I to the Geneva
  Conventions, 44
Additional Protocol to the Geneva
  Conventions of 12 August 1949, and
  Relating to the Protection of Victims of
  International Armed Conflicts, 43, 44
Additional Protocol to the Geneva
  Conventions of 12 August 1949, and
  Relating to the Protection of Victims of
  Non-International Armed Conflicts, 43
adjudication of civil reparation, 151
administrative mechanisms, 5, 6, 10, 11, 80, 111,
  126, 127, 128, 131, 135, 146, 150, 198, 208
affected communities, 143
African Court of Human and Peoples'
  Rights, 31
African Union, 164
aftermath of conflicts, 20
aggression, 3, 7, 36, 75, 118
Agreement for the Prosecution and
  Punishment of the Major War Criminals
  of the European Axis, 52
Al Mahdi case, 107, 110
Alien Tort Claims Act. *See* ATCA
Alien Tort Claims Statute, 191
Aloeboetoe v. Suriname, Reparations
  Judgment, 34
American Convention on Human Rights, 30,
  33, 246

American legal system, 154
Amici Curiae, 195
amnesties, 12, 185
apology, 40, 95, 203, 211
application-based approach, 92
arbitral tribunal, 29
archetype of victims, 4
armed conflict, 43, 44, 46, 98, 156, 214
assault and battery, 191
Assembly of States Parties, 75, 130,
  213
assignment of rights, 203
assistance programs, 3, 132
ATCA, 11, 185, 186, 187
atrocity, xxvi, 18
Austria, 151
average harm, 89, 110

balance of probabilities, 93
Baldeón-García v. Peru, Merits, Reparations
  and Costs Judgment, 31
Balkans, 155, 158
Balkans War, 155
Bámaca Velásquez v. Guatemala, Reparations
  Judgment, 34, 41
Bangui, xxvi
Barrios Altos v. Peru, Reparations Judgment,
  38
Basic Principles and Guidelines on the Right
  to Remedy and Reparation for Victims of
  Gross Violations of International Human
  Rights Law and Serious Violations of
  International Humanitarian Law, 1, 8,
  45
Bassiouni, Cheriff, 176
Bemba case, 118, 120, 121, 139, 211

250 *Index*

beneficiaries, 31, 47, 50, 77, 80, 83, 88, 92, 103, 104, 105, 107
Blake v. *Guatemala*, Judgment, 34
Bogoro, 91
Bosnia and Herzegovina, xxi, xxii, 11, 28, 50, 155, 156, 157, 159, 160, 161, 162, 163, 165, 190–193, 218, 221, 224, 234, 235, 236, 242, 243, 244, 245, 247
  Federation of, 161
  State of, 161
Bosnia Genocide case, 157
Bottigliero, Ilaria, 6
Braithwaite, John, 19
Brazil, 153
broader mass atrocities, 32
Buddhist, 72
budget, 127
burden proof, 194

Cambodia, 73
Canada, 189
Cançado Trindade, Antônio Augusto, xvii, 1, 24, 25, 40, 128, 158, 170, 177, 240, 242
Cantoral Benavides v. *Peru*, Reparations Judgment, 37
CAR situation, 139, 143, 211
Caracazo v. *Venezuela*, Reparations Judgment, 35
Case Concerning Ahmadou Sadio Diallo (Republic of Guinea v. *Democratic Republic of the Congo)*, Judgment, 1, 28
Case Concerning Application of the Convention on the Prevention and Punishment of the Crime of Genocide (Bosnia and Herzegovina v. *Serbia and Montenegro)*, Judgment, 28
Case Concerning Armed Activities on the Territory of the Congo (Democratic Republic of the Congo v. *Uganda)*, Judgment, 28
Case Concerning Avena and Other Mexican Nationals (Mexico v. *United States of America)*, Judgment, 28, 29
Case Concerning jurisdictional immunities of the State (Germany v. *Italy)*, 49
Case Concerning Pulp Mills on the River Uruguay (Argentina v. *Uruguay)*, Judgment, 28
Castillo Páez v. *Peru*, Reparations Judgment, 41
causation, 84, 102, 108
  causal link, 108

Central African Republic
  CAR, 98, 100, 113, 134, 143
Chappell, Louise, 121
charged, 210
charitable purposes, 131
Charter for the International Military Tribunal for the Far East, 52
child soldiers, 89
child victims, 83
Chorzów Factory, 24, 27
civil awards, 194
civil claimant, 153
civil claims, 2, 5, 151
civil judgments, 184
civil litigation. *See* human rights civil litigation
civil party, 69
civil recovery, 184
civil redress, 127
civil remedies, 3
civil reparation in criminal proceedings, 154
civil responsibility, 128
civil suits, 195
Clark, Kate, 159
close personal relationship, 105
Code of Hamurabi, 15
cohesive understanding, 212
collapse of judicial institutions, 207
collective. *See* collective reparation
collective awards, 111
collective reparation, 32, 37, 38, 68, 113, 114, 115, 141
comity, 180
Commission for Real Property Claims of Displaced Persons and Refugees (CRPC), 50, 160, 161
Common Article 3 to the four Geneva Conventions of 1949, 44
common law system, 152
community condemnation, 195
community reparations, 85
compensation, 1, 8, 18, 28, 33, 40, 42, 44, 45, 47, 49, 50, 54, 56, 57, 58, 59, 60, 61, 62, 64, 65, 69, 77, 78, 92, 94, 101, 129, 132, 137, 138, 140, 147, 153, 157, 159, 163, 164, 166, 188, 191, 193, 195, 203, 216, 229, 231
complainant, 152
complementary, 101, 199
composition of the Court, 213
concept of justice, 2
conflict, 2
context-sensitive, 143

contributions from States, xxvi, 134, 213
Convention against Torture and Other Cruel, Inhuman or Degrading Treatment or Punishment, 7, 247
Convention of the Rights of the Child, Article 39, 30
Convention on the Prevention and Punishment of the Crime of Genocide, 158
conviction, 210
conviction-based reparation system, 99
co-perpetrator, 82, 94
corporate liability, 185
corporations, 195
corruption, 98, 106
cost effective, 93
Côte d'Ivoire, 112, 143
court of last resort, 205
crime, 1
  grave nature of, 178
crimes against humanity, 3, 7, 48, 50, 55, 75, 98, 118, 119, 159, 164, 169, 173, 179, 180, 186, 189, 215
criminal conviction, 98
criminal dimension, 3
criminal law remedies, 17
criminal liability, 18
criminal processes, 2
criminal responsibility, 128
Croatia, 158
cruel, inhuman, and degrading treatment, 191
Cryer, Robert, 171
cultural awareness, 105
cultural heritage, 76, 94, 95, 97
cultural sites, 95
customary international law, 44, 45, 171, 172, 173, 182, 183, 196, 207

Dayton Peace Agreement, 160
  Commission for Real Property Claims of Refugees and Displaced Persons, 161
  Human Rights Chamber, 30, 46, 160, 161
de Greiff, Pablo, 25
Declaration of Basic Principles of Justice for Victims of Crime and Abuse of Power, 45
delay, 210
Democratic Republic of the Congo, 82, 134
destruction or unavailability of evidence, 96
deterrence, 16, 17, 86, 190
deterrent effect, 194

deterrent role, 13
development aid, 202
dialogue, xxvi
dignity, xxvi
direct victim, 34
diverging perspectives, 115
Dixon, Peter, 117, 133
dogmas, 199
domestic claims commissions, 208
domestic courts, 3, 197
donors, 73
Draft Agreement between the United Nations and the Royal Government of Cambodia Concerning the Prosecution under Cambodian Law of Crimes Committed During the Period of Democratic Kampuchea, 66
Draft Implementation Plan for collective reparations to victims, 87
Dretelj detention camp, 192
Duch, 70
duties of Judges, 194
Dwertmann, Eva, 6

EAC, 164
earmarked contributions, 134
Eboe-Osuji, Chile, 101
ECCC, xix, 11, 53, 63, 66, 67, 68, 69, 70, 71, 72, 73, 74, 203, 207, 208, 232, 236, 238
  Case 001, 70
  Case 002, 70
economic loss, 96
Economic Resilience Facility, 97
education, iv, 35, 38, 70, 72, 92, 131, 142
Educational, Scientific and Cultural Organization (UNESCO), 97
Egypt, 188
enemies of humanity, 189
enforced disappearance, 34, 161
enforcement of the awards, 197
Eritrea, 216
Eritrea's Damages Claims Between the State of Eritrea and the Federal Democratic Republic of Ethiopia, Final Award, 29
Eritrea-Ethiopia Claims Commission, 29, 50, 216, 239
Ethiopia, 216
European Convention for the Protection of Human Rights and Fundamental Freedoms, 30

252 Index

European Convention on Non-Applicability of Statutes of Limitations for Crimes against Humanity and War Crimes, 175
European Court of Human Rights, xxiv, 2, 31, 32, 45, 46, 48, 160, 244
evidence of damage, 36
ex aequo et bono, 89
exclusion of victims, 201
expectations, 206
expeditious, 209
expertise of Judges, 201
experts, 37, 92, 94, 99, 108, 110, 113
expressive role, 13
external funding, 72
extradition, 180
Extraordinary African Chamber, 164. *See* EAC
Extraordinary Chambers in the Courts of Cambodia, 66–73. *See* ECCC
  civil party, 69
  reparations, xxi, xxvi, 1, 3, 4, 5, 12, 13, 17, 30, 32, 33, 34, 35, 43, 44, 45, 57, 58, 59, 65, 67, 78, 79, 80, 85, 86, 87, 88, 89, 100, 101, 109, 110, 111, 123, 129, 150, 151, 152, 164, 165, 195, 196, 205, 206, 207, 210, 211, 240, 242
extraterritorial litigation, 194
extraterritoriality, 187

fair and impartial trial, 143
familial relationship, 93
family, 105
family member
  death, 89
  loss, 89
Ferida Selimović et al. v. the Republika Srpska, Decision on Admissibility and Merits, 160
Ferrini v. Federal Republic of Germany, Corte di Cassazione (Sezioni Unite), 48
financial contributions, 140
fines, 146
Fletcher, Laurel, 117
foreign courts, 163, 193
forfeitures, 146
forum of necessity, 189, 196
France, 152, 189, 192, 195
freezing assets, 195
fund raising, 138, 141, 146

Gangaram Panday v. Suriname, Merits, Reparations and Costs Judgment, 36
Garrido and Baigorria v. Argentina, Reparations Judgment, 34

gender sensitive, 143
gender-based crimes, 120
General Assembly Resolution 52/135, 66, 67, 245
general contributions, 134
General Framework Agreement for Peace in Bosnia and Herzegovina, 50
genocide, 3, 7, 50, 55, 62, 75, 118, 119, 157, 158, 159, 169, 173, 179, 180, 183, 191, 215, 229
Germany, xix, xx, xxi, xxii, 16, 48, 49, 128, 151, 152, 181, 238, 239, 242, 243
global common, 177
global perspective, 208
grants for survivors, 142
Greece, 48
gross human rights violation, 181
guarantees of non-recurrence, 26
guarantees of non-repetition, 1, 8, 95

Habré, Hissène, 164, 165, 208
Hague Convention (IV) Respecting the Laws and Customs of War on Land, 44
harm, 89
Hart, H. L. A., 14
health and well-being, 143
healthcare, 62, 70
Hema, 82
hierarchy, 123, 124, 201
hierarchy of victimhood, 121
high seas, 177
historic monuments, 131
historical dichotomies, 199
HIV/Aids, 188
hope, xxvi
hospitals, 131
hostis humani generis, 176
housing, 92
Housing and Property Claims Commission, 50
human rights, 2
  bodies, 29
  law, 2
  mechanisms, 2, 9, 162
  norms, 46
  system, 31, 201
Human Rights Center at the University of California, Berkely School of Law, 112, 206
human rights Court, 140
human suffering, xxvi

Index

humanitarian aid, 114
humanitarian assistance, 202
humanitarian purposes, 131
humanity, xxvi
hurt, injury or damage, 108
hybrid criminal tribunals, 2

IACtHR, xx, 10, 29, 31, 32, 33, 34, 35, 36, 37, 38, 39, 40, 41, 105, 239, 239
ICC Rules of Procedure and Evidence
  Rule 85, 93, 103, 130
  Rule 98(2), 107, 130
  Rule 98(1–4), 130
  Rule 98(4), 131
  Rule 98(5), 130
ICC Statute. *See* Rome Statute
ICC Trust Fund Regulations
  Regulation 69, 112
ICRC Commentary on Customary
  International Humanitarian Law, 48
ICTY Rules of Procedure and Evidence of the
  Tribunal
  Rule 106, 157
identification of beneficiaries, 106
identification of victims, 110
identifying information, 97
identity of victim, 34
immaterial damage, 35
implementation of the reparation order, 87, 202, 203
implementation phase, 107
implementation plan, 140
implementation stage, 91
impunity, 171, 208
Impunity of Perpetrators of Human Rights
  Violations (civil and political)Report,
  169
income generating activities, 92
indigence, 73, 85
indigenous group, 34
indirect victims, 34, 83, 89, 104, 105, 141
individual legal duty to repair, 9, 164
information sessions, 142
infrastructure, 70
injuries, 156
Institut de Droit International, 189
Institute for War and Peace, 195
institutional knowledge, 73
institutions, 103
Inter-American Commission for Human
  Rights, 31, 32

Inter-American Convention on Human
  Rights, 30, 46
  Article 25, 31
  Article 63(1), 33
Inter-American Court of Human Rights, 31
Inter-American System of Human Rights, 32
International Center for Transitional
  Justice, 83
International Committee of the Red Cross,
  48
International Convention on the Elimination
  of All Forms of Racial Discrimination,
  Article 6, 30
International Court of Justice, 28, 29, 157,
  159, 162
International Covenant on Civil and Political
  Rights, 30
international crimes, 1, 7, 198, 199
International Criminal Court, 200
  definition of victims, 103
  limits on jurisdiction, 148
  reparation for victims, 80
  reparations for sexual and gender-based
    violence, 119–122
  reparations order, 85
international criminal justice, 2, 8, 198
  criminal dimension, 21
international criminal law, 2, 8, 17, 23, 31,
  199
  individual perpetrators, 52
  role of national courts, 150, 167, 205
  state-based approach, 22, 144
international criminal tribunal, 32
International Criminal Tribunal for
  Rwanda, 56
International Criminal Tribunal for the former
  Yugoslavia, 56, 156, 160
  reparations for victims, 59
international dimension, 150
international human rights law, 24, 25, 30, 31,
  47, 203
international humanitarian law, 24, 25, 41–49,
  57, 66, 112, 199, 216
international justice, 2
international law, 3
International Law Association, 43
International Law Commission Draft Articles
  on State Responsibility, 48
International Military Tribunal at
  Nuremberg, 15
international relations, 180

Index

internationally wrongful act, 27
inter-state agreement, 2
investigation, 3
Iran-US Claims Tribunal, 216
irreparable harm, 120
Italy, 48
Ituri, 2, 82, 87, 91, 92, 135, 141, 144, 242

Jackson, Robert, 16, 52
Jesner at Al. v. *Arab Bank, PLC*, US Supreme Court, 187
Juan Humberto Sanchez v. *Honduras*, Judgment, 33
judicial institutions capable, 166
judicial process, 80
judicial supervision, 140
judicial training, 213
jurisdiction
 exercise of, 170
 national security interests, 170
 nationality of the offender, 170
 territoriality, 163
 territory, 170
 treaty-based, 173
 universality principle, 170
jurisdiction of the ICC, 123
justice, xxvi, 1
justice and reconciliation, 143
justice for victims, 2, 8

Kadić v. *Karadžić*, 70 F.3d 232 (2d. Circ. 1995), 190
Kant, Immanuel, 14
Karadžić, Radovan, 190, 191, 195
Katanga case, 105, 107, 108, 113, 115
Katanga, Germain, 91
Kelsen, Hans, 21
Kenya, 100, 112
Khmer Rouge, 66, 68, 70, 71, 227, 236
Kiobel v. *Royal Dutch Petroleum*, US Supreme Court, 185
Kosovo Specialist Chambers & Specialist Prosecutor's Office, 63
Kouwenhoven, Guus, 175
Kuwait, 216

La Cantuta v. *Perú*, Judgment, 36
La Rochela Massacre v. *Colombia*, Judgment, 35
lack of resources, 210

large-scale community meetings, 142
Lauterpacht, Hersch, 20, 22
lawsuit, 194
Lebanon, 64
 Special Tribunal for Lebanon, 63–64
Legal Consequences of the Construction of a Wall in the Occupied Palestinian Territory, Advisory Opinion, 28
legal entity, 69
legal persons, 103
legal representatives of the Civil Parties, 68
legal systems, xxvi
legislation, 167
legitimacy, 124
Letter of the President of the ICTR to the United Nations Secretary-General, 60
lex specialis, 42
lex talioni, 15
liability, 108, 211. *See* criminal liability
liability of corporations, 151
Liberia, 175
Libya, 188
life imprisonment, 164
Loayza Tamayo v. *Peru*, Reparations Judgment, 34
local organizations, 144
locating and freezing assets, 111
locus delictum, 59
Lomé Peace Agreement, 65
Lopez Alvarez v. *Honduras*, Judgment, 33
loss, xxvi, 105
Lotus case, 172
Lotus principle, 172, 196
 express prohibition, 172
Lubanga, xx, xxi, xxii, 81, 82, 83, 84, 86, 87, 88, 89, 90, 91, 102, 103, 110, 115, 120, 137, 141, 151, 231, 232, 240, 242
Lubanga case, 82, 87, 92, 95, 96, 104, 107, 109, 110, 111, 114, 121, 127, 137, 140, 141, 147, 210
lump-sum agreement, 54

M/V "Saiga" (No. 2) (Saint Vincent and the Grenadines v. *Guinea)*, Judgment, 28
Mali, 94, 97, 113
Malian Cultural Heritage Act, 98
mass arbitration, 161
mass claims process, 2, 10
mass victimization, 7

massacre, 34, 37
Massacre of Plan de Sanchez v. *Guatemala*, Reparations Judgment, 34, 37
material damage, 36
material reparations, 69
material security, 143
material support, 127, 134
mausoleum, 96
McCarthy, Connor, 6
meaningful, 209
medical referrals, 135
Mégret, Frédéric, 78, 113, 138
memorial, 32, 38, 49, 72
methodology, 110
military commander, 98
militia, xxvi
Minow, Martha, 12
MLC, xxvi
Moffett, Luke, 2, 6, 77, 104, 118, 121, 123, 142, 204, 205, 207, 214
Moiwana v. *Suriname*, Judgment, 34
monetary liability, 86, 110
money, xxvi
moral damage, 35, 38, 67
moral or collective reparation, 68
mother, xxvi
multifaceted mandates, 206
Muslin Cham, 72
mutilations, 156

national claims commissions, 197
national court, 3
national dimension, 150
national interests, 189
national justice systems, 124
national remembrance day, 72
natural persons, 69, 103
natural resources
    depletion of, 216
Nazi, 16
Nazi forces, 15
negotiating history, 17
Netherlands, 188, 189
new expert evidence, 96
next of kin, 33
Ngujolo Chui, Mathieu, 91
Nigeria, 186
Nollkaemper, Andre, 167
nongovernmental organizations, 143, 169
noninternational armed conflicts, 44, 47
non-profit activity, 67

nonstate actor, 191
Nordic background, 151
normative, 3
North Kivu, 144
Northern Uganda, 134, 143
Nuremberg, xxiii, 1, 52, 54, 55, 73, 224, 225, 235, 243
Nuremberg and Tokyo trials, 54, 55
Nuremberg Trials, 15, 20, 54, 73

offender, 1
Office of the Prosecutor, 210
OPCV, 106
opinio juris, 182
Optional Protocol to the African Charter, 30
organizations, 103
outreach, 107

pain, xxvi
Panel Banca v. *Guatemala*, Reparations Judgment, 34
participatory rights, 152, 154
partie civile, 53, 152, 166, 167
peace, 132
peace accord, 12
peace treaty, 215
peacetime, 214
pecuniary reparation, 39
Permanent Court of International Justice (PCIJ), 27, 172
physical rehabilitation, 135, 142
piracy, 175, 176, 177, 179, 183, 221, 224, 227
Plato, 13
Plavsić, Biljana, 192
political interference, 207
political will, 166
politics of gender justice, 121
post-conflict, 196, 214
postwar reparation, 163
potential beneficiaries, 88, 107, 202
poverty reduction, 70
Prefecture Voiotia v. *Federal Republic of Germany*, Hellenic Supreme Court, 48
presumption of innocence, 143
prevention, 13, 16
The Princeton Principles on Universal Jurisdiction, 100, 169, 170, 171
principle of fairness, 36

256   *Index*

principle of nondiscrimination, 105
Principles for the Protection and Promotion of
     Human Rights Through Action to
     Combat Impunity, 169
prioritization, 124
private donors, 134
procedural status, 194
prohibitive costs, 106
proprio motu, 56
prosecution, 3
     criminal prosecution, 2
Prosecutor v. Ahmad Al Faqi Al Mahdi, 94
Prosecutor v. Charles Ghankay Taylor,
     Judgment, 66
Prosecutor v. Furundžija, Trial Chamber,
     Judgment, 180
Prosecutor v. Germain Katanga, 76, 90, 91, 92,
     93, 242
Prosecutor v. Jean-Pierre Bemba, xxvi, 76, 98,
     99, 100
Prosecutor v. Thomas Lubanga Dyilo, xx, xxi,
     xxii, 76, 79, 81, 82, 83, 87, 103, 115, 141, 151,
     240, 242
prosthetic and orthopedic devices, 142
Protocol to the African Charter on Human and
     Peoples' Rights on the Establishment of
     an African Court on Human and Peoples'
     Rights, 30
proyeto de vida, 36
psychological harm, 89, 93, 105, 109. *See*
     psychological suffering
psychological impact, 35
psychological rehabilitation, 92, 134, 142
psychological trauma, 87
public apology, 38, 41
Public Prosecuting Authority v. Mirsad
     Repak, 192
punishment, 1
punitive damages, 17, 24, 191, 194
punitive goals, 194
punitive justice, 101

rape, xxvi, 55, 59, 72, 82, 98, 156, 191
rebel, xxvi
reconciliation, 132, 145, 202, 208
reconstructive and general surgery, 142
redress, 2
regional human rights courts, 9, 29
Regulations of the Assembly of States Parties
     (ASP), 129
Regulations of the TFV, 130

Regulation 55, 136
Regulation 50 (a), 136
Regulations 27–30, 134
rehabilitation, 1, 8, 13, 115, 127
religion, 131
remedies
     prompt, adequate and effective, 119
reparation, 1, 39
     access to, 120
     against convicted person, 130
     appropriate, 124
     Article 75 of the Rome Statute, 129, 225,
        231
     Article 79 of the Rome Statute, 3, 129
     award, 58, 90, 139, 164, 205
     caselaw, 115, 118
     community-based, 117
     court-ordered, 127, 132, 136, 143
     duty for states to provide reparations,
        46
     effect of acquittal, 118, 145
     enforcement of awards, 171, 201
     first ICC decision, 116
     funding, 111
     ICC regime, 133
     inclusion in legal texts, 124
     individual and collective, 120
     individual awards, 130
     interim, 120
     large number of victims, 139
     legal duty, 202
     legal duty to reparation, 23, 27
     mandate of the ICC, 125, 147
     mass claims, 127
     modalities of, 139
     operationalization of, 116, 203, 216
     order, 128, 140
     programs, 135
     prompt and adequate, 110
     realization of, 87, 198
     remedial justice, 24
     reparations funds, 209
     reparative dimension, 4
     reparative justice, 2, 31
     right to, 194, 196, 198
     right to reparation, 41, 47
     sexual and gender-based crimes, 120
     sexual and gender-based violence,
        119
     symbolic, 78, 136, 197
     system of, 4, 125

Index

TFV reserve fund, 134
theories, 121
through the Trust Fund, 130
Report of the Group of Experts for Cambodia
   Pursuant to General Assembly Resolution
   52/135, 66
Report of the International Commission of
   Inquiry on Darfur to the United Nations
   Secretary-General, 29, 45
Report of the Special Rapporteur on the
   promotion of truth, justice, reparation
   and guarantees of non-recurrence, 26
Report of the Trust Fund for Victims,
   "Reviewing Rehabilitation Assistance and
   Preparing for Delivering
   Reparations," 143
Report on the Establishment of an
   International Criminal Court, 54
Republika Sprska, 160
reserve fund, 134
Resolution, 63
"Strengthening the International Criminal
   Court and the Assembly of States
   Parties," 75
Resolution of the Establishment of the
   Secretariat of the Trust Fund for
   Victims, 131
Resolution on the Establishment of a Fund for
   the Benefit of Victims of Crimes within
   the Jurisdiction of the Court, and the
   Families of such Victims, 134
resources, 146, 205
restitutio ad integrum, 138
restitution, 1, 8, 28, 39, 47, 54, 55, 56, 59, 61, 77,
   78, 129, 132, 164
restoration, 145
restorative justice, 3, 18, 19
retraumatization, 107
retribution, 3, 12, 14, 15, 16, 17, 18, 22, 23, 24, 62,
   198, 208
   retributive justice theory, 14
retributive justice theory, 14
revenge, xxvi
reversal of conviction, 99
revictimization, 116
rhetoric, 124
rhetoric justice, 124
right to remedy, 8
rights of the accused, 116, 143
rights of the defence, 84, 116
rights of the defense, 116

Romano-Germanic, 152, 153
Rome Statue for the International Criminal
   Court
   Article 75, 77, 129
   Article 75 (1), 78
   Article 75 (2), 78
   Article 79, 126
   Article 79 (3), 136
rule of law, xxvi, 12, 15, 32, 163
Rules of Procedure and Evidence of the ICTY, 56
Ruto and Sang, 118
Ruto and Sang case, 101
Rwanda, 55
   International Criminal Tribunal for
      Rwanda, 50, 60
Ryngaert, Cedric, 173

safe haven, 189
sample, 89. *See* sample of victims
sample of victims, 89
sanctioning effect, 194
satisfaction, 1, 8
science, 131
screening, 90, 95, 96, 107
Second Protocol to the Hague Convention for
   the Protection of Cultural Property, 44
Second Protocol to the Hague Convention for
   the Protection of Cultural Property in the
   Event of Armed Conflict, 44
Second World War, 15, 20, 21, 23, 49, 50, 52,
   54, 55
secondary victimization, 213
Security Council, 45, 56, 57, 60, 62, 63, 65, 216,
   230, 244, 246
   chapter VII powers, 156
   Resolution 1644, 63
selectivity, 124, 205
self-interest, 179
Senegal, 153, 164
Senegalese Code of Criminal Procedure, 164
sentencing, 154
Serbia, 157, 158, 159
sex and ethnic inequality, 191
sexual and gender-based crimes, 109, 119
sexual violence, 83, 155
shared harm, 90
Shelton, Dinah, 2, 24
shock the conscience of humanity, 75
Sierra Leone, 64, 65, 66, 67, 218, 221, 227,
   231, 245
   Special Court for Sierra Leone, 65–66

single, consolidated group, 69
situation under investigation by the
 Prosecutor, 145
slave trade, 179, 183
social justice, 118
social support and integration, 143
society, xxvi
Sosa v. *Alvarez-Machain*, US Supreme
 Court, 182
South Kivu, 144
sovereignty, 172
special chambers, 197
Special Court for Sierra Leone, xxii, 63, 65, 66,
 230, 231, 243
Special Rapporteur. *See* Report of the Special
 Rapporteur on the promotion of truth,
 justice, reparation and guarantees of non-
 recurrence
Special Tribunal for Lebanon, 63, 64, 222, 224,
 226, 228, 230, 232
specific intent
 mens rea, 158
Srebrenica, 157
standard and burden of proof, 84
standard of proof, 108, 201
state immunity, 20, 42
state of indigence, 84, 89
state practice, 182, 199
state responsibility, 9, 10, 22, 23, 31, 32, 46, 50,
 54, 55, 128, 150, 157, 158, 159, 162, 199,
 202, 203
state-based reparations, 4, 199, 203
state-centered, 20
Statement of the ICC Deputy Prosecutor in
 the opening of the Prosecutor's case in
 Katanga and Chui, 2
state-sponsored reparations programs, 197
status quo ante, 24
statute of limitations, 185
Statute of the Special Court for Sierra
 Leone, 65
 Article 17, 64
 Article 19(3), 39, 65
 Article 25(3), 64
stigmatization, 83
Street Children v. *Guatemala*, Reparations
 Judgment, 34
substantive realization of reparations, 204
sufficient link, 189
summary execution, 191
Supreme Court Chamber, 71

TFV, 11
 assistance mandate, 132, 142, 144
 assistance program, 139
 Board of Directors, xxi, 79, 92, 100, 131, 133,
 134, 135, 136, 140, 143, 145, 246
 financial ability, 137
 reparations mandate, 130, 132, 135, 146
 voluntary contributions, 138
The Hague, 158, 188
theories of justice, 10, 13, 200
theory of international justice, 198
therapy groups, 72
Timbuktu, 94, 97
timeline, 209
Tokyo, 52, 54, 55, 73, 247
Tokyo Trials, 54, 73
tort, 3
tort jurisdiction, 181
torture, 7, 55, 59, 82, 164, 179, 180, 183, 185, 186,
 187, 189, 190, 191, 192
Torture Victims Protection Act ("TVPA"),
 185
tragedy, xxvi
transformative reparations, 84
transgenerational harm, 109
transgenerational psychological harm, 93
transnational crime, 7
trauma counseling, 142
trauma sensitive, 143
treaty bodies, 31, 32
Treaty of Peace between the Allied Powers,
 215
Trial of Major War Criminals before the
 International Military Tribunal, 15, 20
Tribunal de Grande Instance, 192
Trust Fund for Victims, 6, 84, 126.
 See also TFV
 establishment, 129
 funding and resources, 146
 mandates, 132
trust funds, 208
truth, 12, 26, 35, 40, 41, 133, 201
truth and reconciliation, 10, 12

Uganda, 112, 134
Union of Congolese Patriots (UPC), 82
United Nations, xxi, 25, 26, 45, 56, 60, 61, 63,
 65, 66, 97, 120, 133, 148, 176, 201, 242, 244,
 246, 247
United Nations Charter, 63
 chapter VII, 63

Index

United Nations Compensation
Commission, 216
United Nations Convention on the Law of the
Sea, 176
United Nations Convention on the Non-
Applicability of Statutes of Limitations for
War Crimes and Crimes Against
Humanity, 175
United Nations Guidance Note of the
Secretary General: Reparations for
Conflict-Related Sexual Violence, 119
United Nations Special Rapporteur on the
promotion of truth, justice, reparations
and guarantees of non-recurrence, 25
United States, 187, 195
universal civil jurisdiction, 11, 151, 163, 168, 180,
181, 182, 183, 184, 185, 186, 187, 188, 189, 193,
194, 195, 196, 200, 207
emerging recognition, 196
international crimes, 189
Netherlands, 188
Norway, 192
Sweden, 193
United States. *See* Alien Tort Claims
Statute
universal civil jurisdiction versus universal
criminal jurisdiction, 181
use of domestic laws, 188
universal criminal jurisdiction, 168
in absentia, 174
Universal Declaration of Human Rights, 30,
62, 238, 247
universal jurisdiction, 3, 168, 178,
180
lawfulness, 181
universal tort jurisdiction. *See* universal civil
jurisdiction
unknown victims, 107

Velásquez-Rodríguez v. *Honduras*, Merits
Judgment, 29, 49
victim, xxvi, 1, 8
empowerment of, 201

individual, 18, 37, 39, 42, 46, 47, 48, 49, 51, 78,
88, 95, 115, 117, 122, 137, 204
invisible, 123
mass victimization, 1
participation in International Criminal
Court, 104
real experiences of, 200
recognized, 123
role in the administration of justice, 15
victim redress, 208
victim-centered approach, 201
victim-centered, 109
victimhood, 4
victimization, 2, 32, 55, 59, 78, 113, 146,
156, 206
victimized, 211
victimology, 122
victim-oriented approach, 180, 194
victim-perpetrators, 122
Vietnamese, 72
violence
sexual and gender-based violence, 4, 82,
119, 120
Vlaming, Frederiek de, 159
vocational training, 142
voluntary contributions, 142
VPRS, 106
Vuckovic, Nikola, 191

war crimes, 75, 82, 94, 118
war-related personal harms, 162
Wemmers, Jo-Anne, 6
woman, xxvi
Women's Initiatives for Gender Justice, 82, 83
wrongful. *See* wrongful act
wrongful act, 25
wrongful conduct, 18
wrongful death, 191

Yugoslavia, 55, 156

Zappalà, Salvatore, 116
Zegveld, Liesbeth, 148

Lightning Source UK Ltd.
Milton Keynes UK
UKHW022323020920
369267UK00005B/29